COURT AND CRAFT

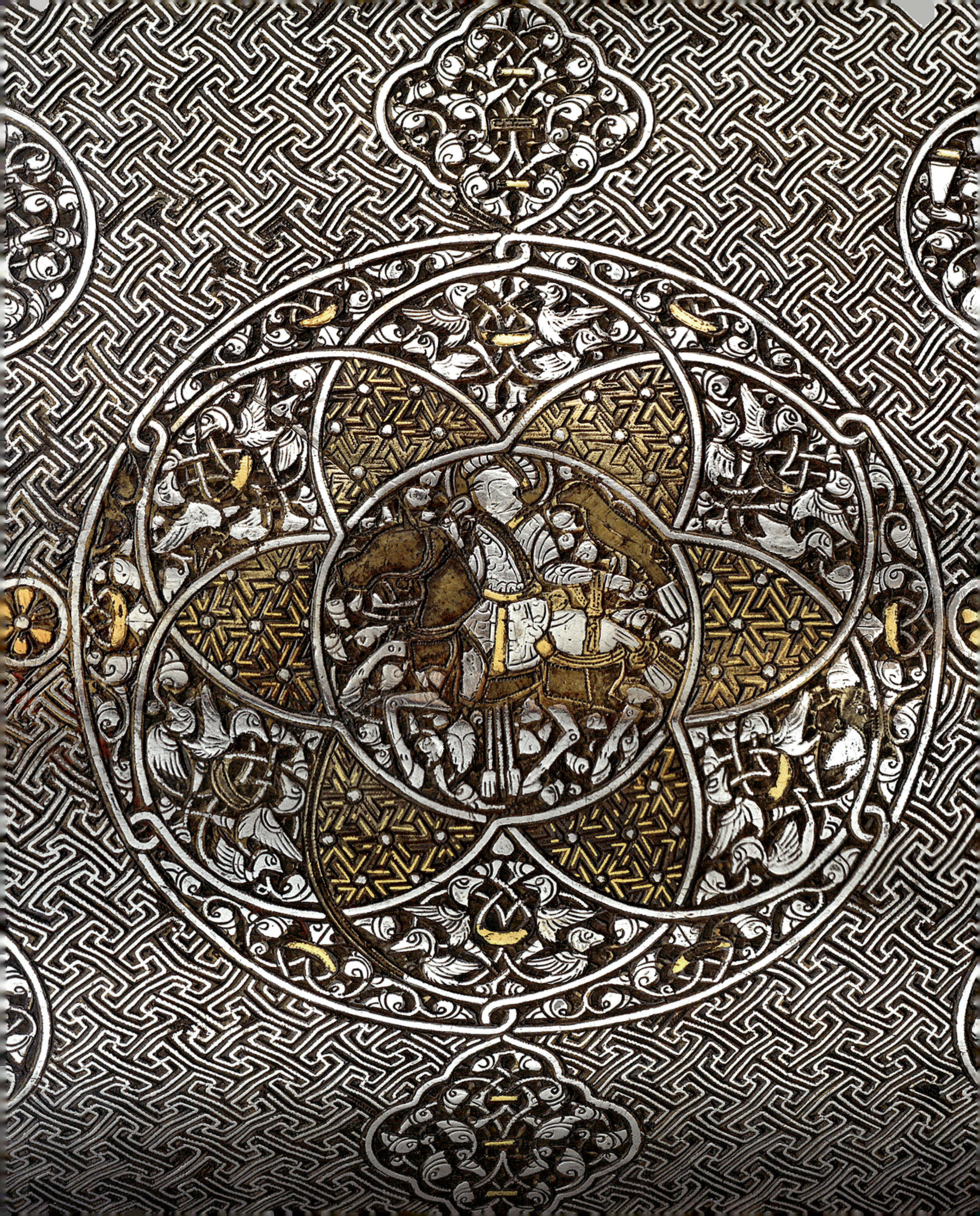

COURT AND CRAFT
A Masterpiece from Northern Iraq

EDITED BY

Rachel Ward

THE COURTAULD GALLERY
IN ASSOCIATION WITH
PAUL HOLBERTON PUBLISHING
LONDON

First published to accompany the exhibition

COURT AND CRAFT
A Masterpiece from Northern Iraq

The Courtauld Gallery, London
20 February – 18 May 2014

The Courtauld Gallery is supported by the
Higher Education Funding Council for England (HEFCE)

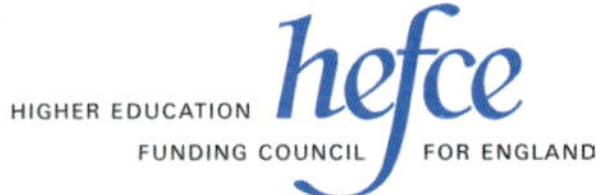

Exhibition Support

SPONSORS

Friends of The Courtauld
Oryx Petroleum

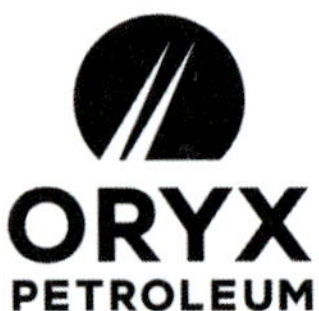

SUPPORTER

GardaWorld

THE GOVERNMENT INDEMNITY SCHEME

This exhibition has been made possible by the provision
of insurance through the Government Indemnity Scheme.
The Courtauld Gallery would like to thank HM Government for
providing indemnity and extends its thanks to the Department
for Culture, Media and Sport, and Arts Council England for
administering the scheme.

Contents

Foreword

THE REMARKABLE inlaid brass bag which is the subject of this exhibition has long been recognised by specialists as one of the most important examples of metalwork from the Islamic world. No other object of its kind survives. And yet despite its status, this exceptional work has been surprisingly little studied; significant questions about its origins, function and imagery have remained unanswered. In providing a forum for the discussion of these questions, *Court and Craft* follows the highly focused approach which has so successfully characterised The Courtauld Gallery's exhibitions over the last decade.

Surprisingly, however, this is the Gallery's first exhibition dedicated to non-Western art. As such it reflects important recent developments in the academic programmes of The Courtauld Institute of Art, including the introduction of a Masters course in Persianate painting and the establishment of The Robert N. H. Ho Family Foundation Centre for Buddhist Art and Conservation. This broadening of scope was prefigured in The Courtauld's first years of operation, when its wide ranging courses and lectures included, for example, Islamic art and architecture and, substantially, Chinese art.

Court and Craft has its immediate origins in 2011 when Rachel Ward joined the Gallery as Visiting Curator to study the distinguished but little known group of Islamic metalwork bequeathed as part of the magnificent collection formed in the nineteenth century by Thomas Gambier Parry. Subsequently, a workshop, attended by most of the contributors to the present publication, helped define the scope and aims of the exhibition. Since then Rachel has led all aspects of the scholarly content of the project. The exhibition and catalogue are fully the reflection of her expertise and unflagging commitment, and The Courtauld is deeply grateful to her. Our ability to appreciate the magnificent craftsmanship of this luxurious object has been greatly enhanced by Diana Heath's sensitive and painstaking conservation treatment. Chief amongst the colleagues from within the Gallery who contributed to the preparation of the exhibition, is Alexandra Gerstein, our curator of sculpture and decorative arts. I extend my warm personal thanks to her. Special thanks are also due to Karin Kyburz and Julia Blanks.

The integrity of The Courtauld's highly focused exhibitions relies heavily on the inclusion of precisely selected loans, for which there are often no substitutes. We gratefully acknowledge the generosity and kindness of the institutions and private owners who have so fully lent important works from their collections.

This exhibition would not have been possible without the generosity of our sponsors and supporters. We are enormously grateful to them. The Friends of The Courtauld (incorporating Samual Courtauld Society members) have helped fund many exhibitions at the Gallery and have once again provided a major and enabling grant. The Courtauld is also very pleased to welcome Oryx Petroleum as a sponsor of the exhibition. Valuable additional support was provided by GardaWorld, where special thanks are due to Oliver Westmacott. Both Oryx Petroleum and GardaWorld embraced this exhibition as a contribution to the public understanding and enjoyment of the history and great cultural wealth of present day northern Iraq and the wider region. Finally, The Courtauld would like to thank Vahid Alaghband for his advice and encouragement, and Kamyar Nemazee for his enthusiasm and his invaluable assistance in securing support for this project.

ERNST VEGELIN VAN CLAERBERGEN
Head of The Courtauld Gallery

Samuel Courtauld Society

Author's acknowledgements

IN PREPARATION for this exhibition, a small workshop on the Courtauld Wallet (as it then was) was held at the Courtauld Gallery on 27 January 2012. It was a good-natured and spirited event and provided an invaluable opportunity for some interested scholars to exchange views about an object with an uncertain context. I am deeply grateful to all the attendees for sharing their knowledge: Doris Abouseif (a virtual presence), Ladan Akbarnia, Aisha Al Khater, Sussan Babaie, Sheila Blair, Jonathan Bloom, Moya Carey, Anthony Eastmond (who initiated the idea for the exhibition), Alexandra Gerstein, Julia Gonnella, William Greenwood, Rosalind Haddon, Irina Koshoridze, Bernard O'Kane, Michael Rogers, Marianna Shreve Simpson, Eleanor Sims, Bas Snelders, Tim Stanley; especially Manijeh Bayani who contributed substantially to the text on the inscription; and James Allan, Anna Contadini, Teresa Fitzherbert, Robert Hillenbrand, Charles Melville, Judith Pfeiffer and Julian Raby who each wrote an essay in this catalogue, expanding the context and delving deeper into the various themes depicted on the bag. The catalogue has benefited immeasurably from the contributions of such a distinguished group of scholars. But the star of the exhibition and the catalogue is the bag, which now sparkles and gleams as it should because of the meticulous conservation work by Diana Heath.

Many institutions and private collections have generously loaned magnificent objects. I and the Courtauld Gallery would like to thank the individuals who helped discover appropriate exhibits, organise conservation and photography where necessary and generally facilitate the loan process. In Baltimore, Barbara Fegley, Amy Landau, Joan Elisabeth Reid and Terry Weisser at the Walters Art Museum. In Berlin, Stefan Weber and Julia Gonnella at the Islamic Museum and Cristoph Rauch at the Staatsbibliothek. In Copenhagen, Kjeld von Folsach and Mette Korsholm at the David Collection. In Dublin, Elaine Wright at the Chester Beatty Collection. In Florence, Marco Spallanzani at the Bargello Museum.

In Tbilisi, David Lordkipanidze, Irina Koshoridze, Nino Kalanddze, Marina Dgebuadze, Natia Demurishvili and Tamara Gugunava at the National Museum of Georgia. In the UK, Colin Baker, Emma Denness, Ursula Sims-Williams and Muhammad Isa Waley at the British Library; Ladan Akbarnia and Venetia Porter at the British Museum; Richard de Unger at the Keir Collection; David Khalili and Nahla Nasser at the Khalili Collection; Ali Sarikhani, Ina Sandmann and Melanie Gibson at the Sarikhani Collection; Lucia Burgio, Moya Carey, Hannah Kauffman, Beth McKillop, Helen Persson, Boris Pretzel, Mariam Rosser-Owen, Tim Stanley and Ming Wilson at the Victoria and Albert Museum.

The exhibition follows in the substantial footsteps of *The Legacy of Genghis Khan 1256–1363,* curated by Linda Komaroff and Stefano Carboni, and Linda Komaroff gave me considerable encouragement during a flying visit to London. Their work has been a great help in the preparation of this catalogue. Many other colleagues responded patiently to specific queries, including Craig Clunas, Susan LaNiece, Carole Michaelson, Souren Melikian-Chirvani, Alison Ohta, Shelagh Vainker, Zoe Ward, Oliver Watson. Particular thanks go to Teresa Fitzherbert who was always ready to help in a myriad of ways, from commenting on my text to supplying copies of obscure articles.

I am grateful to the Courtauld Gallery and to its Head, Ernst Vegelin van Claerbergen, for inviting me to curate this exhibition and for shouldering much of its administration. Everyone in the Courtauld made me welcome and helped me in the preparation for this exhibition, especially Graeme Barraclough, Eva Bensasson, Julia Blanks, Aviva Burnstock, Kate Edmonson, Sarah Green, Henrietta Hine, Jack Kettlewell, Karin Kyburz, Chloe Le Tissier, Douglas Maclennan, Karen Serres and Hannah Talbot. It has been a pleasure to work with Paul Holberton and Laura Parker at Paul Holberton publishing, who have done a magnificent job on this catalogue, and Colin Lindley, Alan Farley and Belinda

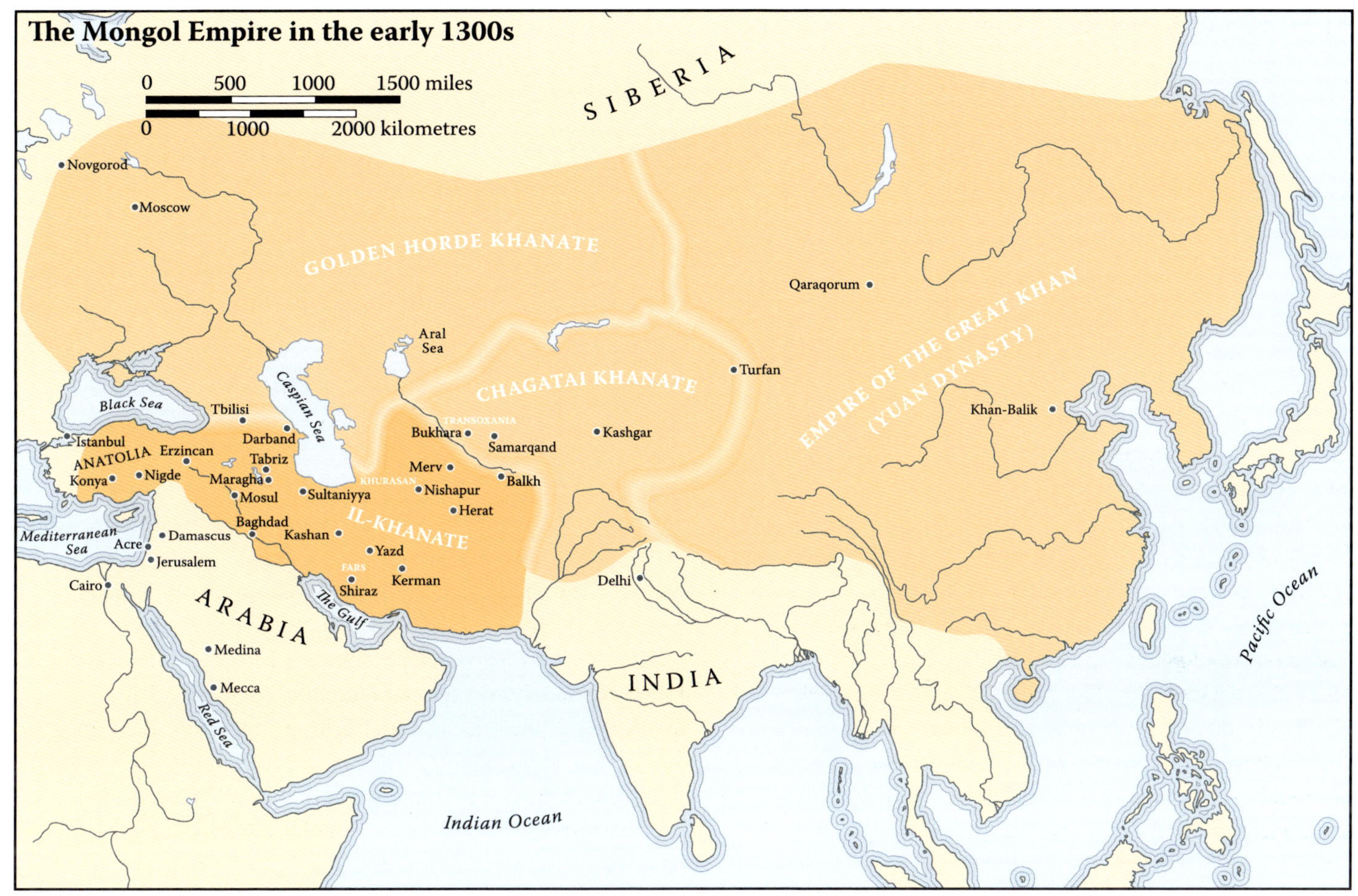

Moore, who were responsible for the attractive design of the exhibition. Hilal Saodiy must be thanked for recording the inscription, and John Hindmarch, Stuart Robson, Melissa Terras and Lindsay Macdonald at University College London for the three-dimensional model in the exhibition.

Special thanks to Alexandra Gerstein, curator of sculpture and decorative arts at the Courtauld Gallery. She has been a great support during the two years it took to bring this project to completion and has involved herself in both the exhibition and this catalogue with enormous enthusiasm.

Finally, my family has been supportive in every possible way, thank you.

All dates are AD or AH/AD.

The most acceptable or usual English spelling has been selected for the many Mongol, Arabic, Turkish and Persian names and words that appear in the text. Arabic script has been kept to a minimum and full transliteration has been included only where essential (and in the bibliography).

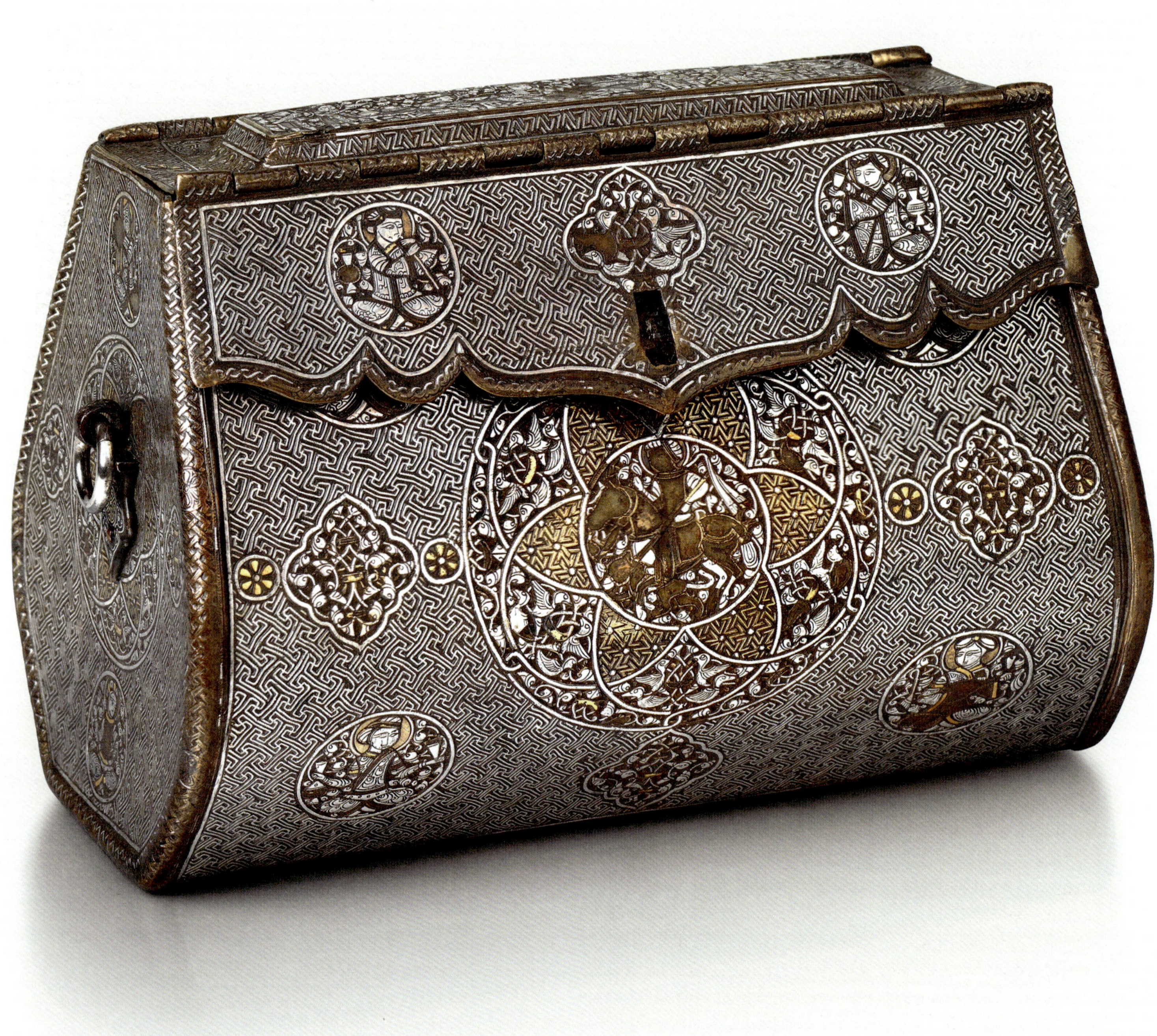

The Courtauld Bag: What's in a name?

RACHEL WARD

THE COURTAULD BAG is one of the finest examples of inlaid brass to have survived from the Islamic world – it is so richly inlaid with gold, silver and black material that the brass ground is only visible where the inlays are missing.[1] Decorated with a court scene, horsemen, musicians and revellers on a geometric ground inspired by Chineses silks, it creates a fascinating picture of princely life during the Il-Khanid period in northern Iraq in the early fourteenth century.

A hundred and fifty years ago the Courtauld bag was in the collection of Thomas Gambier Parry (1816–1888), one among a number of inlaid brass vessels that he collected along with early Italian paintings, Renaissance maiolica and enamels, glass, medals and Gothic ivories. The bag was acquired in 1858, perhaps during an extended trip to the Dalmatian coast and northern Italy (including Venice, where he made several purchases of 'Veneto-Saracenic' metalwork) in the spring of that year.[2] Gambier Parry's collection, including the bag, was bequeathed to The Courtauld in 1966.

No other metal vessel of this shape has survived and its function has always puzzled scholars. In 1858 Gambier Parry referred to it as an "oriental box" and in 1860 as "a cartouche box".[3] In 1875 William Chaffers called it an "oriental damascened work basket".[4] In 1967 Basil Robinson suggested that it was a wallet "to carry a prince's documents and seals", and it has been known as 'the Courtauld wallet' since then.[5] From the front, the Courtauld bag with its lobed flap does look like a leather wallet; but leather wallets never have the curving profile of the Courtauld bag, or straps for suspension.

The Courtauld 'wallet' more closely resembles the rounded shape of a leather or textile bag, and like them, was suspended by a long strap attached to loops on each side. Despite the rigidity of the metal, the double hinge of the lid would have allowed it to be opened and the contents accessed even when it was worn closely against the body. Leather and textile is perishable, but a fragment of leather

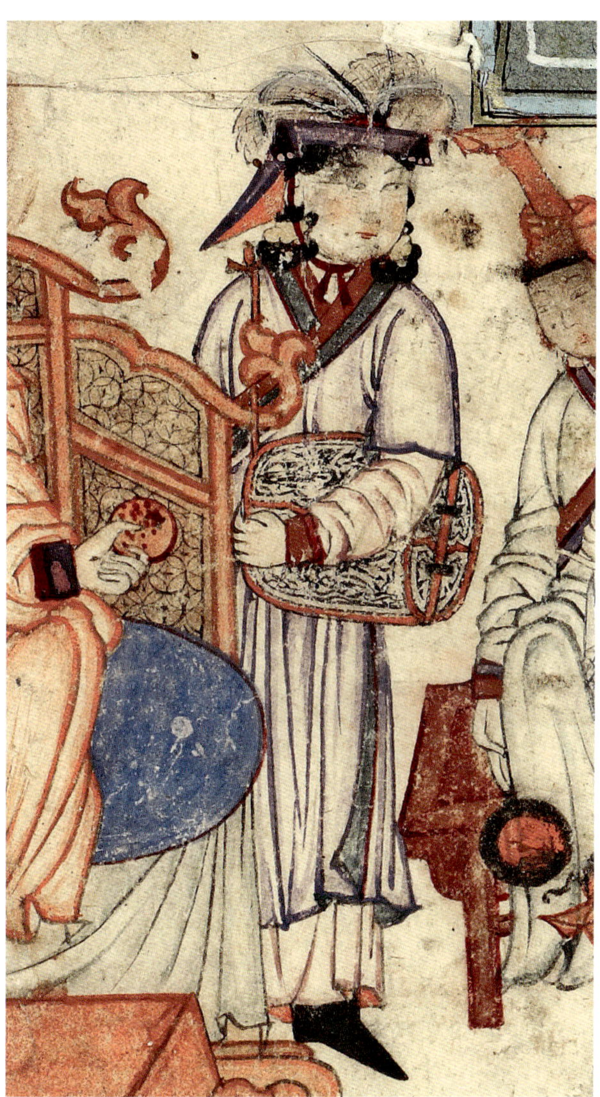

FIG. 1
An enthronement scene, probably Tabriz, early 14th century (cat. 16), detail showing a page wearing a shoulder bag

in the exhibition may be a rare survivor from a leather bag (cat. 15). It is remarkably similar in size and shape to the Courtauld bag and has holes where a loop for a strap might have been attached; it even has a plait border running around its edge. However, bags depicted in Il-Khanid court scenes are rather grander affairs, with patterned silk laid over a solid frame, a lobed flap in front and a long red cord for suspension (fig. 1).

'The Courtauld wallet' needs a new name. 'Bag', defined in the Oxford English Dictionary as 'a flexible container with an opening at the top, used for carrying things', is the most accurate description of its function – even though the abrupt, unglamorous word does not do justice to such an exquisite receptacle.[6]

There is considerable visual evidence to suggest that the Courtauld bag was used by a lady rather than by a prince. A large percentage of the depictions of noblewomen in fourteenth-century Iran and Iraq show a bag being worn or carried by her attendant. The most significant is

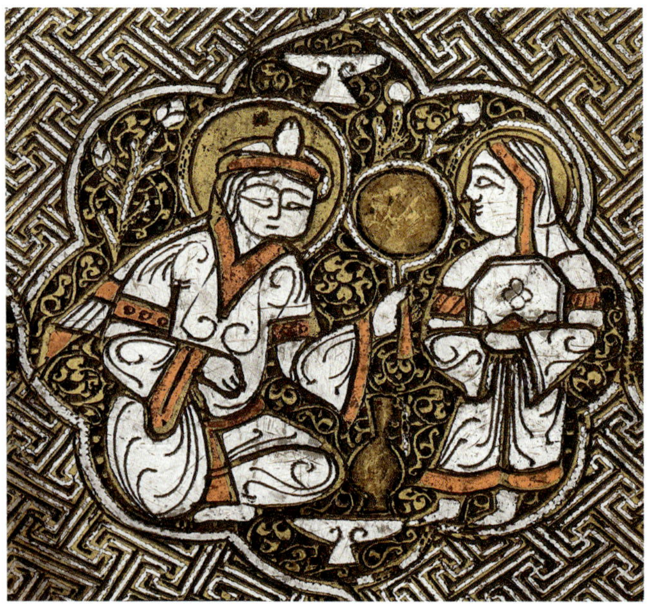

the bag in the court scene on the Courtauld bag itself (detail right) but there are others on metalwork and in illustrated manuscripts (cat. 16–20). To put the numbers into perspective, one should remember that images of noblewomen are rare, even in the Mongol period, whereas there are hundreds of images of male rulers and courtiers in illustrated manuscripts, on metalwork and on other media and there is no page wearing or carrying a bag beside any of them.

The preponderance of related Il-Khanid images suggests that the association between a noblewoman and her bag may have arrived from eastern Asia with the Mongols, but evidence for that is scarce. Paintings of Mongol and Yuan women often include a female attendant behind them holding a box but never a bag,[7] and boxes are associated with women in the Islamic world too: a female attendant holds a box ready for a lady doing her toilette in a medallion on the Blacas ewer (cat. 21, fig. 2).A series of illustrations from the life of Judith in the Arsenal Bible, painted in Acre around 1250, suggests that the custom of bag and bag-carrier attending a noblewoman already existed in western Asia by the mid thirteenth century. In each scene Judith is accompanied by her loyal maid, who carries her bag (fig. 3). Judith's is a utilitarian, open-topped bag in a rough material like wicker or hessian, so much humbler than the Courtauld bag, but the concept is the same. Illustrations to Khwaju Kirmani's story of Humay and Humayun (cat. 19, fig. 4) suggest that bags of the same shape continued to be used, in Iraq at least, until the end of the fourteenth century and that they were sometimes imitated in gold.

We can only speculate what these bags contained, but other items carried by attendants holding bags, or standing nearby, include mirrors (cat. 1, 19, 20), napkins (cat. 1 and detail right, 16, 17) and perfume bottles (cat. 19 and fig. 4). The bag carried by one of the pages assisting a Mongol lady to walk (cat. 18) demonstrates that it was not just a ceremonial accessory but something, like a

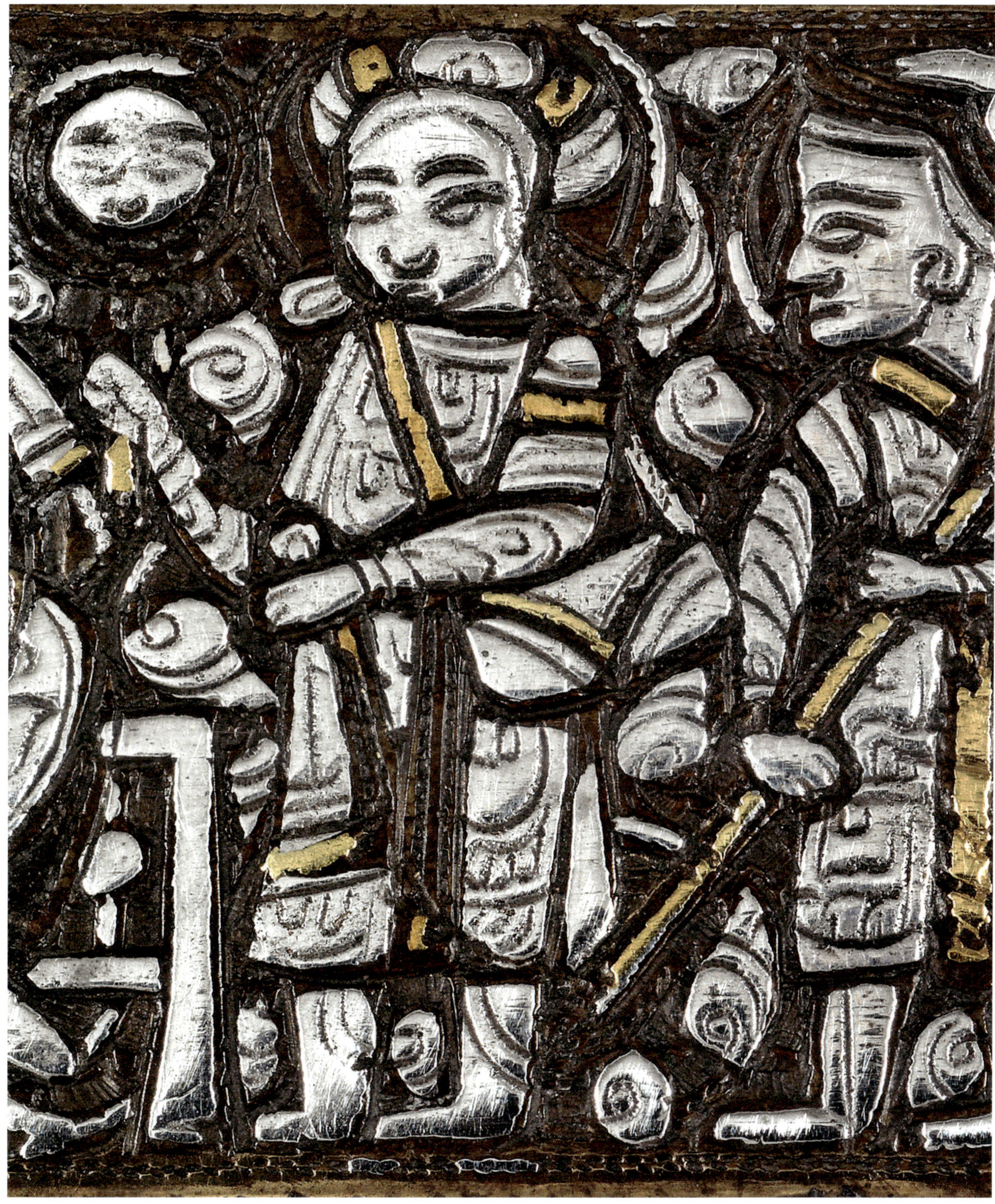

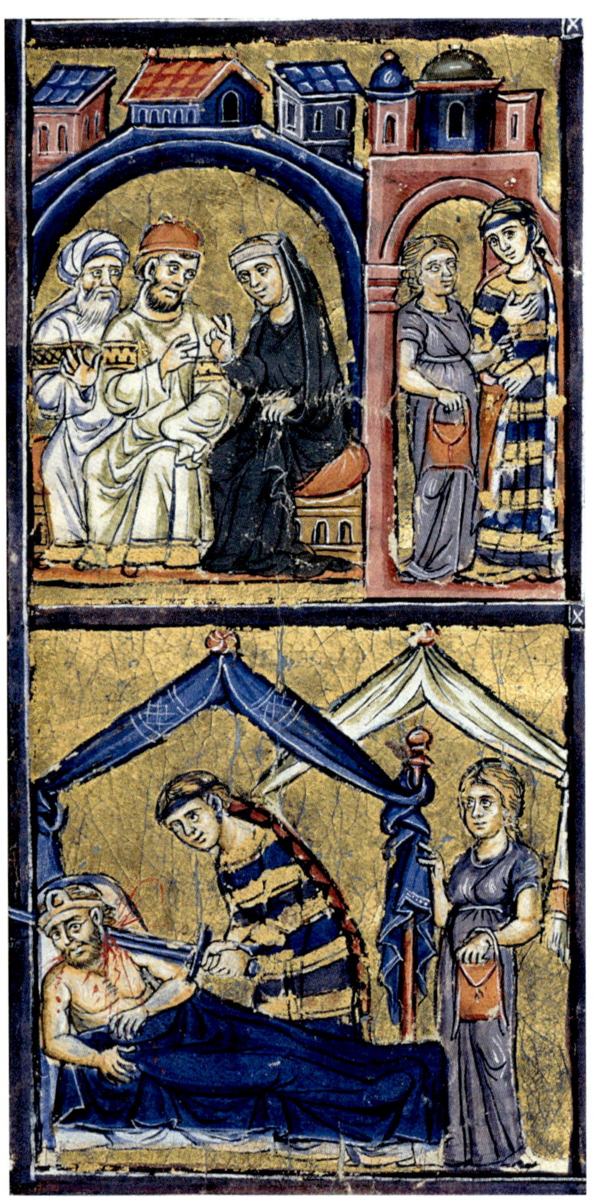

modern handbag, that accompanied the woman at all times. It probably contained items for the lady's comfort or toilette that, unlike a mirror, napkin or perfume bottle, were not appropriate for public display.

The Courtauld bag is one of the finest and best preserved examples of inlaid brass to have survived, yet it has been little published because of scholarly uncertainty about its date and provenance. It was first published in 1967 by Basil Robinson, who compared it to the Blacas ewer, made in Mosul in 1232 (cat. 21 and fig. 2), and attributed it to mid-thirteenth-century Mosul, although he did note some similarity between the figural decoration on the bag and the style of decoration on a Mamluk metal basin, the Baptistère de Saint Louis, then thought to date between 1290 and 1310, and a Mamluk illustrated manuscript of the *Maqamat* of al-Hariri dated 734/1334 (figs. 21, 26).[8] In 1976, the 'wallet' was in the *World of Islam* exhibition at the Hayward Gallery in London. James Allan, who wrote the catalogue entry, published the inscription it bears for the first time in transliterated form with a translation. Allan agreed with Robinson that it should be dated to mid-thirteenth-century Mosul and he also compared it to the Baptistère, suggesting that it 'provides a bridge' between Mosul and Mamluk metalwork.[9] In 1983 the 'wallet' was mentioned and illustrated by Eva Baer, who also attributed it to the mid thirteenth century (although in a later note in the same volume she qualified that to 'probably second half of the thirteenth century'), without suggesting a provenance.[10] I still have my notes of a lively student seminar with James Allan in Oxford in 1981, at which we discussed Mosul in North Iraq, Tabriz in north-west Iran, Shiraz in southern Iran and Damascus in Syria as possible attributions for the 'wallet': no conclusion was reached. At the Courtauld workshop held in January 2012 during preparation for the exhibition this catalogue accompanies, the majority of scholars opted for an Il-Khanid provenance, but no one was certain of the exact location of the workshop and several people argued in favour of Mamluk manufacture.

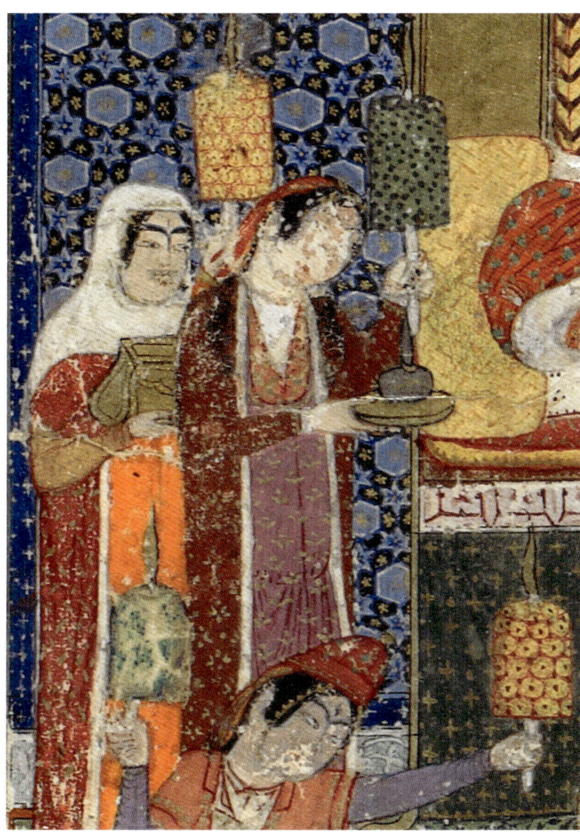

Because there is no documentary inscription, the only way
to identify a context for the Courtauld bag is by comparison
with other material, which is often itself of insecure date
and provenance. My conclusion, for reasons outlined in my
essay on Il-Khanid Mosul (pp. 68–78) and catalogue entry
on the bag (pp. 76–99), is that it was made in Mosul in the
early fourteenth century, when the city was ruled by the
Il-Khanids. The striking similarity of its decoration to a ball
joint in the name of Sultan Öljeitü (fig. 47, p. 88) suggests
that it may have been made within his reign, 1304–16. This
publication, with its detailed photographs of the newly
cleaned bag, will facilitate further discussion.

NOTES

1 In a letter from Anthony Blunt, Director
   of the Courtauld Institute of Art, to
   Thomas Gambier-Parry, 12 October
   1965, he describes the reaction of Basil
   Robinson (then Assistant Keeper of
   Metalwork at the Victoria and Albert
   Museum) on seeing the bag for the first
   time: "The man from the Victoria and
   Albert Museum almost fainted when
   he saw the early Mosul receptacle.
   Apparently the only other thing of
   equal quality known to him was a piece
   acquired by St Louis on his crusade,
   which later formed part of the Treasury
   of Sainte Chapelle and is now in the
   Louvre": Courtauld Gallery Archives.
2 Thomas Gambier Parry, 'Some
   particulars about things bought', dated
   1858, in which he calls it an "oriental
   box". In *c.* 1860 it appears as no. 6 in
   a list of objects and is described as "a
   cartouche box, silver and gold inlaid
   all over it – curious group of figures
   in medallions on very rich diapers,
   probably late 13th century or early
   14th": copies of both documents in
   the Courtauld Gallery Archives. For
   Gambier Parry's trip see Gerstein 2013.
3 See note 2 above.
4 In a manuscript catalogue of the
   Gambier Parry collection written in 1875
   by William Chaffers (copy in Courtauld
   Gallery Archives), the "oriental
   damascened work basket" is no. 209.
5 Robinson 1967, p. 169 no. 1, pls. 81–84.
6 The problem has been solved by modern
   designers who prefix 'bag', or replace it
   altogether, with the name of a celebrity
   owner or fashionable area: the Birkin by
   Hermes, the Bayswater by Mulberry.
7 My thanks to Craig Clunas for
   confirming this point.
8 Robinsen 1967, p. 169, pls. 81–84. The
   Baptistère has since been re-dated to the
   mid fourteenth century: Ward 1999.
9 London 1976, p. 182, no. 199.
10 Baer 1983, p. 120, 126, note 13 on p. 326
   and figs. 98 and 104.

Northern Iraq: Historical and political context

CHARLES MELVILLE

THE TURN OF THE FOURTEENTH CENTURY was a time of turbulence and trauma, but also one pregnant with possibilities – nowhere more so than in northern Iraq, the region in focus here as the suggested provenance of the main object of this exhibition.

Mesopotamia, the territory enclosed between the Tigris and Euphrates rivers, once the centre of the ᶜAbbasid caliphate, not to mention the more ancient civilisations of the Assyrians, Achaemenids and Sasanians, was now caught between two implacable rival regimes, newly established to east and west. The capital, Baghdad, had been sacked by the Mongols under Hülegü Khan in 1258, rounding off the conquest of the eastern Islamic world initiated by his grandfather Chinggis Khan in 1219 – a conquest that wrought spectacular damage on the great urban centres of art and learning in Transoxania and Khurasan. The carnage at Samarqand, Bukhara, Merv, Balkh, Herat and Nishapur claimed many lives and dealt a psychological trauma to the survivors. Although Baghdad itself perhaps suffered less than the contemporary figures would suggest – at least 800,000 people are supposed to have died, according to the hysterical accounts [1] – the fall of the city after a short siege marked the end of an era, specifically the 500-year reign of the ᶜAbbasids and the Perso-Islamic framework that regulated both government and society. It was replaced by the Mongol Il-Khanate, ruled by Hülegü Khan and his successors as 'Il-Khans', notionally subject to the Great Khan residing first in Qaraqorum and later in China.

The early Il-Khans made their capitals in north-west Iran, at Maragha and Tabriz, and were initially of various non-Muslim religious affiliations – Buddhists and Shamanists, with Nestorian Christianity also widespread. It was in these circumstances that Christians, Jews and Shiᶜis too could rise to positions of high rank and influence in government and the administration. As we will see, one of the chief characteristics of the period is the bloody rivalry between the Christian communities of northern Iraq – briefly empowered, or at least more or less protected, by the conquering Mongols – and the Muslims in the region, seeking revenge and the chance to restore their former dominance. As the Mongols gradually adopted Islam, so the position of the Christians worsened.

Two years after the fall of Baghdad, Mongol forces stationed in Syria advanced south to meet an army led up from Cairo by al-Muzaffar Qutuz, the Mamluk sultan who had shouldered aside the last traces of Ayyubid rule in Egypt and elected to resist Hülegü's demands for submission to Mongol supremacy. The outcome was the celebrated Mamluk victory at the battle of ᶜAyn Jalut in September 1260, which put a limit on Mongol expansion and set the stage for a more or less permanent state of hostility. The uneasy border between these rival empires lay along the Euphrates, with contested territories in eastern Anatolia and northern Mesopotamia.[2] Iraq was transformed from a centre to a periphery, from an imperial heartland to a border region.

The Mongol and Mamluk regimes thus came into existence at the same time and in their different ways were both heirs to the ᶜAbbasid caliphate – the Mongols in their control of Baghdad and the Tigris-Euphrates valley that had been at the centre of previous empires embracing the Iranian plateau; the Mamluks as guardians of the refugee ᶜAbbasids, whom they welcomed and set up in a shadow caliphate in Cairo, from which their regime could claim some legitimacy. Open warfare between these rival powers persisted for the next half century as they staked out the ground between them and reached a mutual recognition of the balance of power; this was finally marked by the treaty of Aleppo in 1323.[3]

As for the possibilities at the turn of the new century, the establishment of an uneasy peace was a reflection

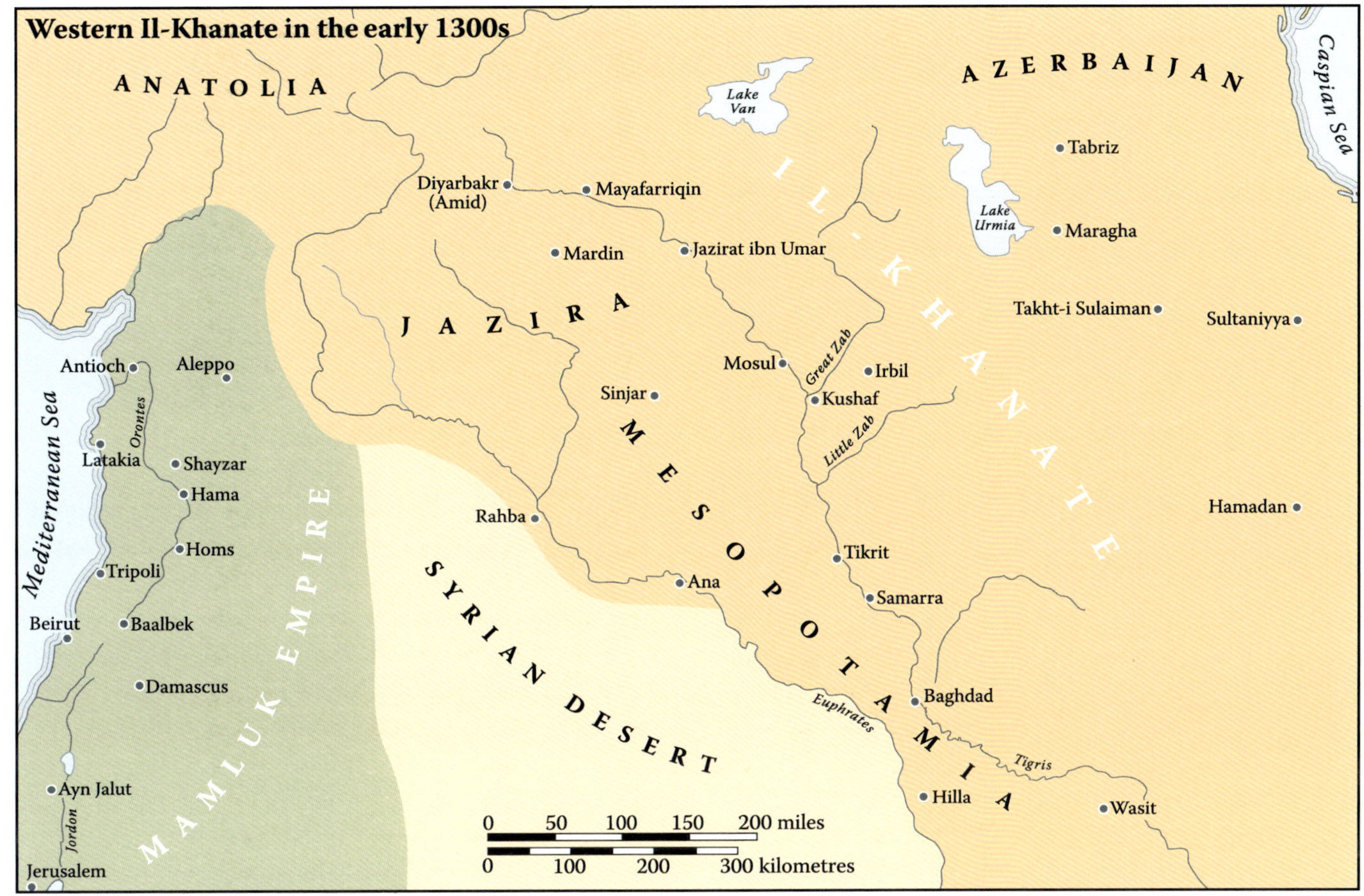

not only of military realities, but also of fundamental changes within the Il-Khanate. After three generations of pagan rule, the Mongols in Iran officially converted to Islam at the hands of a sheikh of the Kubravi order in 1295.[4] Athough this was far from an overnight change of mentality or practice, the very fact that the Mongol regime under the leadership of Ghazan Khan (1295–1304) and his brother Öljeitü (1304–1316) acknowledged Islam as the guiding force in society led to their acceptance – at least in their public role – of the need to conform to the traditional expectations of a Muslim monarch. While this was expressed in the numerous political and financial 'reforms' initiated by the vizier Rashid al-Din (d. 1318), another important aspect was the revival of court patronage and the fostering of an environment in which the arts could flourish.[5] To what extent this holds true for northern Iraq remains an open question – whether artistic production could continue without serious interruption, or awaited the recovery of 'Islamic'

rule. The essential requirement was the return of social and economic stability, a commodity in short supply in the late thirteenth and early fourteenth century.

Turning to the situation on the ground, one factor that assisted continuity across the brutal transition from ʿAbbasid to Mongol rule was the relative absence of the large-scale destructions in Hülegü's westward campaign that had characterised the initial conquests under Chinggis Khan in the east.[6] Although Mongol raids penetrated as far as Hamadan and into Iraq in 1221, the focus of their activity and their eventual route out of Iran was in the northwest, through Azerbaijan and the Caucasus. This left Baghdad and Mosul, the major cities of Mesopotamia, untouched and largely unaffected by the first Mongol invasions; their importance as political and cultural centres continued undiminished.

Mosul at this time was under the rule of the former Zangid atabeg Badr al-Din Luʾluʾ (see figs. 25 and 28), whose control of the city was formally recognised by the caliph al-Mustansir (ruled 1226–42) in December 1233.[7] Lu'lu' entered into various marriage alliances with the caliphal court, marrying one daughter to a senior amir, al-Duwaydar, in 1227, and another to al-Duwaydar's son, Mujahid al-Din Aybak, in 1237.[8] The Mongols continued to make periodic sorties into the area, raiding in the vicinity of Irbil and capturing and sacking the town in 1237 but failing to take the citadel.[9] Lu'lu' was obliged to send supplies to assist the besieging Mongols, an indication of his gradual incorporation into the Mongol sphere and a recognition of their overlordship that allowed him to remain in power in Mosul, on payment of tribute and the despatch of envoys to attend the enthronement of Güyük in Qaraqorum, accompanied by the Mongol viceroy, Arghun Aqa, in 1246.[10] By 1254, having been confirmed as ruler of Mosul by the new Great Khan Möngke, Lu'lu' had clearly seen which way the wind was blowing: he sent his eldest son Isma'il to represent him in Mongolia and the same year struck coins in the name of Möngke (and himself), thus breaking off his allegiance to the caliph al-Musta'sim (ruled 1242–58).[11] As the Mongol armies under Hülegü and Baiju Noyan converged on Baghdad, Lu'lu' had no option but to join the advance, and assisted Baiju's crossing of the Tigris with a bridge of boats (see fig. 5). After the fall of the city, Lu'lu' went in person to pay allegiance to Hülegü Khan in Maragha in August 1258, possibly not least because of doubts surrounding his loyalty[12] – a loyalty that he used to attempt to extend his own power over Irbil, ʿAmid and Mayafarriqin. After the fall of Mayafarriqin in April 1259, Hülegü married Lu'lu's son and heir al-Salih Ismaʿil to the Khwarazmian princess Turkhan Khatun.[13]

When Lu'lu' died later in 1259, aged over eighty, a period of relative calm and security died with him. He bequeathed Mosul to al-Salih Ismaʿil, and other towns to his other sons, who, however, were quick to align themselves with the Mamluks and the growing power of Sultan Baybars al-Mansuri. Al-Salih initially extended his control over Sinjar and assisted the Mongol siege of ʿAmid. He maintained his Mongol allegiance on coinage in 1259–61, before retiring to Cairo to seek the assistance of Sultan Baybars. He and other sons of Lu'lu' then took part in the abortive expedition despatched by Baybars to help the ʿAbbasid refugees recover Baghdad.[14] Al-Salih himself did not take part in the final battle but returned to Mosul, where he found his wife Turkhan Khatun had taken over the citadel at the head of a pro-Christian and pro-Mongol faction and had informed Hülegü of his defection. Al-Salih nevertheless entered the city in November 1261 and issued coinage acknowledging the Mamluks, shortly before the Christian Mongol *noyan* (commander) Samdaghu arrived with a *tuman* (unit of 10,000 troops), followed by a further Persian contingent, to take it once and for all (see fig. 6). In the absence of effective support from his brothers or the Mamluks, al-Salih eventually surrendered and suffered a lingering death at Hülegü's camp by Lake Van in July 1262.[15] Mosul was sacked and the Mongols established the governorship on Shams al-Din Muhammad b. Yunus al-Baʿshiqi, the former Christian governor of Nineveh, whose Christian community had suffered greatly at the hands of al-Salih Ismaʿil. The Mongol *noyan* Nurin was appointed alongside him. The Mongol conquest of northern Iraq was consolidated by the following summer with the fall of Jazirat b. ʿUmar and the appointment of another Christian governor, Mar Hisya.[16]

The level of information available for affairs in northern Iraq decreases significantly after these events, the main contemporary sources being the Syriac chronicle of Bar Hebraeus (Ibn al-ʿIbri), written mainly in Maragha, and an anonymous Arabic chronicle written in Baghdad, formerly attributed to Ibn al-Fuwati.[17]

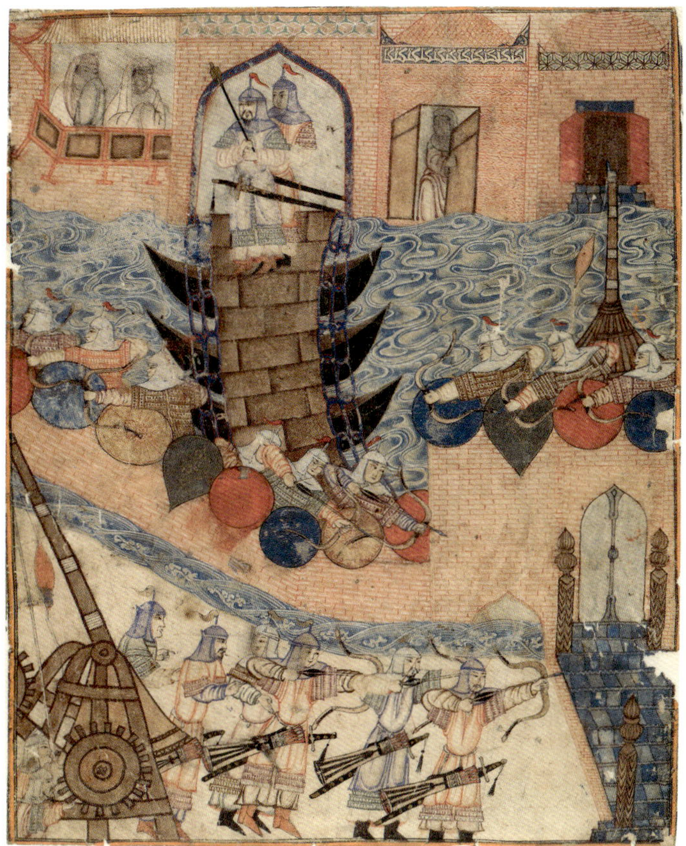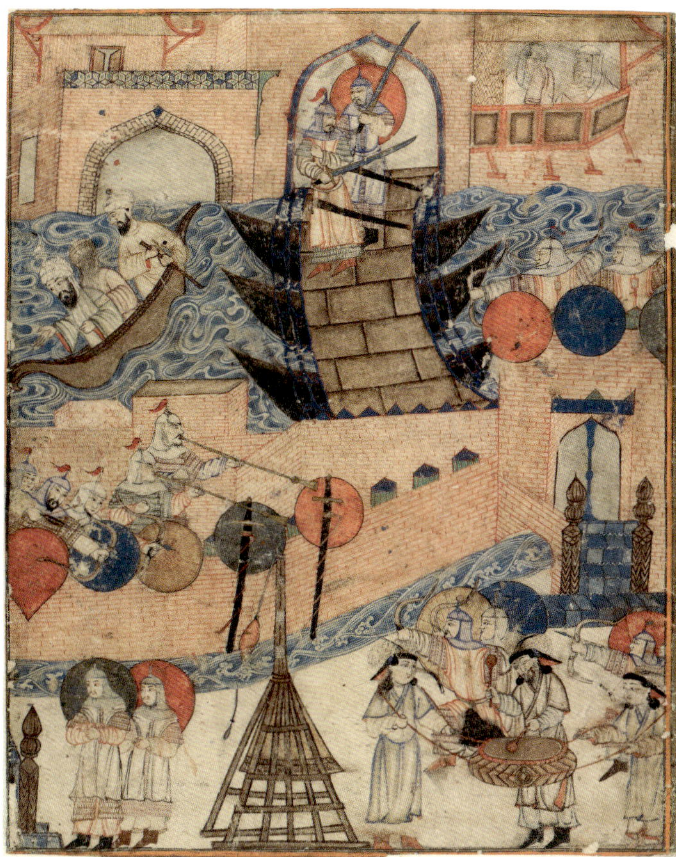

These authors from their different standpoints give brief details of the sequence of governors in Mosul and other towns in Mesopotamia and, especially in the case of Bar Hebraeus, of the ever-worsening position of the Christian communities and their monasteries, as well as of the persecution of the Jews, as the Muslims reasserted themselves after the collapse of caliphal rule. This narrative gives little scope for imagining an environment conducive to artistic patronage and production. On the other hand, the presence of the rulers in the region, and with them the whole Mongol court (*ordu*) including the princesses and womenfolk, might have encouraged the creation of luxury items. We will briefly note both these aspects of the situation.

Governors of Mosul from 1262

There are few details of the changes of governorship in Mosul after the death of Ismaʿil, and some conflicts in the dates given; the turnover was quite rapid and was usually attended by charges of financial corruption. Few lasted more than two years. Many of the governors were Christian and relied on Mongol support (and a Mongol military official, the *shihna*) to maintain their position in an increasingly hostile environment. In 1264, Zaki al-Irbili was able to destroy and replace Ibn Yunus al-Baʿshqi, accusing him of amassing wealth from Badr al-Din Lu'lu''s treasury.[18] Two years later, in 1266, Zaki al-Irbili was himself seized and pursued over his accounts; most of what was due was recovered from him and he was then killed; he was replaced by a Persian, Razi al-Din al-Baba.[19] The latter was replaced in 1268 by another Christian, Masʿud al-Barquti, who had been presented to Abaqa Khan by the Uighur Christian Ashmut (Yoshmut) after his father died on his way to honour Qubilai Khan. Masʿud was made governor of Mosul and Irbil, with Yoshmut as his *shihna*.[20]

The ousted al-Baba, however, returned in 1270 falsely to accuse Masʿud of amassing wealth together with Yoshmut, and they were imprisoned and replaced.

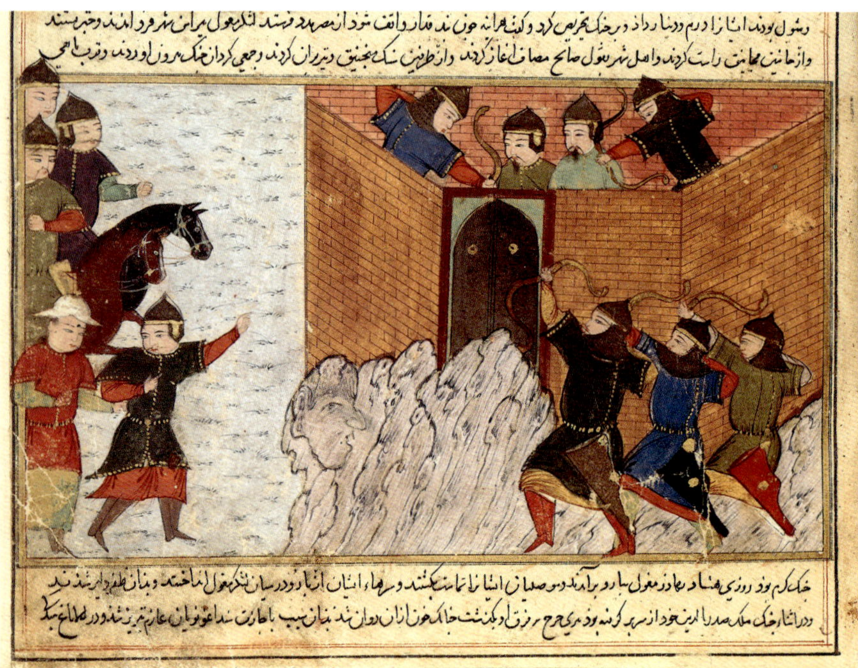

FIG. 6

'Conquest of Mosul by the Mongols', from
Rashid al-Din's *Compendium
of Chronicles*, Herat, *c.* 1425
Ink, colours and gold on paper,
H: 14.5, W: 24.5 cm (image)
Paris, Bibliothèque Nationale,
MS. Supplément Persan 1113, fol. 190

Several Mongol amirs were appointed *shihna*s with the reinstated al-Baba.[21] The feud between these parties continued throughout the reign of Abaqa (1265–82), and in 1277 Masᶜud al-Barquti and Yoshmut were able to secure the execution of al-Baba and their reinstatement in Mosul and Irbil. They paraded his head round the town and it was fixed to the Bab al-Jasr (Bridge Gate).[22] Once again, supporters of the defeated faction took their case to court, accusing Masᶜud of embezzlement; he was arrested and tortured but managed to give his captors the slip.[23] Yoshmut, however, seems to have remained as military governor, accused of siding with Arghun in his conflict with his uncle Ahmad Tegüder.[24]

On Arghun's accession in 1284, Masᶜud was again named governor of Mosul, but his comrade Yoshmut was murdered by the sons of Jalal al-Din Turan, a former enemy.[25] Masᶜud's governorship was faced with severe challenges, among them a raid by an army from Syria in 1285, which was directed against Diyarbakr, Mosul and Irbil, where many people were killed and in Mosul the goods of the merchants were looted from the bazaar. The Christians were the main sufferers in Irbil, as well as in towns and villages in the vicinity of Tikrit and Mosul. The *shihna* fled to Baghdad.[26] Masᶜud's governorship of Mosul came to an end in 1289, when Arghun Khan's chief

minister, the Mongol Buqa, fell from favour and with him his brother Aruq, who was governor of Mesopotamia. At the same time, Taj al-Din, the son of Mukhtatas, the Armenian governor of Irbil, was tortured in order to get him to reveal his wealth.[27]

Masᶜud was perhaps replaced by his accuser, ᶜAbd al-Mu'min, who was in turn challenged by a Coptic jurist called Faraj-Allah and investigated, found guilty of financial irregularities and killed. The new *sahib-i divan* (chief minister), the Jewish Saᶜd al-Daula, sent his brother Amin al-Daula to be governor of Mosul, Mardin and Diyarbakr, together with Taj al-Din b. Mukhtatas.[28] As protests against Saᶜd al-Daula's regime mounted, Arghun's cousin Baidu sent someone to seize Amin al-Daula.[29]

Thereafter, information is lacking about the authorities in northern Iraq and events connected with the Mosul district. Baidu, already based in the region, occupied Mosul and Baghdad in his revolt against Geikhatu in 1295.[30] The tribulations of the Christian communities continue to be lamented in the Christian texts, notably the destruction of churches in Mosul and elsewhere when Ghazan Khan came to power, and particularly the massacre at Irbil in 1310.[31] Early in Ghazan's reign, in 1295, thousands of Oirat Mongols migrated from the region to seek refuge in the Mamluk sultanate.[32]

Il-Khans in the Mosul district

Intermittent warfare between the Mamluks and Mongols throughout this period drew the Il-Khans in person into Mesopotamia. Mosul's geographical position by the crossing of the Tigris and the Zab rivers and its nodal point on the route between north-west Iran and northern Syria put it in the path of the Mongols' major expeditions against the Mamluks. These persisted beyond the Il-Khans' conversion to Islam, as the Mongols sought to overturn previous failures and establish themselves as the paramount rulers of the age.

Thus Abaqa Khan stayed around Sinjar and Mosul with the *ordu* for three weeks in October 1281 before crossing the Tigris at Kushaf and travelling down to Baghdad; his brother Möngke Temür died in the region on his return from the Mongol defeat at Hims shortly afterwards.[33]

In 1299, Ghazan Khan, at the head of the army, left his womenfolk behind in Mosul on his first, successful, Syrian expedition and returned to Tabriz using the same route, passing slowly through Mesopotamia with extended stays round Sinjar and Mosul for about six weeks in March–April 1300.[34] The following year, he remained in the Sinjar area for around ten weeks in February–May 1301, after withdrawing from Aleppo in the face of adverse weather (which aborted a second expedition into Syria), spending the time feasting and hunting.[35] On his third expedition, in 1303, he despatched the advance guard via Kushaf and Mosul, while he himself went to Hilla and hunted around Wasit, and visited the ᶜAlid shrines before travelling along the Euphrates to 'Ana. From there, he despatched the *ordu* of the women and the bureaucracy to return to Iran via Sinjar and Mosul, turning back himself the same way a couple of weeks later.[36] He remained in the Mosul area, rejoining the women and hunting around Sinjar before crossing the Tigris at Kushaf in April 1303. Here,

receiving complaints of the tyranny of the governor of Mosul, Fakhr al-Din ᶜIsa the Christian, he sent Sultan Najm al-Din, governor of Mardin, to execute him.[37]

Fakhr al-Din ᶜIsa b. Ibrahim is otherwise known as the dedicatee of the *Kitab al-Fakhri*, composed by Ibn al-Tiqtaqa in the course of the winter of 1301–02, while delayed in Mosul by heavy snow on his way to Tabriz.[38] The glowing picture he gives of his patron is very different from the reports that led to his downfall very shortly afterwards. Unfortunately, there appears to be no record of when Fakhr al-Din became governor, nor of who succeeded him.

Military hostilities ceased briefly after Ghazan's death, but his brother Öljeitü launched one further campaign, directed at Rahba on the Euphrates; Öljeitü was in the Mosul area for around a month in November–December 1312, reviewing the army at Sinjar, before retiring to Baghdad.[39]

The last effective Il-Khan, Abu Saᶜid, son of Öljeitü (ruled 1317–35), made Baghdad his winter quarters several times during his reign.[40] Thus the *ordu* wintered in the city in 1317–18, 1326–27, and again in 1332–33 and 1333–34; the route taken is not specified.[41] During his reign the governorship was in the hands first of Chupan's son Dimashq Khwaja and then, after their fall, given to ᶜAli-Padshah, uncle of Abu Saᶜid. The occasional presence of the Il-Khans may have created particular opportunities for precious commodities to be commissioned or presented, while the occupation of this prestigious governorship by personalities very close to the court, such as the historian ᶜAta-Malik Juvaini, provincial governor between 1259 and his death in 1283, ensured that Baghdad at least remained an important cultural centre, despite the magnet of the rival Mamluk Cairo.[42]

NOTES

1 *Hawadith* 1997, p. 360; al-Dhahabi/Negre 1979, p. 267, gives 1,800,000!

2 See Amitai-Preiss 1995 and Broadbridge 2008 for authoritative studies of the whole period.

3 Amitai 2005, pp. 359–90.

4 Melville 1990, pp. 159–77.

5 Komaroff 2006, not forgetting earlier patronage at Maragha and Takht-i Sulaiman under Hülegü and Abaqa.

6 Lane 2003 is particularly generous towards Hülegü's mission.

7 Patton 1991, pp. 30–33, citing numerous Arabic sources, for this and most of what follows. See especially *Hawadith* 1997, p. 79.

8 *Hawadith* 1997, pp. 99, 121; Patton 1991, pp. 48–49. The first daughter died in October 1237, *Hawadith* 1997, pp. 130–31.

9 *Hawadith* 1997, p. 128; Patton 1991, pp. 52–53.

10 Juvaini 1912–37, vol. 1, p. 205; Juvaini/Boyle 1958, p. 250; Rashid al-Din 1994, p. 805; Patton 1991, pp. 56–57.

11 Patton 1991, pp. 58–59; although this allegiance was temporarily reversed as the Mongol threat to Baghdad appeared to wane, *ibid.*, p. 60.

12 Patton 1991, pp. 60–61; cf. Rashid al-Din 1994, pp. 1022–23.

13 Patton 1991, pp. 62–64; Juvaini 1912–37, vol. 2, p. 201, Juvaini/Boyle 1958, p. 468; Rashid al-Din 1994, p. 1025.

14 Bar Hebraeus/Budge 1932, pp. 442–43; as Ibn al-ᶜIbri 1986, p. 322. See also Patton 1991, pp. 76–77; Amitai-Preiss 1995, pp. 57–58.

15 *Hawadith* 1997, pp. 375, 377–78; Rashid al-Din 1994, pp. 1040–43; Patton 1991, pp. 79–81; Amitai-Preiss 1995, pp. 60–61.

16 *Hawadith* 1997, pp. 378–79; Fiey 1975, p. 30; Patton 1991, p. 81.

17 See Melville 1997a, pp. 25–26; and Aigle 2008, pp. 25–61.

18 Bar Hebraeus/Budge 1932, p. 444; Ibn al-ᶜIbri 1986, p. 323; Fiey 1975, pp. 30–31.

19 *Hawadith* 1997, p. 385; Ibn al-ᶜIbri 1986, p. 325, calls him Nasir al-Din Baba; Fiey 1975, p. 31.

20 *Hawadith* 1997, p. 393; Bar Hebraeus/Budge 1932, p. 456, Ibn al-ᶜIbri 1986, pp. 334–35, places this in 1276, a discrepancy carried over to the rest of his career. See Fiey [1959], p. 48; Fiey 1975, pp. 36–37.

21 *Hawadith* 1997, p. 401; Bar Hebraeus/Budge 1932, pp. 459–60; Ibn al-ᶜIbri 1986, p. 337.

22 *Hawadith* 1997, pp. 434–35; Bar Hebraeus/Budge 1932, p. 462; Ibn al-ᶜIbri 1986, p. 340 (under 1280); Fiey 1975, p. 37.

23 Bar Hebraeus/Budge 1932, pp. 463–64; Ibn al-ᶜIbri 1986, p. 341; Fiey 1975, p. 38.

24 Mar Jabalaha/Budge 1928, pp. 158–59; Fiey 1975, p. 43.

25 Bar Hebraeus/Budge 1932, p. 472, Ibn al-ᶜIbri 1986, p. 348; Fiey 1975, p. 45.

26 *Hawadith* 1997, p. 482; Bar Hebraeus/Budge 1932, pp. 475–77; Ibn al-ᶜIbri 1986, pp. 351–52; Fiey 1975, p. 45–46, distinguishing several separate disorders at this time.

27 Bar Hebraeus/Budge 1932, pp. 480–81, Ibn al-ᶜIbri 1986, pp. 356–57; Fiey 1975, pp. 51–52.

28 Bar Hebraeus/Budge 1932, pp. 484–85, Ibn al-ᶜIbri 1986, p. 359; Fiey 1975, p. 53.

29 *Hawadith* 1997, p. 503; Bar Hebraeus/Budge 1932, pp. 488–89, records the undoing of Faraj-Allah.

30 Bar Hebraeus/Budge 1932, pp. 497–98; *Hawadith* 1997, pp. 521–23; Fiey 1975, p. 60.

31 Bar Hebraeus/Budge 1932, pp. 507–08; Ibn al-ᶜIbri 1986, pp. 378–79; Mar Jabalaha/Budge 1928, pp. 262–302; Fiey [1959], pp. 51–53; Fiey 1975, pp. 66–70, 76–79; Rashid al-Din 1994, p. 1259; Qashani 1969, pp. 110–16, with an account of earlier sieges.

32 Bar Hebraeus/Budge 1932, p. 508, Ibn al-ᶜIbri 1986, p. 379; Rashid al-Din 1994, p. 1262.

33 Rashid al-Din 1994, pp. 1116–18; Vassaf 1853, p. 98; Vassaf 1967, p. 60, hunting near Rahba.

34 *Hawadith* 1997, p. 544; Rashid al-Din 1994, pp. 1290, 1296.

35 *Hawadith* 1997, 545; Rashid al-Din 1994, pp. 1298–99.

36 Vassaf 1853, pp. 401, 408–09, Vassaf 1967, pp. 242–45, Rashid al-Din 1994, pp. 1309–13.

37 Rashid al-Din 1994, p. 1313.

38 Ibn al-Tiqtaqa 1960, pp. 8–9, 339; Ibn al-Tiqtaqa/Whitting 1947 (1990), pp. 4, 326; Melville 1997b, pp. 58–59. Fitzherbert 2006, pp. 390–406.

39 Vassaf 1853, p. 553, Vassaf 1967, p. 305; Qashani 1969, pp. 305–06.

40 For the whole of this period, see Melville 1999.

41 Mustawfi Qazvini 1999, p. 1451, l. 5; Ahri 2010, pp. 212, 216. Abu Saᶜid was intending to spend the winter of 1335–36 there too, when his attention was directed north to meet the threat of an invasion from the Golden Horde: see Shabankara'i 1984, pp. 289–90.

42 The celebrated calligrapher Yaqut al-Mustᶜasimi continued to work there, for example, till his death in the reign of Ghazan Khan.

"Not every head that wears a crown deserves to rule"[1] Women in Il-Khanid political life and court culture

JUDITH PFEIFFER

THIS ESSAY focuses on elite women at the courts of the Il-Khanate, where the Courtauld bag was probably produced. During the Il-Khanid period women were exceptionally powerful players at the highest echelons of politics, both at the Mongol and at local courts. Mongol women in particular were exceedingly influential in Il-Khanid politics. When they are seen seated next to the Khan in contemporary miniatures (fig. 7, cat. 16–17), this is not merely an expression of marital relations, or of an affectionate relationship between two spouses: it is also a reflection of the matrix of political power on the ground. The Mongol first ladies and princesses of the Il-Khanate had access to their own grazing grounds, taxation rights and share in booty, and played a major role in the election of succeeding Il-Khans,[2] just as they had played a major role in the political assemblies (*quriltay*s) of the Mongol empire.[3] They also had their own camps (*ordu*s), retinue and contingents of military support (*amir*s), made independent endowments,[4] had the right to issue decrees with their own seals, owned large appanages in the provinces of the Il-Khanate, and could move around independently of their husbands for several months at a time.[5] Some of them minted their own coins; their name was mentioned in the Friday prayer (*khutba*)[6] and they wore both male and female titles of sovereignty, including the titles *sultan* and *padishah*.[7]

A distinction needs to be made between Mongol and non-Mongol women. The latter were, at least initially, subject to different legal systems and part of different socio-anthropological frameworks, and appear to have remained largely outside the Chinggisid court circles of the Il-Khanate, even if they married into them. However, these women could also have prominent roles in politics. Local non-Chinggisid dynasties such as the Salghurids of Fars, the Atabegs of Yazd and the Qara-Khita'ids of Kerman, had the same Turco-Mongol steppe traditions

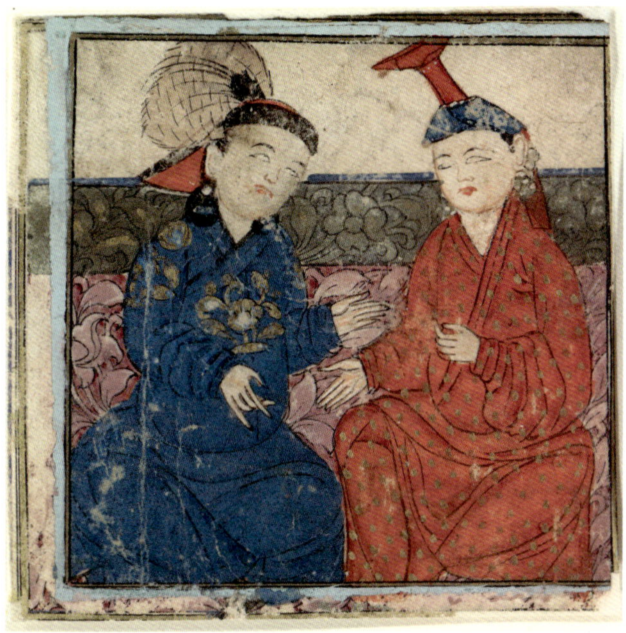

FIG. 7
'Khan and Khatun', probably an illustration to the genealogical charts in Rashid al-Din's *Compendium of Chronicles*, Iran, 14th century, now mounted in the Diez Albums (cat. 16–18)
Ink, colours and gold on paper,
H: 6.9 cm, W: 7.0 cm (image)
Berlin, Staatsbibliothek, Diez A,
fol. 71, S. 42, no. 4

as the Chinggisids, permitting women to direct political affairs at the highest echelons of society. Amongst their most prominent women were the Qara-Khita'id Terken Qutlugh Khatun (d. 1282), who ruled Kerman for 26 years, claiming full rights to both the civil and the military administration of this province; her daughter, and wife of the Il-Khans Abaqa and Geikhatu, Padishah Khatun (d. 1295), who ruled Kerman from 1291 to 1295 and was also known for her poetry (see below), and several female regents and rulers in the province of Fars, notably the Salghurid queen Abish Khatun (ruled 1263–84).

Loyalty to the Chinggisids was often secured through betrothal to a Hülegüid prince.[8] These nominal marriages into the Il-Khanid dynasty appear to have been a control mechanism for the Il-Khans over the women's and their dynasties' power. While women from the imperial house were given in marriage to Mongol military commanders (*noyan*s and *amir*s) without hesitation, only rarely were Chinggisid princesses given in marriage to local, non-Mongol rulers – or at least, the sources don't tell us about them.[9] There is little evidence that marriages between Il-Khans and the daughters of local rulers were actually consummated. Hülegü apparently did not marry any 'local' women at all, and his son Abaqa Khan took Padishah Khatun of Kerman as his sixth, and Tespina (or Despina) of Trabzon as his ninth wife, but had children with neither.[10] Saljuq Khatun, daughter of the Seljuq Sultan of Rum, was Arghun's third wife, but there are no reported children. A sister of Demetrius II of Georgia was married to one of Arghun's sons, and again there are no reports of any offspring.[11] The Qutlughkhanid Shah ᶜAlam, wife of the Hülegüid princes Taraghay and Baidu, who had a son with Taraghay, was a Chinggisid on her maternal side, so was not really an 'outsider.' The one exception appears to be the Salghurid Abish Khatun, who

had a daughter with Hülegü's son Möngke Temür, who never acceded to rule. In general, such marriages appear to have been meant to forge political alliances for one generation, without giving potential offspring the chance to get involved in inner-Mongol affairs in the future.[12]

Conversely, Chinggisid marriages with Mongol women were taken extremely seriously, and spouses were as a matter of principle selected according to their tribal background. Exogamy (marriage outside the tribe) was the overriding principle in the selection of a spouse according to the steppe taxonomies that informed Mongol marriage customs during the early Il-Khanate.[13] These customs led to clashes with Islamic law after the Mongols' conversion to Islam, as cousin marriage is both common practice and legal according to the *shariᶜa*, and was often used in western Asia to prevent the parcellation of landed property by keeping it 'in the family.' In contrast, the Mongols strongly disapproved of cousin marriage, which they perceived as incestuous and despicable, and some recent Mongol converts to Islam almost abandoned Islam because of this practice.[14] Levirate marriages (re-marriage to a close family member after the death of a husband), however, were widespread and often used by successors to the Chinggisid throne to gain access to the property, including the armies, that belonged to the wives of a deceased brother, father or uncle.[15] The same applied, at least initially, to the highest echelons of the Il-Khanid political class. There are no known marriages between members of the Hülegüid Chinggisid (royal) dynasty before their conversion to Islam.[16] The Chinggisids took wives from non-Chinggisid tribes, often acquiring these from outside the Il-Khanate, requesting wives from Mongolia and China. Among these, the Qonqirat was the preferred consort tribe.[17]

Keeping track of their genealogy was therefore exceedingly important for the Mongols, as expressed in

Rashid al-Din's *Compendium of Chronicles* and *Five-fold Genealogies*.[18] In political terms, only Chinggisids could become rulers; all others were considered commoners (*qarachu*) and had no right to the throne. Only after the Chinggisid line died out in the Il-Khanate did commoners – especially from the Jalayirids and Chupanids – dare to aspire to rule, but they always did so by electing a so-called 'puppet khan', a lateral descendant from the Chinggisid line, or by marrying one or more princesses of the Chinggisid blood line. During the later Il-Khanate, Hülegüid and Chinggisid princesses and former wives of Il-Khans therefore became coveted as potential wives by commoner warlords, who hoped to boost their legitimacy through such alliances.[19] Thus, in 1319 the powerful amir Chupan of the Suldus clan married the Il-Khan Abu Saʿid's half-sister Sati Beg (*fl.* 1316–45), who became a ruler in her own right in 1338–39.[20] Sati Beg minted coins in a large number of cities, stretching from Erzincan (in modern-day Turkey), Hilla (in modern-day Iraq), Tbilisi and Isfahan all the way to Tus (near Mashhad in modern-day Iran), mostly in areas under Chupanid rule.[21] Her coins bear the Muslim *shahada* and the names of the first four caliphs on the obverse, and her name and the titles 'Khan' and 'Sultana' on the reverse.[22] After the execution of her husband Chupan in 1327, she allied with the founder of the Jalayirid dynasty, Hasan Buzurg, who, as she was from the Hülegüid blood line that was needed to claim the title *khan*, helped her to the throne: she duly claimed title – title that was then used by her second and third husbands respectively, the 'puppet khans' Arpa Khan (ruled 1335–36) and Sulaiman Khan (ruled 1339–46), who, while Chinggisid, were not direct descendants of Hülegü and thus reinforced their standing by marrying into the Hülegüid line.

While female affluence was curbed through Ghazan's reforms and his confiscation of some of the women's *ordu*s without, apparently, later restituting them,[23] this did nothing to diminish the Chinggisid ladies' standing through their blood line either on the paternal or maternal side, or indeed, in some cases, the standing of non-Chinggisid Mongol women who had been wives of former Il-Khans and had acquired substantial influence through connections, wealth or, most importantly, Chinggisid offspring.

Wealth was only one among several factors in a woman's standing. One of the most coveted women was Baghdad Khatun (d. 1335), the daughter of the amir Chupan (a two-time Chinggisid son-in-law through marriage to the Il-Khan Öljeitü's daughters Sati Beg and Dowlandi Khatun).[24] She was first married to Hasan Buzurg, the founder of the commoner Jalayirid dynasty, but was wooed by the Il-Khan Abu Saʿid, who forced her to divorce her husband and marry him instead. After Abu Saʿid's death, Baghdad Khatun was executed by one of the successor puppet khans, Arpa Khan, apparently because he was afraid of her power, and he married instead Sati Beg, the sister of his predecessor on the Il-Khanid throne, Abu Saʿid, and widow of Baghdad Khatun's father Chupan.

Some historical accounts provide romantic narratives surrounding Abu Saʿid's infatuation with the beauty of Baghdad Khatun, and some modern scholars have inferred that he must therefore have been able to see her face and that Mongol women at the time were not veiled.[25] Baghdad Khatun occupied a central position in the web of power that cemented the alliance between the two major competing commoner groups (the Chupanids, represented by her father Chupan, and the Jalayirids, via her husband Hasan Buzurg) who challenged Abu Saʿid and Chinggisid power. In the light of the highly entangled marriage politics outlined above, this may have been a more important factor in her appeal for Abu Saʿid than her physical appearance. In the chess game of Mongol marriage politics, she was a 'queen' in the true sense of the word, being able to move in all directions, both vertically and horizontally. As soon as she was married to Abu Saʿid, her moves were restricted – like those of the 'king' in the chess game (the Il-Khan) himself.

While modern scholars have argued that the social and political roles of Mongol women in western Asia eventually adapted to Islamicate customs and values,[26] women at the height of the Il-Khanate retained much of their social and political authority. This was expressed in the seating order at court, as articulated in the visual representation of women in the images of the period.

The Il-Khanid vizier Rashid al-Din's *History of the Mongols* distinguishes several dozen different Turkic and Mongol tribes and affords invaluable insights into the inner dynamics of Turco-Mongol society. Rashid al-Din also composed detailed genealogical charts of the Mongols.[27] These genealogical charts list each of the amirs and women with their role and status (e.g. commander of ten thousand, or parasol bearer in the case of the amirs, and wife (*khatun*)[28] or concubine (*egechi*)[29] in the case of the women) together with the names of their tribes, their 'horizontal connection,' so to speak. In addition, each woman's children (her 'vertical connection') are also listed. In contemporary texts and paintings that have survived from Rashid al-Din's *History of the Mongols*, women play a central role (see fig. 7 and cat. 16). The Mongol military commanders were seated to the right of the Chinggisid Il-Khan and the women were seated to his left in order of rank, with the first lady next to the Il-Khan.[30] In a society in which the seating order clearly reflected the political hierarchies this was of extreme importance. Further distinctions in the rank of the women were expressed by a special headgear, the *boghtaq* (fig. 8).

Whereas we know the names of dozens of women of the Il-Khanate who were married to members of the Il-Khanid family, Turco-Mongol commoners, and local notables,[31] we know very little about their lives, personality and appearance. What we hear about them are topoi, often expressed through symbols and comparisons such as 'jewel,' 'moon' or 'untouched pearl,' regardless of their age and marital status. Thus, the Qara-Khita'id ruler of Kerman, Turkan Khatun (ruled 1257–82) was described as a "world-illuminating sun" and "beauty" when she was over fifty years old.[32] Similarly, the appearance of her daughter Padishah Khatun, who was also known as a poetess,[33] remains elusive, as descriptions remain within the boundaries of oft-repeated common-places: she is said to possess "beauty" (a quality also ascribed to male potentates) and is described as a "fragrant rose".[34] Quade-Reutter, who has studied these two women extensively, has concluded that despite their non-Chinggisid background and local rule, both Turkan and Padishah Khatun "certainly wore the clothes that were usual for Mongol women at the court" and that "like her mother [Turkan], she [Padishah Khatun] appeared in public without the veil; the poem ascribed to her about the *miqnaʿa* is probably to be interpreted symbolically".[35] Since the poem (*qitʿa*) in question contains one of the few self-descriptions of a contemporary woman, it is quoted here in full:[36]

I am that woman all of whose works are good deeds,
Underneath my veil (*miqnaʿa-yi man*) there is plenty
    of sovereignty (*kulah-dārī*).
Behind the curtain (*parde*) of chastity (*ʿiṣmat*) which
    is my refuge,
It is difficult for the travellers of the east wind to
    intrude.

Not every woman who wears two ells of veil (*miqnaᶜa*)
  is a lady,
Not every head that wears a crown deserves to rule.[37]
Whoever I give a *miqnaᶜa* to asks:
What is the rank of the *miqnaᶜa*? It is a crown worth
  a thousand dinars.
I am that king (*shah*) from the seed (*nizhād*) of
  powerful rulers (*shahān-i ulugh-sulṭān*).
They take their wives from us [our family] for as long
  as rule exists in this world.

While a symbolic reading is certainly appropriate,
there is no reason not to believe that Padishah Khatun
wore a *miqnaᶜa*: there is no contradiction between
wearing a veil, even a light one, like a *miqnaᶜa*, which
leaves the full face visible, and being a political leader
– as Padishah Khatun forcefully expresses in her poem.
Between the famous 'religious tolerance' of the Mongols
and the exceedingly fast acculturation of the Qara-Khita'i
(to the extent that their women were capable of writing
poetry in Persian that is still quoted in the literary
histories of Iran today),[38] the idea of a first lady wearing a
Muslim headgear – the *miqnaᶜa* – instead of the *boghtaq*
appears entirely plausible. While the evidence is sparse,
we know too little about this time to be able to discard
the evidence that we do have – such as Padishah Khatun's
poem, and the Courtauld bag.

Padishah Khatun's "beauty" has been interpreted as
inner beauty and integrity – symbolised by the *miqnaᶜa*
in her poem, which she clearly juxtaposes to the crown,
which, according to her, not everyone was fit to wear.
Corruption was rife in the Il-Khanid period, both at
the courts and among amirs and viziers, and this was
true for her family, too. Padishah Khatun had her own
half-brother Soyurghatmish strangled, because he had
interfered with state affairs that she thought he was not fit

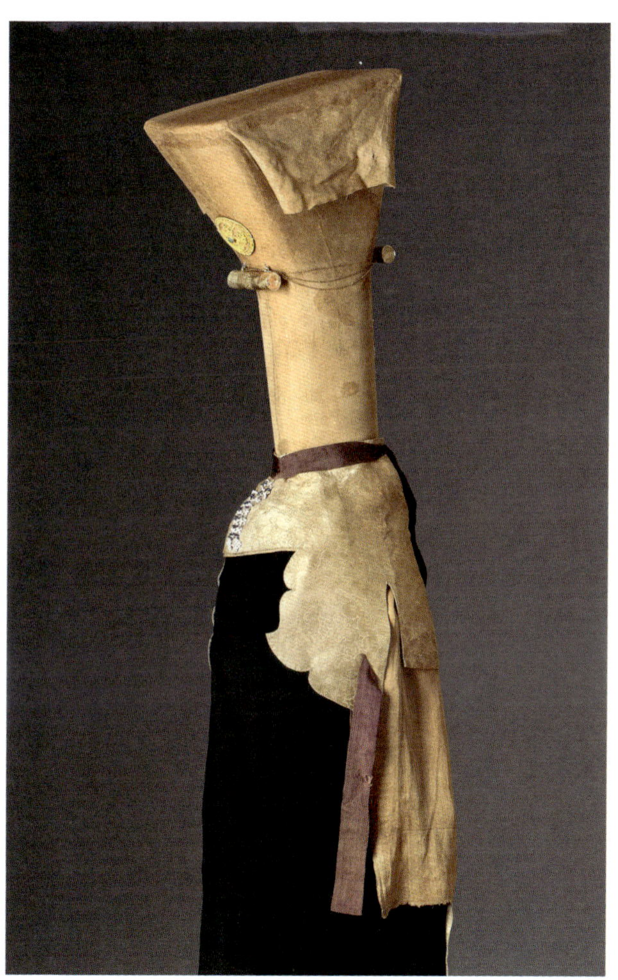

to handle: he had reached for the crown that she thought he was not fit to wear, but which he had won through back-hand politics at the Il-Khanid court.[39] The poem is clearly about more than female chastity: it is *Sozialkritik* before the term, and an apologia of a woman who firmly asserted that gender did not matter in state affairs: whether the ruler was the wearer of a *miqnaᶜa* or a crown was secondary to their aptitude for the job. Padishah Khatun was intensely conscious of her value both by descent (*nizhad*), as a benefactor in society (through "good deeds") and as a leader in politics, and she did not hide it.

Wielding significant power under the Il-Khans, women were weighty players in marriage strategies, and were an important tool with which to bind generals, scholars and administrators to the royal house, to hand power down from father to son, and to add major economic assets and military power to the groom's. The application of the Muslim *shariᶜa* to Mongol day-to-day life, especially in the area of marriage law, probably resulted in a major restructuring of the society in the long term, but that subject still awaits in-depth study.[40]

NOTES

1 The quotation is taken from Kirmani 1328 sh./1949, pp. 70–71. I am indebted to Evrim Binbaş for his comments on this article, and to Rachel Ward for an inspiring correspondence on the art historical side of this paper while it was in the making. For all remaining errors I claim responsibility. Funding for research for this article was made available from the European Research Council under the European Union's Seventh Framework Programme (FP7/2007–2013) / ERC Starting Grant 263557 IMPAcT.

2 Pfeiffer 2003, ch. 3.

3 Franke 1994, p. 36.

4 For the endowments made by Turkan Khatun of Kerman (d. 1283), see Quade-Reutter 2003, pp. 145–54; 545–48; for those of her daughter Padishah Khatun (d. 1295) in Erzerum and Kerman, ibid., pp. 204–05; Karamağaralı 1971a; 1971b. On the endowments of Turkan of Fars (d. 1263), see Quade-Reutter 2003, p. 258, and those of the Timurid princess Gawharshad (d. 1457), ibid., p. 513.

5 Blochet 1910, p. 13.

6 Lambton 1988, pp. 282, 289; Mernissi 1993.

7 For the titles of female rulers and regents during this period, see Quade-Reutter 2003, pp. 417–18; 553–57. See also the references in fnn. 21 and 22.

8 On Terken Qutlugh Khatun see Juvaini/ Boyle 1997, pp. 476–77; Quade-Reutter 2003, pp. 75–165. On Padishah Khatun, see Quade-Reutter 2003, pp. 175–213. On Abish Khatun, see Spuler 1982; Quade-Reutter 2003, pp. 270–302. For further elite women from both local and Chinggisid dynasties under Mongol and Timurid rule, see Quade-Reutter 2003.

9 Lambton 1988, pp. 287–88.

10 He took the former in his mother Yesünjin Khatun's stead, an honor that may have come together with the sexual abstinence that he would have exercised vis-à-vis his mother, as no children issued from this marriage.

11 Lambton 1988, p. 288.

12 Pfeiffer 2003, ch. 2.iii ('Marriage politics and conversion in the Ilkhanate: Radical choices in appropriate mates').

13 Zhao 2008, pp. 15–30.

14 Qashani 1348 h.sh./1969, pp. 97–98.

15 A famous example is the Il-Khan and convert to Islam Ghazan Khan's wish to marry his father's primary wife (but not Ghazan's biological mother) Bulughan Khatun after his father's death, which was Mongol custom, but forbidden by Islamic law. Had not a Muslim scholar declared that it was licit for Ghazan to marry Bulughan because she had never been married to his father according to Islamic law (a marriage which could thus be considered as virtually not having taken place), Ghazan might have returned to the Mongol *yāsā*. On the levirate among the Mongols, see Holmgren 1986.

16 The situation clearly changed after the Mongols' conversion to Islam. For instance, the Il-Khan Ghazan's daughter Öljei Qutluq was first betrothed to her nephew Bistam (son of Ghazan's brother Öljeitü), who died in infancy, and then married to another cousin of hers, Bistam's younger brother and later Il-Khan Abu Saᶜid. See Melville 1998.

17 For the Yüan, George Qingzhi Zhao has established that "The Onggirat tribe was … the most important marriage partner of the Chinggisid ruling clan, with 67% of the imperial consorts selected from this tribe and 25% of Mongol Princesses married into this tribe. Among the 22 women who received the title of Empress … fourteen originated from the Onggirat tribe": Zhao 2008, pp. 207–08. See also Togan 2006.

18 Rashid al-Din, *Shuᶜabi panjgāna,* Istanbul Ms. Ahmet III. 2937; Binbaş 2011.

19 Woods 1999, pp. 1–23; Melville 1999.

20 Spuler 1985, p. 209.

21 Diler 2006, pp. 533–42.

22 E.g.: "*al-sulṭāna al-ᶜādila Sātī Beg Khān khallada Allāhu mulkahā;*" "*al-sulṭān al-aᶜzam Sātī Beg Khān khallada Allāhu mulkahu*": Diler 2006, pp. 539, 541; Aydın and Aykut 1992, p. 111.

23 Lambton 1988, pp. 293–94.

24 On Baghdad Khatun, see Savory 1960; Quade-Reutter 2003, pp. 353–65.

25 Gilli-Elewy 2012.

26 Gilli-Elewy 2012.

27 Binbaş 2011.

28 On the Turkic term *khātūn*, meaning 'wife of a khan,' later 'wife' in general, see Doerfer 1963–75, vol. 3, pp. 132–41 (no. 1159); Boyle 1978; Bosworth 2006.

29 On the Mongol term *ēgǎčī*, meaning 'concubine,' see Doerfer 1963–75, vol. 1, p. 191 (no. 67).

30 For the importance of the seating order in Turco-Mongol societies, and the rituals attached to it, including the custom of seating the ladies to the left of the ruler, see, e.g. Ibn Fadlan 1939, pp. 159–60 (§ 46a); İnan 1968–91; and McChesney 1983. It remains debated whether the royal ladies were seated to the right or the left of the Khan. Miniatures show them to the right, but it has been argued that from the ruler's perspective, this would mean that they were seated to his left, which is confirmed by the above textual evidence. In either case, it is beyond doubt that the first lady was seated close to the khan.

31 Quade-Reutter 2003, pp. 315–35.

32 Quade-Reutter 2003, pp. 119–24.

33 Quade-Reutter 2003, pp. 192–97.

34 Quade-Reutter 2003, pp. 197–99.

35 Quade-Reutter 2003, p. 199.

36 Kirmani 1328 sh./1949, pp. 70–71. Quade-Reutter 2003, pp. 194–195 (including variants from later text witnesses and a German translation).

37 This distich appears to be an adaptation of a distich ascribed to Zahir al-Din Faryabi (d. 1201). See Dihkhuda, *Lughatnama,* 'Miqnaᶜa.'

38 Safa 1358/1980, vol. 3.1, p. 658.

39 Lambton 1988, pp. 280–87.

40 İsenbike Togan has suggested that the role of women and patterns of domination, authority and privileges during this period changed according to the greater or lesser level of decentralisation at the state level, and that in non-centralised state structures in Iran and Central Asia "women […] appear in their microcosms as more powerful matriarchs who organised the lives of their immediate but extended families" because they were less of a "threat to the non-centralised state authority." Togan 1999. For a chapter on elite women in the Il-Khanate, see Lambton, 1988, pp. 258–96; Mernissi 1993; Manz 2003. In-depth scholarship on Mongol elite women, and women under Mongol rule in general, is still in its infancy, though the recent works of Karin Quade-Reutter 2003, Shai Shir 2006, Bruno De Nicola 2011, and Yoni Brack 2011 provide excellent examples of what can be achieved in this area.

The hunt

TERESA FITZHERBERT

THOMAS ALLSEN'S EPITOME of the Eurasian hunt in pre-modern times as the pursuit of protein, profit, power and pleasure[1] is nowhere more amply demonstrated than in the lands under Mongol rule during the thirteenth and fourteenth centuries. In the steppe tradition of their ancestors, the Il-Khanid court and its government administration were peripatetic, on the move not only for seasonal pasturage and food resources but also strategic and political purposes, in which the hunt played a crucial role.[2]

Hunting was not only a necessity but also a pleasure shared across geographical, cultural, ethnic and social divides. For nomadic rulers, the skills needed for marshalling manpower, logistics and particularly

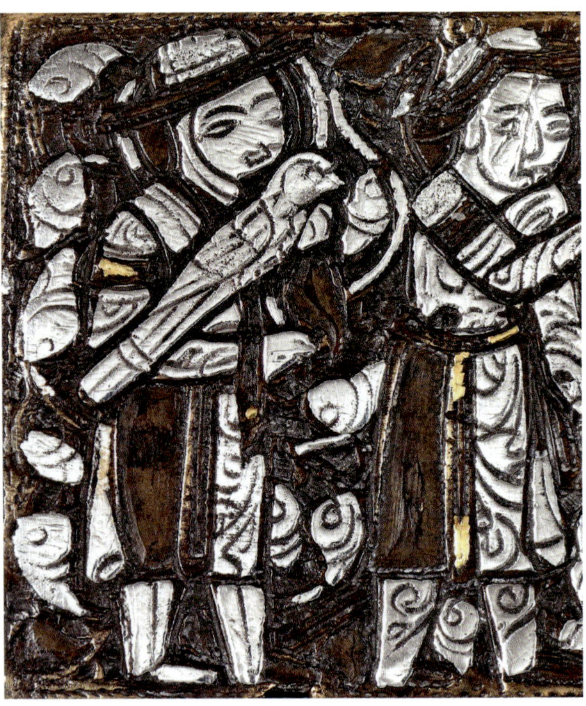

The Courtauld bag (cat. 1), detail of falconer on lid

manoeuvres such as the ring hunt or *battue* were largely interchangeable with those of the battlefield, and when not on campaign the hunt played a major role in maintaining an army in readiness for war. It also provided a useful cover for intelligence gathering in the remoter areas of a realm, and opportunities for showcasing the qualities, both moral and material, expected of a ruler, his entourage and his army. Feasts that followed the hunt provided occasions not only for socialisation and demonstrations of wealth, but also for the granting of appointments and favours, the distribution of largesse as rewards for loyalty, and bolstering state consolidation generally.[3]

For example, the presence of Ghazan Khan during a hunting expedition west of the Caspian in the autumn of 701/1301 encouraged the trespassing Ulus Jochi to withdraw across "the great river"[4] and the rebellious amirs of Lagzistan to surrender voluntarily. After fishing and shooting swans and other water-fowl in the vicinity of Govbari, Ghazan moved on to Talishan and Ispahbad. There he ordered two walls of trunks and branches to be built, stretching one day's distance between the mountains, to funnel "… wild oxen, *jür* [deer], antelope, wild asses, jackals, foxes, wolves, bears and other wild animals and beasts" into a hunting circle created by the army, "… and the Padishah of Islam and Bulughan Khatun sat in a pavilion constructed of wood in the midst and watched the animals. Some were shot and others were released."[5]

Depictions of the general mêlée of a hunt are known from pre-Il-Khanid metalwork (fig. 9) and also from the early Mamluk period (fig. 17). Il-Khanid equivalents for such complex scenes have yet to be identified. However, the description of Ghazan fishing, shooting water-birds and hunting in the vicinity of the Caspian relates closely to images on two magnificent inlaid brass basins

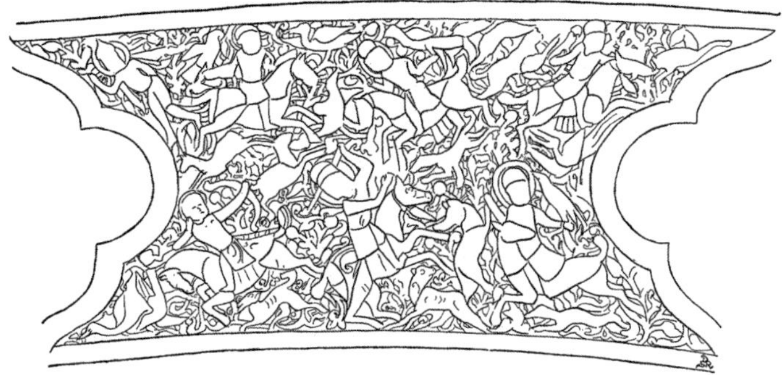

FIG. 9
A hunt, detail from an inlaid brass
basin made for the Ayyubid Sultan
al-ᶜAdil (1238–40), probably in Mosul
Paris, Louvre, OA 5991 (drawing after
D.S. Rice 1957, pl. 6d)

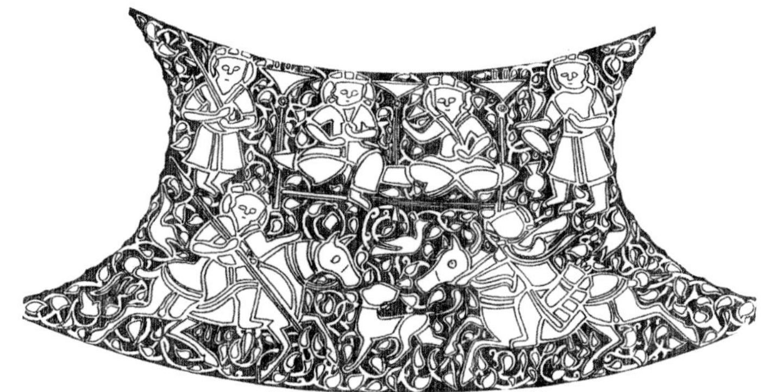

FIG. 10
Seated figures watching a hunt,
detail from an inlaid brass basin,
Mosul or western Iran c. 1300
Berlin, Museum für Islamische Kunst, I. C.
1069 (drawing after Enderlein 1973, fig. 8)

with specifically Il-Khanid features such as phoenixes, *qilins* and dragons integrated into their designs, and provide insights into how the Il-Khanids engaged in and celebrated the chase. Of the five narrative cartouches on the Berlin basin, one shows a scene of two seated figures flanked by attendants as they watch horsemen lancing and shooting an animal and various birds (fig. 10), two specifically depict water-fowl, a third shows members of the elite bibbing wine in a boat.[6] The five narrative cartouches on the rim of the basin in the Victoria and Albert Museum, of which two are illustrated here (figs. 11–15)[7] depict a *fête champêtre* of a type that played an important role in state procedures associated with the chase. Although now lacking the fine detail that the silver and gold inlay once supplied, the cartouches still provide glimpses of the Il-Khanid court at ease in its hunting environment: khans and members of the *corps d'élite* either crowned or wearing feathered headdresses, a khatun wearing a *boghtaq* (fig. 41), Mongol and non-Mongol attendants, some holding the shortened crook used for training feline charges.[8] One of the crowned figures stands with a raptor on his right hand and a ceremonial staff with a stylised vegetal top in his left;[9] others hold leafy branches, maybe as part of New Year celebrations or, more prosaically, to use as fans and ward off flies or mosquitoes. They are feasting in the company of a 'mews' of raptors, a cheetah and a young gazelle. Here too, one complete cartouche shows a hawk or falcon harrying waterfowl, in another a plump specimen

is being offered to a crowned figure, while in a third a less fortunate quacker, held by its neck, is surely destined for the pot. In the register below, a wide variety of fauna including a wild ox and a couple of harpies gambol and pursue one another in merry perpetuity.

Horses, raptors, hunting leopards (Asiatic cheetahs) and gazehounds – particularly greyhounds and salukis – were required in vast numbers. Since semi-domesticated raptors and felines breed poorly, if at all, in captivity, replenishment stocks were needed on an annual basis and trafficked as important trade commodities.[10] Trainers and handlers carried the status of skilled artisans, with their lives spared if captured by the Mongols in war.[11] Grooms, cheetah keepers and falconers held offices in the extensive personal household of the Il-Khans, the *keshig*.[12] A snapshot of numbers is provided in Ghazan's legislation to redress the extortion and abuses being perpetrated by the corps of falconers and cheetah keepers at the time of his accession. This reform limited the number of falcons and cheetahs to be brought in per year to a thousand falcons and three hundred cheetahs.[13] Trained hunting animals also functioned as prized diplomatic gifts. In letters to the European powers dated 1289 the Il-Khan Arghun included requests for gerfalcons and jewels of all colours. In 1291, Edward I of England sent three falconers with a return mission, led by Geffrey de Langley; Arghun's successor, Geikhatu, returned this courtesy by sending a leopard in a cage – presumably a trained cheetah – to the English king.[14]

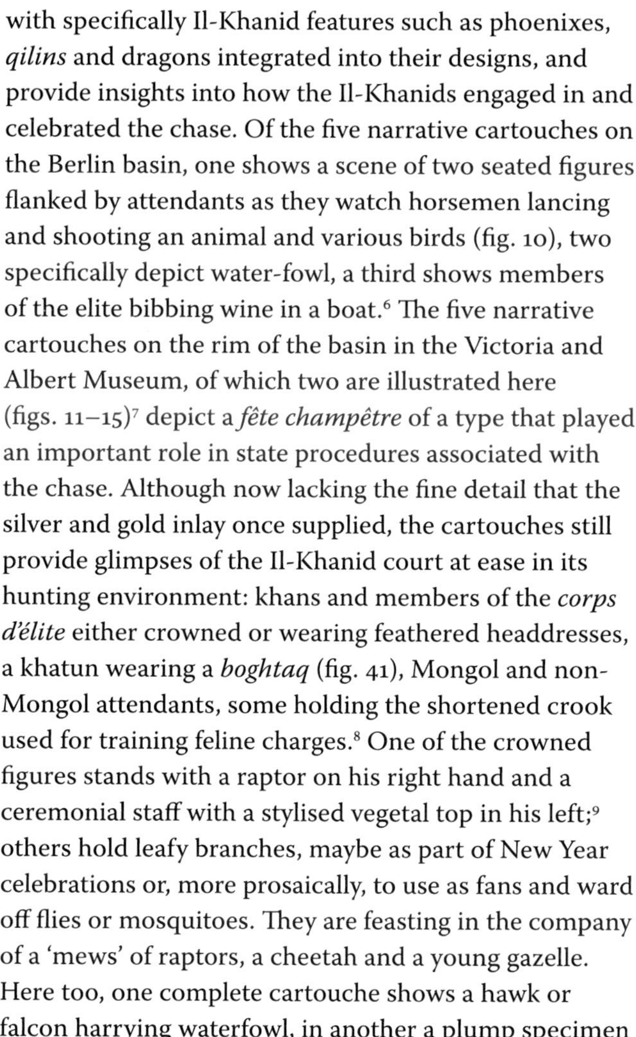

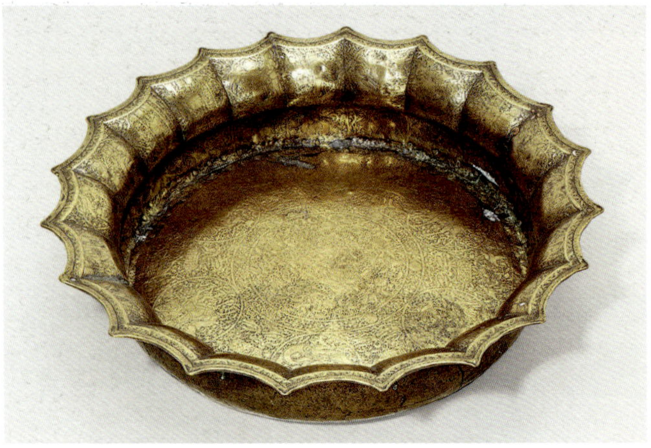

On the Courtauld bag three figures are specifically associated with the chase – the falconer in Mongol dress standing at the far left of the enthronement scene on the top of the bag (see detail p. 30); the turbaned horseman spearing a lion in the central roundel on the front (see detail p. 82); and the turbaned horseman with raptor on his left wrist in the central roundel on the back of the bag (see detail p. 2).

Taking the falconers first, while the status of eagles was never in doubt, and their symbolic value internationally recognised, for practical reasons they were less commonly used in the field. In the thirteenth and fourteenth centuries, gerfalcons and goshawks were the raptor hunting companions of choice among Mongol and Turkic peoples, favoured for their size and hunting skills as well as their appearance. In the *Nuzhatu'l-qulub*, completed in 740/1339–40, Hamd Allah Mustawfi Qazvini says of the gerfalcon: "It attacks its prey with great fury, and is capable of being trained. In body it is larger than the hawk, but resembles it in form. It lives in cold countries, and is plentiful in Europe. It circles round its prey in the air, and however many there are they never escape."[15] It was these qualities that encouraged the use of the pseudonyms 'Aq Sunqur' (white falcon) and 'Qara Sunqur' (black falcon) for Turkic military commanders. For example, in 1312, the Mamluk governor of Damascus, Qara Sunqur, defected to the Il-Khan Öljeitü (ruled 703–17/1304–17), who renamed him Aq Sunqur, apparently on account of his riper years.[16] Both gerfalcons and goshawks breed in northern or temperate zones, and the colours of gerfalcons correlate to their natural habitats.

Throughout Eurasia those of white plumage were in particularly high demand.[17] However, for the Mongols the white gerfalcon also carried an additional significance.

Embedded in the ancient traditions of the Turkic tribes of Central Asia, raptors representing authority and as a metaphor for the soul that ascends to the heavens at death had already travelled west with the Seljuqs, and become integrated into the multi-cultural artistic and literary traditions of Greater Iran, Atabeg Jazira and Seljuq Anatolia.[18] The arrival of the Mongols provided this raptor symbolism with fresh potency. For the still-shamanist Mongols, birds of prey represented mankind's link with the all-powerful sky god, Tengri,[19] through the intermediary of a shaman, and Tengri had designated the young Temujin (later Chinggis Khan) to rule the world. According to the thirteenth-century *Secret History of the Mongols*, this event had been heralded in a dream to Temujin's future father-in-law by a white gerfalcon holding the sun and the moon,[20] and Chinggis used a white gerfalcon as a metaphor for himself.[21] White was also traditionally a colour of good omen for ancient Iranian and Turkic peoples.[22] The thirteenth-century Armenian monk-chronicler Grigor of Akanc` records the tradition that the Chinggisid law code, the *Yasa*, was delivered to the Mongols by an angel in the guise of an eagle with the power of speech and golden feathers.[23] Marco Polo, travelling across Asia between 1271 and 1295, notes that: "To certain very great lords also there is given a tablet[24] with gerfalcons on it; this is only to the very greatest of the Kaan's [Khan's] barons, and it confers on them his own full power and authority; so that if one of those chiefs wishes to send a messenger any whither, he can seize the horses of any man, be he even a king, and any other chattels at his pleasure."[25] For the Mongols, therefore, the white gerfalcon symbolised the right to rule through their all-important Chinggisid genealogy.

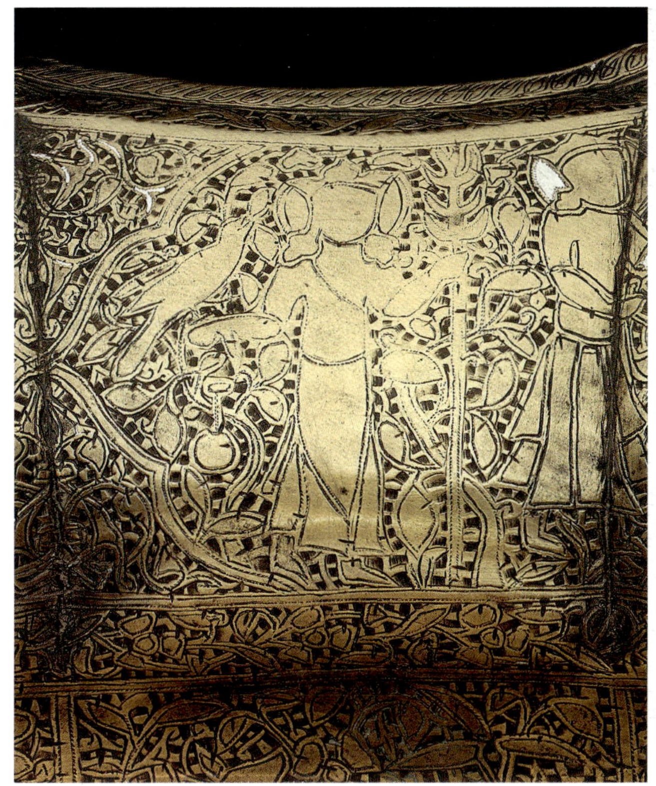 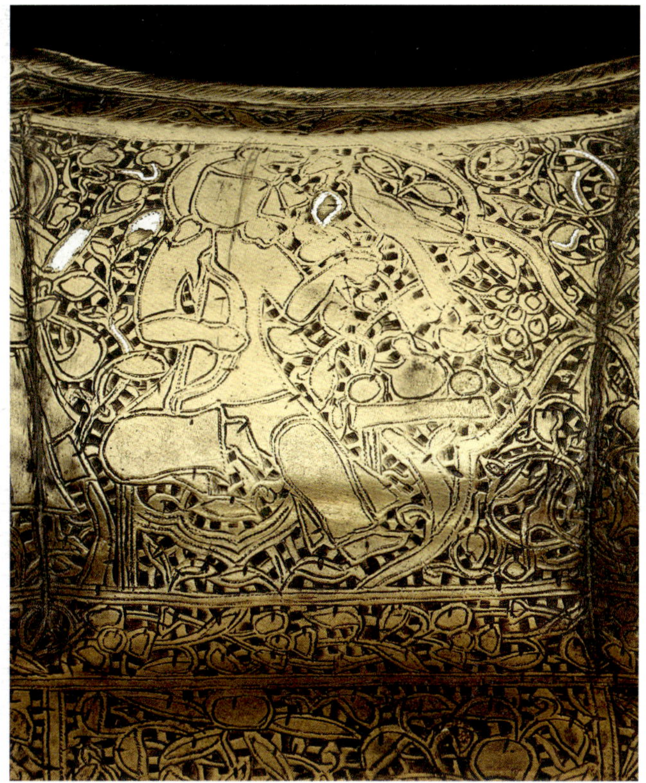

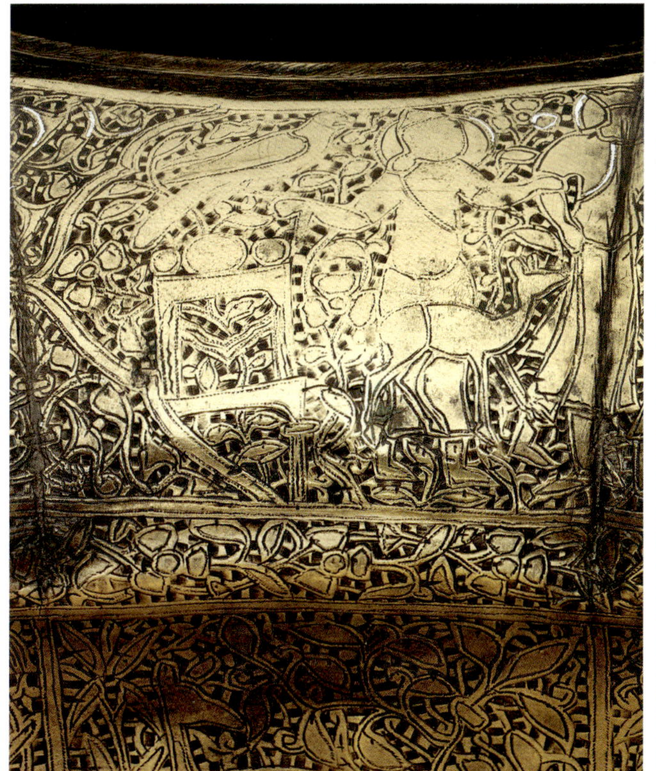 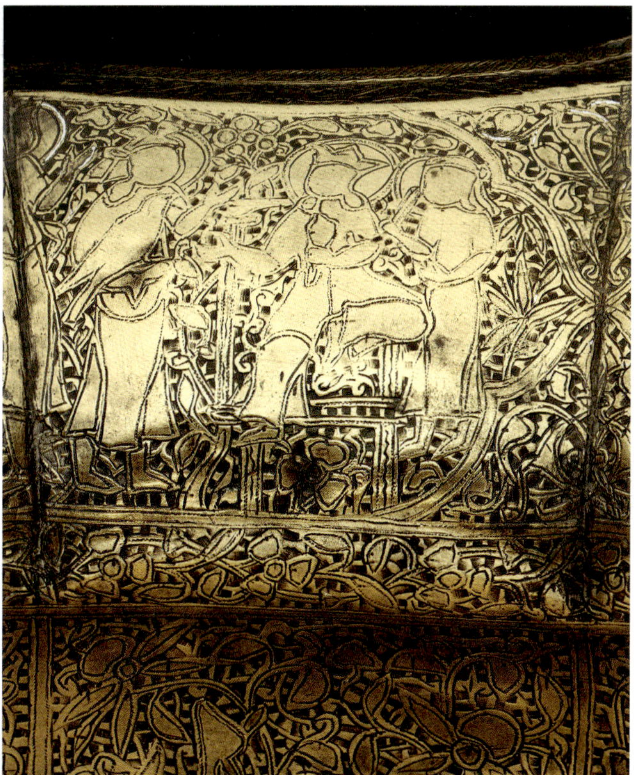

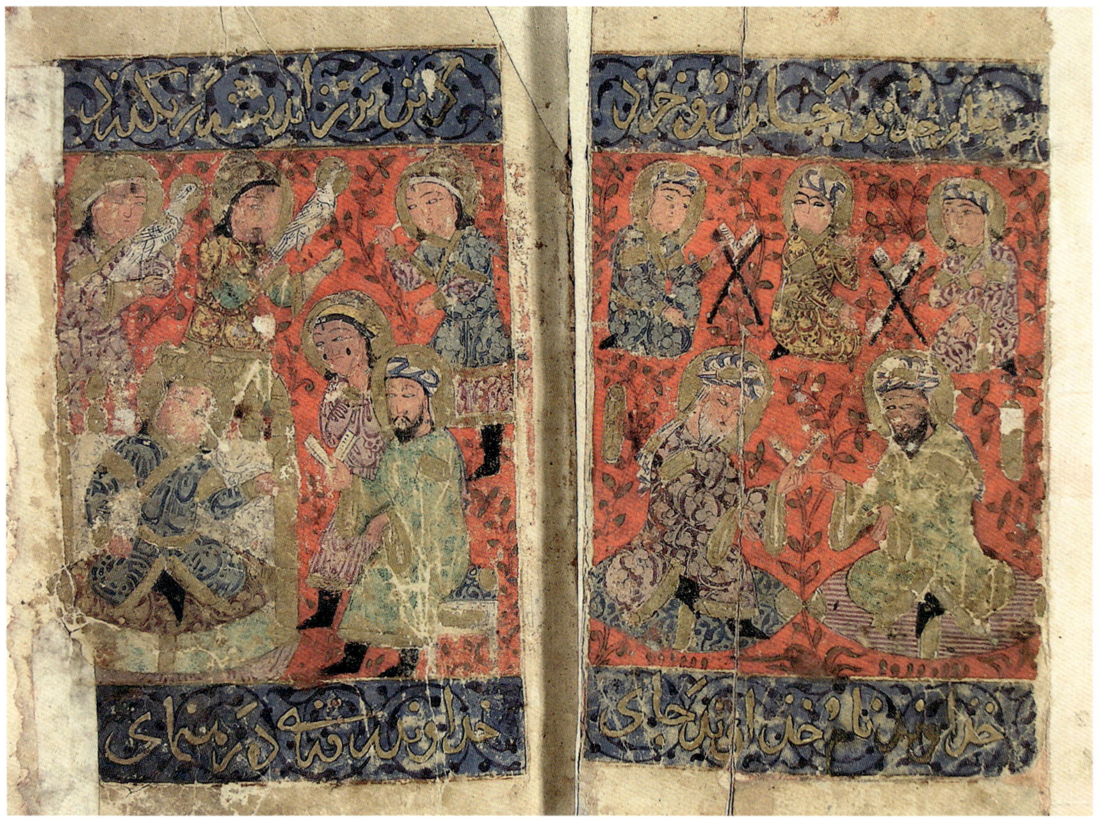

To read layers of meaning into every raptor would be absurd, but they were effective as commonly understood symbols of temporal and supernatural power and hierarchies, and Chinggisid hunting practices set precedents that were followed through succeeding centuries.[26] White gerfalcons are included in contemporary paintings, as, for example, in the left-hand enthronement scene from the double frontispiece to the Topkapı Palace Library's *Kalila and Dimna*, probably from late thirteenth- or early fourteenth-century Jazira or Anatolia (fig. 16).[27] The raptor on the wrist of the standing falconer on the Courtauld bag cannot be identified by colour, but the clear banding on its tail feathers suggests it is a goshawk (see detail p. 30).

Depictions of the ruler as falconer and the presence of official falconers can be traced in the iconography of the eastern Islamic world from at least the tenth century onwards. It is noticeable that in the Il-Khanid period the Central Asian Mongol and Turkic preference for flying raptors off the right hand rather the left – as generally favoured in more westerly and Arab lands –

is depicted on a more regular basis, even if some of the images may have been reversed when transferred from paper to three-dimensional objects. The headgear worn by the Courtauld standing falconer causes pause for thought. A similar hat with horizontal brim is worn by a member of a reception committee greeting a mounted Il-Khanid grandee in a Diez Album folio,[28] but is otherwise rare in courtly settings, despite the variety of other types of hat and headdress regularly worn by courtiers, and often plumed with official owl and eagle feathers as in the Diez Album court scene (cat. 16). Unfortunately, owing to the confines of the strip format on the top of the bag, the craftsman was not able to include in his representation the central attachment for securing feathers that might denote status or skill in marksmanship.[29] However, since a similar hat is worn by the galloping falconer on the Keir ball joint (cat. 10), and the leading horseman on the hunting scene on the Walters pen box (cat. 29), perhaps this type was part of an attire more practical than ceremonial, or specific to a particular region or people.

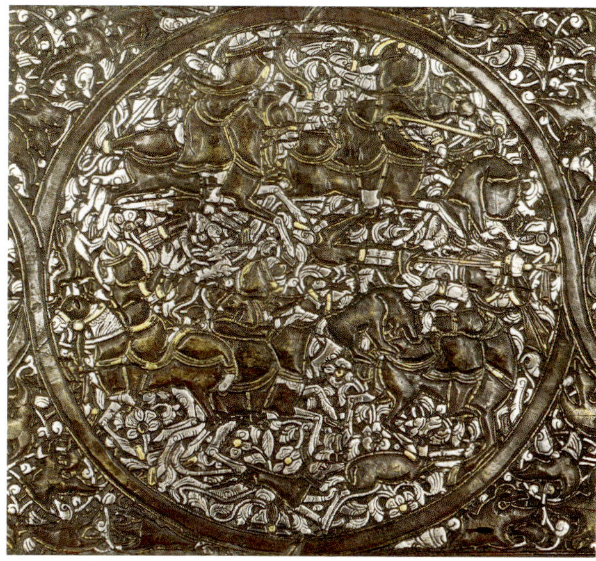

While the standing falconer clearly belongs to an
Il-Khanid retinue, the cavaliers on the body of the
bag reflect continuing links with a pre-Mongol world,
familiar from images on metalwork and in paintings from
lands under Seljuq rule or influence. This is particularly
true of the horses on the Courtauld bag, which, in
contrast to the Il-Khanid preference for horses with
lighter frames and more flowing tails, as on the ball joint
(cat. 10), continue the stocky, muscular type with Turkic
knotted tails of earlier times. This older type is seen
on the Blacas ewer, decorated in Mosul in 629/1232
(cat. 21), and in the frontispiece to volume 20 of the *Kitab
al-Aghani*, dated Ramadan 616/1219, probably painted in
Mosul (fig. 28), and in the *Kitab al-Diryaq,* undated but
probably with a similar provenance (fig. 20). This horse
type continued into the fourteenth century on Mamluk
objects, as in the dramatic hunting scene in the roundel
on the pen box bearing the name of the Mamluk Sultan
al-Nasir Muhammad ibn Qalawun (ruled 1293–94,
1310–41), which probably dates to the first decades of
the fourteenth century (fig. 17).[30]

The mounted falconer on the back of the Courtauld
bag comes from a long tradition of such images carrying
both general and authoritarian connotations, as in the
frontispiece to volume 20 of the *Kitab al-Aghani* (fig. 28).
The turban of the rider on the bag associates him with
an Islamic cultural milieu and the convoluted design on
his tunic – perhaps representing watered silk – suggests
pre-Mongol dress, similar to that worn by the rider in the
Kitab al-Aghani frontispiece, probably representing the
Atabeg ruler of Mosul, Badr al-Din Lu'lu'.[31] Decorations
hanging beneath the horse's belly may represent either
the tassels from a bag hung from the far side of the
saddle for carrying falconry impedimenta or small game,
or straps for securing game to the saddle itself.[32] The
purpose of the loosely looped and knotted swag of cords

hanging from the left forearm of the falconer is
unclear, as nothing appears to be attached. Jesses
would be held within the grip of the falconer's fist, as in
the *Kitab al-Aghani* frontispiece and in the illustration
of a falconer in the *Book of the Wonders of Creation*
(cat. 34b).

The mounted lion killer on the front of the Courtauld
bag is also turbaned and rides a horse similar in type
to that of his companion on the back, but loss of inlay
hinders defining his garb. The genealogy of the mounted
lion killer reaches back into antiquity and the Sasanian
legacy of the hunt, particularly in the person of Bahram
Gur (ruled 421–38), which was widespread. Bahram Gur
mounted on a camel with his harpist, Azada, appears on
the Blacas ewer, and also in one of the central roundels of
the Il-Khanid basin in the Victoria and Albert Museum.[33]
The hunt as a rite of passage from youth to manhood
crossed cultural divides. When Ghazan, at the age of
eight, first "brought down prey" in 678/1279–80, while
hunting with his grandfather, Abaqa, it was followed by
three days of celebration.[34] Rashid al-Din does not specify
Ghazan's prey, whereas the teenage prince Bahram Gur,
as recounted in Balʿami's tenth-century *Tarikhnama*,
was tested in front of the army, and by felling a lion, an
onager, a gazelle and a dragon demonstrated his skills
both as a provider of protein and as a protector against
the threats of this world and beyond (fig. 18). In the Freer
manuscript, probably from Mosul *c.* 1300, the figure of
the great hunter has been cast as an Il-Khanid monarch,

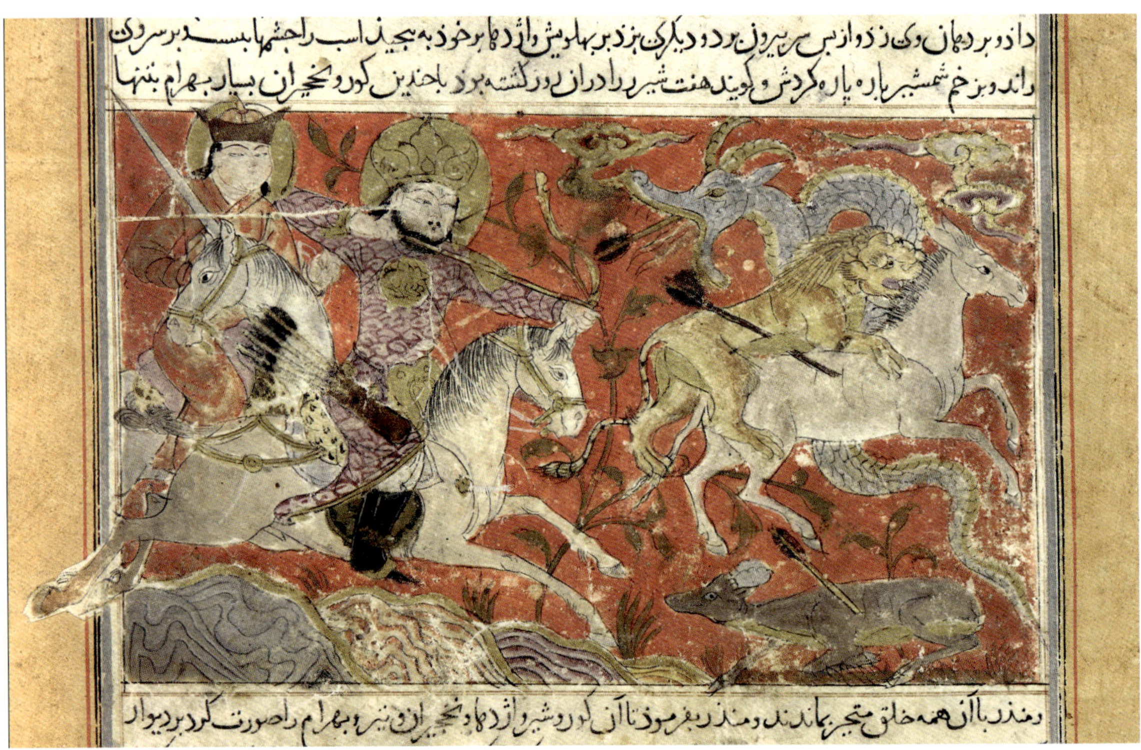

reflecting the political reality of Mongol rule, while his horse remains in pre-Mongol mode.

The ethnic and cultural interface of the times is also evident in the treatment of the men of the chase and their mounts on the Courtauld bag. While the standing falconer in the line-up on the top appears entirely at home in his Il-Khanid courtly setting, the two horsemen placed centre stage on its front and back have been drawn from the pre-Mongol repertoire. While this may be due to the longevity of particular design formulae rather than intentional juxtaposition, it nonetheless contrasts with the scene on the Walters pen box, in which hunters sporting flat-brim, upturned-brim and turban headgear are shown pursuing game together (cat. 29).

Weighty motives might underpin the hunt, but for the elites who took part it was also a source of private pleasure. Written some 75 years before the fall of Baghdad to the Mongols, no one catches the excitement of a day with horse, hound, falcon and cheetah more vividly than Usama ibn Munqidh in his *Kitab al-Iᶜtibar* (Book of Contemplation), completed in Diyarbakr around 1183. Reminiscing of hunting with his father at their castle at Shayzar, in northern Syria, and over an area ranging from Mosul to Aleppo, he vividly captures the world of the mounted riders on the Courtauld bag:

"But when we rode out in pursuit of waterfowl and francolin, *that* was a day of real amusement. We would start off … for the hunt from the town gate. Then we could reach the cane-brakes, which we would go in with the goshawks. If a francolin flies up, the hawk will take it. If a hare is roused, we slip one of the hawks on it. If she takes it, splendid. If not, then the hare will just run out towards the cheetahs, which will be slipped after it. Likewise, if a gazelle is roused, it leaves the cane-brakes in the direction of the cheetahs, which are slipped after it. If a cheetah takes it, splendid. If not, they would slip the sakers after it. Thus, hardly any game escaped us, except by some twist of fate."[35]

Allsen's definition of the hunt as the pursuit of protein, profit, power and pleasure certainly rings true for the Il-Khanid period, and the hunt and the feast which followed were important elements in the complex package of Mongol rule. However, if the images on the Courtauld bag reflect one of the hunt's pursuits more than another, it is surely pleasure and *joie de vivre*.

NOTES

1 Allsen 2006, in particular pp. 1–13 and 274–77; I am indebted to Thomas T. Allsen's study of this subject, which provides that rare thing, an encyclopaedic work that is a compulsive read. I also owe many thanks to Tim Stanley, Moya Carey and Rowan Bain at the Victoria and Albert Museum, Martin Kauffmann at the Bodleian Library, James Allan for his insights on metalwork, Judith Pfeiffer for checking Mongol and Turkic terminology, James White for sharing images and ideas, my brother Anthony Fitzherbert for advice on falconry and the wildlife of Iran, Julian Raby for discussion and guidance, and above all to Rachel Ward for many years of friendship and sharing her expertise, and now for letting the genii out of the Courtauld bag. All errors are entirely my own.

2 Melville 1990a, pp. 55–70, especially map fig. 1 p. 58, and Appendix I, pp. 64–66.

3 For general discussion see Allsen 2006, pp. 197–201.

4 Presumably, the river Aras.

5 Rashid al-Din/Thackston 1998–99, vol. 3, pp. 650–52; Rashid al-Din 1994, vol. 2, pp. 1301–03. No feast is mentioned immediately after this hunt, but the reception at Ujan the following July is described in dazzling detail soon after.

6 Inv. no. I.C. 1061, See Enderlein 1973, pp. 7–21, especially figs. 2–11.

7 Inv. no. 546–1905, Melikian-Chirvani 1982, no. 93 pp. 202–207, and Melikian-Chirvani 1997a, pp. 173–177 and pls XIII–XXII.

8 Allsen 2006, p. 79.

9 A similar standard is held above the head of an enthroned Mongol figure in the left hand folio of a double frontispiece now in the Topkapı Album, MS H. 2152, fol. 60b, Ipsiroglu 1965, p. 51–54 and ill. 11.

10 Allsen 2006, pp. 6–10, and Ch. 12, pp. 223–64.

11 Allsen 2006, p. 261.

12 Allsen 2006, p. 83; Melville, 2006, pp. 150–55, especially 153–54.

13 Rashid al-Din/Thackston 1998–99, vol. 3, pp. 751–54, especially p. 753; Rashid al-Din 1994, vol. 2, pp. 1518–23.

14 Lockhart 1968, pp. 26–28; Paviot 2000, pp. 314–15; on the intercultural nature of falconry in the Middle Ages, see Akasoy 2007, pp. 46–64.

15 Mustawfi Qazvini/Stephenson 1928, p. 76, text p. 108.

16 Boyle 1968a, p. 403.

17 Macdonald 2006, pp. 16–18; Potapov and Sale 2005, pp 46–51.

18 For raptor totems of the Oghuz tribes see Rashid al-Din/Thackston 1998–99, vol. 1, pp. 33–34; and more generally and in shamanism and eastern monotheism, Potapov and Sale 2005, pp. 198–207; for Konya see Gierlichs 1996, pp. 191–92 and pl. 35.1–2; for the Artuqid mirror in the David Collection, Folsach 2001, no. 503, pp. 314–15; and for raptors with spread wings in the stucco frieze surmounted by the titles of Badr al-Din Lu'lu' in the Qara Saray, his palace in Mosul, see Herzfeld and Sarre 1911–20, vol. 1, pp. 18–20, and vol. 3, pls. VI and XCVI.

19 According to Roux, 'Tengri' is the oldest Turco-Mongol word known, and by the second century BC had subsumed all other words for deities: Roux 1984, p. 110–11; see also Bira 2004, pp. 1–12.

20 *Secret History*/Rachewiltz 2004, vol. 1, pp. 13–14.

21 For an example see Boyle 1978a, p. 184, and Rashid al-Din 1994, vol. 1, p. 390.

22 Allsen 2006, p. 145.

23 Allsen 1997, pp. 61–62; Grigor of Akanc`/ Blake and Frye 1949, pp. 289 and 291.

24 The *paiza*, or passport of the Mongol empire.

25 Polo/Yule–Cordier, 1903, vol. 1, p. 351 and notes pp. 353–34.

26 Mirza 1996, pp. 33–34; Mirza/Thackston 1996, pp. 29–30.

27 Topkapı Palace Library, MS H. 363, fol. 2a.

28 Berlin State Library, Diez A fol. 71.s.54, Bonn 2005, p. 274, no.302.

29 Esin 1970, p. 112.

30 Paris 2002, p. 184–5, no. 152; Ward 2004, pp. 59–61.

31 See Allan below, p. 52.

32 For a comparable bag see de Chamerlat 1987, pp. 273–74; for incantations over the straps attached to Mongol saddles used for tying game, Heissig/Samuel, 1980, pp. 67–68; for similar tasselled straps see the *Kitab al-Aghani* frontispiece (fig. 28).

33 Melikian-Chirvani 1982, p. 203, ill. 93D; on the enduring image of Bahram Gur, see Ettinghausen 1979, pp. 25–31.

34 This initiation ceremony, known as *yaghlamishi*, involved greasing of thumbs, according to Thackston, or the middle finger, according to Boyle; Boyle 1968b, pp.1–7; Rashid al-Din/Thackston 1998–99, vol. 3, p. 591, and vol. 2, p. 260; Rashid al-Din 1994, vol. 2, p. 1211; and also vol. 1, p. 259.

35 Usama/Cobb 2008, p. 210; Usama ibn Munqidh 1930, pp. 201–02.

Wine in Islamic art and society

ROBERT HILLENBRAND

CONVENTIONAL WISDOM, disdaining the nuances of a complicated subject, insists that Islam prohibits the consumption of alcohol. And there can be no doubt that in this case conventional wisdom is correct, both as regards the medieval period and in the Islamic world today, as epitomised by the frequently repeated saying that alcohol is 'the mother of all evils'.[1] Yet the very definition of what constitutes alcohol has been hotly contested.[2] A typical case is that of a mild fermented liquid called *nabidh*, usually made from raisins or dates; its consumption was legal if it was no more than two days old, though thereafter it became stronger – and illegal.[3] It seems that orthodox attitudes to alcohol hardened over time. A Qur'anic verse (5:90–1) forbids prayer by anyone who is intoxicated, while Qur'an 2:219 brackets strong drink with games of chance as something to be avoided. A very clear distinction is traditionally drawn between earthly wine that causes drunkenness and the wine of Paradise, which does not and is delicious.[4] Anecdotes reflecting orthodox Muslim distaste for wine

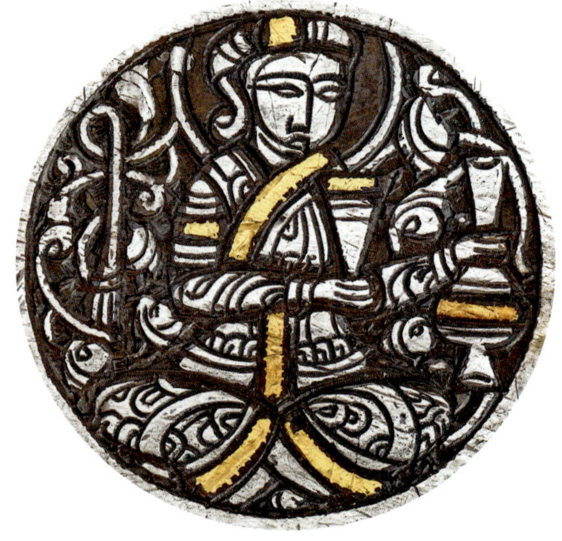

are frequently found in the literary sources. Thus the traveller Ibn Jubayr, when working as a secretary for the governor of Granada in 1182, was forced to drink seven cups of wine. The penitent governor thereupon rewarded him with seven cups filled with gold dinars, money which he used to perform the *hajj*.[5] And when the army of the Mongol Il-Khan Hülegü entered Damascus, the triumphant Christians sprinkled the Muslims with wine.[6] But such stories need to be balanced against an overwhelming body of evidence indicating that, from Umayyad times onwards, caliphs, nobles and courtiers habitually drank alcohol, often to excess.[7] Among Umayyad rulers ᶜAbd al-Malik, Yazid I, al-Walid I, Sulaiman and Hisham drank wine regularly,[8] the latter directly after the Friday prayer; and al-Walid II surpassed them all.[9] And most of the ᶜAbbasid caliphs also drank wine, some coming back to it after having forsworn it as a vice;[10] indeed, the stock reason for deposing a ruler was that he was addicted to wine,[11] a vice often associated with an equally reprehensible love of music. Some of the practices associated with wine-drinking in early Islamic times may have Sasanian origins, for a complex ceremonial surrounded the consumption of wine at the Sasanian court. It was to be perfumed, consumed with dried fruit, a sandwich or candied myrobalan, taken with a meal (a practice not followed in Islamic times)[12] or used as a dip for oily pastry.[13]

Conventional wisdom of a more specialised kind, but equally unconcerned with the finer details of the matter, insists that scenes of wine-drinking are common in medieval Islamic art. It therefore comes as something of a surprise to discover that no general survey of the pictorial evidence for this assertion has been published, although scholars have investigated in close detail wine-drinking in the art of Samarra[14] and of the early Turks.[15] Those two themes converge in the

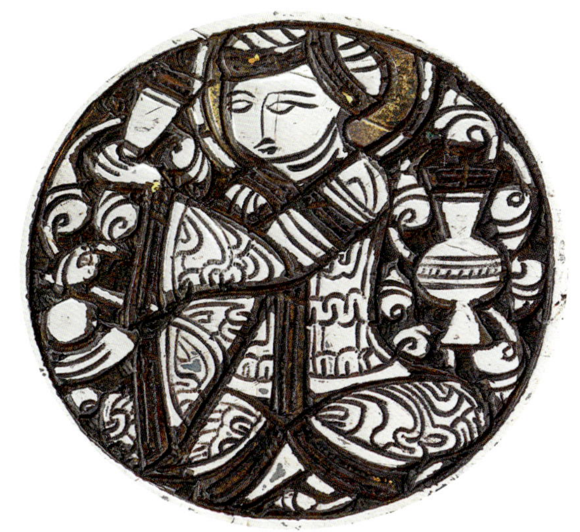

The Courtauld bag (cat. 1),
details of roundels with revellers

many reports that the Turks of Samarra were notorious for their drunkenness. The literary references to wine-drinking from early Islamic times onwards are copious, as is the scholarship on wine poetry (*khamriyyat*), a distinct specialised genre. Clearly, then, there is a significant information gap between the written sources execrating wine-drinking and the pictorial evidence to the contrary. But scholars agree that the aristocracy drank freely from early Islamic times onwards; indeed, a treatise on good manners specifies what a gentleman should know about the types and vintages of wine; and in the same spirit, the caliph al-Mustakfi convened a symposium on cooking at which the court poets vied with each other to describe the most recondite dishes in appropriately extravagant terms.[16] A drinking party where the host (the vizier Hasan b. Makhlad) drank many pints of wine before passing out and keeling over backwards on to his cushion is recorded. There is even a reference to taxes on wine in Diyar Rabi'a in the early tenth century.

The most sustained evidence for this widespread drinking of alcohol lies in wine poetry.[17] Yet one of its most constant themes, alongside love and obscenity, hedonism and blasphemy, is repentance for indulgence in alcohol. The undisputed master of this genre was the courtier and libertine Abu Nuwas (d. 815), who greatly extended its range of expression by means of the dialogue form, by evocations of the setting for serious drinking (descriptions of cup-bearers and singers, flowers and gardens, and even drinking vessels), and by the introduction of bold similes (fire, jewels, light and perfume). And wine figures in many other types of poetry too: thus the ʿAbbasid caliph al-Mahdi wrote: "In song and wine is my felicity; And perfumed girls, music and gaiety".[18] A favourite trope in erotic poetry was to liken the saliva of the beloved to wine,[19] and the colour

of wine to blood. Mystical *khamriyyat* poetry abounds and uses wine as a metaphor denoting the intoxication felt by the Sufis as they achieve closer proximity to God. The imagery can be extravagant, as in the "wine-coloured" or "drunken" eyes of the beloved.[20] Often it is liberally sprinkled with paradoxes, as in the lines by Bayazid Bastami (d. *c.* 874): "I am the wine drinker and the wine and the cupbearer".[21] Or, as al-Hallaj put it: "When in my thirst I stooped my face to wine, Dark in the cup I saw a shadow. Thine!"[22]

But yet other quotations make it clear that wine could also serve as an entirely religious metaphor. Thus Ibn al-Farid (d. 1235) wrote in the *tawil* metre: "We drank upon the remembrance of the Beloved a wine wherewith we were drunken before ever the vine was created. The full moon was a cup for it, itself being the sun."[23]

Drunkenness is frequently recorded, from al-Walid II with his wine pool at Khirbat al-Mafjar[24] to the Il-Khan Abaqa, who succumbed to delirium tremens,[25] and many a prince in Mughal India died of drink. The Seljuq sultan Alp Arslan threw a tent-peg at his venerable vizier Nizam al-Mulk in a drunken rage ("I bumped against a tent-pole", said the vizier tactfully when his master enquired about his bruise the next morning).[26] The Turkish warlord Il-Ghazi celebrated his victory over the Crusaders at the Field of Blood by retiring to his tent for a drunken debauch that lasted a week,[27] while the fearsome Zangi was assassinated in his cups.[28] The standard issue of wine to the Mongol army, following a decree by Chinggis Khan, led to widespread alcohol abuse. Al-Jahiz, a person of encyclopaedic knowledge who was widely regarded as the finest of all classical Arabic stylists, wrote a scintillating disquisition on the very varied behaviour of drunken people, with no hint of disapproval; its climax is the account of a litigator who never appeared before a judge until he had drunk ten bottles, and then his brilliant oratory would infallibly win the day.

How, then, is the theme of drinking presented in medieval Islamic art?[29] Even a rapid and superficial overview of the visual material that falls most easily to hand is enough to reveal some interesting anomalies. For example, surviving images, it seems, offer no clue as to the nature of the liquid in question; it could as easily be water, sherbet (a word of Arabic derivation) or fruit juice as wine or spirits. One looks in vain for diminutive bottles of the kind that might hold spirits, although the frontispiece to a manuscript of Saʿdi's *Bustan* from the Herat school, dated 1488, depicts a working still.[30] Instead, the standard containers are large jugs or ewers, most of them with a capacity of several litres, though wine-skins were also used. Amphorae were used for storing larger quantities of wine. Vessels for holding alcohol of lesser strength, such as beer[31] and fermented mare's milk (*kumis*), much favoured by the Mongols and others of Turkic origin, were of different shape. According to William of Rubruck, *kumis* was made and stored in skins with a mouthpiece tied with string. [32] It was served in cups called *kasa* and there was often a strong ceremonial element in the use of these at court.[33] Jugs were also used.[34] As for the drinking vessels used for wine, they too were very varied, and might be of glass, ceramic, brass or precious metal. They ranged from delicate beakers or shallow bowls or ewers[35] to hefty goblets or even the skulls of enemies.[36] A special category concerns the ritual drinking of wine in crescent-shaped cups evoking the merging of the sun and the moon at sunset, and giving rise to the image of a boat sailing in a sea of wine. This concept, which can be traced back to Achaemenid times, has been thought to have acquired mystical significance in Sufi thought and to have found visual expression in the boat-shaped beggar's bowl (*kashkul*) used by wandering dervishes into modern times.[37] While rhytons of Greek and thence Parthian form appear to have fallen into disuse with the coming of Islam, a closely related and still more ancient type – the wine leg – is recorded, and survived into the Islamic era.[38] Bull-shaped containers for drinking wine also have a long tradition behind them and had Zoroastrian associations;[39] other forms of vessel included horns[40] and birds,[41] and wine-drinking played a key part in the celebration of Nowruz, the Iranian New Year, from pre-Islamic times onwards.[42]

The absence of scenes of conviviality in which many people are shown drinking is noteworthy, nor do scenes of competitive drinking or wine tasting survive. Instead, a strict formality is maintained, signified for example by an isolated figure of authority sitting cross-legged in a rigidly frontal pose. Indeed, scenes of actual drinking – as distinct from images of a person of rank holding a goblet or beaker – are virtually unknown. There is too little sense of how far the custom of wine-drinking spread to the wider world outside the court. Sometimes a specific sense of context enriches images of the royal drinker, featuring such elements as the recitation of poetry, music-making, dancing or acrobatic displays. The conclusion that gradually imposes itself is that wine-drinking as depicted in medieval Islamic art is not an independent iconographic theme that is developed in its own right. It quickly stabilised as a visual cliché – clearly the fact that wine was forbidden in orthodox Islam caused artists no embarrassment. On the other hand, it is an indispensable component of the visual panorama

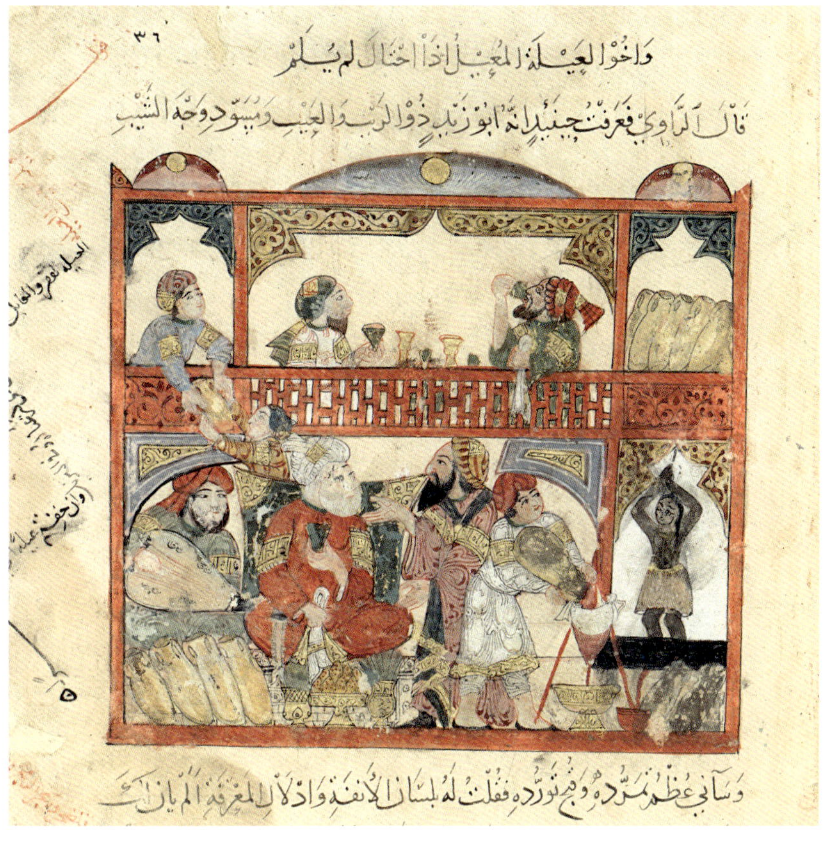

of what might be termed the good life – the pictorial equivalent of the formulaic blessings called down on the owner of an object by its benedictory inscriptions. On the Courtauld bag, leaving aside the major narrative band in which drinking plays perhaps the key role, no less than six independent roundels depict people holding wine beakers, sometimes a wine jug too or a beaker in each hand. This is counterbalanced by an astonishing nine roundels depicting music-making. Riders account for only two roundels. No other piece of medieval Islamic metalwork comes close to this sustained emphasis on wine and music, to the virtual exclusion of other amusements. It reflects the close interdependence of these two themes and is a clear signal that these were the principal entertainments of at least one contemporary court. The accounts by al-Mas῾udi, al-Tabari, al-Isfahani and others of high life in ῾Abbasid Baghdad flesh out this statement with abundant corroborative detail, and it is this gilded ambience which set the gold standard for subsequent courts.

It is time to consider how the theme of wine is treated in the art of the twelfth to fourteenth centuries, the period which provides a broad context for the Courtauld bag. Here the choice of medium is decisive. This is precisely the time from which the earliest Islamic (mainly Arab) illustrated manuscripts survive, and by a fortunate coincidence it also saw the *floruit* of Islamic inlaid metalwork. These are the two major sources for images of drinking in the medieval Islamic world, closely followed by luxury ceramics, in which lovers may be shown in intimate conversation, one plucking a harp and the other holding a goblet of wine, or a monarch holding a goblet may be presented amidst serried ranks of courtiers. Similar themes turn up in the ivory carving of Umayyad Spain and Fatimid Egypt – in the latter case (a long strip of animated figures in constantly varied poses), a seated figure serenaded by a quartet of female musicians pours himself a drink from a ewer, while further along a youth flanked by female lute-players and holding a beaker reclines languidly on cushions.[43] The

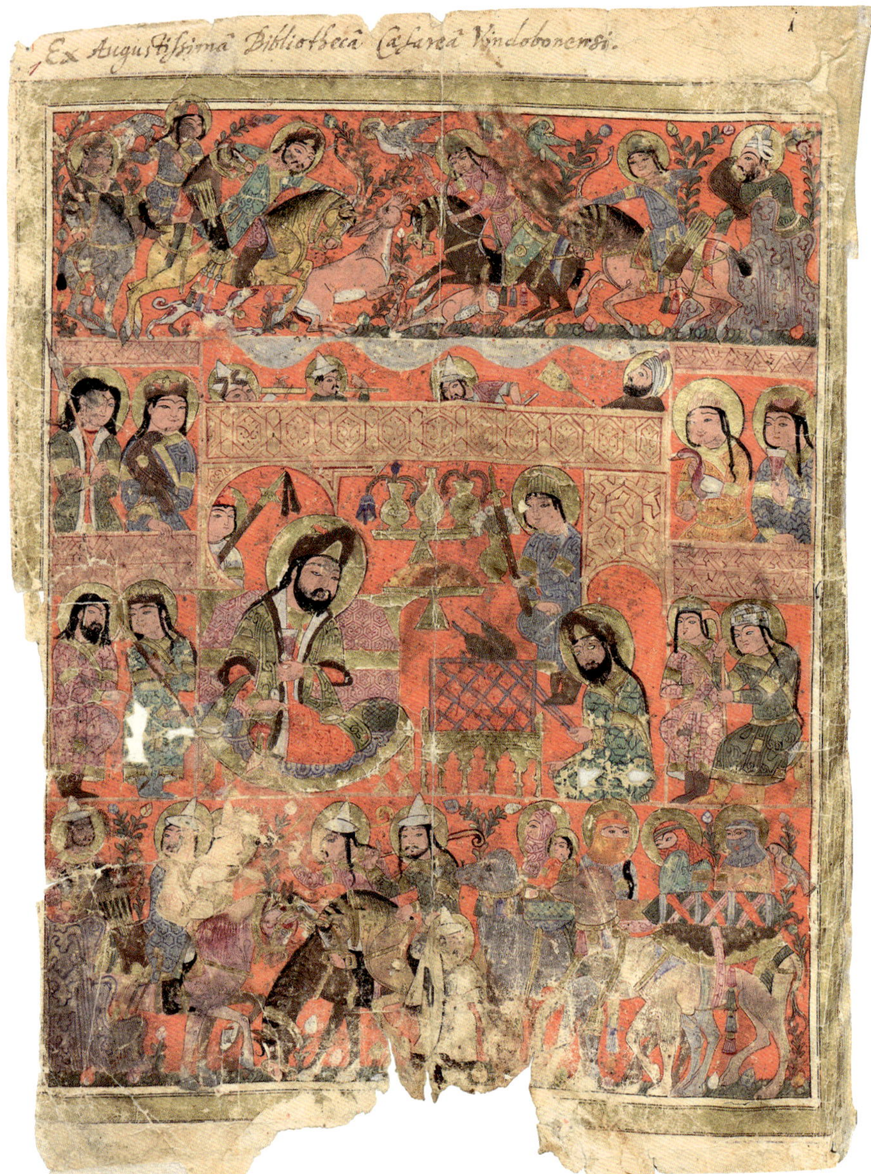

FIG. 20
Frontispiece from the *Book of Antidotes* (*Kitab al-Diryaq*), probably Mosul, mid 13th century
Ink, colours and gold on paper,
H: 32 cm, W: 25 cm (folio)
Vienna, Nationalbibliothek,
A.F.10, fol. 1r

close connection already noted between drinking and music could not be clearer.

And so to the evidence of manuscripts.[44] Obviously enough, painting on paper allows far more latitude for the depiction of detail. Thus a copy of al-Hariri's *Maqamat* dated 643/1237, whose 99 pictures hold up an unsparing mirror to life in the raw in thirteenth-century Baghdad, the foremost metropolis of the Islamic world, contains its full share of images of feasting, merry-making – and the pleasures of the tavern. In one such image the confidence trickster Abu Zayd occupies

the place of honour, enthroned in a broad parody of a standard contemporary ruler image (fig. 19).[45] Like the well-bred gentleman that he is not, he sports a *mandil*, the napkin that was a must-have accessory for any drinking bout. Beside him a musician strums his lute. Other nattily dressed drinkers occupy the upper storey, and large wine storage jars are stacked at both levels. A topless slave-girl standing in a trough crushes the fruit with her feet; the juice runs into a bowl, while next to her a boy pours the liquid from a storage jar into a straining cloth over an amphora suspended by a tripod, with the

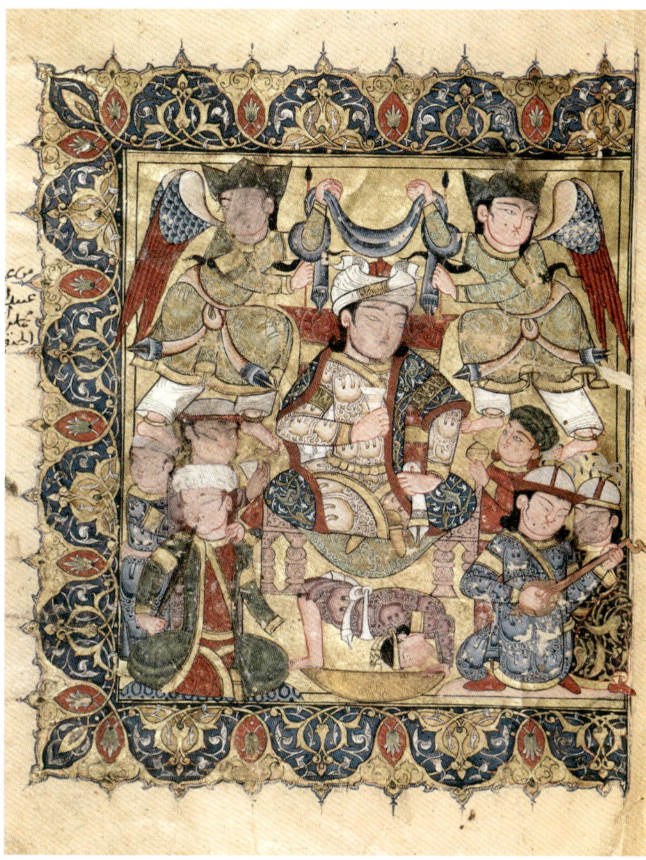

purified red wine dripping into a bigger bowl. Meanwhile a servant leans over the balcony to hand a colleague a small two-handled wine jar. Despite its simplified format, this image presents several stages in the operation of a wine shop, from the making of the product to its consumption, though there is no reference to the spices that were added to finer wines – cardamom, turmeric, ginger, musk and so on. Nor is there any sign here of the Christians (and Jews)[46] who were traditionally associated with this industry. In fact Christian monasteries were, from Umayyad times onwards, a favoured discreet location for Muslims intent on heavy drinking.[47]

This *Maqamat* image has an unmistakable flavour of low life. On the other hand, two frontispiece paintings – the prestigious location is important, for it shows that the patron felt no need to hide his drinking – for books of science or light entertainment vividly evoke the aristocratic context in which wine-drinking was normal. Here they must do duty for a number of broadly similar painted images of the same period. The first, probably

produced in Mosul or Northern Iraq *c.* 1250, illustrates a manuscript dealing with antidotes to snakebite (fig. 20). Here an entire court is on display,[48] with the central band depicting at each side the principal officials bearing the attributes of their posts, while an oblong panel above shows a hunting scene and a matching predella has court ladies and their attendants. At centre stage sits the ruler, holding a glass beaker full of red liquid. Meat is being roasted on a barbecue, while a table in the background holds a ewer and a wine-jug. The second prefaces a copy of al-Hariri's *Maqamat* probably produced in Damascus in 734/1334 and its atmosphere is noticeably more formal; this is largely due to the presence of winged angels holding a cloth over the ruler's head, mimicking a baldachin (fig. 21). An acrobat contorts himself into an improbable pose on a bowl directly at the foot of the throne, with musicians playing on either side. The ruler himself, again enthroned cross-legged, holds a *mandil* and a beaker.[49] Even closer in date and spirit to the Courtauld bag is the image from the *Compendium of Chronicles* of Rashid al-Din (714/1314–15) depicting the Seljuq Sultan Malikshah holding a wine cup just presented to him on a matching salver by a kneeling servant, while a seated female harpist plays to the assembled company (fig. 22).[50] The best parallel of all, however, comes from a series of scenes in the Diez and Istanbul albums depicting Mongol court receptions. In several of these the ruler shares his throne with his consort and both are drinking or are about to do so (cat. 16, 17).[51] Several Il-Khanid *Shahnama*s feature, as components of a royal image, a low table in front of the royal throne bearing a pair of long-necked ewers, clear evidence that the consumption of alcohol was an established element in court ceremonial (cat. 2).

A drinking vessel, whether cup or beaker, held against the chest sometimes had a symbolic function,[52] for from

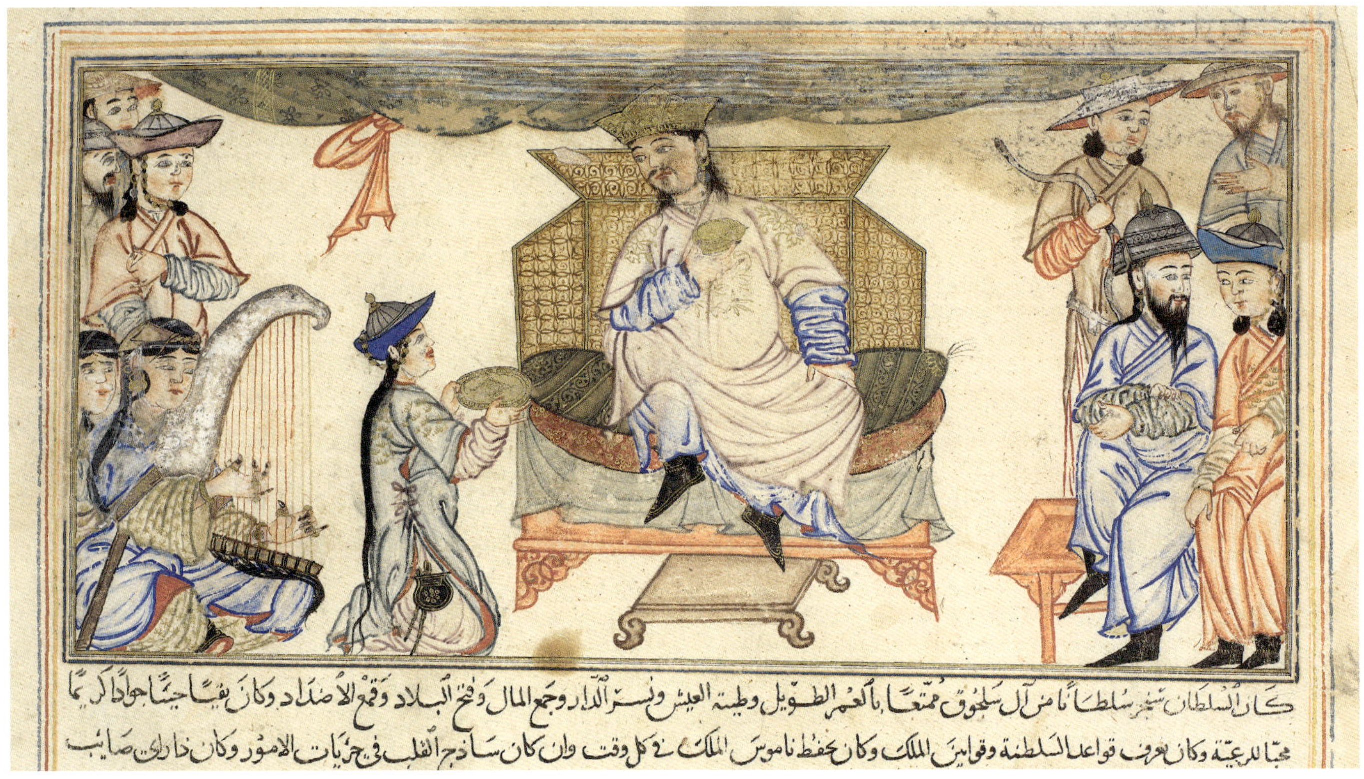

pre-Islamic times a Turkic icon of royal authority was the cup, as shown by the stone figures (*balbal*s) distributed widely over the inner Asian steppe. A famous image from the painted ceiling of the Cappella Palatina in Palermo (after 1143) shows a seated ruler holding before him a large beaker filled with red liquid; this is at the centre of the image, and is clearly intended as an attribute of sovereignty since an attendant is pouring him a much smaller beaker of wine from a pitcher.[53] Thus in images of the royal wine-drinker one must be alert to a possible ceremonial dimension in its meaning. And the cup has yet further symbolic significance as a symbol of the sky itself. A related issue (to which Hafiz refers in his *mathnawi* beginning "*Biya Saqi …*")[54] is the notion of the magical world-revealing cup of the mythical ruler of ancient Iran, Jamshid, who himself is credited with inventing wine.[55] The difficulty here is that there is no standard format for either a drinking vessel or a ceremonial cup.

The other medium in which wine-drinking is a favoured theme is inlaid metalwork of the twelfth to the fourteenth century. Several standard scenes (excluding the ruler and his consort enthroned while drinking) occur – the drinker reclining on a couch, served by an attendant with a pouring vessel; a seated ruler turning to an attendant to have his outstretched beaker replenished; and, most common of all, the frontally depicted figure of authority seated cross-legged with a drinking cup or similar receptacle held at chest level (see fig. 39). This last formula is sometimes enriched by the addition of flanking attendants and musicians below. None of these compositions are new, and indeed many can be paralleled in Sasanian or post-Sasanian silverwork. What distinguishes the later versions of these themes is above all their visual context, which is one of merrymaking – not only drinking but eating, music-making, dancing, hunting and so on. These interconnected themes are, moreover, explicitly linked by the layout of these metalwares, which comprise a series of roundels, medallions or cartouches each devoted to one aspect of the good life. As the Ghaznavid poet Manuchihri Damghani writes:

> "We're men of drinking, feasting and singing.
> Hurray for the *rebab*, kebab and wine."[56]

NOTES

1 Karic 2002, p. 557; cf. Fulton 1948 on al-Firuzabadi's list of the ills connected with wine and his compilation of almost 450 names for wines.
2 Ahsan 1979, p. 111, with copious references.
3 On *nabidh* see Wensinck 1978, p. 996a; Sadan 1977, p. 134; Jahiz/Pellat 1969, pp. 52–53; McAuliffe 1984, pp. 164–65.
4 McAuliffe 1984, pp. 160–63, 166 and 168–70.
5 Ibn Jubayr/Broadhurst 1952, p. 16.
6 Spuler 1985, p. 173.
7 For a learned survey of the whole subject, see Sadan 1977.
8 R. Hillenbrand 1982, pp. 13 and 28. But the evidence for Hisham is contradictory; see Hamilton 1988, p. 111.
9 Derenk 1974, pp. 33–35, 59–62; R. Hillenbrand 1982, pp. 11–14, 18 and 28–29; Hamilton 1988, pp. 35–37, 88–89, 91–3, 118–19, 122, 124–25, 149 and 164; and Rotter 2004, pp. 105, 109, 115, 117, 122, 125 and 130.
10 E.g. al-Qahir, al-Radi and al-Mustakfi (Mez 1937, pp. 397–98, quoting respectively Miskawayh, al-Suli and al-Mas'udi).
11 As in the case of the deposition of the caliph al-Rashid in 1136 (C. Hillenbrand 1990, p. 78, quoting Ibn al-Azraq).
12 Mez 1937, p. 396; Ahsan 1979, p. 164.
13 Azarnouche 2013, p. 57.
14 D.S. Rice 1958, with detailed descriptions of particularly select wines.
15 Esin 1969, pp. 241–57.
16 Arberry 1967, pp. 156–64 (a translation of al-Mas'udi, *Muruj al-dhahhab*).
17 Bencheikh 1978; Kennedy 1997; Noorani 2004, pp. 345–46, explores, in the context of the wine poetry of Abu Nuwas, the notion that "the elite excesses of enjoyment … are rooted in the same moral order that allies political dominance with virtue".
18 Tr. Schroeder 1955, p. 281.
19 Hamilton 1988, p. 105.
20 Nurbakhsh 1980, p. 80.
21 Rumi/Barks 1999, p. 288.
22 Tr. Schroeder 1955, p. 525.
23 Arberry 1965, pp. 126–27.
24 Hamilton 1959, pp. 53–55.
25 Spuler 1985, p. 369.
26 C. Hillenbrand 1995, p. 240.
27 C. Hillenbrand 1981, pp. 277 and 289, with copious references to the largely Arabic sources.
28 C. Hillenbrand 2001, p. 120.
29 For a rapid inventory of examples of this theme, see Sadan 1977, pp. 137–38.
30 Washington 1989, p. 261.
31 Ghouchani and Adle 1992.
32 Dawson 1966, pp. 96 and 98.
33 Spuler 1985, p. 367; Dawson 1966, p. 96. For an impressive list of citations to the ceremonial use of *kasa* see Rashid al-Din/ Quatremère 1836, p. 354, n. 155.
34 Spuler 1985, p. 146.
35 Ghouchani 1999 deals with the content of the wine poems that they bear.
36 It is recorded that in 1108 the Seljuq warlord Tughtegin drank from the skull of his scalped enemy, the Crusader knight Gervase de Basoches (C. Hillenbrand 2011, p. 463; see pp. 465 and 467 for further examples of the practice among the Scythians, Tibetans and Safavids, and cf. Dawson 1966, p. 142 for more details of Tibetan practice).
37 Melikian-Chirvani 1991 explores these themes with an impressively wide range of reference, drawing extensively on the evidence provided by medieval Persian poetry.
38 See Melikian-Chirvani 1997b, pp. 82–84, for an example from Afrasiyab.
39 Melikian-Chirvani 1991 and 1992.
40 Melikian-Chirvani 1996; cf. also Melikian-Chirvani 1991.
41 Melikian-Chirvani 1995. The wine leg, used for both beakers and decanters, and sometimes spouted, is an even more remarkable receptacle for wine-drinking than a boat or a bird. For its survival into the medieval period in Iran, see Melikian-Chirvani 1997b, especially pp. 82–87.
42 Melikian-Chirvani 1996, pp. 115–24.
43 Spuler and Sourdel-Thomine 1973, p. 261, pl. 191 (entry by J. Zick-Nissen).
44 For a tally of some significant examples of the theme, see Sadan 1977, pp. 132–33 and 138.
45 Stewart 1967, repr. p. 95.
46 Rotter 2004, pp. 118 and 212.
47 Ahsan 1979, p. 271, quoting Shabustari.
48 Ettinghausen 1962, pp. 91–92.
49 Ettinghausen 1962, pp. 147–49.
50 D.T. Rice 1976.
51 New York 2002, pp. 80 and 82.
52 Barry 2010, p. 151.
53 Ettinghausen 1962, pp. 45 and 47.
54 Arberry 1962, pp. 129–30; Hafiz 1941, p. 356.
55 Simpson 2013, pp. 353–54.
56 Clinton 1972, p. 12 (translation slightly adapted).

Picturing music in Islamic art

ANNA CONTADINI

MUSIC MAKING and musicians are widely represented in the arts of the Islamic Middle East, both in manuscript painting and on objects in all materials.[1] The main areas of representation are:

1. entertainment, often related to the princely cycle (everywhere, all times, all regions).
2. ceremonial,[2] birth, circumcision and other celebrations (usually in later periods).
3. warfare, i.e. music to spur on the soldiers and/or frighten the enemy. This is less common, but is present from earlier periods.[3]
4. religious ceremonies, usually Sufi (less common, and in later periods).

The musicians on the Courtauld bag are certainly to be assigned to the first group, and are possibly to be associated with the princely cycle, depending on the

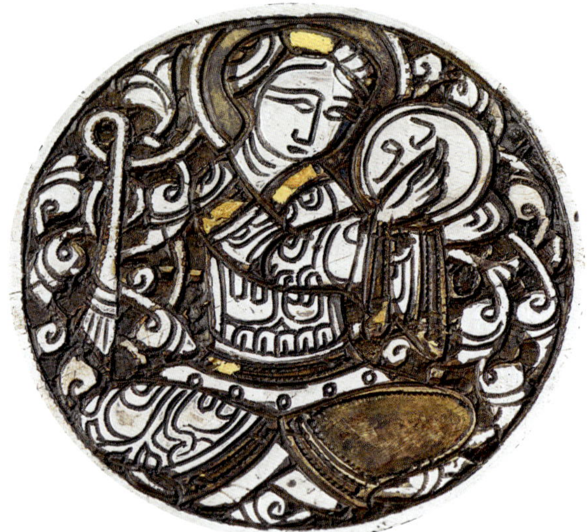

The Courtauld bag (cat. 1),
detail of roundel with musician

interpretation given of the scene on the lid. They are integral to scenes of entertainment, whether princely or not, where they are portrayed together with, variously, food, drink, perfume and hunting, as on the bag.[4] As the association with entertainment was a constant, it was also possible to imply it through the portrayal of a musician in isolation, and of this we have numerous examples in all media.[5] So, the fact that the musicians are represented alone on the bag, within their roundels, is not surprising. Considered together, the ensemble they form, consisting of flute, lute, harp and frame drum (see roundel below), is a typical one for intimate – and frequently indoor – entertainment.

The connection with entertainment is reinforced, or made explicit, by a reference to a related activity, most obviously drinking, through the inclusion of beakers and bottles. The inclusion of floating scarves may suggest dancing, as this is a feature normally associated with dancers. They contrast with the floating scarf of the rider in the central medallion, which is definitely a double scarf going around his neck (a motif that goes back at least as far as Sasanian and early Islamic iconography), for they emerge, incongruously, from the side of the haloes surrounding the heads of the musicians playing the frame drum, flute and lute. Further, they turn around to form a loop before descending to a wider lower end with horizontal stripes probably denoting decorated *tiraz* bands. However, turbans in early thirteenth-century metalwork are often represented with a floating and looping tail, and a more prosaic explanation would be that in later metalwork, as in the case of the bag, the connection was lost and it became just a decorative motif.

The iconography of the flowing and looping scarf coming out from the halo is also found in other pieces of metalwork depicting musicians, such as in the image of the harpist with a flutist on the Blacas ewer

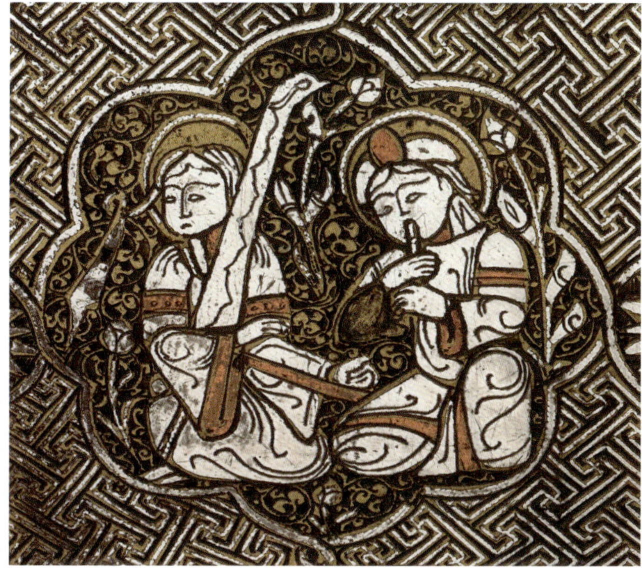

(cat. 21 and fig. 23).[6] But while its inclusion in scenes with musicians might suggest that it represents a scarf worn by dancers, it also appears in other contexts, such as in the figure of a mounted knight with a crossbow,[7] in a bird-hunting scene[8] and (without a closed loop) beside the figures of two sword fencers with shields.[9] Whether or not dance is implied on the bag by the floating scarves, representations of dancers with such scarves are present from early periods. One example is a dancer in the painted ceiling of the Cappella Palatina in Palermo, placed close, moreover, to a frame-drum player who, like the one on the bag, is striking the instrument with a beater. This playing technique is also found elsewhere, for example on an ivory plaque made in Egypt in the twelfth century,[10] and on the Vaso Vescovali made in Afghanistan around AD 1200.[11] The iconographic record thus suggests that this technique was geographically widespread, from the Mediterranean to eastern Iran, but it is not consistently shown and is in any case confined to early representations: all later examples show the modern technique of using open-hand strokes (at the centre) and finger strokes (at the rim). The instrument, which is of particularly frequent occurrence, is represented played by both men and women. It is still played today, and it is principally at festivities, and in particular at weddings, that there are women performers.

One question is whether we can use musical information to say something more precise about the date and provenance of objects. The answer is both yes and no but, unfortunately, more frequently no. Even if we may assume a generally high level of realism in the representations of instruments, some of which are extremely detailed, there is no archaeological record against which they can be matched, and in most cases textual references and descriptions are insufficient to supply a very precise dating or distribution for a given instrument.[12] A particular feature, the number of pegs (and hence strings) on a lute, say, might give a crude indication of date, but such evidence would do no more than confirm a case already made on the basis of art-historical analysis. Some instruments are ubiquitous (lute, flute, frame drum), while others do seem to be used more in one area than another (hornpipe in Spain,[13] qanun (large zither-type stringed instrument) in Mamluk territories, harp in the Persianate and Ottoman worlds), but the dividing line is seldom sufficiently sharp to serve as a reliable diagnostic tool: an instrument with generally Persian associations may be encountered on an Egyptian artefact. As might be concluded from this, the grouping together of instruments in an ensemble is equally unlikely to provide any clear indication, particularly as depictions coming from the same period and place may show a degree of variation in the size of the ensemble and the nature of its constituents.

For later periods it is usually easier to match an instrument with a date and a geographical area, but such information is potentially more useful for musicologists than for art historians. It may be helpful for the art historian to know that by the eighteenth century the harp had become obsolete in western Asia,[14] but we already knew that later representations of Bahram Gur with Azada and her harp are prolongations of a well-established iconographical tradition rather than a reflection of contemporary practice. The harp is, in fact,

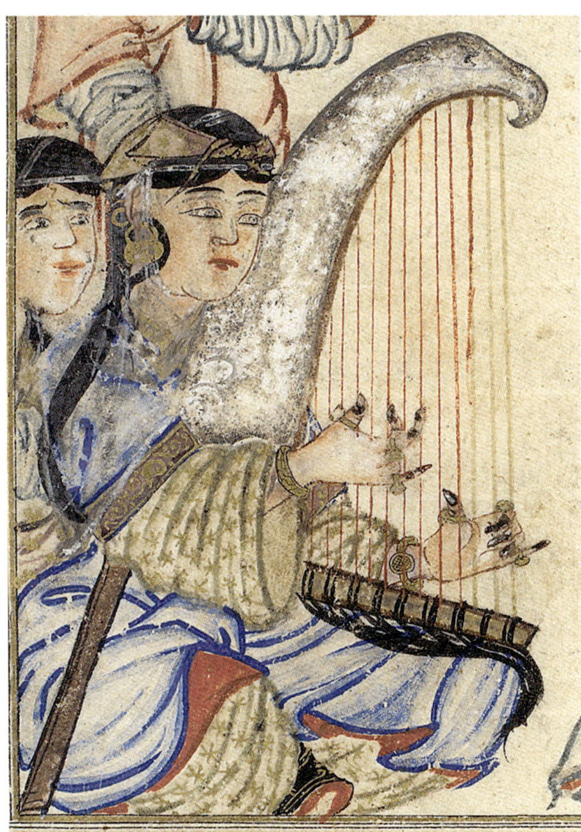

one of the more commonly represented instruments, from the earliest Babylonian representations and the Sasanian Taq-i Bustan reliefs.[15] Closer in date to the Courtauld bag is the illustration of a heavily bejewelled lady playing for Sultan Sanjar ibn Malik Shah in a manuscript of the *Compendium of Chronicles* dated 714/1314 (fig. 24).[16] Depictions of the harp are frequently very realistic, with the performer portrayed using a thumb-and-first-finger plucking technique, as on the bag (see roundel p. 98). The only significant difference between this harp and those in miniature paintings lies in the reduction of the number of strings resulting from the constraints of the medium. Otherwise the morphology is standard, clearly belonging to the zoomorphic type, where the soundboard terminates in the shape of the head of an animal, usually a bird. Another very beautiful metalwork example is provided by the probably Southern Italian casket in the Treasury of San Marco, Venice, which shows both a barbed lute player and a harpist, again using the thumb and first finger technique.[17] The

size of the harp increases with time, at least in the Persian environment, as we can see in Timurid and Safavid paintings from 1481 and 1509–10.[18]

It is difficult to draw conclusions about gender: most instruments can be found being played by either men or women in different places and at different times. To generalise, iconography suggests that after the thirteenth century women generally played the harp, men the flute, and especially the shahrud (extra large-bellied lute), while both could play the frame drum and the lute. Earlier accounts of singing slave-girls associate them with a variety of instruments, including the frame drum;[19] at the ʿAbbasid court they performed mainly on the short- and long-necked lutes (oud and tunbur),[20] while later the qanun was also favoured by Mamluk female singers.[21] In one of the frontispieces of the *Kitab al-Aghani* (fig. 25), painted in Mosul, *c.* 1215–19, we actually find, in a row at the bottom of the page, an all-female ensemble playing the same instruments as represented on the bag – frame drum, flute,[22] lute and harp. This combination of percussion, wind and string instruments is quite typical. Various types of plucked string instruments are found represented on artefacts and paintings, and one may suggest that less important than the differences in sonority between them was the contrast between the sustained notes of the wind instruments and the sharper attacks and quicker decay of the string instruments, the attacks reinforcing the rhythmic structure articulated by the frame drum.

A striking painting of a female lute-player is found in the Mamluk *Maqamat* now in the Nationalbibliothek in Vienna, dated 734/1334 and probably produced in Damascus (fig. 26).[23] This is an all-male party scene, with the exception of a woman wearing sumptuous garments, and a light, transparent veil so her face is visible, and with henna marks on both hands and feet. She is playing, left-

FIG. 25
Frontispiece to the *Kitab al-Aghani*
(Book of Songs), vol. 4, Mosul, *c.* 1215–19
Ink, colours and gold on paper
Cairo, Dar al-Kutub, Adab Farsi, 579

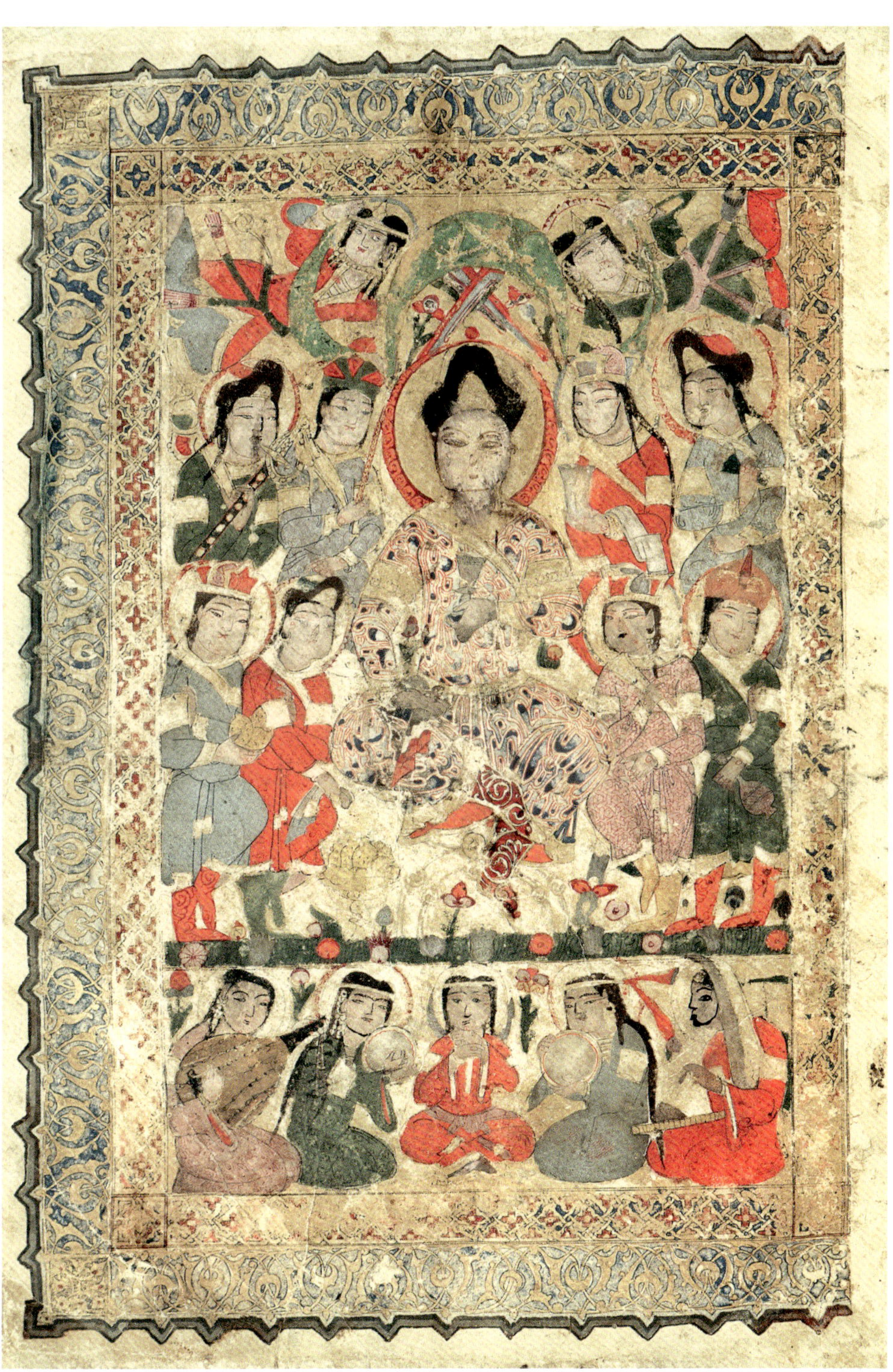

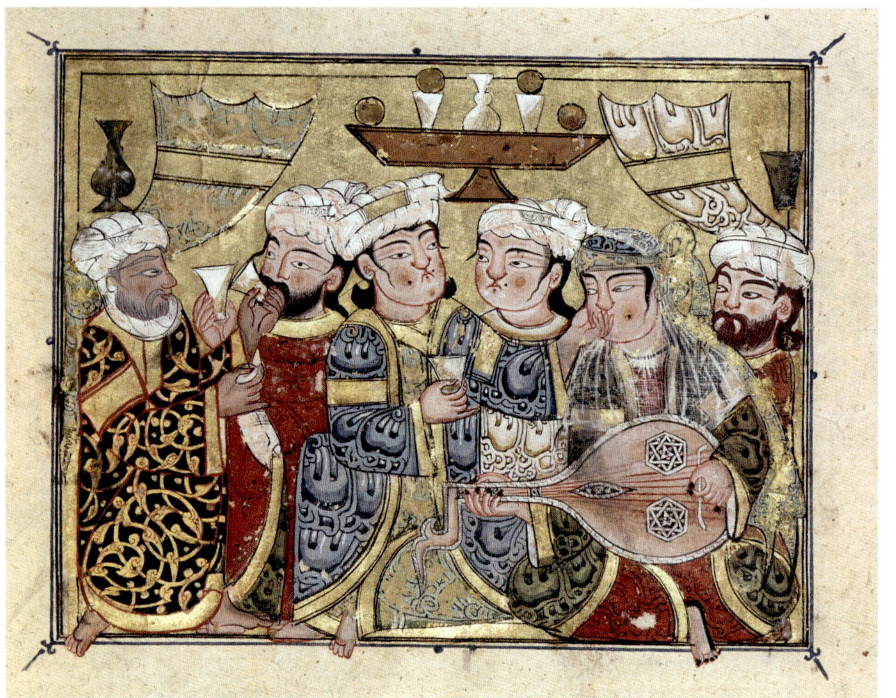
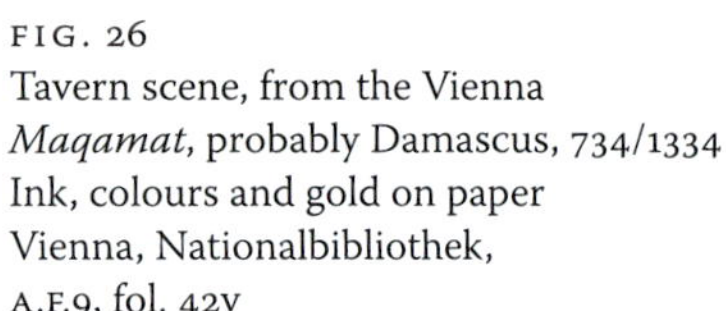
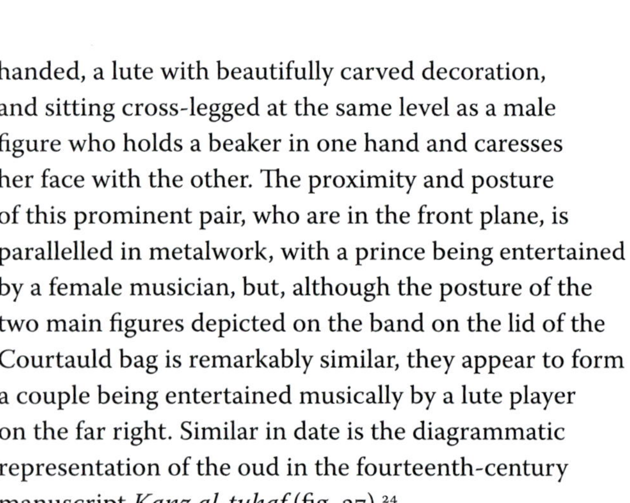

FIG. 26
Tavern scene, from the Vienna
Maqamat, probably Damascus, 734/1334
Ink, colours and gold on paper
Vienna, Nationalbibliothek,
A.F.9, fol. 42v

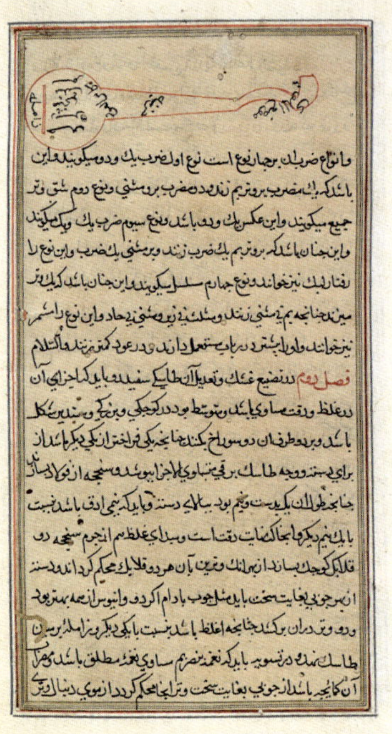

FIG. 27
Drawing of a lute (oud) from the musical
treatise *Kanz al-tuhaf*, Iran, 14th century
Ink, colours and gold on paper
London, British Library, I.O. Islamic
2067, fol. 17v

handed, a lute with beautifully carved decoration,
and sitting cross-legged at the same level as a male
figure who holds a beaker in one hand and caresses
her face with the other. The proximity and posture
of this prominent pair, who are in the front plane, is
parallelled in metalwork, with a prince being entertained
by a female musician, but, although the posture of the
two main figures depicted on the band on the lid of the
Courtauld bag is remarkably similar, they appear to form
a couple being entertained musically by a lute player
on the far right. Similar in date is the diagrammatic
representation of the oud in the fourteenth-century
manuscript *Kanz al-tuhaf* (fig. 27).[24]

In the medium of metalwork, comparison of the bag
with the earlier Blacas ewer (cat. 21 and fig. 23), made in
Mosul in 629/1232, is particularly instructive. Here we
have two couples, lute and frame drum, harp and wind
instrument, the same combination of instrument types
as on the bag, but now with the gender of one of the
musicians clearly indicated, as the lute player wears a veil
that covers her face up to the eyes.[25] We have a similar
disposition of the figures, with roundels of musicians,
dancers and also drinkers, surrounding the larger ones
of riders and hunting scenes, so that, despite differences
of shape as well as date, the compositional strategy of the
two pieces is remarkably similar.

NOTES

1 A broad survey is found in Farmer 1976. Although by no means comprehensive, this is still an essential reference work.

2 As in the *hajj* send-off in the *Maqamat* manuscript dated 634/1237, Paris, Bibliothèque nationale de France, MS arabe 5847, fol. 94v. See Ettinghausen 1962, p. 119.

3 For example, an illustration in Rashid al-Din's *Compendium of Chronicles* dated 714/1314, Edinburgh University Library, Ms. Ar. 20, fol. 156v. See D.T. Rice 1976, pp. 114–15, no. 38.

4 For general background on musical behaviour at the ᶜAbbasid court see Sawa 1989; and for the Timurid court see Subtelny 1984.

5 For example, a fragment of a Fatimid lustre-painted bowl, where the lute, played by a female musician, has a piriform shape with a lovely bent peg-box with eight pegs (that is with four doubled courses) very clearly marked, Athens, Benaki Museum, inv. no. 11121. See Philon 1980, pl. XXII, A. Or on a *mina'i* bowl where a musician takes central stage, New York, Metropolitan Museum of Art, no. 57.61.16. See Fehérvári 1985, p. 148.

6 See also the lute player with a dancer on a brass candlestick made in Cairo, *c.* 1270, Allan 1982, p. 83. Also a woman playing the lute on the basin made for the Ayyubid Sultan al-ᶜAdil II (1238-40) in Syria or Mosul, Paris, Musée du Louvre, OA 5991, published in D.S. Rice 1957, p. 306, fig. 31a and pl. 6a.

7 This figure is on the Freer Canteen, possibly made in Mosul, *c.* 1230-40, Washington D.C., Freer Gallery of Art, F1941.10. See Raby 2012, p. 51, fig. 1.25a.

8 It appears next to a figure holding a blowtube on the Barberini Vase, made in Mosul or Syria for the Ayyubid Sultan al-Nasir Yusuf (ruled 1237-60), Paris, Musée du Louvre, OA 4090; see D.S. Rice 1957, fig. 23.

9 On the aforementioned basin made for Sultan al-ᶜAdil II in the Louvre see D.S. Rice 1957, pl. 8d.

10 Florence, Museo Nazionale del Bargello, inv. 80c 3. See Contadini 2005, fig. 132.

11 London, British Museum, OA 1950.7-25.1. See Farmer 1976, p. 65, fig. 52.

12 The most important early account is that by al-Farabi in his *Kitab al-musiqi al-kabir*, translated in d'Erlanger 1930. His concern, however, is primarily with the scales produced on the instrument in question, so that materials, structure and use are largely ignored. On materials and structure the most precise information is provided by the mid-fourteenth-century *Kanz al-tuhaf* (Tsuge 2013, pp. 165-84), while the early fifteenth-century *Jamiᶜ al-alhan* of al-Maraghi (al-Maraghi 1987, pp. 198-20) gives a general catalogue, with brief descriptions, of the instruments encountered in Timurid Samarkand. With the exception of the oud, for which a certain amount of factual descriptive material is available (see Neubauer 1993, pp. 279-378), modern attempts to reconstruct earlier forms have had to rely on the iconographical record. See Franke and Neubauer 2000.

13 See Reynolds 2006.

14 See Feldman 1996, pp. 154-56.

15 Farmer 1976, p. 17.

16 See D.T. Rice 1976, pp. 174-75, no. 68.

17 Venice, Tesoro di San Marco, inv. no. 123. M.V. Fontana in Venice 1993, no. 297, pp. 477-80.

18 Dublin, Chester Beatty Library, Per. 162, 886/1481, fol. 229r, and Per. 182, 915/1509-10, fol. 256r.

19 Farmer 1929/1973.

20 Sawa 1989.

21 al-Baqli 1984.

22 It is not always possible to distinguish between flutes and reed-pipes.

23 See discussion in Contadini 2012, pl. 32 and p. 81.

24 Tsuge 2013, fig. 11, p. 181. There is also a small miniature in the *Kashf al-humum wa-'l-kurab fi sharh alat al-tarab*, a probably fifteenth-century work dealing with instruments (Cairo, Dar al-kutub, *funun jamila* 1).

25 Ward 1986, fig. 78.

Chinese silks and Mosul metalwork

JAMES ALLAN

ONE OF THE MOST striking aspects of the Courtauld bag is the background fret – an ornamental design consisting of a repeated, interlocking and symmetrical figure in the form of a double-ended T (called T-pattern elsewhere in this catalogue). Its angular pattern contrasts with the curved frames of the roundels and quatrefoils and the figural and vegetal motifs within them. This fret pattern is not unique to the bag. The same design as a background to roundels and medallions occurs on a number of other inlaid brass vessels which can be attributed to the city of Mosul in the first half of the thirteenth century (cat. 21 and 22). Islamic art is full of geometric patterns, but this fret is not seen earlier. This essay briefly explores its likely source and what that tells us about the bag and its cultural milieu.

Ibn Saʿid, who visited Mosul in 1250, writes: "Mosul …. There are many crafts in the city, especially inlaid copper vessels which are exported and presented to rulers, as are the silken garments woven there."[1] Ibn Saʿid's claim that fine inlaid metalwork was produced in Mosul is borne out by surviving vessels.[2] Silk is less durable than brass and so we need to seek evidence of its production in other media.

At the time of Ibn Saʿid's visit, Badr al-Din Lu'lu' was ruler of Mosul. Lu'lu' had commissioned a set of manuscripts of Abu'l-Faraj al-Isfahani's *Kitab al-Aghani,* of which seven volumes survive: six have their frontispieces more or less intact and five of them feature Lu'lu' himself as a Turkic atabeg, dressed in a splendid garment of blue and gold, sometimes with angelic supporters holding a canopy of the same design over his head (figs. 25 and 28). The name and title of Badr al-Din Lu'lu' appear in the corners of the frontispiece of the surviving volume 17, while his name also occurs on the gold *tiraz* bands on his sleeves in the frontispieces of others of the surviving volumes, making clear that

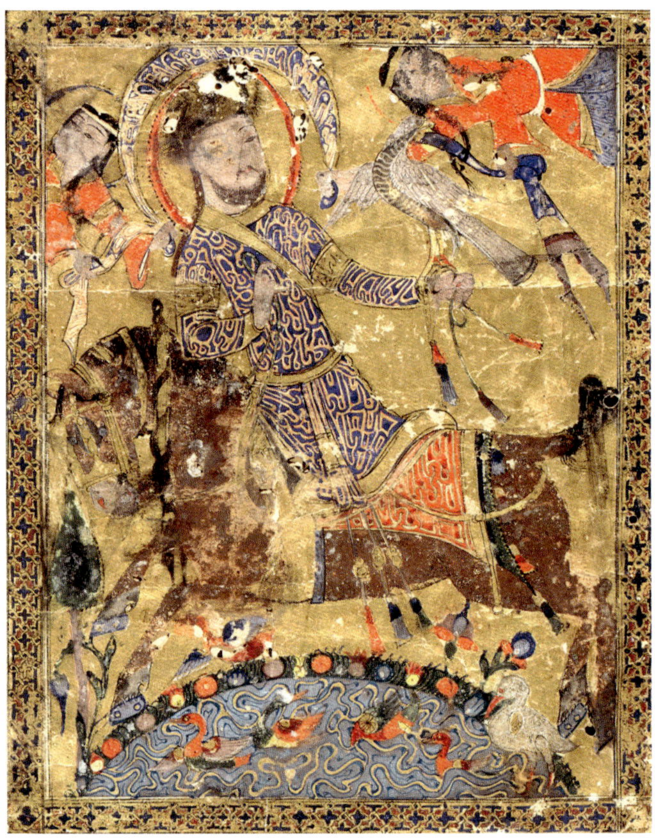

FIG. 28
Frontispiece to the *Kitab al-Aghani* (Book of Songs), vol. 20, Mosul, dated 610/1219
Ink, colours and gold on paper,
H: 28.5, W: 21.5 cm (folio)
Copenhagen, David Collection, D.1/1990
(on loan from the Royal Library)

it is indeed him who is illustrated in the frontispieces. Given Ibn Saʿid's testimony to the quality of the garments produced by the Mosul silk weavers and Badr al-Din's pretensions to greatness, it is inconceivable that he would have been dressed in anything but silk, and the way his costumes have been painted suggests that he was in fact wearing the highest quality of silk, watered in blue and gold.[3] This has intriguing consequences when we look at other early thirteenth-century illustrated manuscripts, for the likelihood is that other costumes depicted in a similar fashion are also meant to indicate silk garments. Thus, for example, the clothes of the seated ruler figure and three central horsemen along the top in the frontispiece to the *Kitab al-Diryaq* (fig. 20) probably painted in Mosul in the mid thirteenth century. We might note also the use of this silk patterning for the costume of the ruler wearing a *sharbush*, whose hand is being kissed by a turbaned figure, on the inlaid ewer dated 1246 in the Walters Art Gallery in Baltimore.[4]

After Lu'lu''s death in 1260, Mosul passed to his son, al-Salih Rukn al-Din Isma'il. However, Mosul did not remain independent for long: it was captured by the Mongols in 1262, its walls were destroyed, and the city was looted (see fig. 6).[5] Many cities which suffered Mongol conquest were forced to give up their weavers to the conquerors for transport to Mongolia or China, but this does not seem to have happened to Mosul, and it continued to be an important silk-producing centre. For Marco Polo, writing sometime after 1295, records: "All the cloths of gold and silk that are called *Mosolins* are made in this country; and those great Merchants called *Mosolins*, who carry for sale such quantities of spicery and pearls, and the cloths of silk and gold, are also from this kingdom."[6] We can therefore be confident that Mosul continued as a major silk-producing centre under Mongol rule.

It should also be noted that Mosul had for many centuries before the Mongol conquests been a major textile centre. Jahiz (d. 869) stated that curtains (*sutur*) and striped robes (*musuh*) came from Mosul, while Tha'alibi's *Lata'if al-Ma'arif*, written in the early

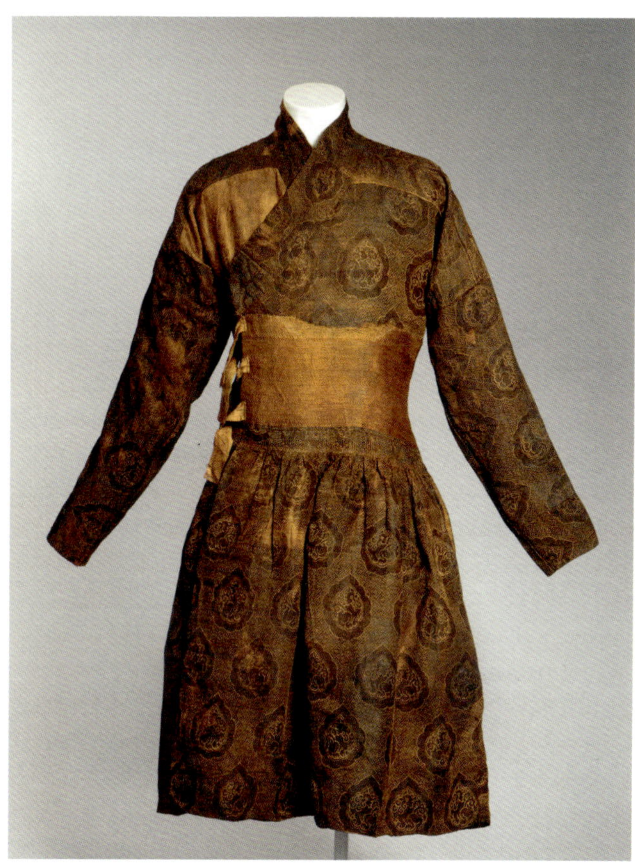

eleventh century, also mentions the curtains of Mosul in a long list of fine stuffs.[7] It should not therefore surprise us if textiles are found to play an important part in the designs used for inlaid metalwork, a technique newly arrived in western Asia in the late twelfth century.

But what of Chinese silks? An extraordinary Chinese silk in a polychrome weave of a Song design known as *tianhua* (heavenly splendour) has been unearthed in Sichuan province (fig. 30). Shelagh Vainker writes: "According to Song texts there were many names for this

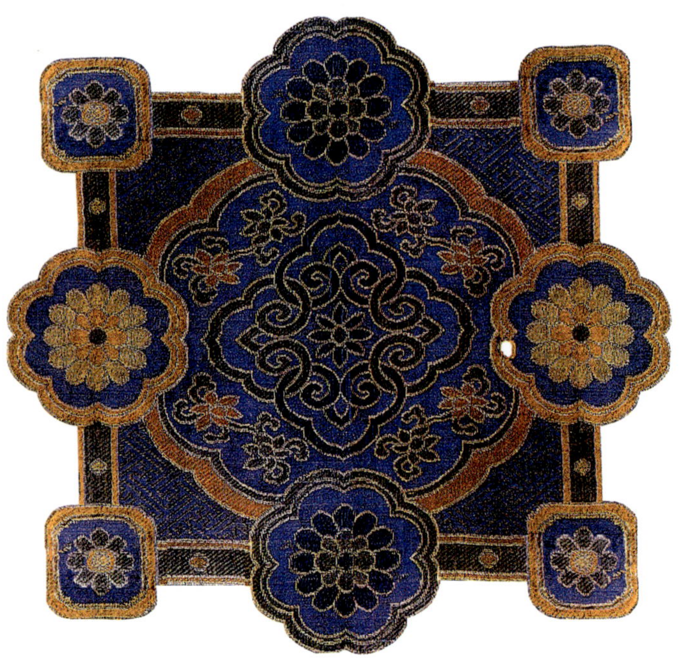

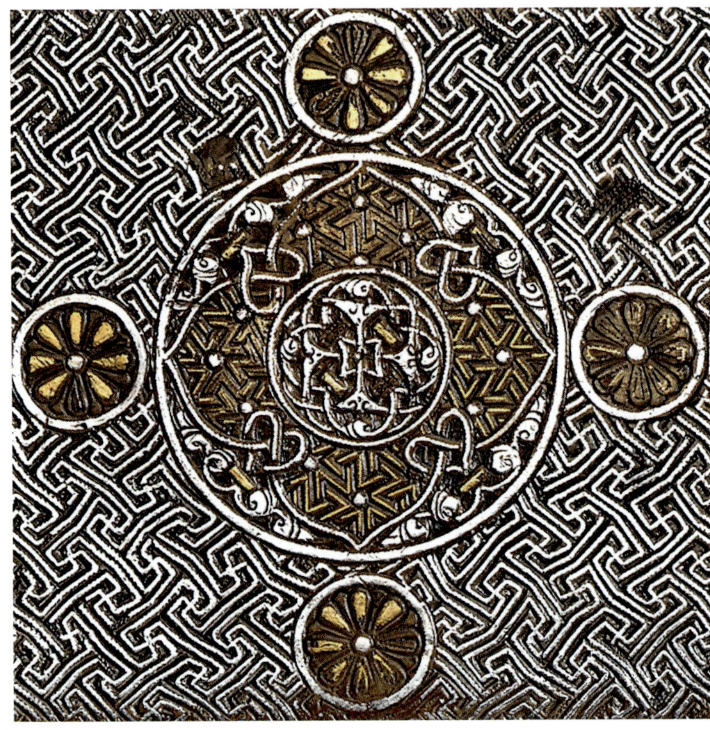

and other ornamental designs that were used on painted architecture as well as on textiles. The architectural decoration is preserved in a manual of building practices commissioned by the emperor and published in 1103 …. The design was known in two versions – 'large brocade' used for curtains, bed covers and so forth, and 'small brocade' for scroll mounts and wrapping cloths".[8] This particular example shows a cusped roundel with four smaller ones, one either side, joined to square medallions by narrow bands, the field being the same fret pattern as on the Courtauld bag. Feng Zhao expands on this: "Characteristic of Liao to Yuan textiles is the use of reserved panels on a background of geometric pattern. This derived from the popular use of geometric patterns on northern Song textiles. These are known as *suo wen* (tiny pattern) in the northern Song text on architectural decoration *Ying zao fa shi* (Manual of Architecture), which lists six types of geometric patterns under *suo wen* – interlinked rings, ingots and squares, turtle shells or hexagons, coins, I-shapes, swastikas and wave pattern. In actuality, these patterns are not only used on wall paintings for architectural decoration, but they are also commonly found on textiles …. Damask-weave textiles from the tombs of the Xixia kingdom bear I-shaped patterns which correspond to the wave pattern of the

text. Patterns of gold ingots, hexagons, and coins in six are found on textiles from Liao tombs."[9] The close resemblance to designs on Mosul inlaid metalwork is striking, and the visual link between the *tianhua* design (fig. 30) and the design on the Courtauld bag (detail above) could hardly be more persuasive.

Textile designs in China were very traditional, and these background designs continued for many centuries. A piece of *nasij* (cloth of gold) of the late thirteenth or early fourteenth century from the Wang family tomb in Zhang County shows an eight-lobed roundel against a background of hexagonal patterning.[10] Notable examples from the early fourteenth century show a dragon roundel, or roundels with abstract designs, on various geometric grounds.[11] These types of arrangement continued into the fifteenth and sixteenth centuries and indeed into the nineteenth century.[12] We know that weavers were taken by the Mongol conquerors from the eastern Islamic lands to work in Mongolian or Chinese textile workshops, and an early fourteenth-century *nasij* caftan from China or the eastern Islamic world, now in the David collection, illustrates the combination of East Asian and Islamic taste popular during Mongol times (see fig. 29). Its drop-shapes with stylised lions, against a background of swastikas, are taken from eastern Asia, while its shoulder bands of pseudo-Kufic and animals of the hunt are typical of the Islamic world.

There remains the question as to whether Chinese silks reached Mosul, bringing with them the designs which the metal inlayers could adopt. The likelihood is strong. Silks were of the highest importance throughout China and Central Asia, and were a commodity of exchange even before the Mongol empire, with large numbers of bolts of silk and robes of silk being used for gifts or for annual payments in the complex political relationships of the Song and the Khitans.[13] Such a role for silk would inevitably have spilled over into the culture of Islamic Central Asia, raising its value throughout the area, and further westwards into the central Islamic lands. Moreover, the literary sources of the pre-Mongol Islamic world constantly emphasise the importance of the silk industry in the central Islamic lands: Serjeant comments that "The importation of Chinese silks into Islamic countries was continuous, and the authors frequently mention 'Chinese silk' (*harir sini*)".[14] So the taste for silk was widespread, and the exotic, the Chinese, would surely have been part of that desire for luxury textiles.

Importantly, Ibn al-Athir relates how, in 1231, "the people of Azerbaijan submitted to the Tatars and supplied them with money, 'Chinese', Khoy and Attabi textiles and other items".[15] When the Mongols reached Tabriz, he continues, "the inhabitants sent him much money and rare textiles of all kinds, silks among other". But he then says that the Mongol general asked the city's notables "to assemble before him some makers of 'Chinese' textiles and the like, so that they could be put to work for their great ruler, for this man was one of that ruler's subjects. The craftsmen were summoned and he

employed them to produce what it was they wanted. The people of Tabriz met the cost." So in Tabriz the textiles called 'Chinese' (*khita'i*) were actually locally produced (a point independently confirmed by Yaqut, incidentally)[16] and presumably therefore copied from imported Chinese silk designs. Thus, Mosul, as a textile-weaving centre, and particularly as a silk-weaving centre, would certainly have been involved in the same sort of business – the manufacture of imitation Chinese silks. There is every likelihood that the metal inlayers took their designs from these imitations.

If the Courtauld bag's decoration is indeed a reflection of Chinese silk designs, be they imported Chinese or local imitations, then we have a bag pretending to be dressed up in precious textile, a dressing-up emphasised by the inlayer's use of curving, rather than straight, lines to give silk-like movement to his fret pattern!

NOTES

1 D.S. Rice 1957, p. 284.
2 Raby 2012, pp. 11-86.
3 See, for example, his endless list of titles on the Munich dish, in Allan 1982, p. 23.
4 D.S. Rice 1953, fig. C.
5 Patton 1991, pp. 70-81.
6 Polo/Yule 1875, I, p. 62.
7 Serjeant 1942, pp. 91-92.
8 Vainker 2004, fig. 82.
9 Zhao 1999, p. 185 and figs. 06.00c, 06.00d, 06.00e.
10 Zhao 1999, fig. 06.10.
11 Zhao 1999, figs. 06.00f, g, h.
12 Zhao 1999, figs. 07.08, 07.08b, 07.00i.
13 Wyatt and Wardwell 1997, p. 10.
14 Serjeant 1942; Serjeant 1951, p. 81.
15 Ibn al-Athir/Richards 2008, pp. 308-09. My gratitude for this reference to Teresa Fitzherbert.
16 Yaqut 1866-70, vol. 1. p. 822.

Mosul metalworkers after the Mongols

JULIAN RABY

WHEN the Andalusian traveller Ibn Saᶜid visited Mosul in Northern Iraq in AD1250, he wrote admiringly about its silver-inlaid metalwork: "There are many crafts in the city, especially inlaid brass vessels which are exported to rulers."[1] Nine years later Badr al-Din Lu'lu' died, after controlling Mosul for 42 years. Under him the city had prospered through his ever-changing alliances, but his sons lacked his political acumen and drew down the ire of the Mongols. After a lengthy siege, Mongol forces seized Mosul in 1262, killed many of its inhabitants, and executed Badr al-Din's eldest son.[2] An era had ended.

Badr al-Din's rule saw the heyday of metalworking in Mosul. Ibn Saᶜid's praise for Mosul metalwork is borne out by the survival, from about 1200 to 1325, of 35 objects made by some 27 craftsmen who signed themselves 'al-Mawsili' (of Mosul). As most metalwork of this period lacks such information, this ratio among the documentary items testifies to a considerable production. In addition, many objects exist in the name of princes and princelings of the Jazira and Syria, which might bear out Ibn Saᶜid's claim, though only a few are actually signed by 'Mawsilis'.[3]

Surviving documentary objects reveal, however, a marked change in the second half of the thirteenth century. First, the number of signed items decline. Secondly, several of the named craftsmen are based in Damascus or Cairo, yet persist in calling themselves 'Mawsili'. Thirdly, the quantity of silver-inlaid objects made for named Mamluk and Rasulid patrons contrasts with the dearth of items for named patrons in the Jazira and Iran. This shift appears at first to confirm the assumption that the Mongol sack of Mosul was the death-knell for metalworking in the city – Mosul's loss was the Mamluks' gain.

A host of issues undermine our understanding of inlaid metalwork production in western Asia in the second half of the thirteenth century. Foremost is a reluctance to accept Mosul as the major centre of inlaid metalwork even in the first half of the thirteenth century, despite the number of items signed by 'Mawsilis'. Even scholars who have credited Mosul as a major centre of metalworking have viewed the Mongol advance as the demise of its industry, on the grounds that 'Mawsili' metalworkers are documented working in Damascus and Cairo in the second half of the thirteenth century, and in the belief that the Mongols were uncompromisingly destructive. Both factors, though, require qualification. First, the majority of 'Mawsili' metalworkers in Damascus or Cairo came from a single family that left Mosul some years before the Mongol attack.[4] Secondly, a Mongol victory did not inevitably entail the elimination of a city's craftsmen.

Mongol practice was to spare the lives of artisans, sometimes allocating them to members of the Mongol elite. This could mean they were removed to other parts of the Empire, but it did not necessitate the end of a tradition. Herati silk-weavers, for example, were transferred to other regions and allowed to return on the death of the ruling Khan, a custom that probably applied to other deported craftsmen.[5] In 1259 the Mongols seized Harim, a town between Aleppo and Antioch, and Hülegü ordered the execution of all men, women and children, with the exception of an Armenian goldsmith.[6] Mosul metalworkers could likewise have been spared the fate of many of the city's inhabitants. Bar Hebraeus (d. 1286), the Syriac Bishop based at the monastery of Mar Mattai just outside Mosul, talks broadly about the population of Mosul being killed, whereas the Il-Khanid vizier and historian Rashid al-Din states specifically that "some of the artisans (*pishe varan*) were taken prisoner".[7]

The Mongols would not only spare craftsmen's lives, but they also gathered them to work on projects. An example is provided by Bar Hebraeus, who describes an embassy from the Il-Khan Ahmad Tegüder to the Mamluk Sultan Qala'un in 1283 led by the Il-Khan's spiritual mentor Shaykh ͨAbd al-Rahman al-Mawsili, a former Greek slave who had once been in the service of the last ͨAbbasid caliph and eventually rose to become the head of religious endowments under the Mongols. ͨAbd al-Rahman "being ready to go to SYRIA, received a large amount of money from the royal treasure of the MONGOLS, and precious stones, and marvellous pearls, and gold, and silver, and apparel, and bales of stuffs (i.e. brocades) wherein much gold was woven. And he left ͨALATAK and came to TABRIZ, and he sat down there for about a month of days. And he gathered together handicraftsmen of all kinds, jewellers, and sewers (i.e. weavers), and others, and he made everything to a royal pattern. And from there he came to MAWSIL."[8] The value of the materials being used by the craftsmen doubtless demanded oversight, which in this case may only have been a temporary arrangement. Following his stay of a month in Tabriz, ͨAbd al-Rahman went to Mosul, which he knew well because after the fall of Baghdad in 1258 he had lived in the city, where, according to Bar Hebraeus, he "dwelt in the bazâr and did carpentry work, for he loved it and had learned the trade".[9] Whether he took the opportunity in 1283 to acquire inlaid metalwork as presents for the Mamluks is not recorded, but the dates of his mission suggest he could have stayed there several months, and, as illustrated by the gift of silver-inlaid candlesticks the Mamluk sultan Baybars presented to the ruler of the Golden Horde in 1263, inlaid metal objects were deemed suitable diplomatic gifts even at the highest level.[10]

We should be wary of too apocalyptic a vision of the sack of Mosul. Metalworkers either survived in or returned to Mosul. Despite the city's travails, some luxury metalworkers lived in Mosul just before and after the Mongol conquest. As Bar Hebraeus records, in 1260 renegade mamluks of Badr al-Din Lu'lu"s heir forced the city's Christians to convert, putting to death the few who remained true to their faith, including "Nafis the jeweller"; in 1275 a Jewish goldsmith was killed in Mosul; and in 1286 a Christian described as a "marvellous jeweller" was killed in an attack on the city by brigands.[11] In 1306 Timur *al-sa'igh* ('the jeweller') wrote an inscription in Arabic for a niche in the church of Mar Behnam, south-west of Mosul.[12]

Documentary evidence that Mosul continued to produce inlaid metalwork is to be found in a note inserted into a sixteenth-century poetic miscellany in the Mevlana Museum in Konya. It records that in 728/1327–28 the Il-Khan Abu Saͨid (ruled 1316–35) ordered a gift for Mevlana's tomb from Mosul.[13]

1. Gift of the superlative sultan, the possessor of the necks of nations, lord of the sultans
2. of the Arabs and Persians, creator of the supports of justice in the land, founder of the paths of felicity
3. for the servants, Abu Saͨid Bahadur Khan. And he ordered its production in the city
4. of Mosul in the year 728 [16 November 1327– 3 November 1328], and despatched it to
5. the blessed and pure tomb in search of intercession, under the escort of Amir Sunqur
6. Aqa in the year 734 of the Hijrah and the Chosen one ('Mustafa') [12 September 1333–31 August 1334].[14]

This surely refers to the Nisan Tası, which with a diameter of just under a metre is the most imposing known Il-Khanid inlaid brass vessel (fig. 31). Its body and pedestal are indeed inscribed in the name of Abu

Saᶜid.[15] The transcription of the manuscript text may be late, but its specificity and appropriate use of titulature suggest that it copies or derives from a credible source, for it records details not documented on the object, such as the date of manufacture and the fact that Abu Saᶜid dispatched the basin to Jalal al-Din Rumi's tomb in 734/1333–34 through the offices of Amir Sunqur Ağa (the ruler of Niğde who constructed a mosque-madrasa there in 1335). This, then, is substantive evidence that Mosul metalworkers were highly regarded enough to

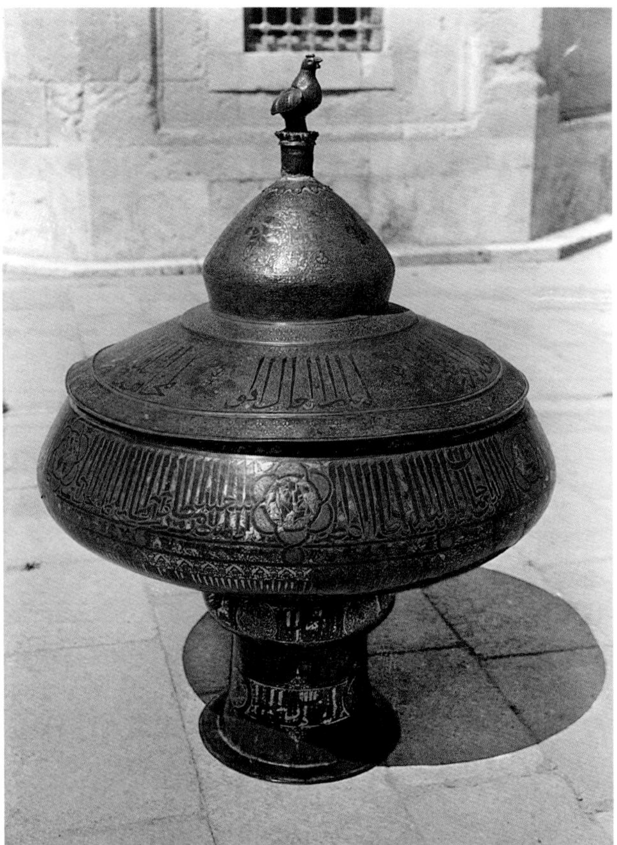

receive an imperial commission in the very last years of the Il-Khanid dynasty. Metalworking in Mosul ultimately survived the Mongol sack of the city.

What, then, can we learn from the works signed by 'Mawsili' metalworkers in the Il-Khanid period? Ten 'Mawsili' metalworkers are known to have been active after the fall of Mosul to the Mongols. Two produced celestial globes, one in 674/1274–5, the other in 718/1318. These globes caution us against assuming the total demise of Mosul's noted scientific tradition after the Mongol sack, but they belong to a largely separate tradition of production from the silver-inlaid vessels that are the remit of this essay.[16] Of the remaining eight metalworkers, five worked for the Mamluks, all but one stating that they worked in Cairo or Damascus. This leaves a trio whose domicile and affiliations are unknown – ᶜAli ibn Hamud al-Mawsili, who was working in the third quarter of the thirteenth century; ᶜAli ibn ᶜAbdallah al-ᶜAlawi al-Naqqash al-Mawsili, who was most likely active in the last quarter of that century; and Ustadh ᶜAli ibn ᶜUmar ibn Ibrahim al-Sankari al-Mawsili, who was working in the first quarter of the fourteenth century. As the work of ᶜAli ibn ᶜAbdallah relates most closely to the Courtauld bag, we shall turn to him last.

ᶜAli ibn Hamud al-Mawsili

ᶜAli ibn Hamud's work is known from three signed objects, two with dates that span the fall of Mosul – a vase from 657/1259 (fig. 32),[17] and a ewer from 673/1274–75.[18] The vase was made for a Christian named Haqta bin Tudra,[19] the ewer for an amir Atmish or Itmish al-Saᶜdi, but neither patron has yet been identified. The ewer was found with a large basin and they are probably a set, although the basin is undated and bears no record

58

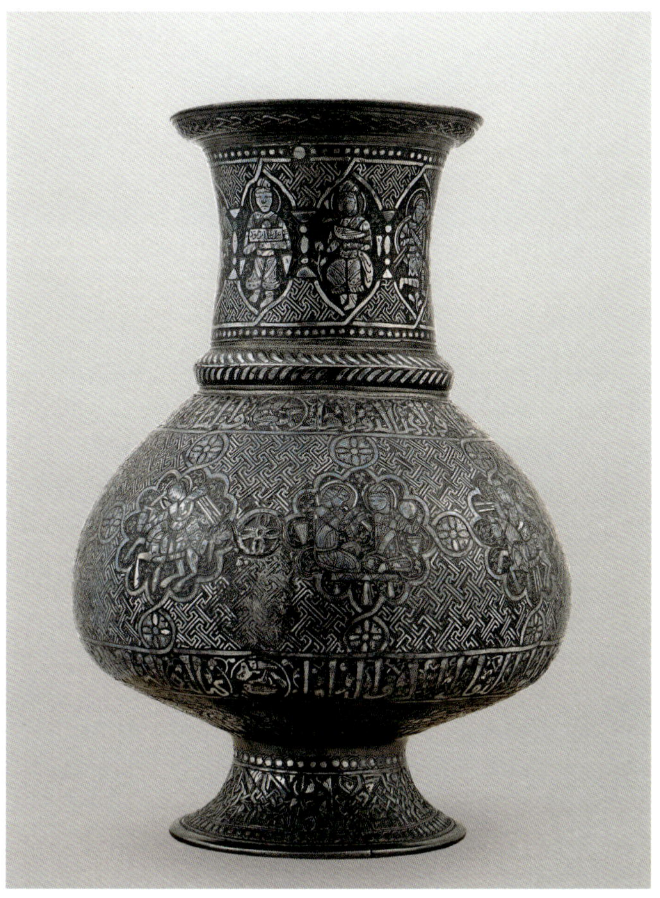

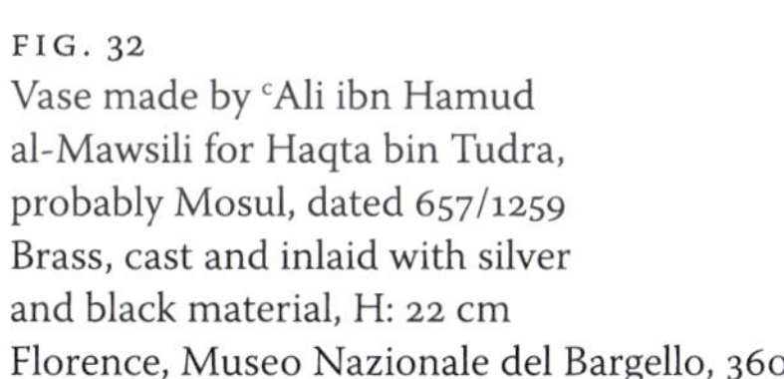

FIG. 32
Vase made by ᶜAli ibn Hamud
al-Mawsili for Haqta bin Tudra,
probably Mosul, dated 657/1259
Brass, cast and inlaid with silver
and black material, H: 22 cm
Florence, Museo Nazionale del Bargello, 360

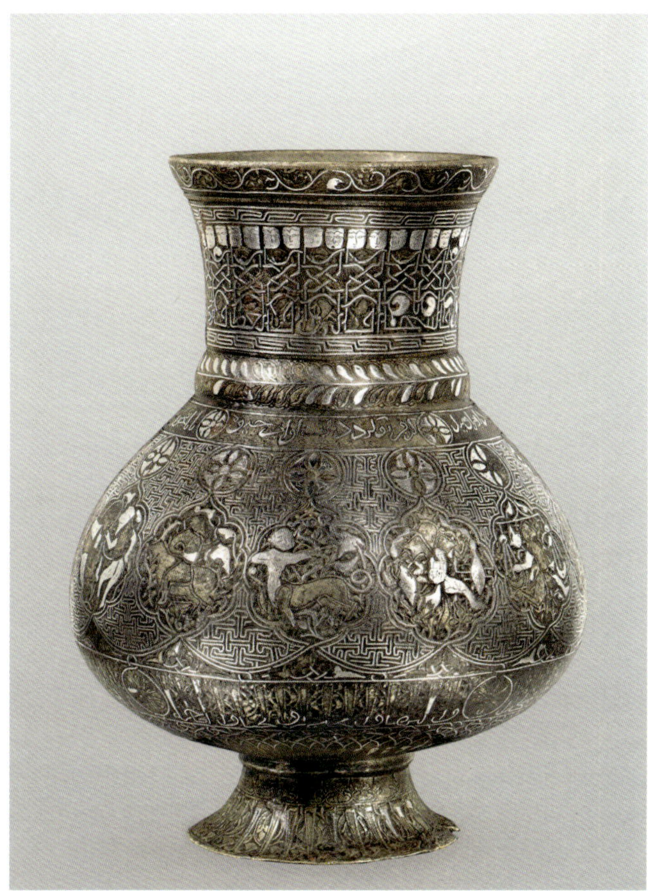

FIG. 33
Vase, probably Mosul, *c.* 1250–75
Brass, cast and inlaid with silver
and black material, H: 16.5 cm
Sold Sotheby's, 13 October 2013, lot 116

of a dedicatee.[20] The ground of the vase is decorated with
a T-pattern of a type found on items in the name of Badr
al-Din Lu'lu' and on the Blacas ewer made in Mosul in
1232 (cat. 21). However, the same type of ground is used
in 1282 by one of the 'Mawsili' artists working in Cairo,
so this element is insufficient to determine where ᶜAli ibn
Hamud worked. There are, though, other pointers.

A vase formerly in a London private collection, and
sold at Sotheby's in October 2013, bears similarities
in shape and decorative layout (fig. 33).[21] Both have a
ground of T-pattern, although on the London vase the
motifs are not arranged on a diagonal grid as on the
Florence example. Both have bodies decorated with
lobed medallions which are linked above and below

by distinctive rosettes to horizontal inscription bands.
The London vase has eight-lobed medallions filled with
a planetary cycle; the Bargello vase has twelve-lobed
medallions filled with courtly and equestrian images
typical of Mosul metalwork. Both have necks connected
to the body by a torus moulding decorated with a
chevron pattern.

The London vase is squatter by about a quarter, and
markedly less elegant, particularly in the proportions
of its neck. The handling of the figural medallions also
differs, and the inlay has a stuttering quality absent from
ᶜAli ibn Hamud's work. Nonetheless, the London vase
appears to depend on the same tradition as ᶜAli ibn
Hamud.[22] This is significant as the London vase is the

only known thirteenth-century Mosul-style object with a Persian inscription.[23] The use of Persian strongly suggests that it was made for a member of the Persian-speaking bureaucracy working for the Il-Khanids, either in Mosul or, if the craftsman/men had moved or been forced to move from Mosul, an unknown location in western Iran.

ʿAli ibn Hamud's ewer and basin also have an Iranian connection. They come from a hoard of mostly Il-Khanid metalwork found at Baznegerd near Hamadan.[24] Their protocolary inscriptions are not Mamluk in style, and the basin carries a laudatory ode used by the two other members of our trio of 'Mawsili' artists and to which we shall return shortly. It is not known if the ewer's dedicatee, Atmish al-Saʿdi, was an amir in the service of the Il-Khans or of a vassal, but his *nisba* al-Saʿdi could indicate he was a mamluk of a Salghurid of Shiraz.[25]

ʿAli ibn Hamud also uses on his ewer and basin a seated figure holding a large crescent that frames his face, a symbol of the Moon. Used as part of a planetary cycle on metalwork, the moon figure was astrological.[26] Yet it often occurs without other planetary signs, repeated alongside scenes of courtly and daily life. In these instances the motif has been read as Badr al-Din Lu'lu'''s personal emblem or an emblem of the city of Mosul. While little credence is now given to the first, the second should not be dismissed out of hand.[27]

In his *Nafa'is al-funun*, which he wrote between AD 1335 and 1342, the encyclopaedist Muhammad ibn Mahmud Amuli devoted a section to the qualities of the planets and their association with different regions. Jupiter, for example, was linked with Babylon (*Babil*), Khurasan, Turkey and western Barbary. The Moon Amuli linked specifically with Mosul and Azerbaijan.[28] As it is unlikely he invented this association, it is feasible that the independent moon figure was used on inlaid metalwork to refer to the city of Mosul.[29] Many of the objects that use the motif have a good claim to be associated with Mosul, whereas no object of certain Syrian or Egyptian provenance is known to use it. Only in the second quarter of the fourteenth century does the moon figure occur on metalwork likely to have been made in another city – Shiraz – and this I would take as one of several indications that Shiraz metalworkers owed a considerable debt to Mosul.

Between 1259 and 1274 ʿAli ibn Hamud's figural style hardened. This can be seen in his treatment of the 'standing courtier', who adopts a distinctive pose – one leg raised, the foot pointed towards the ground – that is a distinctive trait of paintings produced for Badr al-Din Lu'lu' between 1217 and 1219 (see fig. 25).[30] The pose creates a billow at the front of the robe, but in ʿAli ibn Hamud's later work the back of the robe sweeps in, creating billows back and front that are more about symmetry than sense. The headgear also becomes increasingly stylised: on the 1259 vase it is more rounded and looks less like a flat crown than in his later work.

Ustadh ʿAli ibn ʿUmar ibn Ibrahim al-Sankari al-Mawsili

A candlestick dated 717/1317–18 (for a detail, see fig. 34) is the sole known work by ʿAli ibn ʿUmar ibn Ibrahim al-Sankari al-Mawsili, who is the only 'Mawsili' artist to use the title *ustadh* (master), a term more common in signatures by Iranian than Syrian or Egyptian metal-workers.[31] Elements connect it to the work of both ʿAli ibn Hamud and ʿAli ibn ʿAbdallah, even though it was produced some two generations later.

The candlestick's inscriptions do not state where or for whom it was made, but a Mosul origin is probable. The titulature is Jaziran, which led Étienne Combe to propose

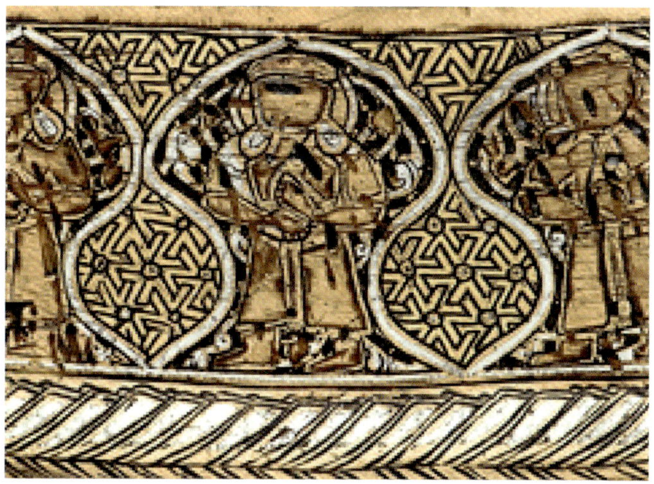

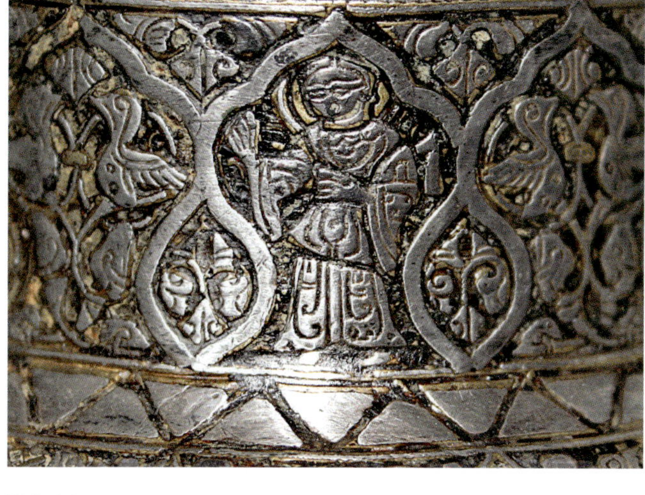

FIG. 34
Candlestick made by ʿAli ibn ʿUmar ibn
Ibrahim al-Sankari al-Mawsili in
717/1317–18, probably in Mosul, detail from
base showing standing figures
Brass, raised and inlaid with gold, silver and
black material, H: 53 cm, Diam: 41 cm
Athens, Benaki Museum, 13038

FIG. 35
Ewer made by ʿAli ibn ʿAbdallah al-ʿAlawi
al-Naqqash al-Mawsili (cat. 24), detail
from the neck showing standing figures

the Artuqid ruler of Mardin Shams al-Din Salih (ruled
712–65/1312–64) as the likely patron.[32] The candlestick
was later owned by Mirjan Agha, a freedman of the Il-
Khanid sultan Öljeitü (d. 1316), who became the governor
of Baghdad under the Jalayrids and in 758/1357 built the
Mirjaniyya madrasa in Baghdad. Mirjan Agha dedicated
the candlestick to the Prophet's shrine in Medina.

The body of the candlestick is dominated by a full-
height inscription with the anonymous dedication.
An inscription on the shoulder divides into two sections
– a poem in three couplets that is both a description
of function and an allegory for the ruler, as it extols the
virtues of the candlestick as the bringer of light to the
assembly;[33] and three lines of a panegyric to the ruler
which reads in translation:

1. Glory, and victory and prosperity and [divine] grace
   and good fortune and grandeur and virtues and
   generosity
2. Forbearance and learning – things in which you
   excel, so that the Arabs and Persians are flustered
   in describing you,
3. Creatures are humbled before you for they see you
   as the root of existence while others had ceased to
   exist.

These three lines or variants appear prominently on
the basins by ʿAli ibn ʿAbdallah and ʿAli ibn Hamud,
linking the work of our trio of 'Mawsili' craftsmen.
As a central girdling band they form the principal
inscription on the exterior of ʿAli ibn ʿAbdallah's basin,
though the last few words of the last hemistich on
ʿAli ibn ʿAbdallah's basin differ in grammar from the
version on the candlestick.[34] A variant, without the last
hemistichs, occurs on the monumental inscription band
on the interior of ʿAli ibn Hamud's basin in Tehran.[35]
The poem is not recorded earlier, but occurs on a
bucket made by a 'servant' of the Inju ruler of Shiraz,
Mahmud Shah, in 733/1332–33, and on work attributed
to the mid-fourteenth-century Fars school.[36] This
pattern of use suggests an origin in the Jazira in the
thirteenth century.

The candlestick includes figural imagery – a planetary
cycle on the shoulder, and five friezes of 116 standing
Il-Khanid-style courtiers under lobed arches (fig. 34).
The strong incurve of the arches occurs on several other
items of Jaziran inlaid metalwork, where the figures
are often recognisably Christian (fig. 35).[37] The 1317
candlestick includes three motifs typical of Il-Khanid
metalwork:

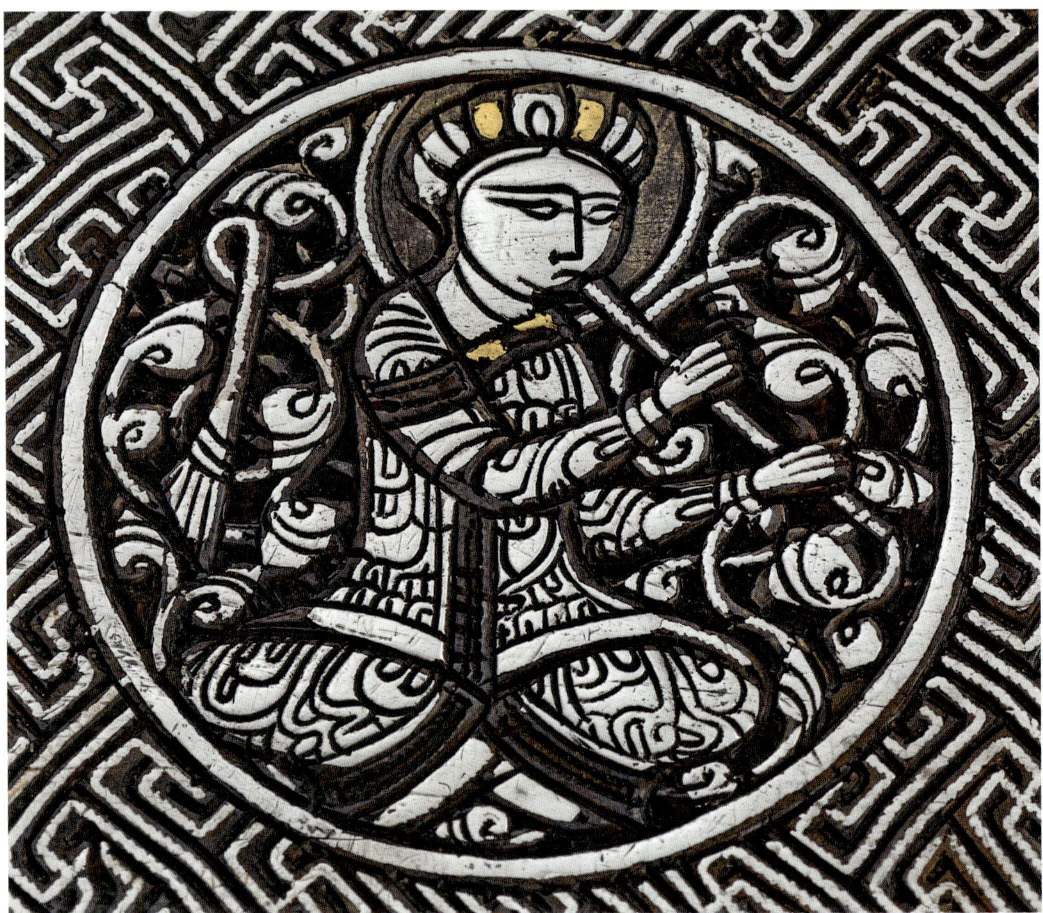

The Courtauld bag (cat. 1),
detail of roundel with a flutist

1. medallions or lozenges occupied by two confronted birds;
2. diamonds occupied by a trefoil (in the well of the candlestick);
3. a Z-pattern inlaid in gold that is used to fill roundels or to cover a ground, in this case the interstices between the foiled arches (fig. 34).

ᶜAli ibn ᶜAbdallah al-ᶜAlawi al-Naqqash al-Mawsili

These motifs also connect ᶜAli ibn ᶜUmar's work to that of ᶜAli ibn ᶜAbdallah al-Mawsili, who is known from a matching basin and ewer that are among the most lavish examples of inlaid metalwork of the second half of the thirteenth century, and revel in a baroque overload of competing elements (cat. 24, 25).[38] His use of arabesques or birds as a ground filler, for example, creates a more turbid look than the T-pattern on ᶜAli ibn Hamud's Bargello vase (fig. 32) or the Courtauld bag.

Although neither ᶜAli ibn ᶜAbdallah's basin nor his ewer is dated or inscribed in the name of a patron, stylistic considerations suggest that they date to the 1280s or thereabouts.[39] Ernst Kühnel argued strongly that ᶜAli ibn ᶜAbdallah was active in Mosul; Eva Baer assumed Syria.[40] His work is pivotal, because it includes key decorative and figural components of a distinctively Il-Khanid style, yet also relates to 'Mawsili' objects. He employed the laudatory ode used by the other two in our trio of 'Mawsili' artists, and motifs such as Z-medallions, confronted birds,[41] and tiny Christian

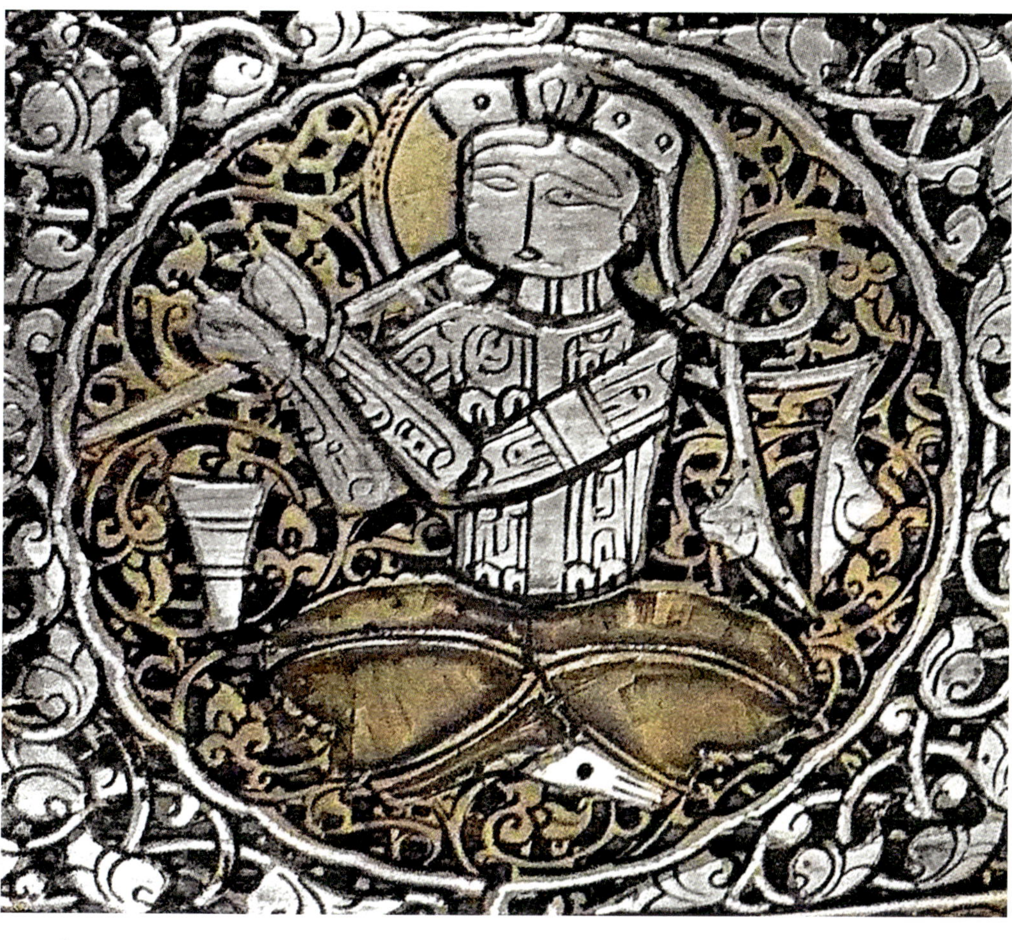

FIG. 36
Basin made by ᶜAli ibn ᶜAbdallah al-ᶜAlawi
al-Naqqash al-Mawsili, Mosul, 1275–1300
(cat. 25), detail of roundel with a flutist

figures under an arcade of lobed arches, with the trefoil device in the interstices (fig. 35). He used both a planetary cycle and independent moon figures. The latter point to an origin in Mosul rather than Syria, while a later graffito on the ewer records the name of a Persian owner, lending support to a provenance in the Jazira or western Iran.[42]

ᶜAli ibn ᶜAbdallah used three main figural groups. None were original as types, but each had distinctive features of iconography and style – an enthroned prince (fig. 39), riders fighting wild beasts (fig. 37) and seated revellers and musicians (fig. 36), including a tambourine player and a flute player, with each figure enclosed in a separate roundel (fig. 36). Very similar figures recur on the Courtauld bag, though an attached scarf in ᶜAli ibn ᶜAbdallah's version becomes a floating motif on the bag (see roundel, p. 62).[43]

ᶜAli ibn ᶜAbdallah's idiosyncratic manner is echoed on a group of high-quality wares that include a spherical incense burner in Berlin (fig. 38) and pen boxes in Pesaro and Doha.[44] Several other objects include imitations of his style, the influence of which continued into the fourteenth century. Characteristic is his manner of rendering a prince holding a beaker, seated on a throne with a back delineated by vertical stripes (fig. 39).[45] Another is his somewhat 'pinched' treatment of the face, and his greater use of facial detailing than is standard in the thirteenth century: this includes a moustache, and extended lines from the lateral canthus of the eyes. He also used a *semée* on costumes rather than standard vertical folds.[46]

A distinctive motif on ᶜAli ibn ᶜAbdallah's ewer is a rider who turns round to shoot his bow, wearing a tell-tale turban that sits at a 75° angle, looking as if it might fall (fig. 37). This rider, accompanied by a hunting cheetah, recurs on the Berlin incense burner (fig. 38), on the pen box in Doha and, in variant fashion, on the pen box in Pesaro, as well as on a tray in Tehran that includes the independent moon image.[47] The moon figure provides a pointer to Mosul. Possible confirmation of a Mosul connection is what may be the earliest occurrence of a rider wearing a similar turban – on the David Collection pen box, with an inscription stating it was made in Mosul in 1255.[48] The shape of ᶜAli ibn ᶜAbdallah's ewer, and the design of its cast handle, also point to Mosul, for close precedents can be found on three 'Mawsili' ewers, dated 1223, 1232 and 1246.[49]

Mosul has been dismissed – either overtly or tacitly – as a centre of inlaid metalwork in the Il-Khanid period.

Yet several strands of evidence indicate that our trio of craftsmen were trained in Mosul and largely upheld the stylistic, and, as Rachel Ward emphasises in her essay below, the technical traditions of the city. Our trio used the appellative 'al-Mawsili' as personal descriptor and professional badge, and in both senses to indicate a direct association with Mosul.

ᶜAli ibn Hamud's work straddles the eras before and after the fall of Mosul, and warns us against assuming the events of 1262 ended its metalworking tradition. The extant work of our trio covers the period from about 1260 to 1320 – thus almost the full span of the Il-Khanid dynasty. On present evidence we cannot be certain where they spent the majority of their working life, but we should not dismiss Mosul, for the city's metalworkers retained or regained sufficient eminence that in the late 1320s the Il-Khan Abu Saᶜid commissioned the extraordinary Nisan Tası from them. It is easier to understand how Mosul merited this commission if

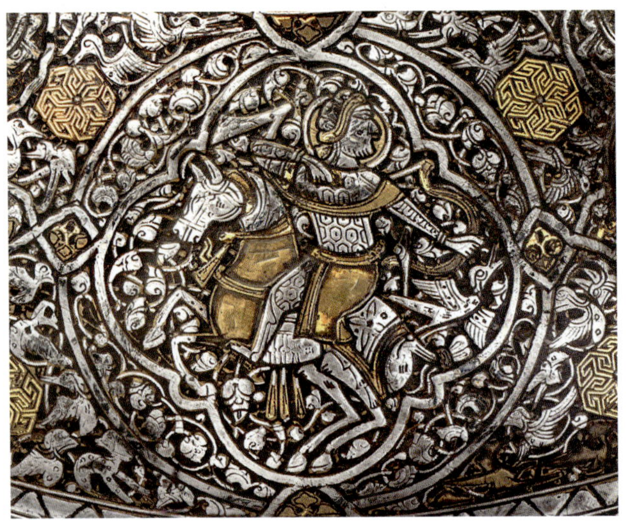

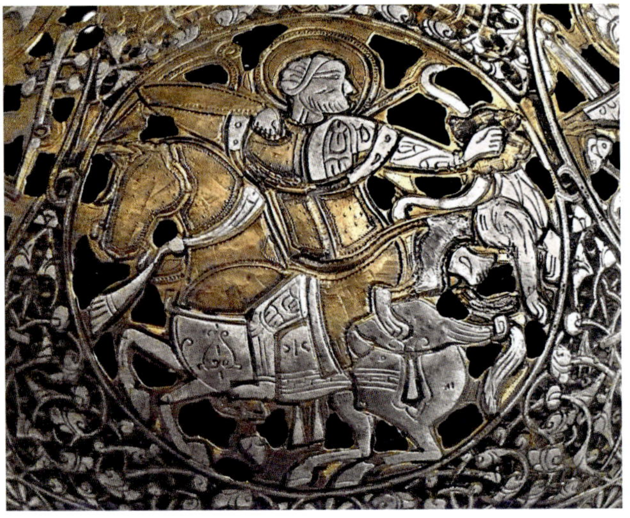

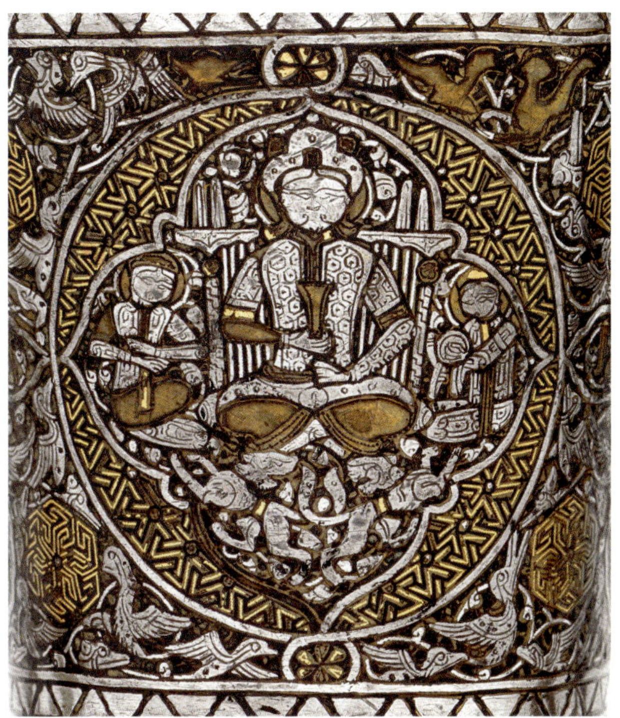

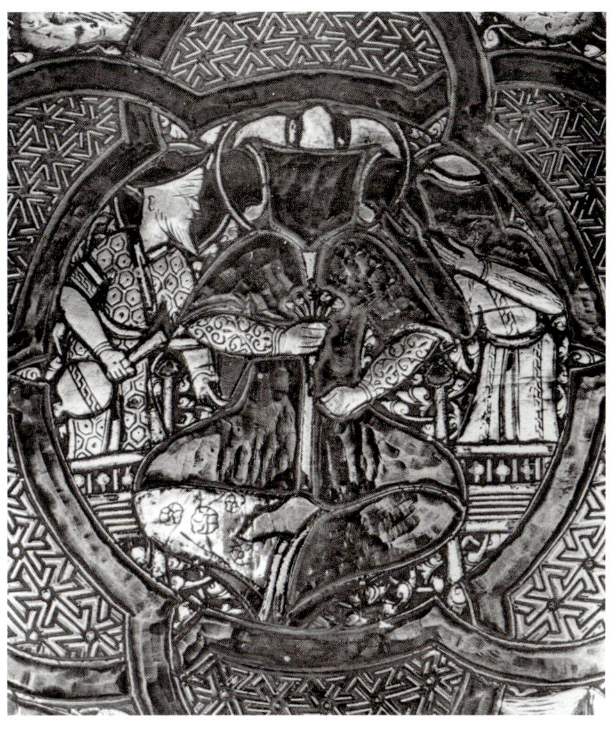

artists of the calibre of ʿAli ibn ʿAbdallah, ʿAli ibn Hamud and ʿAli ibn ʿUmar had continued to work there.

Our trio of artists were largely traditional in their choice of shapes, and of figural and epigraphic styles, but they should not be dismissed as second-rate descendants of the craftsmen of Badr al-Din Lu'lu''s era. On the contrary, they produced some of the most extravagant surviving inlaid metalwork, including the only two extant sets of ewer and basin. Nor were they unresponsive to Il-Khanid innovation. ʿAli ibn ʿUmar's small-scale figures under arcades (fig. 34) reflect a more Il-Khanid fashion of dress and coiffure than earlier Jaziran equivalents, such as those on the neck of ʿAli ibn ʿAbdallah's ewer (fig. 35). The manner in which Mosul metalworkers adapted traditional styles to reflect Il-Khanid taste and iconography can be seen in the depictions of two seated rulers, one from ʿAli ibn ʿAbdallah's ewer (fig. 39), the other from a section of the Nisan Tası that is in the name of Abu Saʿid and datable to between 1327 and 1334 (fig. 40). Given the gap of some forty or fifty years, the changes are understandable.

In other words, Mosul traditions were formative in the emergence of Il-Khanid metalwork styles, and, vice versa, Il-Khanid fashions influenced the Mosul aesthetic.

This should not surprise us, for as the history of calligraphy and of ceramics in Iran demonstrate, there was not the total rupture with the past that an apocalyptic reading of the Mongol invasions postulates. The Courtauld bag is proof that in metalwork there was, on the one hand, continuity from the traditions of Badr al-Din Lu'lu''s Mosul and, on the other, a shift in emphasis with the adoption of the miniscule style that ultimately led to the triumph of pattern over figuration in the fifteenth century.

I would like to thank James White for help with some of the research, and Teresa Fitzherbert for her insights. I owe thanks to Venetia Porter and Ladan Akbarnia of the British Museum; to Beatrice Paolozzi Strozzi, Director of the Bargello Museum, and to Marco Spallanzani also in Florence; to Sheila Canby and Annick de Roches of the Metropolitan Museum; and to Tim Stanley, Moya Carey, and Mariam Rosser-Owen of the Victoria and Albert Museum; to Stefan Weber and Gisela Helmecke of the Museum für Islamische Kunst in Berlin; to Kjeld von Folsach of the David Collection, Copenhagen; and Nahla Nassar of the Khalili Collection.

1 D.S. Rice 1957, p. 284; Raby 2012, p. 22.

2 Patton 1991, p. 80.

3 Raby 2012, especially pp. 22–23, 58–64. The geographical relative 'al-Mawsili' cannot be used on its own to argue where a craftsman was working, as it was used both by craftsmen who were working in Mosul and by others who had left the city.

4 Ward 1995, pp. 154–55; Raby 2012, pp. 37–44.

5 Allsen 1997, pp. 30–37; Rossabi 1998, pp. 87–89.

6 Howorth 1876–1888, III, pp. 150–51, evidently relying on Bar Hebraeus/Bruns and Kirsch 1789, p. 556, where the artisan is called an 'aurifex'. Budge's translation gives him as an 'Armenian blacksmith' (Bar Hebraeus/Budge 1932, I, p. 436), but the Syriac word can mean either goldsmith or blacksmith.

7 Rashid al-Din 1983, pp. 730–31; Howorth 1876–88, III, p. 182; Bar Hebraeus/Budge 1932, I, p. 443; in his *Mukhtaṣar fi'l-duwal* Bar Hebraeus mentions eight days of plunder and killing, with no reference to the sparing of artisans (Bar Hebraeus/Salihani 1890, p. 496).

8 Bar Hebraeus/Budge 1932, I, pp. 467–68. This passage does not occur in the account of Teküder Ahmad's reign in Bar Hebraeus' Arabic version of his history: Bar Hebraeus/Salihani 1890, pp. 505–20.

Bar Hebraeus was buried in the monastery of Mar Mattai, just outside Mosul.

9 Bar Hebraeus/Budge 1932, p. 474.

10 ʿAbd al-Rahman was denigrated in Mamluk sources as a charlatan, who used his knowledge of alchemy to trick the Mongols: Holt 1986; Allouche 1990, esp. p. 443. The Il-Khan's letter to Qala'un was dated July 1283 and the Il-Khanid embassy only arrived in Damascus in March 1284. On Baybars's gift, see Little 2006, p. 41.

11 Respectively, Bar Hebraeus/Budge 1932, I, pp. 441, 452, 477; cf. Conrad 1994, p. 330.

12 Snelders 2010, pp. 97, 277, 569–70; Monneret de Villard (1940, p. 86) refers to Timur as "l'artigiano"; Harrak and Ruji 2004.

13 Oral 1954, pp. 2–3: it occurs in a poetic miscellany, MS. 2906, p. 486.

14 ١ — هدية السلطان الاعظم مالك رقاب الامم سيد سلاطين
٢ — العرب والعجم واضع دعائم العدل فى البلاد مؤسس
مناهج السعادة
٣ — على العباد ابو سعيد بهادور خان وامر باعمالها فى مدينة
٤ — الموصل فى سنة ثمان وعشرين وسبعماية وارسلها الى التربة
٥ — المقدسة المطهرة لاجل الاستشفاع بصحابة الامير سنقر
٦ — آقا فى سنة اربع وثلثين وسبعماية الهجريه المصطفويه

15 Oral 1954; Baer 1973–74. Its diameter is 95 cm.

16 Carey 2009. Doubts have been expressed about the true date of the globe dated 718/1318, which is signed by ʿAbd al-Rahman ibn Burhan al-Mawsili. See Savage-Smith 1985, no. 60, pp. 34, 247–48. Links have been drawn between the manner of rendering of some of the faces on two globes from the 1270s and the 1280s and on some Mosul painting and metalwork, notably the Blacas ewer: Carey 2009, p. 106; Pinder-Wilson 1976, p. 319.

17 Wiet 1931; Wiet 1933, no. 36, pp. 36–37; Combe, Sauvaget, Wiet et al. 1931–, XII, no. 4454. Atıl (1981, p. 51) assigned him to Syria, Mayer (1959, p. 102) to Mosul, though with no discussion.

18 Wiet 1931; Wiet 1933, no. 40, pp. 39–40; Combe, Sauvaget, Wiet et al. 1931–, XII, no. 4697; Pope and Ackermann 1938–39, pl. 1342A.

19 There has been some doubt over the reading, but the inscription is large and fully pointed: Ḥaqtā b. Tudra.

20 Wiet 1931; Wiet 1933, no. 41, pp. 40–41; Combe, Sauvaget, Wiet et al. 1931–, XII, no. 4698; Pope and Ackermann 1938–39, pl. 1341. Kühnel (1939, p. 10) thought the basin and ewer were of different dates, and not a set. Mayer (1959, p. 34), presumably relying on London 1931, no. 233C, p. 149, and Pope and Ackermann 1938–39, p.2497, say the basin is also in the name of Amir Atmish al-Saʿdi. This is not attested in Wiet's publications.

21 Sotheby's 2013, lot 116. I would like to thank the owner for allowing me to see the object well before its consignment to auction.

22 For an object of similar form, but with a different style of decoration, see Scerrato 1967, pp. 13–15, no. 9.

23 For the inscription, see Sotheby's 2013, lot 116.

24 Mayer 1959, p. 33. See Melikian-Chirvani 1982, index p. 409, s.v. Baznegerd.

25 He might possibly have been a mamluk of either the short-reigned Saʿd b. Qutlugh Khan (ruled 1260) or, at a stretch, his grandfather ʿIzz al-Din Saʿd ibn Zangi (ruled 1198–1226), after whom the poet Saʿdi derived his pen-name. Salghurid Shiraz became part of the Il-Khanid domains in 1264 when the daughter of Saʿd b. Qutlugh Khan married one of Hülegü's sons, Möngke Temür, with whom she jointly ruled Shiraz until her husband's death in 1284.

26 On the planetary sequence, see Baer 1983, pp. 248–58; New York 1997.

27 Both Aga-Oglu (1945, pp. 42–43) and D.S. Rice (1957, p. 321) rejected van Berchem's suggestion it was an emblem of the city (1906, p. 201, note 1.)

28 Amuli 1379/1959, III, p. 294 on Jupiter (cf. Donaldson 1939, p. 156) and p. 298 on the moon.

29 Kühnel 1939, p. 14; Raby 2012, p. 32.

30 Raby 2012, pp. 46 and 48.

31 Combe 1931; Ballian 2009. ᶜAli ibn ᶜUmar's first *nisba* has been misread as Yashkuri (Combe 1931, pp. 51–52) and Sunquri (Los Angeles 2011, no. 119, p. 67). On the titles used by metalworkers, see Mayer 1959 *passim.*

32 Combe 1931.

33 Combe 1931. See Ballian 2009, fig. 17 for excellent photograph of the inscription.

34 Kühnel 1939, p. 6.

35 Baer 1989, fig. 91; see also Giuzalian 1960, p. 1. The poem occurs on a candlestick in Berlin of similar shape and proportions as the Benaki one, though it is of poor materials and manufacture; it was purchased in 1902 in Iran: Sarre and Mittwoch 1906, no. 55, pp. 25–26.

36 Giuzalian 1960; Melikian-Chirvani 1971a, pp. 376, 389–90; Melikian-Chirvani 1973, pp. 80–81.

37 For examples see Baer 1989, though she generally prefers a Syrian origin (pp. 22–23). Cf. Snelders 2010, esp. pp. 280–83.

38 Gladiss 2012, pp. 90–97; Kühnel 1939; Baer 1989, pp. 15–16; Berlin 2006, no. 34, pp. 85–89.

39 Kühnel (1939, p. 13) proposed a date of *c.* 1255; Berlin 2006, pp. 85–89, dates it to the third quarter of the thirteenth century (cf. Baer 1989, p. 15). A ewer in Bologna echoes ᶜAli ibn ᶜAbdallah's style, but is dedicated to Turuntay al-Tabbakhi, identified as one of the leading Mamluk viziers in the 1280s and 1290s (Venice 1993, no. 173, pp. 302–04; Gabrieli and Scerrato 1979, figs. 564–69; Northrup 1998, *passim,* but especially pp. 143, 207). The ewer could have been a gift from the Il-Khanids. The ewer also needs close examination to determine whether all parts of the handle, including the dedication, are from the original object.

40 Kühnel 1939; Baer 1973–74, p. 13; cf. Baer 1989, p. 16.

41 His surviving work does not show the use of these motifs in a frieze, as was to become common later.

42 Kühnel 1939, p. 7.

43 For an example of how images on Mosul metalwork were transformed over time, see Raby 2012, fig. 1.25 a–f.

44 For the incense burner, see Gladiss 2012, pp. 98–99; Berlin 2006, no. 35, pp. 89–90. For the Doha pen box see Allan and Maddison 2002, no. 4, pp. 26–29. For the Pesaro penbox see Spallanzani 2010, pp. 77, 155, fig. 35.

45 In addition to the three items in the previous note, similar scenes occur on a pyxis (Pope and Ackermann 1938–39, pl. 1335), a ewer (Kühnel 1924–25, p. 55), and a candlestick (Riefstahl 1922, p. lix and fig. 38).

46 Kühnel 1939, p. 19. Varyingly debased derivations of his style include three items in the Metropolitan Museum in New York, acc.no. 17.190.1716: Aga-Oglu 1945, p. 37, fig. 13; acc.no. 17.190.1717: New York 1997, pp. 8–9; and acc.no. 91.1.596, a fragmentary candlestick (unpublished). See also a diminutive tray in Copenhagen (David Collection, inv. 13/1966); an incense burner in Bologna (Spallanzani 2010, p. 155, fig. 41); and a casket in the Victoria and Albert Museum (Melikian-Chirvani 1982, no. 89, pp. 195–97).

47 Pope and Ackermann 1938–39, pl. 1331.

48 See Folsach 2001, p. 317, no. 506.

49 Raby 2012, p. 30, figs 1.8 a, b; cf. the handle on the ewer in St Petersburg (Kühnel 1924–25, pl. 55). The ewer was not the only form associated with Mosul that continued well into the Il-Khanid period (see cat. 24 and 25).

Il-Khanid Mosul: More craft than court

RACHEL WARD

THE ICONOGRAPHY of the Courtauld bag places it securely within the Il-Khanid cultural milieu and there is sufficient comparable material to suggest that it was made during the first decades of the fourteenth century, possibly during the reign of Sultan Öljeitü (1304–16). Its place of manufacture is less certain. The exhibition presents Mosul as the likely provenance of the bag for the historical and art historical reasons outlined in this essay.

Terror of the Mongols preceded them, and no wonder, for some of the stories of their cruelty haunt the memory even after centuries. Jeremiah Curtin's Gothic description, gleaned from contemporary sources, of al-Salih Isma'il, vanquished ruler of Mosul, tied in an animal skin and left in the summer sun to die slowly of heat and maggots is hard to erase.[1] Signatures by Mosul craftsmen on Mamluk metalwork confirm our negative assumptions that, faced with the impending Mongol invasion, skilled craftsmen left Mosul to avoid having their goods sequestered and workshops trashed and to escape being killed, taken prisoner or moved elsewhere.[2] As Melville relates in this volume, after the conquest of Baghdad in 1258 Iraq became a peripheral region rather than a heartland, and after the conquest of Mosul in 1262, the city no longer had an independent court, just a rapid succession of governors that are unlikely to have rivalled Badr al-Din Lu'lu''s patronage of the arts earlier in the century – a bleak picture. It is hardly surprising that the Mongol conquest was assumed to have decimated the luxury metalwork industry in Mosul. But did it?

No doubt the conquest was gruesome for the political and military leaders of the city who, like al-Salih Isma'il, suffered the revenge of the Mongols. But it was in the Mongols' interest to have functioning cities which could provide services and taxes. Rashid al-Din claims that financial reforms in Ghazan's reign, including the abolition or reduction of taxes on trade and crafts, and investment in agriculture and infrastructure, helped revive areas which had suffered from the conquests – and so produce greater tax revenues for the Il-Khan. He describes a large building project near Mosul in which twenty thousand men were employed (and paid wages) to build a canal and fourteen new villages, whose occupants were supplied with seed, animals and tools and encouraged to farm.[3] Attempts to restore the viability of Herat after its conquest in 1221 and sacking in 1222 – punishment for the rebellion of its inhabitants – included the return of a substantial number of its weavers to re-establish its textile industry between 1236 and 1239.[4] The historian 'Ata-Malik Juvaini, governor of Baghdad between 1259 and his death in 1283, presided over the restoration of the city, which was often used as winter quarters by the Il-Khanid court.[5] The description of the famous calligrapher Yaqut al-Musta'simi hiding in a minaret and continuing to write while Baghdad was sacked may be apocryphal, but he certainly survived and continued working there until his death in 1298, establishing a lasting calligraphic tradition in that city.[6]

Mosul – the name itself means 'point of junction' – had been an important trade centre since ancient times as it was located on the main route between Iran and Syria. The thirteenth-century geographer Yaqut al-Hamawi wrote: "I have often heard that the great cities of the world are three: Nishapur because it is the door to the east; Damascus because it is the door to the west; and Mosul because it is the short way to the two directions, through which few do not pass".[7] Mosul remained a trade centre after the conquest. Marco Polo, who travelled through the Il-Khanid realms in the last quarter of the thirteenth century, describes goods arriving in Tabriz from India, Baghdad, Hurmuz and Mosul.[8] He wrote of Mosul: "All the cloths of gold and silk that are called *Mosolins* are made in this country; and those great

Merchants called *Mosolins*, who carry for sale such quantities of spicery and pearls, and the cloths of silk and gold, are also from this kingdom".[9]

After 1262, Mosul no longer had its own resident dynasty and court but it had two of the world's most powerful dynasties nearby – the Mongols and the Mamluks. The Mongol court was peripatetic, but, as relations were tense between these two super-powers, it was never far away from its vulnerable western frontier.[10] Numerous embassies passed through Mosul and some of these may have picked up diplomatic gifts en route (see Raby above, p. 57). Because of their mobile and pastoral lifestyle, Mongols were accustomed to commissioning specialist objects from different urban centres.[11] Mosul had a sophisticated retail infrastructure and was well used to supplying foreign courts: in this context it is worth remembering Ibn Saᶜid's comment, made in 1250: "There are many crafts in the city, especially inlaid brass vessels, which are exported to rulers". The many surviving metal objects inscribed to Ayyubid sultans suggest that he reported truthfully.[12] Mosul's merchants must have relished having easier access to the lucrative Mongol market.[13]

It is undeniable, however, that the Mongol threat created an unsettled situation for craftsmen, and metal inlayers in particular had alternative sources of patronage, for their products were in great demand.[14] In the early thirteenth century, before the Mongol invasion, metalworkers from Khurasan moved west and probably helped start the inlay industry in Mosul.[15] In the middle of the thirteenth century, as the Mongols advanced, some Mosul metalworkers moved to Damascus, Cairo, Konya and elsewhere.[16] After the fall of Mosul, the direction of migration may have been reversed. Although there is no evidence for the forced migration of luxury metalworkers from Mosul (on the contrary, in his essay

in this volume Raby has gathered three clear references to goldsmiths working in Mosul in the second half of the thirteenth century and makes a strong case for the continuity of the city as a metal inlay centre), it is likely that some craftsmen from Mosul moved, voluntarily or involuntarily, to start up new workshops within Il-Khanid territory elsewhere.

The changing status of cities, the shift in patronage, the mobility of craftsmen – all contribute to an uncertain picture for the Il-Khanid period. As Melikian-Chirvani wrote in 1982, "Our present understanding of the development of Iranian metalwork in the thirteenth and fourteenth centuries somewhat resembles a puzzle full of gaps".[17] Despite much more published material, after thirty years the picture is still patchy, especially for the later thirteenth century.

By the early fourteenth century, however, the situation for craftsmen was more stable, as the Il-Khanids were focused on succession rather than expansion. New workshops established by migrant inlayers from Mosul, before or just after the Mongol invasion, had been in operation for decades. When first set up, their products would have been virtually indistinguishable from the products of their native cities, but during the intervening years techniques and styles had begun to diverge. Mamluk inlaid metalwork is a good example of the evolution one can expect in response to a new group of patrons. By the early fourteenth century, the scenes of princely pursuits and varied calligraphic scripts typical of Mosul metalwork had been phased out in favour of clear, bold inscriptions that proclaimed the power and authority of the Mamluk ruling class and non-figural ornament more in line with its orthodox beliefs.[18] Within the mass of metalwork attributed to the Il-Khanate, often labelled 'western Iran', are groups of identifiably different techniques and styles. Here I would like to focus on one

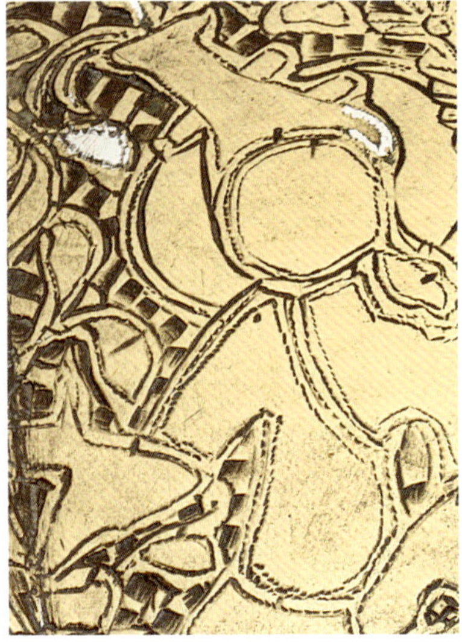
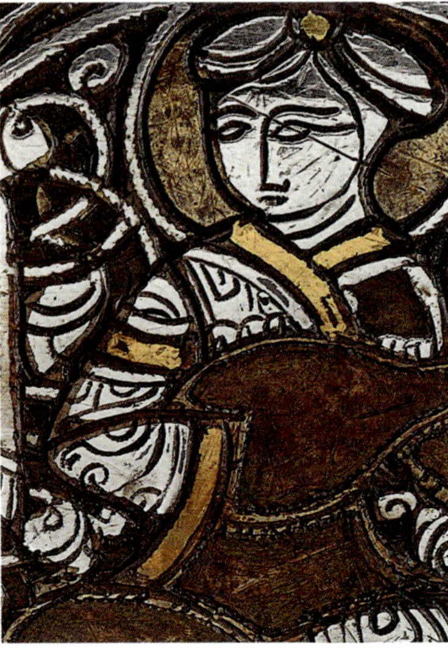

large group of objects (represented in the exhibition by cat. 1, 26–30), which in form, manufacture, technique and style continue the metalworking traditions of thirteenth-century Mosul and so have the greatest claim to have been made in that city.

Mosul was famous as an inlay centre, but its other speciality was working sheet metal. The group contains a range of objects that continue and expand the earlier Mosul sheet-metal repertoire: for example, facetted candlesticks (cat. 26) show how traditional shapes could be elaborated by the metalworkers. The group includes some of the most complex objects of the period, such as the Courtauld bag (cat. 1) and Walters pen box (cat. 29), which both involved several different processes and intricate construction techniques. Most metalwork produced outside this group has simple, hammered forms which could be spectacular in effect, like the star-shaped basins (fig. 11), but were not so difficult to produce.

The group also includes objects which, for reasons of function, were made from cast brass. A type of incense burner produced continuously with little change in method of manufacture or shape for at least eighty years has its roots in the heyday of Mosul metalworking – one is dated 641/1243–44 (cat. 22) and another was made for the Ayyubid Sultan al-ʿAdil (ruled 1238–40).[19] More than fifty of these are known and developments in Mosul metalworking can be tracked through them. One in the British Museum is so close to the style of ʿAli ibn ʿAbdallah al-Mawsili that it may have been inlaid by

him.[20] This provides some additional evidence that ʿAli was working in Mosul, but the style of decoration on cast objects is an unreliable indicator of provenance as they were sometimes traded as blanks to be decorated in workshops in other cities.[21] At least one of these incense burners was decorated in the Mamluk empire and another was decorated in another Il-Khanid city, perhaps Tabriz (see cat. 23).

The objects in the group are inlaid in the traditional Mosul manner – recessing the areas to be inlaid, bevelling the brass down towards the edges, which were undercut so that they could be hammered over the sheet inlays to hold them securely in place. Most fourteenth-century metalwork attributed to western Iran (and later Fars) did not recess the ground behind the inlays. A punch was used at a slight angle to create pits around the area and push the displaced metal up into a shallow ridge which could be hammered over the sheet when it was in place (fig. 41). While this allowed craftsmen to be both faster and more economical, as thinner sheets of the precious metal could be used to the same effect, the fixing was much less secure and many of these objects have now lost their sheet inlays. The black inlays were also more carefully prepared and applied in the Mosul group. A small flat-ended chisel was used to chip out the brass, leaving a neatly stepped ground. Scrolling stems and leaves, all inlaid with silver, were arranged to reduce the areas of black material to a size that would adhere properly to the surrounding brass. On objects

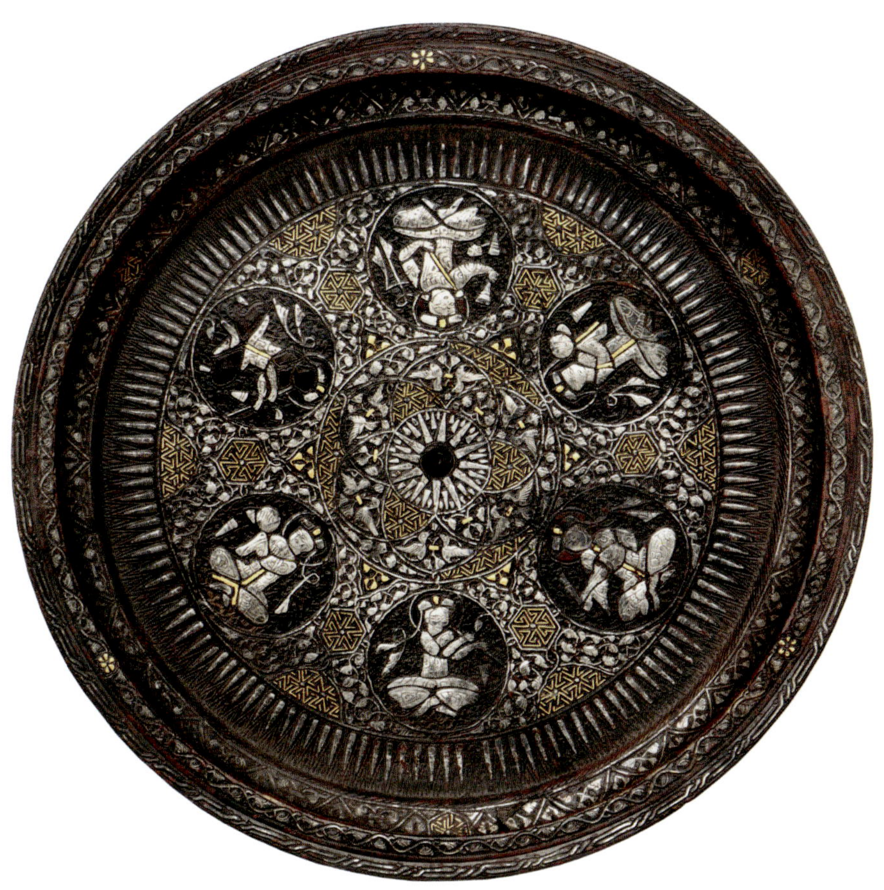

made elsewhere, the ground was more roughly excavated and the inlaid stems were often given small brass shoots either side to give the black material traction. These regular small 'floaters' of visible brass create a lacy effect which would have been even more distinct when the ground was filled with black inlay (fig. 41). A candlestick dated 708/1308–09 already shows both features.[22]

The style of the group evolves seamlessly from earlier Mosul metalwork. In his essay (see above, pp. 56–67) Raby has outlined many of its characteristics as represented by three Mosul-trained craftsmen. The successful repertoire of designs from thirteenth-century Mosul was continued, with some inevitable standardisation, as certain motifs or patterns established themselves as favourites, whether it was an archer on horseback or musicians in roundels (figs. 36 and 42). Perhaps to advertise the superior skill and technique of its craftsmen, the group specialises in increasingly intricate designs featuring geometric patterns, intersecting circles, lattice designs with tiny birds or

leaves, knots and small inscriptions in gold. At first these are combined with figures, as on the Metropolitan Museum dish (fig. 42), British Museum pen box (cat. 28) and Courtauld bag (cat. 1) but sometimes the patterns are shown on their own (figs. 43–45).

The group includes some extraordinarily fine pen boxes which have been variously attributed to Syria, western Iran and Shiraz in southern Iran (figs. 44 and 45).[23] The inlays are dizzyingly tiny and presage the move towards miniaturisation seen in fifteenth-century inlaid metalwork, which has encouraged most scholars to date them to the late fourteenth or even the fifteenth century.[24] But their form, manufacture, inlay technique and every element of their decoration is already present in the group under discussion, and the inscriptions are typical of the Jazira and western Iran. They consist of wishes rhyming with *ā'*, which is not usual on Shiraz metal and unknown anywhere after 1400,[25] and of non-specific titular inscriptions, including the title *al-ghazi*, which is also not found on metalwork attributed

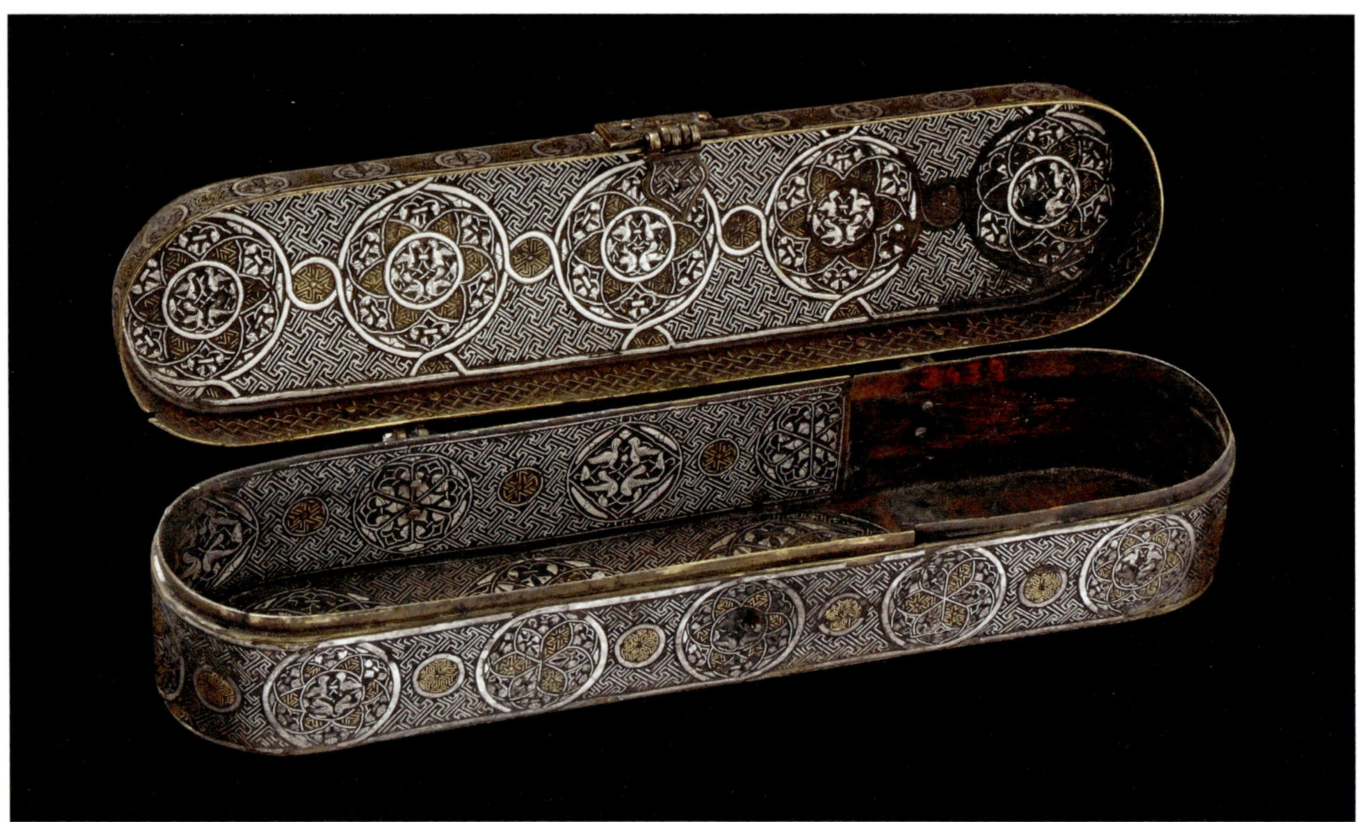

to Shiraz.[26] Allan compared them to a pen box made for Abu'l-Fida, ruler of Hama in Syria, between 1320 and 1331, which has miniscule inlays and many similar elements in the decoration, and suggested that the group was made in Mamluk Syria.[27] The comparison is valid, but Hama was not a metalworking centre and so the pen box, or a metalworker, must have been brought in from elsewhere. It could have been ordered or sent as a gift from Mosul; alternatively it might be the work of a Mosul-trained craftsman newly arrived in Syria.[28] The influence of immigrant inlayers can often be seen in Mamluk metalwork.[29] In any case, the date of the pen boxes is unlikely to be much later than the death of Abu'l-Fida in 1331.

The Nisan Tası (figs. 31, 40 and 46) is the most important object in the group because it is documented as having been ordered from Mosul by Sultan Abu Saʿid in 728/1327–28 (see Raby above, pp. 57–58). Abu Saʿid ruled the Il-Khanate between 1317 and 1335. He was an enthusiastic patron of literature and the arts and is

thought to have commissioned the finest illustrated manuscript of the period, the Great Mongol *Shahnama* (see fig. 50).[30] He commissioned metalwork from at least two different cities. His name is on a concave candlestick of a type thought to have been made in Konya, which he probably also donated to the shrine there.[31] The inscription on the candlestick is abbreviated and may be based on a coin.[32] The inscriptions on the Nisan Tası, which give Abu Saʿid's titles in full, were probably provided when the bowl and stand were commissioned (the lid is too big for the bowl and in a completely different style and so must be from another vessel).[33] They may even have been drawn out by a court calligrapher, although the inlayer would have had to adapt any design to the tapering spaces on the object and the interruptions of the roundels. The inscriptions on the Bargello incense burner, also in the name of Abu Saʿid (cat. 30), are very similar in content, layout and calligraphy. They may both have been part of a much larger commission for inlaid metalwork from Mosul by Abu Saʿid in 1327–28.

FIG. 43
Pen box, Mosul, *c.* 1300–30
Brass inlaid with gold, silver
and black material, L: 26 cm
Paris, Musée du Louvre, Islamic
Department, Koechlin Collection, 3439

FIGS. 44, 45
Pen box (general view and detail
from inside lid), Mosul, *c.* 1325–50
Brass inlaid with gold, silver and
black material, L: 28.3 cm
New York, Metropolitan Museum of Art,
Islamic Department, 17.190.822

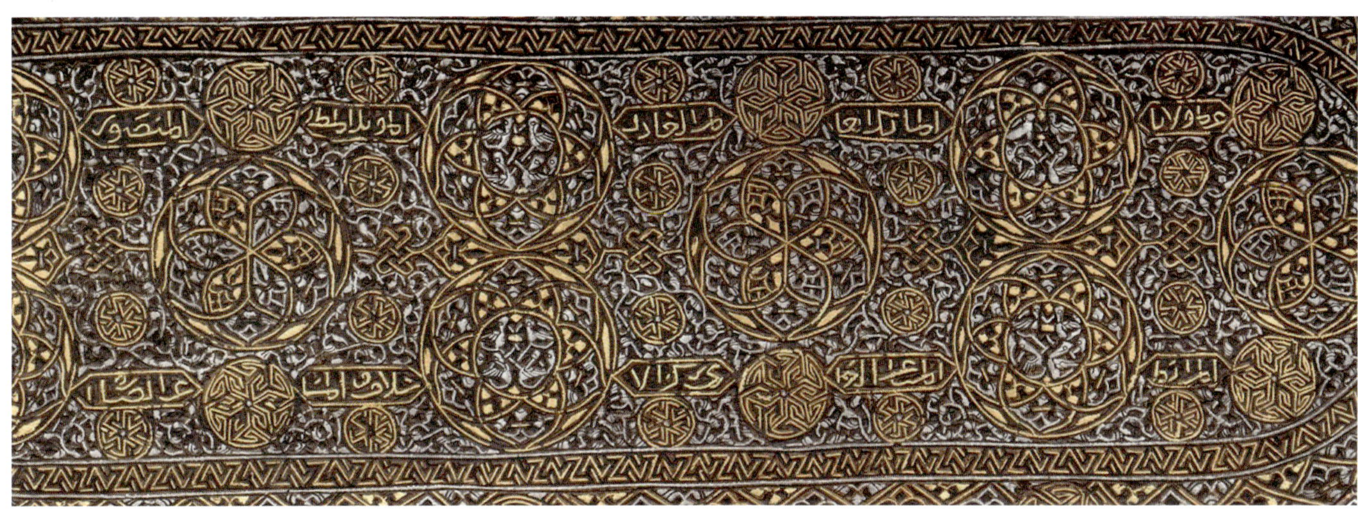

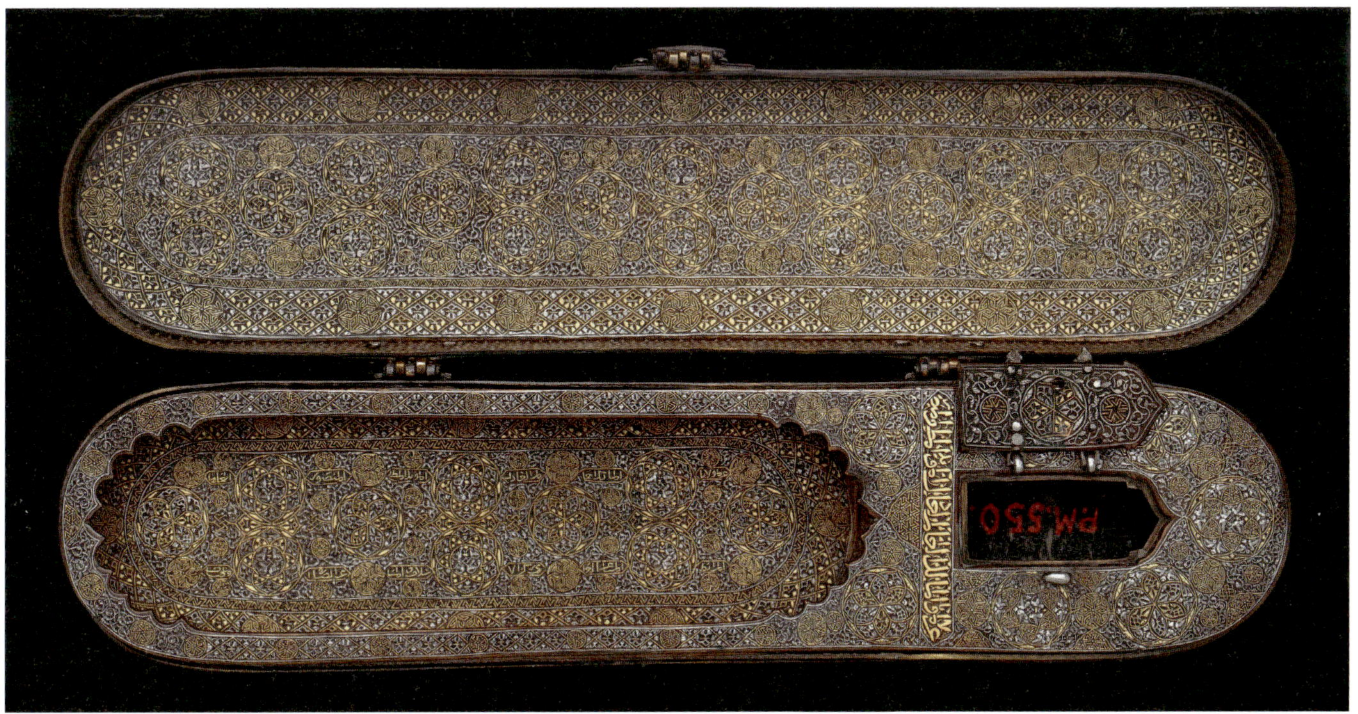

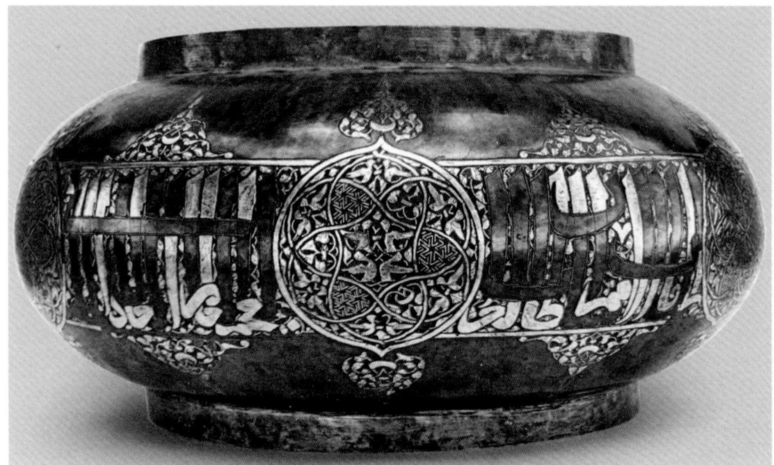

The Nisan Tası was inlaid in the Mosul manner, with the inscriptions well recessed and bevelled towards the edge.[34] The roundels on the pedestal and ball support include intersecting circles filled with birds, Z-pattern, and leaves seen frequently in the group (see cat. 26, 30, figs. 42–45). The figural scenes in the roundels on the bowl are unusual and appear to have an esoteric theme, but the style of the figures is comparable to the cross-legged figures on the Courtauld bag, with pointed facial features, lop-sided turbans and wiggly folds on their garments. One figure is seated on a dais supported by ball joints (fig. 40), like the dais in the court scene on the Courtauld bag (illustrated pp. 86–87).

The objects in this group are of the highest technical quality. Their decoration is traditional and less exposed to Central and East Asian influences than other groups of contemporary metalwork, which suggests that they were produced some distance from the Il-Khanid court. However, all of the surviving metalwork in the name of an Il-Khanid ruler belongs to this group – various ball joints made for Öljeitü to decorate windows or furniture (fig. 47), the Bargello incense burner (cat. 30) and Nisan Tası bowl and stand inscribed with the name and titles of Abu Saʿid (figs. 31 and 46). Other workshops produced simple vessels, with striking and innovative decoration, but it seems that special commissions were ordered from Mosul. A parallel situation existed in the Mamluk empire, with Damascus providing much of the inlaid metalwork for the court in Cairo in the thirteenth and early fourteenth century.[35]

Evidence presented here suggests that Mosul remained a provenance for inlaid metalwork after the Il-Khanid conquest.[36] Although the city suffered from Mongol depredations in 1262, its geographical position helped it to recover and continue as an important trade centre. A variety of luxurious goods are known to have been produced in Mosul in this period, including a magnificent royal Qur'an (cat. 35 and 36) and fine textiles (see Allan, above, pp. 52–55), and innovative illustrated manuscripts (cat. 34, figs. 16, 18) were produced in Mosul or nearby. Mosul was the pre-eminent centre for inlaid metal before 1262, producing high-quality vessels for local and foreign markets, and Raby (above, pp. 56–67) puts forward a strong case for the continuity of metalworking in Mosul. There is no evidence that metalworkers were forcibly removed from the city by the Mongols. On the contrary, similarities in the work of three metalworkers using the *nisba 'al-Mawsili'* confirm that they were trained there in the late thirteenth and early fourteenth century. Mosul metalwork retained its prestige, with third-generation Mosul metalworkers in Cairo using the *'al-Mawsili' nisba* till the end of the century and the reigning Il-Khanid Sultan Abu Saʿid making a documented commission in 728/1327–28. In form, manufacture, technique and style, the Nisan Tası, the Courtauld bag and the group of associated inlaid brass objects discussed above continue the metalworking traditions of Mosul and provide a substantial body of work that can be attributed to the city in the first decades of the fourteenth century.

NOTES

1 Curtin 1907, p. 281. Jeremiah Curtin's *The Mongols: A History* was originally published in 1907 with an enthusiastic endorsement by President Theodore Roosevelt, who wrote the foreword.

2 The Mongols often moved craftsmen to other centres. For the Mongols' transportation of large numbers of weavers to different locations, see Allsen 1997, especially pp. 30–45.

3 Shields 2000, p. 4; Lambton 1981, pp. 302 and 311 note 65.

4 Allsen 1997, pp. 39–40.

5 Simpson 1979, pp. 308–12, 322–33; Melville 1990a.

6 Bloom 2001, p. 109. See James 1988, pp. 76–131, for Qu'rans produced by Yaqut's pupils in Baghdad in the fourteenth century.

7 Shields 2000, p. 4.

8 Jackson 2005, p. 297.

9 Polo/Yule 1875, I, p. 62. See Allan above, p. 53.

10 Öljeitü's annual travels are tracked in Melville 1990a.

11 Allsen 1997, p. 101.

12 Raby 2012 makes the case that metalwork in the name of Ayyubid sultans was made in Mosul.

13 Jackson 2005, p. 290.

14 In fifteenth-century Spain entrepreneurial noblemen facilitated lustre potters to set up workshops in their region: see Caiger-Smith 1985, pp. 101–03.

15 Melikian-Chirvani 1982, especially pp. 136–44.

16 Ward 1995, pp. 154–55; Raby 2012, pp. 37–44.

17 The quotation comes from the start of the chapter 'Western Iran and Fars in the 13th–14th Centuries', which provides the only overview of metalwork of this period: Melikian-Chirvani 1982, pp. 136–230.

18 The change from Mosul to Mamluk style is best illustrated by a series of cast candlesticks produced in a Cairo workshop known to have employed inlayers from Mosul. See Ward 1995.

19 Keir Collection: see Fehérvári 1976, no. 129.

20 Ward 1993, figs. 61 and 63. Notice, for example, the chased line extending his thumb into his wrist.

21 Sometimes blanks have survived. The Khalili Collection has a blank cast candlestick of a form produced in large quantities in the fourteenth century and decorated in several different styles (MTW 1306, unpublished).

22 Boston, Museum of Fine Arts, inv. 55.106, illustrated in Melikian-Chirvani 1987, fig. 7: he suggests Tabriz as its possible provenance.

23 Paris, Musée Jacquemart-André, I 1959 (D980), Melikian-Chirvani 1973, pp. 84–85; New York, Metropolitan Museum of Art, inv. 17.190.822, Komaroff 1988, fig. 6; New York, Metropolitan Museum of Art, inv. 91.1.536, Komaroff 1988, figs. 3–5 and p. 93; Komaroff 1992, pp. 147–49; Paris, Musée du Louvre, OA7531, unpublished; London, British Museum, Godman Bequest 1983, no. 509 (unpublished).

24 The exterior of one pen box decorated in mid fifteenth-century style appeared to support a late date for the group (Melikian-Chirvani 1973, p. 84; 1982, pp. 233–34 and fig. 59). Komaroff 1988, fig. 3–5 and p. 93; 1992, pp. 147–49, first observed that the exterior had been re-engraved. Washington 1989, nos. 48 and 47, compared them to illumination done for Iskandar Mirza and attributed them to Shiraz, 1400–25, but the comparison is unconvincing.

25 Melikian-Chirvani 1982, p. 246 note 39. This rhyme is found, for example, on the ewer by ᶜAli ibn ᶜAbdallah (cat. 24).

26 Melikian-Chirvani 1987, p. 121 and note 21.

27 Allan 1982, p. 90. The pen box is illustrated in Washington 1981, pp. 84–85.

28 The inscription on the lid with Abu'l-Fida's titles with birds squashed between the letters is strikingly similar to the inscriptions in the name of Abu Saᶜid on the Nisan Tası and Bargello incense burner, which might suggest that it was a gift ordered by the Il-Khanid court.

29 Several scholars have commented on similarities between the Courtauld bag and the Baptistère de Saint Louis, a Mamluk basin signed by Muhammad ibn al-Zayn which is strongly influenced by Il-Khanid metalwork; see Ward above, p. 14.

30 For a discussion of Abu Saᶜid's likely involvement with the Great Mongol *Shahnama* see Soudavar 1996.

31 Melikian-Chirvani 1987, pls. 1–2. He argues that it was a royal gift to the Konya shrine in commemoration of Abu Saᶜid's victory near Zanjan in 1319.

32 Melikian-Chirvani 1987, p. 231.

33 Melikian-Chirvani 1987, p. 232.

34 See Baer 1973–74 for many small black-and-white photographs, including details of most of the decoration.

35 According to Maqrizi, in 692/1292–93 the Mamluk Sultan Al-Ashraf Khalil ordered from Damascus 100 brass candlesticks inlaid with his name and titles (as well as 50 in gold and 50 in silver): D.S. Rice 1952, p. 573.

36 Unwillingness to accept Mosul as a provenance for inlaid metalwork even before the Conquest, despite substantial documentary evidence, is discussed in Raby 2012.

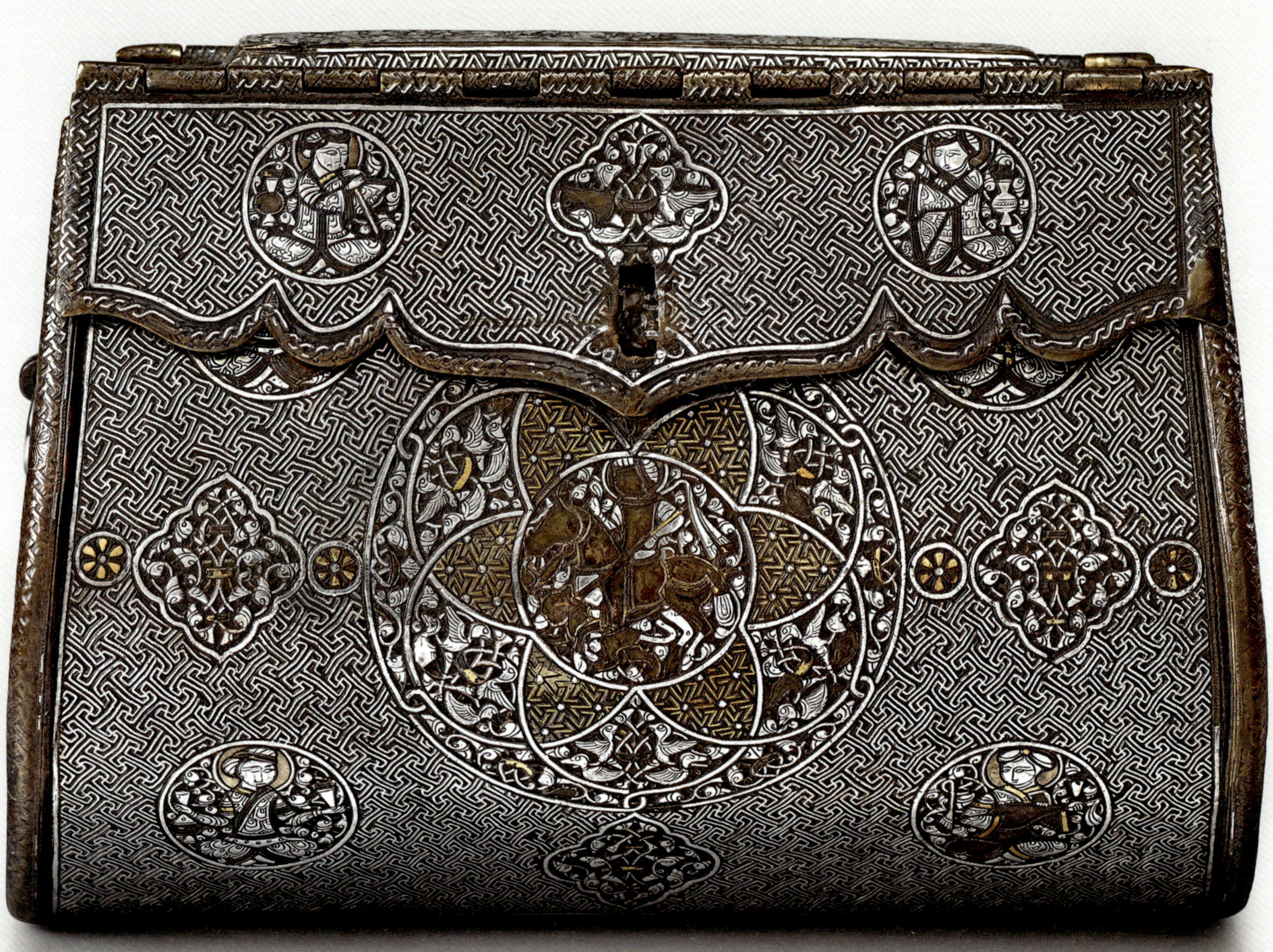

1

The Courtauld bag

Mosul, 1300–30 (possibly during the reign of Sultan Öljeitü, 1304–16)
Brass sheet hammered to shape and inlaid with gold, silver and black material
H: 15.2 cm, W: (base) 22 cm, (aperture) 19.2 cm, D: (max) 13.5 cm
London, Samuel Courtauld Trust, The Courtauld Gallery, O.1966.GP.209

Manufacture

The Courtauld bag is constructed from brass sheets soldered or hinged together. The likely stages of manufacture are as follows. Fives sheets of brass were cut to shape to form the body, the two sides, the lid and its flap. The curved edges of the two sides were hammered to create rounded cavities; the regularity of these suggest that the sheet was hammered into a mould or over a thick rod bent to shape. The body sheet was inserted into the cavities and soldered in place to form the front, base and back of the bag. The lid was hammered to create a raised central panel with slanting sides and the outer edge of the lobed flap was hammered to create a shallow convex moulding; both of these features are decorative but they also help increase the rigidity of the lid and flap. 'Knuckle' hinges run along the long edges of the lid and its flap and the back of the body: these were formed by folding the sheet to create a narrow 'hem', which was soldered in place. Sections of this were then cut away to allow the three sheets to be hinged together by inserting rods through the remaining sections of hem. Two small plaques with integral loops were separately cast and attached to each side with three rivets. The present copper rivets are replacements, but the plaques themselves are original. They fit precisely within spaces left undecorated to receive them and the small visible areas of the circles are filled with scrolling arabesques matching those on the plaques. The loops are too small to thread with a leather or fabric strap and so the missing strap was probably attached to larger metal rings similar to the silvered copper ones there now; the upper part of the loop's interior is very worn, which is consistent with wear from a metal ring. The interior of the bag is now bare but it was probably lined with fabric or coloured leather (illustrated p. 97).[1]

There is a wide variety of shapes used for suspension plaques, hinges and other attachments on metalwork in the thirteenth and fourteenth century. The cast plaques used to anchor the rings for the missing strap on the Courtauld bag are most similar to attachments on Mosul metalwork. Mosul pen boxes are hinged by plaques riveted to the body and lid. Where the original plaques have survived (many are replacements), the lower ones have a pointed tip swelling into a rounded shape below the hinge (plaques the same shape are used on the front of the pen boxes as closers). The particular outline of the plaques on the bag, in which the swelling rounded part is also lobed, is typical of hinges on fourteenth-century pen boxes also here attributed to Mosul (figs. 43 and 44).[2] The traditional cast handles on Mosul ewers often have a single loop at one or both ends, perhaps for a chain to attach the lid (none have survived with a chain attached but it is hard to imagine what else they could be for; see cat. 24). The finishing of that section of the handle, a pointed tip swelling into a rounded shape with a pronounced ridge before the loop, is again similar to the plaques on the bag.

Some of the closest comparisons in style, technique and ingenuity to the Courtauld bag are boxes, such as the pen box in the Walters Art Museum with its clever side opening (cat. 29), the unusual kidney-shaped box in

NOTES

1 The penbox in the British Museum made by Mahmud ibn Sunqur in 680/1281 has green leather lining its base, protected by a pierced brass screen: Ward 1993, pp.90–91 (the leather is not visible in any published photograph).

2 Plaques for hinges on other pen boxes of this period can be rectangular or long and thin, solid or openwork. Plaques on inkwells are closer to the curved shape seen here but the suspension method is quite different, for they are cast with two loops: the loop for the suspension ring fits neatly between them and all three are hinged together by a short rod.

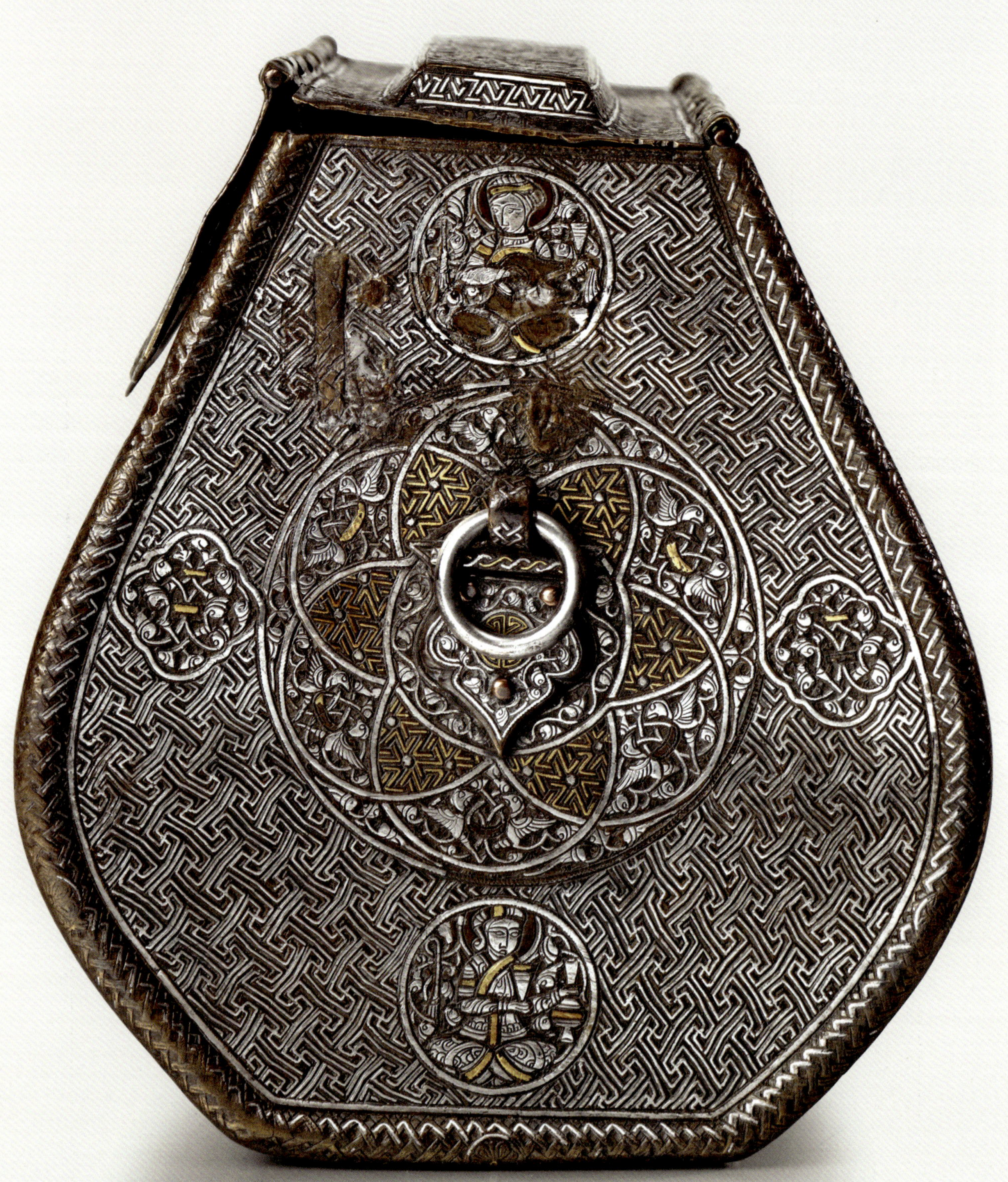

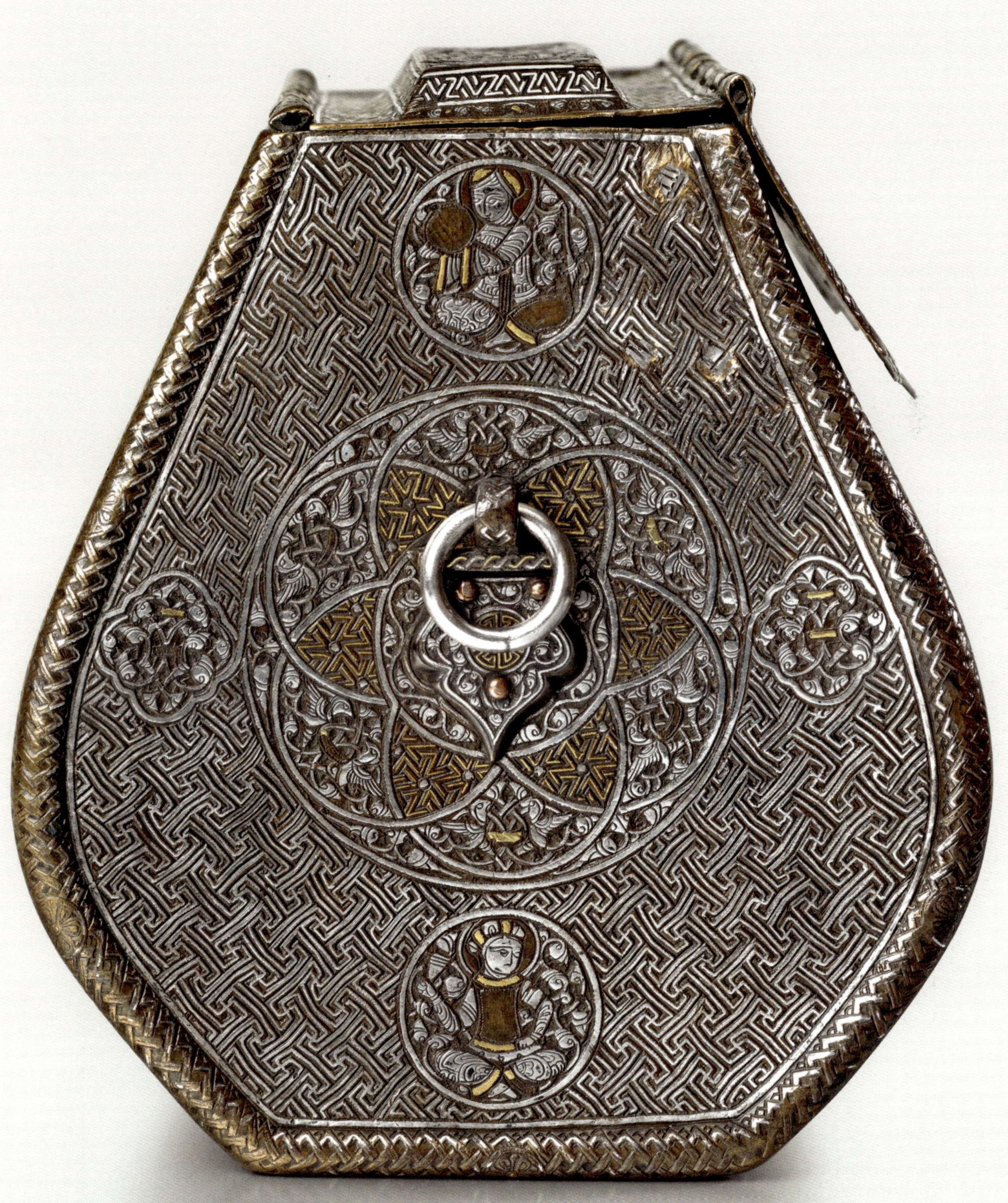

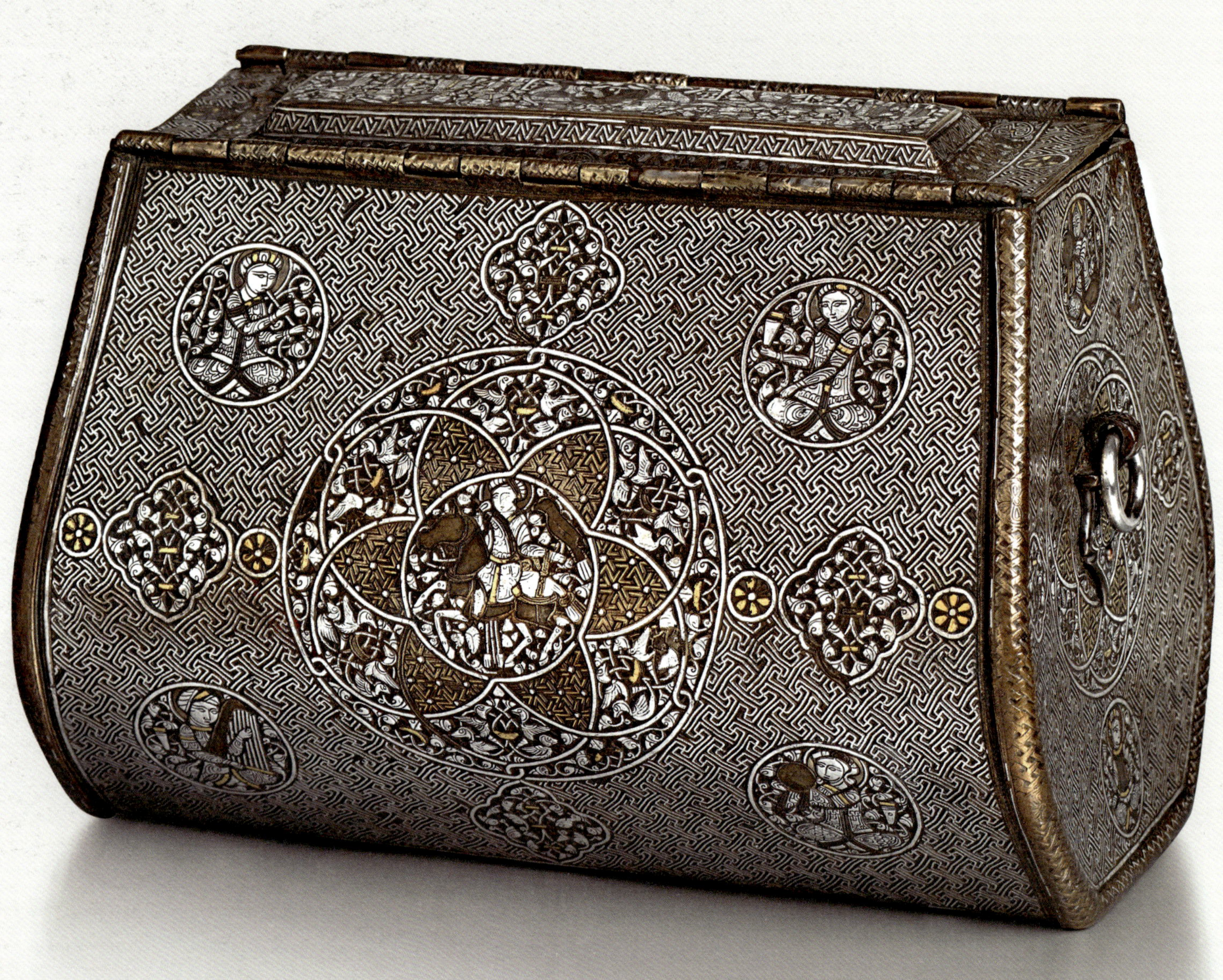

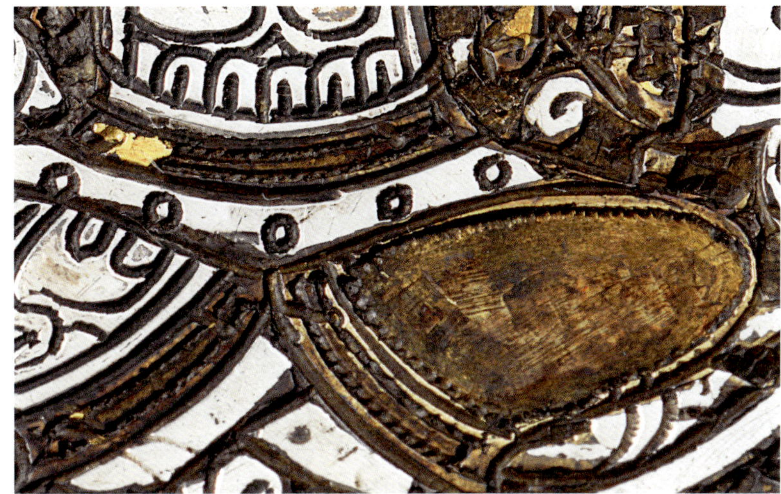

the British Museum (cat. 27) and a series of round-ended pen boxes with increasingly miniscule inlaid decoration (cat. 28 and figs. 43–45). Perhaps the workshop that produced the bag specialised in sheet-metal boxes of various types.

Several features suggest that the manufacture of the bag may have been influenced by gold or silver bags. Very little gold and silver has survived from this period, but two gold containers of the same shape, set with precious stones, in two illustrations to the story of Humay and Humayun, painted in Baghdad *c.* 1396, indicate how they may have looked (cat. 19 and fig. 4, p. 15).[3] The body of the Courtauld bag could have been hammered to shape rather than constructed from sheet, a technique more typical of gold and silver objects. Gold and silver are relatively soft metals, and thin sheets were preferred for economic reasons so they had to be supported by a rigid frame of wood or wire.[4] The gold containers in the paintings have rounded edges, probably because they were wrapped around thick wire. The Courtauld bag also has rounded edges, even though there is no wire inside because the brass sheet is thick enough not to need extra support. The hinges of the bag, made from the metal sheet that forms the object itself, also suggest a knowledge of goldsmiths' work. Similar hinges were used, for example, on gold bangles, whereas hinges on brass vessels were made separately and fixed to the lid and body of the object with rivets (cat. 24, 28, figs. 43, 44).[5] Several goldsmiths are documented in Mosul after the Mongol conquest (see Raby above, p. 57). The probable use of

moulds in forming the rounded edges of the bag and its flap suggests that this was not a unique object: perhaps bags of gold or silver were made in the same or a neighbouring workshop. The paintings suggest that bags of this type continued to be produced throughout the fourteenth century.

Decorative techniques

The whole surface of the bag is inlaid with silver, gold and a black material (probably bitumen or conifer resin).[6] The brass ground was carefully prepared to receive the precious metal inlays. Large areas are well recessed and bevelled towards the outer edge, where there is a border of neat pits to help secure the sheet inlays when the edges had been hammered down upon them. The ground for thin wire inlays was prepared with two parallel rows of pits hammered into the surface, so close together that they form two shallow grooves with a ridge between. Gold wire was laid on top of the ridge and hammered lightly so that it was secured within the grooves, but remained proud of the surface. The silver wire is thicker and laid into a single deep groove formed by a series of pits, which is why very little of it is missing. The haloes are polished brass (the only exposed brass on the bag), encircled by a thin silver wire. The ground behind the decoration

3 Gold and silver has a particularly poor rate of survival in the Islamic world because there is no tradition of burying objects with the dead, and above ground they were melted down and refashioned when damaged or outmoded. The sources are full of descriptions of gold and silver vessels and these valuable items inspired the shapes of many brass objects.

4 The sixteenth-century Ottoman pen box in the Topkapı Palace Museum is gold sheet laid over a wood core: London 1988, no. 69, pp. 134–35.

5 Jenkins and Keene 1982, no. 25, p. 54–55, for a gold bangle, attributed to twelfth-century Iran, with similar hinge construction.

6 See the analyses of black inlays by Raymond White in Ward *et al.* 1995, p. 250, table 4.

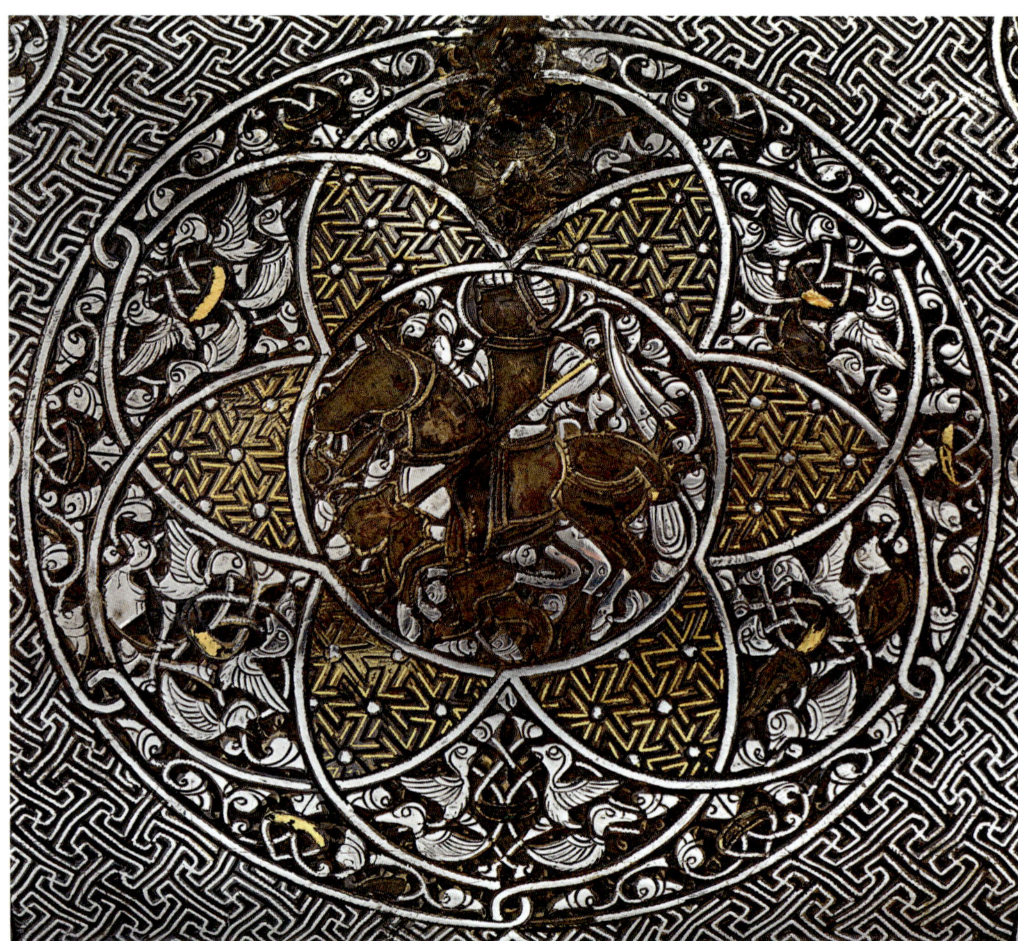

has been excavated with a small flat-ended
chisel leaving a distinctive stepped surface to
receive the black inlay.

Three technical innovations of the
thirteenth century are all seen on the
bag – gold inlays, a recessed ground filled
with black inlay and background scrolls
inlaid with silver. Gold was rarely used as
an inlay material before the last quarter of
the thirteenth century and did not become
widespread until the fourteenth century,
by which time it had completely replaced
copper as an inlay material.[7] The black inlay
material was introduced before the Mongol
conquest, but was not consistently used until
the second half of the thirteenth century.[8]
Susan LaNiece has demonstrated that the
black inlay had to be applied hot and semi-
viscous. Although it seems counter-intuitive,

it must have been applied before the brass
was prepared for inlays because the sticky
black material would have filled any recessed
areas.[9] Even when the black inlay is missing,
the stepped appearance of the ground
beneath it is quite different to the engraved
circles or parallel incisions used to texture the
ground of earlier objects (cat. 22). Previously,
the scrolling foliage behind the main designs
had been left as plain brass, which together
with the textured ground helped to create a
dark backdrop for the metal inlays. The new
material provided a completely black ground
for the designs and the scrolls were inlaid
with silver to contrast even more dramatically
with it. All three technical innovations are
already seen in the work of ᶜAli ibn ᶜAbdallah
(*fl. c.* 1275–1300), but the roundels on the
exterior of his basin (cat. 25) still have brass

7 An astrolabe made for al-Malik
   al-Ashraf Musa dated 625/1227–28
   uses gold for the dedicatory
   inscription: Gunther 1932, p.
   233, pls. LIII-LIV. A ewer dated
   644/1246 in the Walters Art
   Museum, inv. 54.456, uses gold
   very sparingly in a few areas. The
   pen box by Mahmud ibn Sunqur
   dated 680/1281 is the earliest dated
   example of the extensive use of
   gold as an inlay material: Ward
   1993, figs. 69–71.
8 Black inlays are already seen on the
   box made for Badr al-Din Lu'lu'
   before his death in 1259: Ward 1993,
   fig. 58.
9 Ward et al. 1995, pp. 241–42.

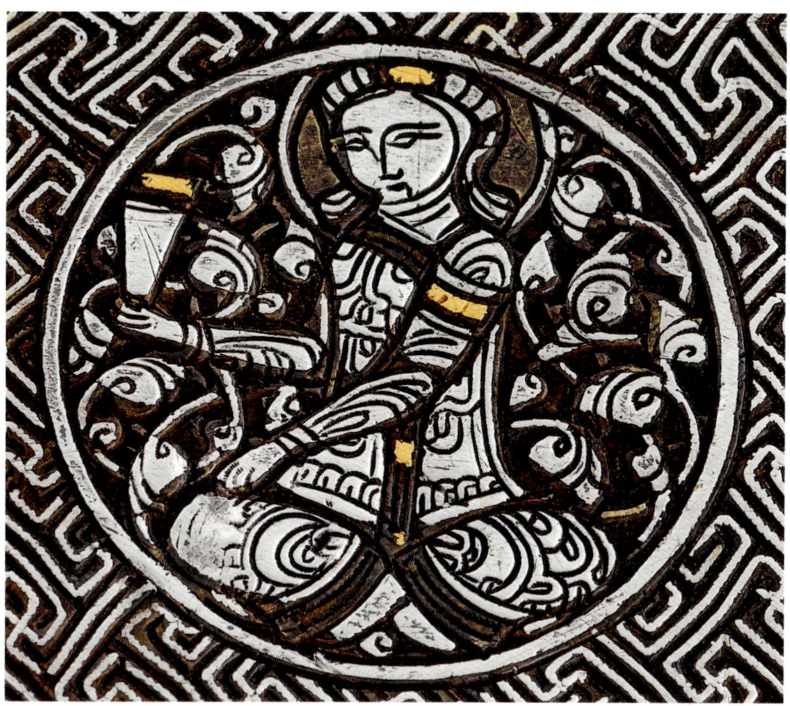

scrolls without inlay in the background, marking it out as a transitional piece.

The decorative techniques on the bag, especially the careful preparation of the brass ground for the inlays, are markedly different from other groups of fourteenth-century metalwork (cat. 20, 23, figs. 11–15, 41). They relate most closely to Mosul metalwork of the first half of the thirteenth century, and to metalwork here attributed to Mosul in the second half of the thirteenth and first half of the fourteenth century.

Decoration

On each side of the bag is a large roundel surrounded by smaller roundels and quatrefoils which contain single figures, flying birds, foliage or interlinked Zs (Z-pattern) on a geometric ground of interlinked Ts (T-pattern).

A roundel of intersecting circles, the interstices filled with birds and Z-pattern, dominates all sides. The birds sprouting symmetrically from stems in the large roundels and some of the quatrefoils are a more formal version of the birds made popular by ᶜAli ibn ᶜAbdallah al-Mawsili in the later thirteenth century (cat. 24 and 25). The Z-pattern inlaid with gold wire in the interstices of the intersecting circles was also introduced in the work of ᶜAli ibn ᶜAbdallah. It was a cost-effective way of using gold inlays because only thin wire was needed to create a rich golden effect with the Zs. Large roundels of intersecting circles became popular in the early fourteenth century and are seen on many objects attributed here to fourteenth-

century Mosul (cat. 26, 30, figs. 31, 42–46).[10]

On the sides of the bag, the central area of the large roundels is covered by the suspension plaques but on the front and back it contains a horseman. The horseman on the front is spearing a lion with a long lance. Like all the figures on the bag he is haloed (haloes were used to draw attention to the heads of figures and sometimes animals at this period, they have no religious significance). He wears a wide turban with the two ends floating out behind him and a three-quarter-length tunic with tight sleeves and boots. The horse has a looped tail tied with a gold band, and a decorative plume dangling below its head. The horseman on the back has a large bird of prey perched on his left wrist with loops of rope around his forearm which may represent equipment to tether the bird. A gold shape just below his buttock may be a misunderstood lure hanging from his belt, as on the Keir ball joint (cat. 10). He wears a wide turban and a three-quarter-length tunic which crosses over in front, with tight sleeves and boots. The horse has a looped tail, a decorative plume dangling below its chin and

10 A surprisingly early example of this motif appears on a pen box, sold Sotheby's, 30 April 2003, lot 68, inscribed with the name and titles of Shams al-Din Muhammad Juvaini (high office 1263–85, executed in 1285), which has other decoration which also appears mid-fourteenth-century rather than thirteenth-century. Such a high-ranking patron may well have owned a pen box with innovative decoration. However, I have not handled this object and would prefer to check that the inscription is contemporary before accepting it as a documentary object: If this pen box is excluded, the earliest dated example of this motif is inside a pen box made for the Rasulid Sultan Da'ud in 702/1302–03 in the Victoria and Albert Museum, inv. 370-1897 (the roundel is not visible in any published photographs).

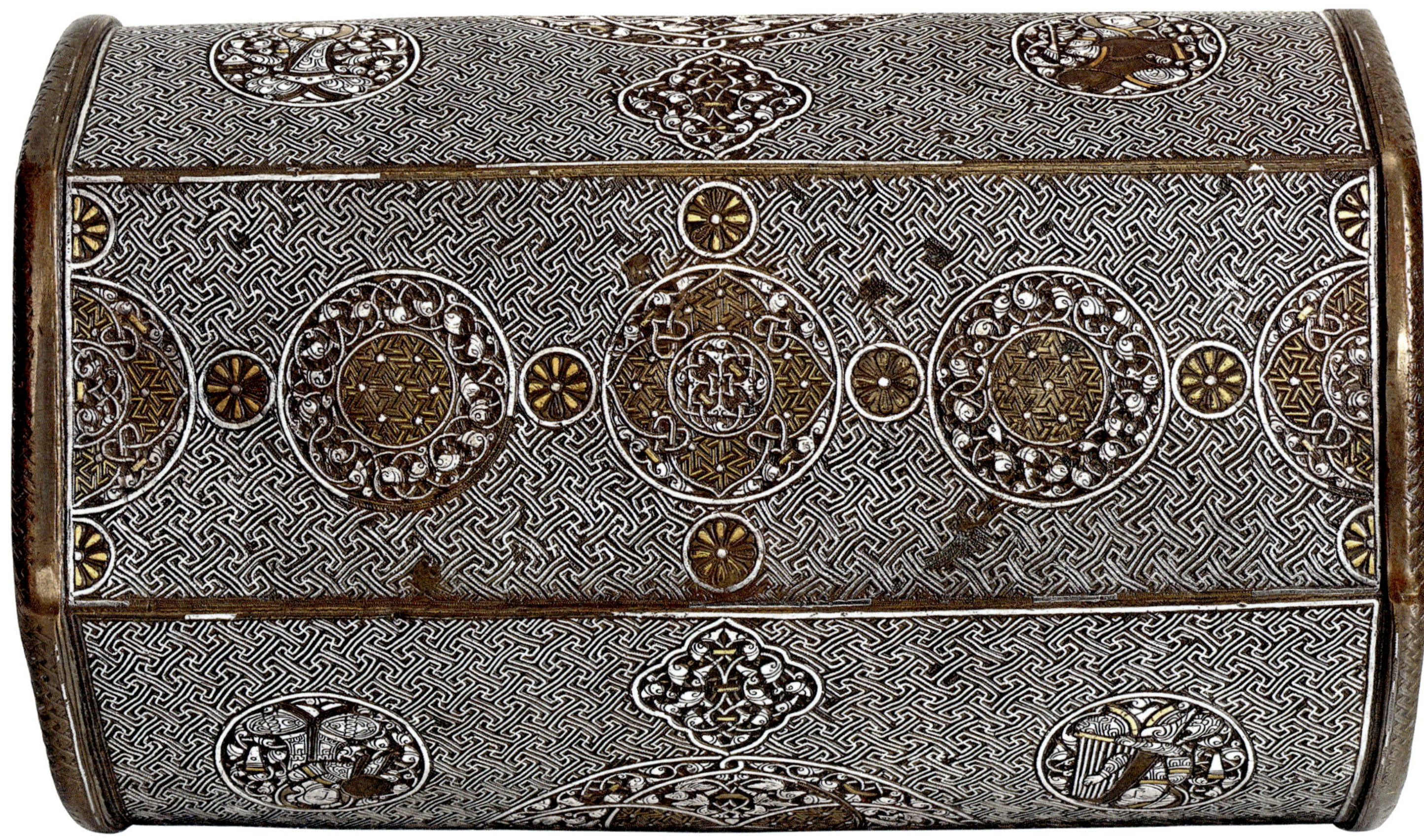

three long straps hanging below its belly. The joints of the beast are articulated with small incised circles. The bird of prey is shown in profile and, although it has lost most of its inlay, the incised hooded eye is visible on the bare brass. Horsemen are ubiquitous in all media but this falconer relates directly to an Arab tradition: the three straps below the belly of the horse are seen in manuscripts (figs. 20, 28) and metalwork (cat. 25, figs. 37, 38) from Mosul. The plume attached to the stirrup of the horse is an idiosyncratic feature of many horsemen on Mosul metalwork, both before and after the Mongol conquest (fig. 37).

The small roundels all enclose a cross-legged figure. Eight of the figures are playing a musical instrument (one harp, two flutes, three tambourines, two lutes) and most of them also have a beaker or bottle in the background. The remaining six figures hold a tall conical beaker and three of them also have bottles in their other hand or beside them. To avoid the monotony created by the repeated cross-legged position of the figures, the craftsman has varied their headgear, clothes (narrow or wide sleeves, central or crossover join, gold belt or not, gold *tiraz* or not) and drapery (loops within loops, small loops bordering a straight line and often a band of wiggly lines that crosses the area). The figures in these roundels are direct descendants of the figures of musicians and drinkers on earlier Mosul metalwork, such as the ewer and basin by ᶜAli ibn ᶜAbdallah (cat. 24 and 25). The musician and drinker in an illustration to Qazvini's *Wonders of Creation* attributed to Mosul or the Jazira *c.* 1300 are remarkably similar to the figures in the roundels on the bag, even in details of their dress and the depiction of the folds of its drapery (cat. 34a). A painting of the same subject in the Diez

FIG. 47
Ball joint inscribed with the name and
titles of Sultan Öljeitü (ruled 1304–16),
probably made in Mosul
Brass, cast, inlaid with gold, silver
and black material, Diam: 13 cm
Cairo, Museum of Islamic Art, Harari
Collection (photograph after Pope and
Ackermann 1938–39, pl. 1357)

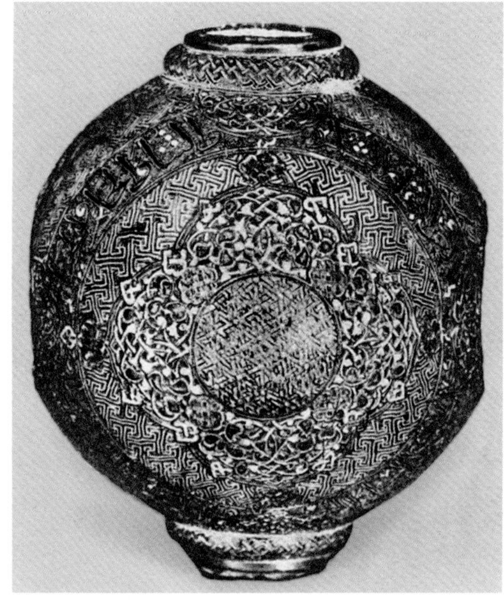

Albums in Berlin is even closer in style, with clearly delineated wiggly folds that provide an interesting pattern but bear little relation to the behaviour of fabric.[11] They suggest that there was some relationship between painting and inlaid metalwork in Mosul.

The base of the bag has a series of roundels containing geometric ornament or foliage and eight-petalled gold rosettes. Apart from the gold inlays, the layout, the roundel with a leafy scroll around a Z-pattern and the rosettes are all extraordinarily similar to the decoration on the Mosul incense burner dated 641/1243–44 (cat. 22). One feature shows Mongol influence. A 'cloud collar' motif appears in three roundels (the two end ones have been cut in half). Cammann has outlined the possible meaning of this motif in Central and East Asia as 'the Gate of Heaven' and has traced its appearance in significant positions – around the neck of clothing, around the tops of tents, around the openings of jars and bottles, and as crowns.[12] It was introduced into Iran and Iraq during the Il-Khanid period, perhaps through textiles such as a silk from Sichuan which features a cloud collar motif at its centre (fig. 30). The earliest examples include a tapestry roundel in the David Collection attributed to early fourteenth-century Iraq or western Iran, where it is worn as a collar or embroidered design around the neck of the enthroned Khan and also as a crown;[13] an embroidered design around the neck of a kneeling prince in an illustration to the Great Mongol *Shahnama*, usually attributed to 1330s Tabriz,[14] and several crowns in the same manuscript (see fig. 50); around the necks of

bottles in an illustration to the Freer Small *Shahnama* from Iraq or western Iran of *c.* 1300–30;[15] and in illustrations intended for Rashid al-Din's *History of the Mongols* (cat. 16). The motif had certainly entered the artistic repertoire in Mosul by 1310, the date of volume 25 of the Öljeitü Qur'an (cat. 35–36), which has a cloud collar framing its commissioning certificate.[16] It became popular on inlaid metalwork here attributed to Mosul around the same time (cat. 26), including the ball joint also commissioned by Öljeitü (fig. 47). Indeed the similarity of the decoration on the ball joint to the decoration on the bag (the cloud collar design with knots, the Z-pattern roundels and T-pattern ground, the plait on the convex moulding) is sufficiently close to suggest that they were made around the same time and that the bag should also be attributed to Öljeitü's reign (1304–16).

The lid of the bag features a rectangular panel with a court scene surrounded by an inscription with narrow bands of fretwork with six-petalled gold rosettes at either end. The rhyming inscription is written in informal cursive script in gold on a ground of silver scrolling stems and leaves and is punctuated by Z-medallions.

11 New York 2002, fig. 260.
12 Cammann 1951. Rawson 1984, pp. 132–38, suggested that the motif had a separate development to the cloud collar garment, but in the Il-Khanate they appear simultaneously in both clothing and objects.
13 Folsach 2013 p. 231, fig. 220.
14 Soudavar 1996, p. 120 and fig. 18.
15 Simpson 1979, fig. 65.
16 Baker 2007, fig. 30.

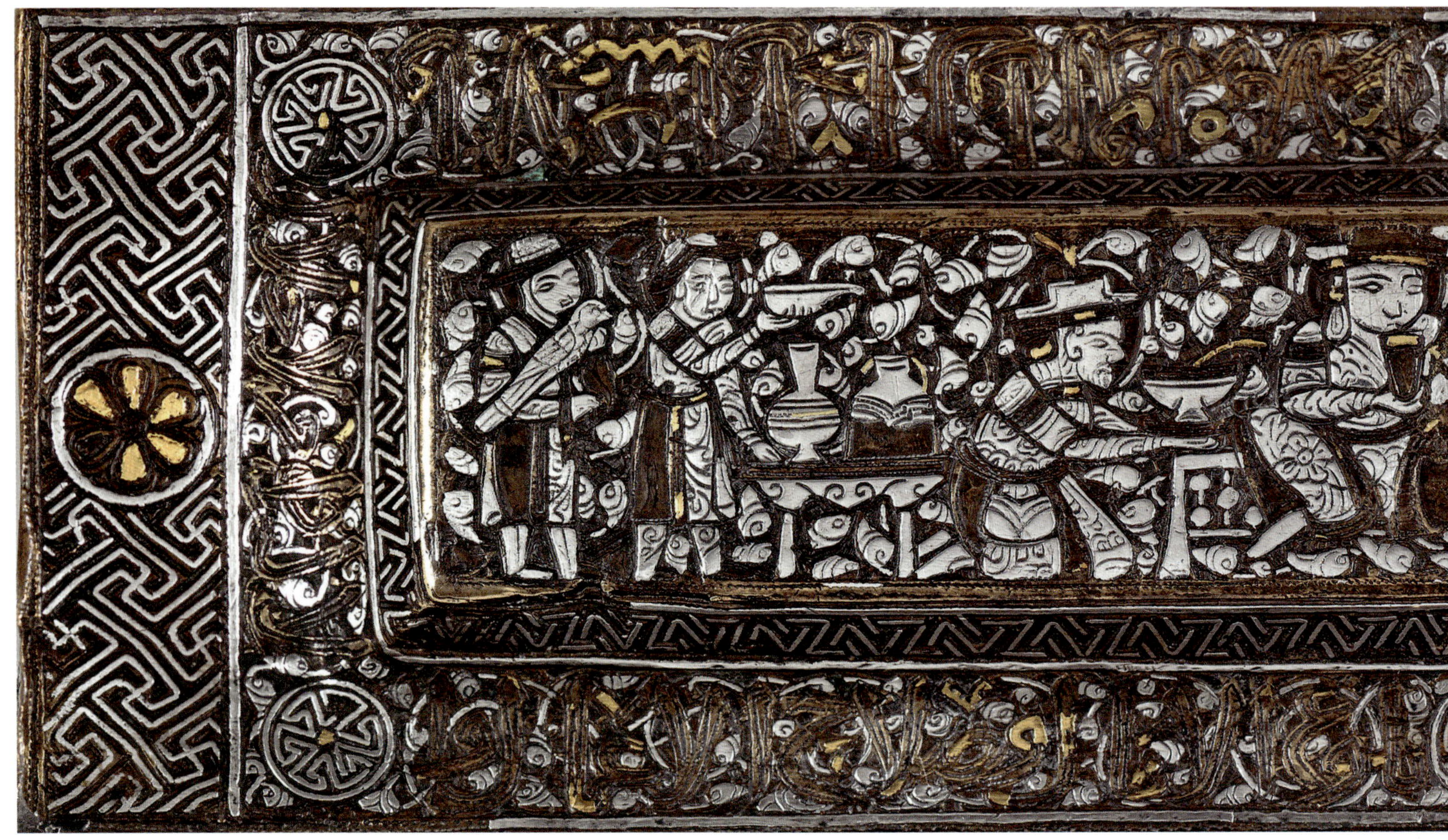

Arabic inscription

Glory and prosperity and (God's) grace and eminence	العز و الاقبال و النع[ـمـ]ة و الافضال
And fulfillment of wishes and prudence in deeds	و (ا) بلوغ الآمال و صلاح الاعمال
And respect and honour	و ا لاكرام و [ا] لاجلال
And benevolence and decent act (?)	و الاحسان و اجمال (كذا) [الاجمال]
And undiminishing good-fortune	و الدولة بلا زوال
And uninterrupted happiness	و السعادة بلا انفصال
And perfection and excellence	و التمام و الكمال
And that is all.	و السلام

al-ʿizz wa al-iqbāl wa al-niʿmah wa al-ifḍāl
wa (a) bulūgh al-āmāl wa ṣilāḥ al-aʿmāl
wa al-ikrām wa [a]l-ijlāl
wa al-iḥsān wa [al-]ijmāl
wa al-dawlah bi-lā zawāl
wa al-saʿādah bi-lā infiṣāl
wa al-tamām wa al-kamāl
wa al-salām

Reading and translation by Manijeh Bayani.[17]

The inscription was specially composed for the bag. It is in Arabic and consists of nouns arranged in rhyming pairs, with the second words all ending with āl. It is written in a good, legible hand, but there are some omissions and additions, which is surprising in a specially composed inscription on an object of such quality, and may be the consequence of errors by the inlayer. The letter *mīm* of *al-niʿmah* is either missing

17 I am extremely grateful to Manijeh Bayani for discussing this important inscription with me.

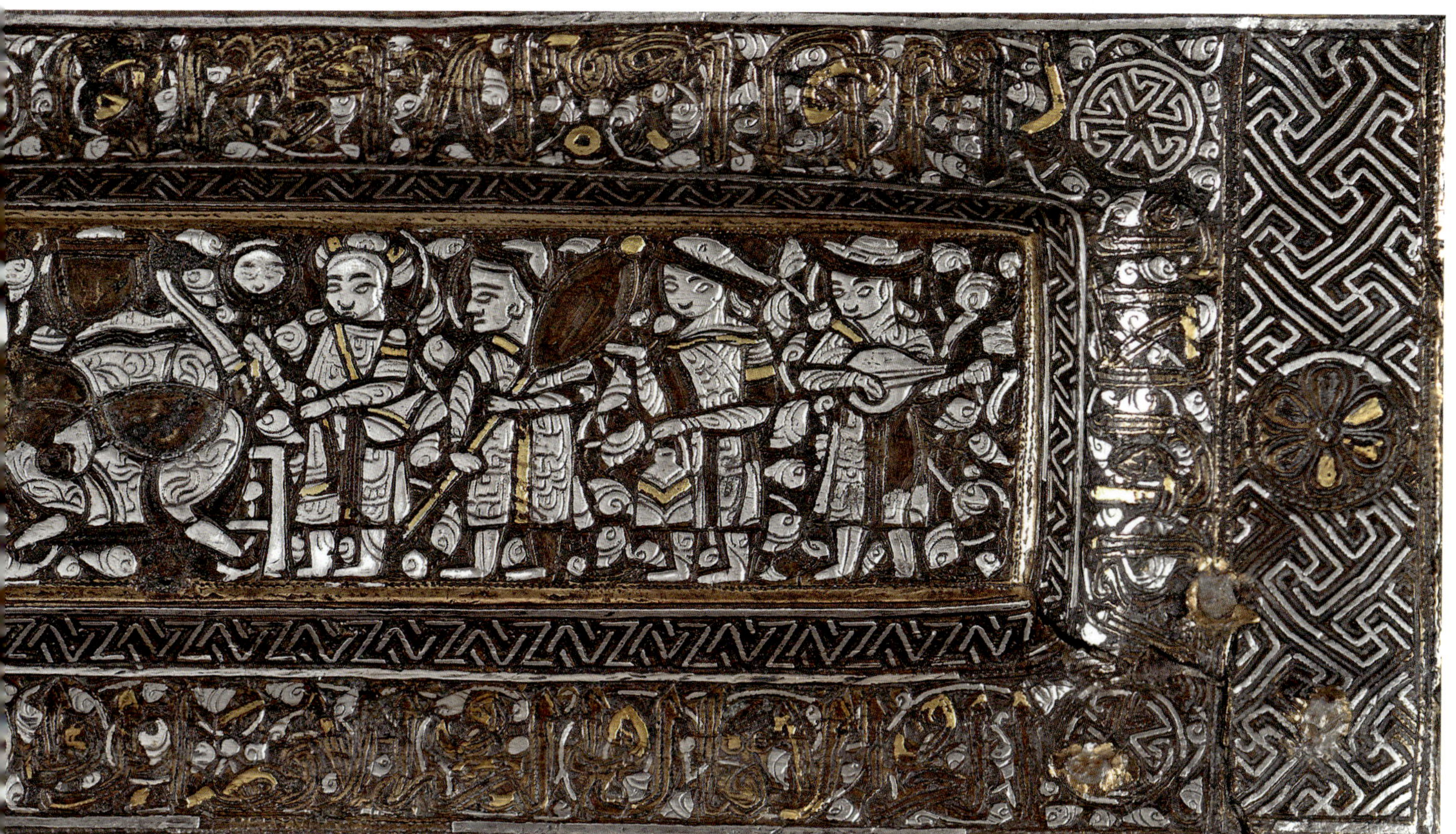

Lid of bag

or extremely small (the inlay has fallen out of that area; it is possible that the *mīm* was visible originally). There is an additional *alif* in the second line, just before the first Z-medallion that punctuates the inscription. It is not uncommon to insert an *alif* if there is some space left at the end of a section, but not enough for the next word or a sensible part of the next word.[18] There is a missing *alif* in the third line. In the fourth line there is a word that is difficult to interpret which also appears to be missing its definite article, which has been read here as [*al*]-*ijmāl* (decent act). The final word, *al-salām*, is also a puzzle. It needs a partner word ending in *āl* to complete the rhyme. The inlayer may have omitted the second word accidentally or because he ran out of space. Alternatively, *al-salām* on its own could be translated 'and that is all', an expression used to mark the end of a text but not usually found in inscriptions on

objects.[19] Various small symbols inlaid in gold appear in the inscription, especially where there is a large space between letters; in the majority of cases these are just decorative.

Wishes such as the ones expressed in this inscription are common on inlaid metalwork and most of the words are popular throughout the Islamic world; it is the choice of words and their arrangements that vary.[20] Nouns with qualifying adjectives arranged as rhyming pairs was a western tradition, and they are often seen on metalwork, as well as objects in other media, from Syria and Egypt in the eleventh and twelfth centuries.[21] Different nouns and qualifying adjectives were also often presented in rhyming pairs on Mosul metalwork of the early thirteenth century and, unlike the earlier examples, these inscriptions included the definite article. The sequence often begins *al-ʿizz al-dāʾim wa al-ʿumr al-sālim* (cat. 22, 24).[22]

18 For several examples of this in a single inscription around the base of the candlestick in the Victoria and Albert Museum, inv. 333-1892, see Melikian-Chirvani 1982, p. 168.

19 For example, the last verse in the section in praise of the Prophet in *Saʿdi's Būstān* reads *alayka aṣ-ṣalāt ey nabī wa's-salām*: 'Salutation be upon you O Prophet! And that is all' (quoted under *salām* in Dikhuda 1946–).

20 For the Il-Khanid period see Melikian-Chirvani 1973 and especially the chapter 'Western Iran and Fars' in Melikian-Chirvani 1982, pp. 136–230.

21 Ward 1995, pp. 151–52.

22 These sequences of nouns and qualifiers, rhyming or not rhyming, are first seen in western Iran and the Jazira in the 1220s: see Melikian-Chirvani 1982, pp. 133–34, 142.

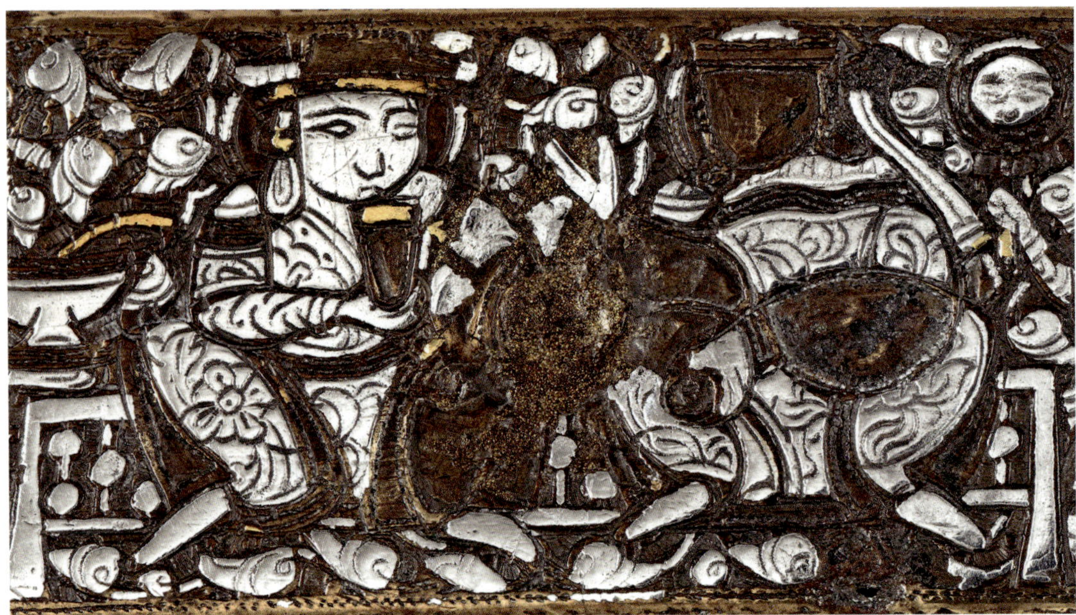

Pairs of nouns rhyming with *ā'*, occasionally seen on metalwork from Khurasan in the early thirteenth century (such as a high-spouted ewer from Herat in the British Museum),[23] are introduced into western Iran and the Jazira in the thirteenth century, probably by craftsmen fleeing the Mongol invasion of Khurasan.[24] The rhyme was being used in Mosul by the second quarter of the thirteenth century, when it features in an inscription on a candlestick decorated by Muhammad ibn Fattuh al-Mawsili, an employee of Shujaᶜ bin Manᶜa al-Mawsili who made the Blacas ewer in Mosul in 1232 (cat. 21).[25] The same rhyme continues to be used in inscriptions on objects here attributed to Mosul, such as the ewer by ᶜAli ibn ᶜAbdallah al-Mawsili (cat. 24) and the pen box in the Metropolitan Museum of Art (figs. 44, 45), and also appears on objects attributed to western Iran in the fourteenth century.[26]

The introductory pair of words seen on the bag, *al-ᶜizz wa al-iqbāl*, often begin inscriptions on twelfth- and early thirteenth-century metalwork from Khurasan (see cat. 8), but are rarely used on Mosul metalwork unless copying an inscription from the east.[27] The bag is the only object known so far that begins *al-ᶜizz wa al-iqbāl* and continues with pairs of nouns rhyming consistently with *āl*. Inscriptions on some objects attributed to later fourteenth-century Fars also begin *al-ᶜizz wa al-iqbāl* and include other words ending with *āl*, but not in pairs.[28]

Many metal objects of this period are decorated with sequences of wishes seen on multiple objects. As Melikian-Chirvani has often emphasised, these repetitive inscriptions can be the most reliable indicators of a particular workshop or region.[29] The inscription on the bag must have been specially composed, which makes it harder to compare to other inscriptions – there are none like it – but increases its significance and importance.

The court scene

In the centre of the lid, on a raised rectangular panel framed by the gold inscription and a Z-border, is the court scene which is the focus of the decoration on the bag. The scene measures only 14 × 2.5 cm yet it is executed in such exquisite detail that contemporary furnishings and vessels are easily identifiable within it, and parallels

23 See London 1976, no. 188, p. 175.
24 For a range of objects bearing inscriptions rhyming with *ā'* see Melikian Chirvani 1982, nos. 53, 58, 75, 77, 92, 93, fig. 46. and p. 153 note 33.
25 For the inscription on the Mosul candlestick see London 1976, pp. 182–83.
26 For similar inscriptions on objects attributed to western Iran see Melikian-Chirvani 1982, nos. 75–77, pp. 169–78, and nos. 92–93, pp. 201–07.
27 For numerous examples from Khurasan see Melikian-Chirvani 1982, especially pp. 55–135. For an example of a similar inscription on an object made in the west, see the ewer made for Mahmud ibn Sanjarshah: Allan 1982, pp. 54–57. The words occur in a human-headed inscription which may have been copied from an object from Khurasan.
28 Candlestick in the Victoria and Albert Museum, inv. 1947-1899: Melikian-Chirvani 1982, no. 101, pp. 217–20; candlestick in the Sarikhani collection, I.MW. 1018: *Sarikhani Collection* [2011], pp. 74–75; a bowl in the Freer Gallery, inv. 49.11: Melikian-Chirvani 1982, p. 155 note 60.
29 Melikian-Chirvani 1982, pp. 74–75.

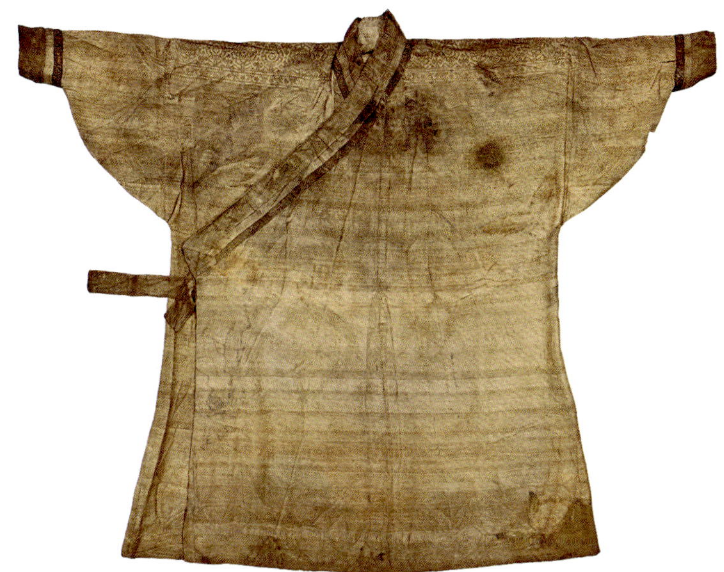

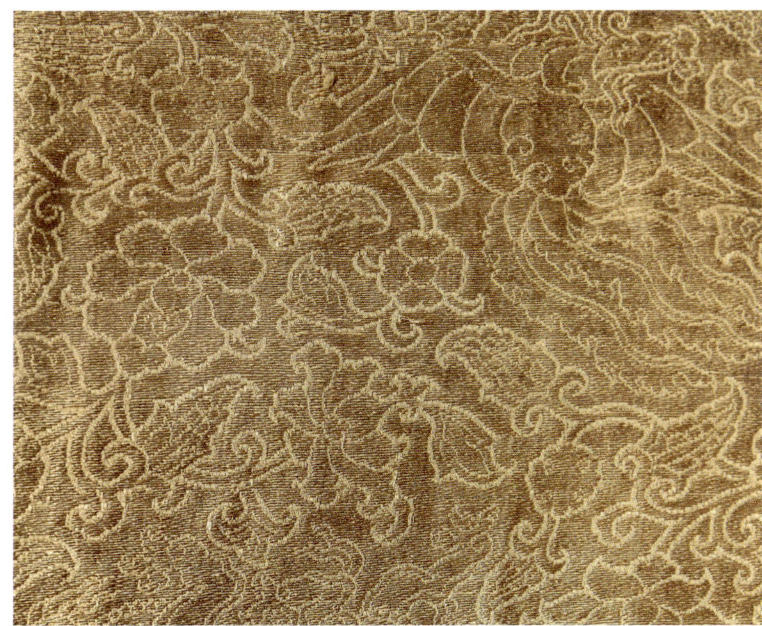

for these have been included in the exhibition
(cat. 3–13).

In the centre, a man and woman are seated
together on a dais, turned slightly towards
each other. The dais is wide and low without
sides or back and appears to be made of wood,
or perhaps wood and metal, with ornamental
ball joints decorating the struts (cat. 10).

The man, on the left, sits with his knees
wide apart, his right hand holding a beaker
to his lips (cat. 11), his left arm bent to rest in
his lap with a napkin in the hand (the inlay
is missing but a bunch of cloth is visible
above where the hand should be). Like all the
figures in the scene, he has a round face and
nose which are quite different to the facial
features of the figures in the roundels and
are obviously intended to portray the Mongol
ethnic type. His hair is looped and gathered
by a gold clip below his ears in the Mongol
style described by Friar Rubruck: "at the rear
corners of the head they leave the hair and
make it into plaits, which they braid up round
to the ears".[30] He wears a wide-brimmed hat,
chased to create narrow panels above a gold
rim; small pointed shapes either side have
lost their inlay but were probably chased to
represent the feathers that adorned this type
of hat (for many similar hats see cat. 16).[31]
His short-sleeved tunic crosses diagonally
across his chest and is richly patterned
with chinoiserie flowers and leaves. Similar
textiles, painted in gold, are often seen in
fourteenth-century miniatures (cat. 2) and
appear to represent *nasij* (cloth of gold),
which was highly prized at the Mongol courts
(figs. 48, 49). He also has gold-inlaid *tiraz*
around his upper arms (inscribed bands on

30 A Franciscan friar, who travelled
    from the Holy Land to Qareqoru
    and back again, 1253–55: Rubruck/
    Jackson 2009, p. 88.
31 For a survey of the huge variety
    of Turkish and Central Asian
    headgear see Esen 1970.

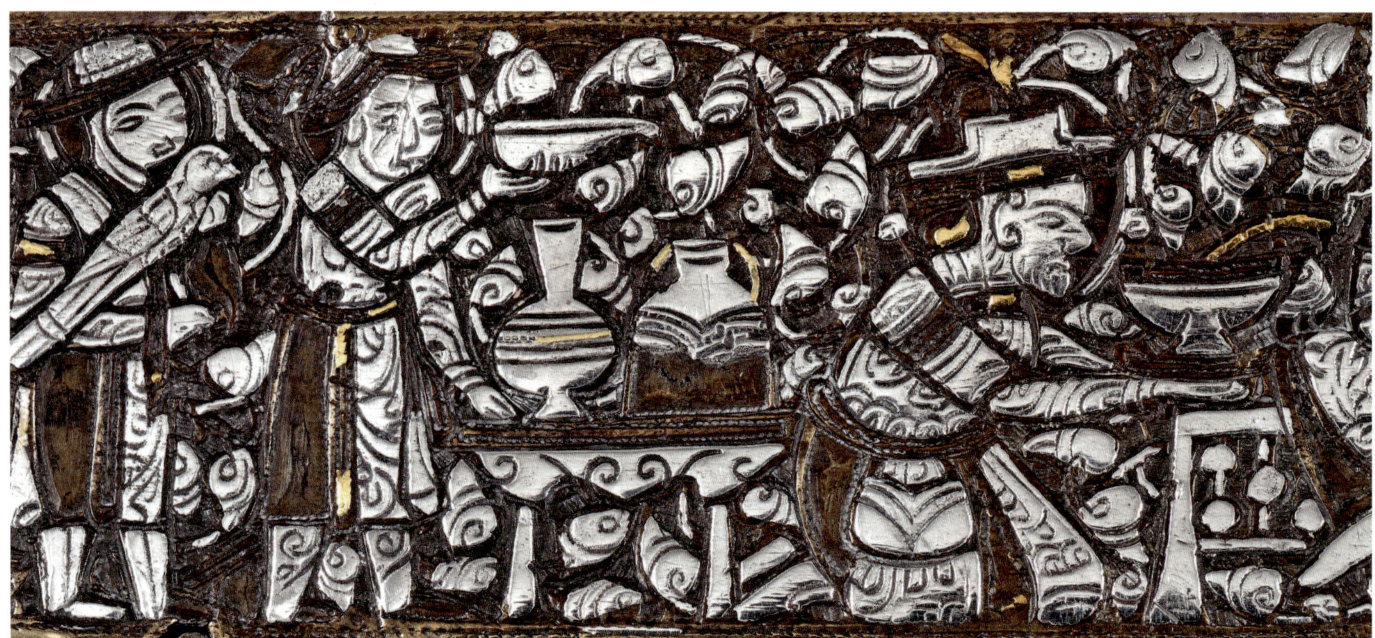

garments often produced in royal factories and worn by the elite). The narrow sleeves of an unpatterned chemise cover his lower arms; the numerous folds create a rippling effect like that on the tunic of Badr al-Din Lu'lu' (figs. 25, 28) and suggest that the fabric is silk (see Allan above, p. 52).

The woman sits to his left, correct Mongol protocol for a consort.[32] Like him she sits with her knees wide apart. Her left arm crosses her body and she holds a round fruit in her left hand, probably a pomegranate, symbol of fertility. Her open-palmed right hand gestures towards the man to indicate conversation. Her face is missing its inlay but she is wearing a gold diadem or headband with a stiffened, pointed front, the fabric knotted and falling to one side, over a *miqnaʿa* (a female veil that covers the head and shoulders but leaves the face visible) hemmed in gold. Her robe has huge puffed sleeves gathered in tight at the wrists and, like the man's, is richly patterned with a leafy design. The shape and textile of her robe is almost identical to one made from *nasij* belonging to the Mardjani Foundation (figs. 48, 49). She wears large gold earrings; the inlay has fallen out but they seem to be crescent-shaped with pearls around the outer edge (cat. 12).

A courtier kneeling to the left of the prince bends forward and holds out a bowl containing a spoon on a flat dish (cat. 7–9). The bowl is hemispherical with a flaring foot and could be gold, silver or porcelain (cat. 9). The spoon has a gently curving handle which must be made of metal – gold, silver or high tin bronze (cat. 7). The courtier is shown in profile; he has a short nose, a strange-looking ear (perhaps because profile views are rare on Mosul metalwork) and a beard. He wears a wide-brimmed hat with a bunch of gold and silver feathers issuing from the top and his looped hair is held by a gold clip. His unpatterned tunic appears to have long narrow sleeves with gold *tiraz* bands on the upper arms and is belted at the waist. On the belt he wears a small bag with a flap opening (cat. 6).

Directly behind the kneeling courtier is a table supporting two bottles. The table has a decorative top with lobed pendants hanging down and may be imported Chinese lacquer (cat. 3). One bottle is round-bodied with a tall neck widening towards the top on a low

Detail of left side of court scene on the lid

32 Rubruck/Jackson 2009, p. 75.

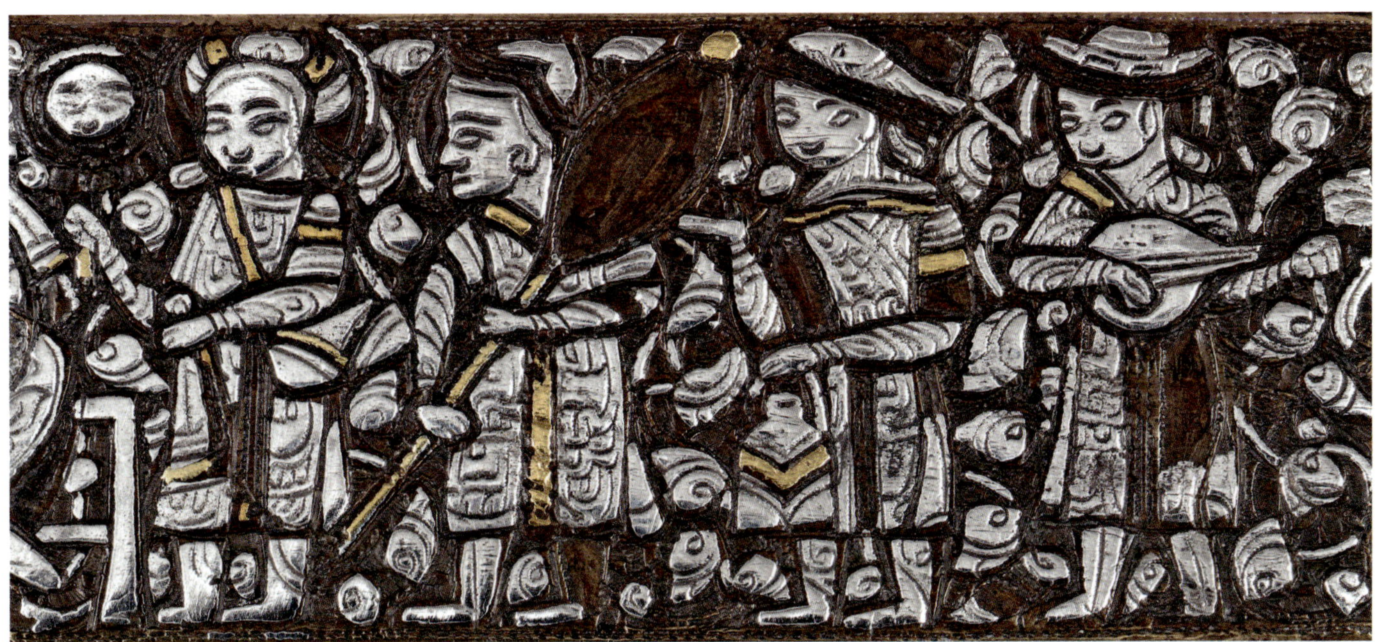

flaring foot, similar to bottles seen in the
roundels; its shape suggests metal, porcelain
or glass (cat. 4). The other bottle is flat-
bottomed with sloping shoulders and a short
wide neck and it has a loop handle attached
to its shoulders. Its shape is unparalleled
by surviving vessels of the Il-Khanid period
but it may be a special container for *kumis*,
fermented mare's milk, which was the
traditional drink of the Mongols (see cat. 4).

Behind the table stands a man holding out
a bowl with a long curving spout (cat. 5). He
wears a three-quarter-length tunic which has
tiraz bands on its narrow sleeves and boots,
presumably leather, which are decorated with
a spiral design. His distinctive domed hat
with a four-pointed brim does not appear
in the detatched illustrations to Rashid al-
Din's *History of the Mongols*, but can be seen
in several paintings in the Great Mongol
Shahnama, probably painted in Tabriz in the
1330s (fig. 50).

Before the left edge of the scene, a man
stands with a bird of prey on his arm and
also coils of rope, perhaps to tether the bird
or swing the lure. He wears a wide-brimmed
hat with a chased top that suggests it may be

wicker. His three-quarter-length tunic has
gold *tiraz* bands and he wears leather boots,
the seam visible up each side.

To the right of the woman stands her page.
He appears to be wearing a turban rather
than a Mongol hat but he has Mongol facial
features and is dressed the same as the other
men, in a three-quarter-length tunic with
narrow sleeves and *tiraz* bands over boots.
In his right hand he holds up a circular
mirror on a long handle; it is identifiable as a
mirror because there is a reflection of a face
within it (cat. 13). In his left hand he holds a
napkin with a gold border. Suspended from
his right shoulder by a gold strap, and clearly
visible beneath his left elbow, is a bag with a
V-shaped flap opening, which must represent
the Courtauld bag itself.

Behind the page are three other attendants,
all wearing three-quarter-length tunics
crossing across the chest from left to right,
with narrow sleeves and gold *tiraz* bands and
long boots. First is a man holding a folded
parasol on a long pole.[33] His face is shown
in profile and he wears a a domed hat with
a four-pointed brim similar to that of the
attendant second from left. Next is a man

33 Robinson 1967, p. 169, identified
this item as a mace, but it is too
large for a mace, and parasols,
open or folded, appear in several
Il-Khanid court scenes (see cat. 16).

carrying, by its loop handle, a bottle which is identical to the one on the table (see cat. 4), while gesturing towards the couple on the dais with his other hand. His hat has a straight brim that slopes diagonally down behind his head to create a flat flap at the back (see similar hats in cat. 16 and 17). Behind him, at the far right of the scene is a man in a wide-brimmed hat playing a lute.

The court scene displays a developed Il-Khanid figural style which is in a different league to images of single figures in Mongol dress that appear regularly on metalwork and pottery (cat. 10, 23, 31, 33) and must have been specially designed for the lid of the bag by an artist with a detailed knowledge of courtly customs and dress. Indeed, drawings for special commissions such as the Courtauld bag could have provided the means of transmission of such images to the metal workshops.

Parallels between the court scene and surviving illustrations of the Il-Khanid court are striking.[34] The tiny image contains almost all of the elements seen in one of the much larger double-page paintings of the Il-Khanid court from Rashid al-Din's *History of the Mongols*, composed in the early fourteenth century (cat. 16). In that painting, the seated couple are at the centre of the composition (or as close as possible to the centre). He holds a cup in his right hand and a napkin in his left hand, and turns towards his wife, who is seated on his left. She inclines towards him and holds a pomegranate in her left hand. Immediately to her left is a page carrying her bag, suspended across his chest by a narrow red cord. The courtiers are

much more numerous and include women as well as men, but the categories are the same – courtiers offering and preparing food and drink, falconers, musicians. The figures all have Mongol features and the men wear their hair looped below the ears in Mongol style. The dress of the courtiers is broadly similar – three-quarter length tunics, boots and elaborate hats. A rolled parasol is placed within a stand on the left rather than carried by a courtier as on the bag. A red (lacquer?) table supports various vessels and bottles. Descriptions of visitors to the Mongols confirm the arrangements depicted in these scenes – the enthroned couple, women on the right side and men on the left, musicians, and the ubiquitous presence of alcohol.[35]

There are some small differences which may suggest that the craftsman of the bag had no personal experience of the Mongol court and was working in an Arab environment. The man holds a beaker not a cup. A beaker was the traditional shape of drinking vessel in the Arab world (see, for example, fig. 20); beakers were also used in Iran but in the Il-Khanid period a small cup was more usual in ruler images (cat. 16, 17). The tunics cross from left to right. Surviving Il-Khanid tunics and depictions of them in paintings invariably cross from right to left and fasten under the arm (cat. 16–18), whereas garments in the Arab world crossed from left to right (figs. 20, 21). The tunics all have long narrow sleeves with gold *tiraz* bands, whereas in Il-Khanid paintings courtiers wear a top coat with short sleeves over a chemise with narrow sleeves; *tiraz* bands, if present, are not visible (cat. 16–18).[36] The page wears a turban or headdress

34 The earliest surviving paintings with comparable Mongol influence are late thirteenth-century but only a tiny percentage of illustrated manuscripts – and virtually no wall paintings – have survived from the Il-Khanid period, so we cannot be sure that it had not developed earlier.

35 See, for example, Rubruck/Jackson 2009, pp. 74–78.

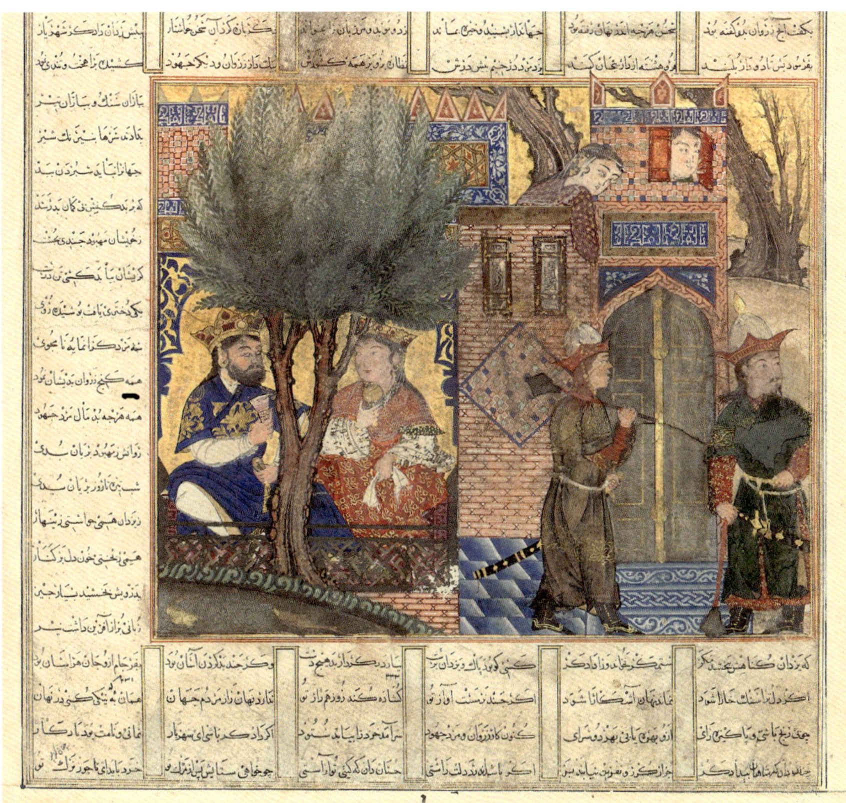

similar to those worn by the figures in the roundels and other Mosul metalwork (cat. 24, 25) rather than a Mongol hat.

Perhaps the most surprising difference is the lady's headdress: on the bag she wears a *miqna'a* but in the paintings for Rashid al-Din's *History of the Mongols* (cat. 16–18), the *khatun* and other noblewomen all wear a *boghtaq*, a tall headdress worn by Mongol married women (fig. 8).[37] Was the *boghtaq* omitted because it was too tall for the narrow panel (the Khan has lost most of the feathers from his hat)? Or because the woman is not a Mongol? Is that why her page wears a turban rather than a Mongol hat? Or was the *miqna'a* an acceptable alternative to the *boghtaq* for Mongol women during the Il-Khanid period? (See the discussion by Pfeiffer above, pp. 26–27, of a poem by Padishah Khatun in which she describes herself wearing a *miqna'a*).

It is probably unwise to read too much into the absence of a *boghtaq* on the Courtauld bag because, whether or not it was always worn by Il-Khanid ladies, it does not appear to have entered the general repertoire of artists outside Rashid al-Din's scriptorium near Tabriz. Even in illustrations to the *Shahnama*, the Persian national epic, which pre-dates the Mongol conquest by centuries and describes events of much earlier times, men are often shown in Mongol hats, boots and tunics decorated with Chinese designs and women wear Mongol dress and textiles, but, if the text does not call for something more elaborate, on their head women wear a semi-transparent *miqna'a* on its own or with a crown, diadem or headband on top. For

example in the painting of Nushirvan eating the food brought by the sons of Mahbud (fig. 50), the king wears a contemporary Mongol tunic and crown and the two men to the right wear Mongol tunics, boots and hats, whereas the three women wear a *miqna'a* (the seated lady wears hers with a crown on top). Soudavar has suggested that the illustration also has a contemporary interpretation and depicts the plot to poison the Il-Khanid Khan Arghun. He identifies the lady as Tughachaq Khatun, who would certainly have been eligible to wear a *boghtaq*.[38] There are a few depictions of *boghtaq*s on metalwork but they are all misunderstood. A *boghtaq* is worn by an Il-Khanid lady on a basin in the Victoria and Albert Museum (fig. 41) but the *boghtaq* has lost its circular peacock feathers and acquired instead a small fountain of ordinary feathers and an unexplained projection like a handle. The lady enthroned on the Tbilisi tray

36 Surviving Mongol garments sometimes have a band of pseudo-script across the shoulders on the back, which may have evolved in response to *tiraz*: Moscow 2013, pp. 170–77.

37 See Rubruck/Jackson 2009, pp. 88–89, for a description of the way they were made and decorated.

38 Soudavar 1996, p. 117 and fig. 15.

93

(cat. 20) also wears a *boghtaq*, but she seems to be wearing it on top of a *miqnaᶜa*, as is a lady on an unpublished bowl in the British Museum, both vessels probably made in Shiraz using Il-Khanid pictorial models.[39]

The paintings of the Il-Khanid court produced for Rashid al-Din's *History of the Mongols* are heavily influenced in composition and style by eastern Asian models and demonstrate a sophistication of composition and understanding of Il-Khanid protocol and customs that are also seen in narrative illustrations to the Great Mongol *Shahnama*, attributed to a court atelier, probably also at Tabriz (fig. 50). The court scene on the bag is closer to illustrations in manuscripts attributed to various provincial workshops, which often combine a local narrative tradition with contemporary Mongol details. In scale, format and style it can be compared to the tiny horizontal illustrations in the Small *Shahnama*s, a group of manuscripts of the Persian national epic (cat. 2).[40] They both have bustling crowded compositions, usually arranged on the front plane and occupied by short figures with round faces. Frontispieces to these manuscripts traditionally included an image of the patron or ruler (often one and the same) surrounded by his court, and so their painters were aware of royal protocol, dress and furnishings, and these often make an appearance in the narrative scenes also: the painting of Zal and Rudaba includes red lacquer furniture and *nasij* or cloth of gold, the fabric most prized by the Il-Khanid elite (cat. 2).[41] The date and provenance of the Small *Shahnama*s is unresolved but current

opinion is that they date between 1300 and 1330 and were made in a provincial workshop somewhere within the western Il-Khanate.

Other provincial schools of painting show a similar mix of local tradition and imported Mongol details. Illustrated manuscripts attributed to Mosul or the Jazira[42] continued the style established since the late twelfth century, which is characterised by Saljuq Turkic physiognomies and dress and a liking for strong coloured backgrounds, particularly red. The influence of this style continued well into the Il-Khanid period, which saw the introduction of Mongol figures, costumes and motifs, and a move from Arabic into Persian illustrated texts (cat. 34, figs. 16, 18). Manuscripts illustrated in this style have been attributed to Mosul on the grounds of likely patronage rather than of textual evidence. Suggested patrons include the ruler of Mosul Badr al-Din Lu'lu' (d. 1259) (figs. 25, 28) and a governor of Mosul under Il-Khanid rule, Fakhr al-Din ᶜIsa b. Ibrahim the Christian (d. 1303), who is known to have been a bibliophile.[43] The artist who provided a model for the court scene on the bag probably came from one of these provincial schools rather than an atelier in the Il-Khanid capital.

During the Il-Khanid period, an interest in paintings of historic and contemporary events and people evolved. Rashid al-Din's illustrated *Compendium of Chronicles* (fig. 22) is the most prominent instance. Less obvious are contemporary glosses on seemingly traditional compositions. Various scholars have suggested double meanings to the illustrations in the Great Mongol *Shahnama* (fig. 50) parallelling actual political

39 British Museum, ME 1938.1212,1. The candlestick inscribed to Abu Ishaq which shows a woman wearing a very peculiar *boghtaq* over a *miqnaᶜa* has been excluded from this discussion because I believe its body, where the court scenes and documentary inscription occur, to be modern work (the inlaid decoration on the neck and shoulder of the candlestick is certainly original and is amongst the finest of all fourteenth-century work): Allan and Maddison 2002, pp. 34–39.

40 The seminal work on the Small *Shahnama*s is Simpson 1979.

41 For a recent survey of the frontispieces see Simpson 2006.

42 For painting, the Jazira is understood as the lands between the Tigris and Euphrates in northern Mesopotamia, bounded to the south-west by Syria and including the cities of Mosul, Mardin and Diyarbakır.

43 Carboni 1992, especially pp. 533–37; Fitzherbert 2001 and 2013, especially pp. 404–06; and Contadini 2012, especially pp. 149–51.

events and personalities of the Il-Khanid court.[44] Simpson has suggested that even the frontispieces of manuscripts produced in provincial centres, typically images of enthroned rulers surrounded by their court, could be "transformed, through the addition of specific details, from formulaic scenes of homage into representations of special occasions or events" such as a visiting delegation bearing gifts.[45]

The court scene on the bag is not a formal enthronement image because the format is horizontal rather than vertical. The distinction between vertical, often double-page enthronement images (cat. 16, figs. 16, 21) and smaller, horizontal narrative scenes (cat. 2, figs. 18, 22) was still current in manuscript illustration in the early fourteenth century (narrative scenes became increasingly vertical through the fourteenth century). Inlaid metalwork respected the distinction between hieratic (vertical) and narrative (horizontal) images seen in illustrated manuscripts but was wedded to a layout based on roundels and panels, so enthronements were placed in roundels, the most vertical space available. A traditional enthronement could have been placed in the large roundel on the front of the bag, but instead the designer chose the horizontal format of a narrative scene. Furthermore, the couple sit on a low dais rather than a throne and there are none of the usual trappings of enthronements such as angels to indicate the divine right to rule (compare the scene on the Tbilisi tray, cat. 20). Animated gestures indicating speech and emphatic actions, particularly the courtier proffering the

bowl and spoon to the couple, all create an immediacy, as if the viewer has interrupted an event at a particular moment in time. The presence of the bag in the scene is significant. If it is supposed to represent the Courtauld bag itself, then the woman should represent its real owner accompanied by her husband and attendants. Who are they?

Images of a man (ruler or nobleman) surrounded by his courtiers are common at all periods. Images of a man enthroned or seated alongside his consort are much rarer, even in the Mongol period.[46] The Khan and Khatun appear together in three different types of illustration in Rashid al-Din's *History of the Mongols* – the enthronement scenes (cat. 16), the small images that head up the genealogical tables of each ruler and his family (fig. 7) and sometimes in the illustrations to the main events that occurred during the reign of each Khan (cat. 17).[47] In almost all of the images the Khatun holds a pomegranate and when she does not it is held instead by one of her attendants. The pomegranate is an ancient symbol of fertility and its presence in these images illustrates the obsessive concern of the Il-Khanids for the continuation of the dynasty and the royal blood line. The presence of the Khatun alongside the Khan in the small images carries the same message, even without a pomegranate, as they appear at the top of the genealogical tables. On the other hand there are no surviving images which can be positively identified as a non-royal man seated alongside his consort – which is perhaps not surprising if the women appear in these images because they are the

44 Soudavar 1996; Hillenbrand 1996; Grabar and Blair 1980.
45 Simpson 2006, especially p. 238.
46 Wright 2006, p. 260.
47 Ruhrdanz 1997, pp. 297–98.

guardians of the royal blood line. This may be just an accident of survival but the evidence, such as it is, suggests that the couple on the bag are likely to be royal.

Even if we could be sure that they are royal, it will probably never be possible to identify the couple on the bag. The Il-Khans all had numerous wives, and we cannot exclude the possibility that other royals, many of whom were independently powerful, were also depicted in this way. Sati Beg Khanum, daughter of Öljeitü, who was briefly an Il-Khan (or Sultan) in her own right, and married to the powerful Amir Chupan and later to two 'puppet khans' is just one example of a number of royal women who could be candidates for the lady on the bag.[48]

Scale is a traditional way of indicating status. In the illustrations for *The History of the Mongols*, the royal couple are considerably larger than their courtiers and attendants (cat. 16 and 17). On the bag, the couple are also much bigger than their attendants, indeed they both have to lean inwards to fit within the space, even though they are seated, whereas their smaller attendants stand erect. But there is another figure who is as big as they are, although his size is disguised by his stance – the kneeling courtier. Separated from the attendants behind him by the table, he has a beard suggesting that he is an older man of some authority. He has a hat of the same design as the seated man and he wears a bag on his belt, a mark of status. His kneeling position and outstretched arms proffering the bowl to the royal couple, are reminiscent of Christian iconography in which the patron of a church holds out a model of it to Christ or the Virgin. Such imagery would have been familiar in Mosul, which had a large Christian population. Could this be the person who commissioned the bag?

The Mongol court was peripatetic, travelling from one area to another for military or agricultural reasons or just for pleasure. The various regions of the Il-Khanate were overseen by a *shihna*, a Mongol official, alongside a local governor. If the court was expected, the *shihna* and governor would have made preparations for hunting and other festivities and ordered gifts ready for the arrival of the royal party. The decoration on the bag should, as was usual for inlaid metalwork, be seen as an iconographic unit. The musicians, drinkers and huntsmen suggest that the court scene depicts the sort of drinking bout that would follow the hunting expeditions that were so popular with the Mongol court. Like the paintings discussed above, the decoration on the bag may have been designed to work on two levels. Superficially it was an object depicting activities associated with the Mongol court, but the bag and the main players within the scene could also be identified with the real bag and the real individuals that were participants in the particular event at which the bag was presented. It should not surprise us that neither the owner nor the event is mentioned in the inscription. Il-Khanid objects are only occasionally inscribed with their owner's name and there is no reason to think ladies' bags ever were – if only because most of them were made from fabric. Illustrations in manuscripts were often untitled: the textual context was enough to identify them.

48 Öljeitü had twelve wives, according to Qashani 1969, pp. 7–8, and Abu Saʿid had six, according to Hafiz-e Abru, Dhail-e Jamiʿ al-tawarikh, British Library ms. Or. 2885, fols. 391v–92r. I am grateful to Charles Melville and Judith Pfeiffer for this information.

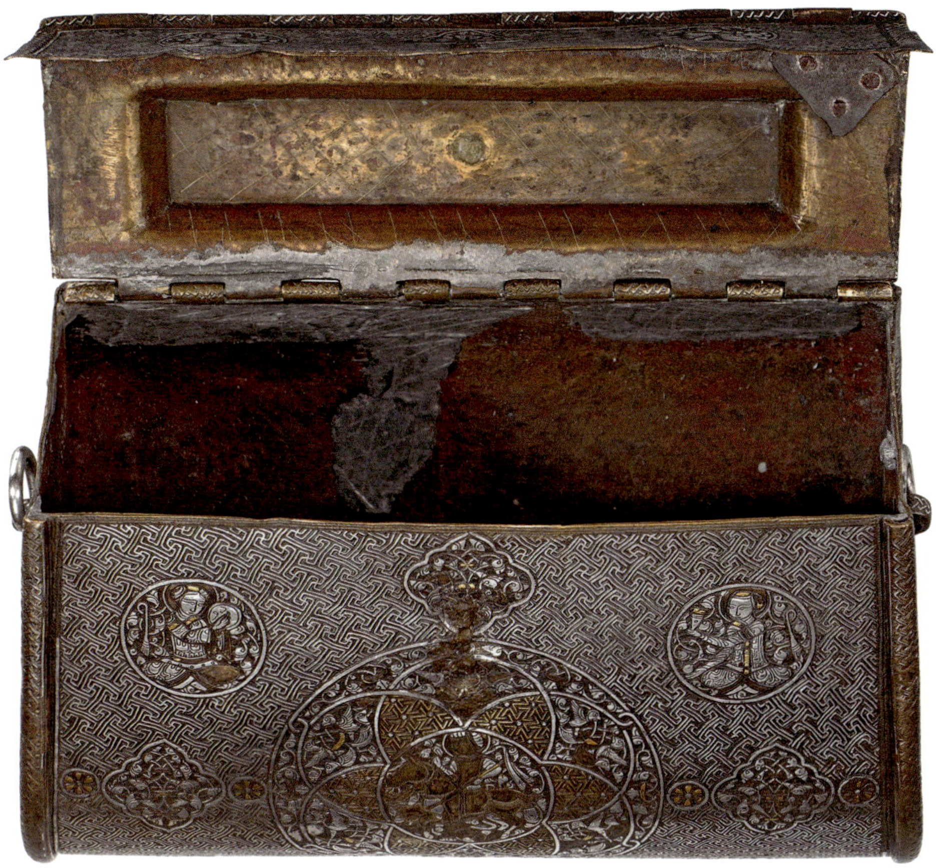

Similarly, the context within which the bag was presented would have clarified its iconography.[49]

A Mongol courtier would have known that a bag would be an appropriate gift for an Il-Khanid noblewoman. Perhaps the Courtauld bag was a gift presented to a Khatun or royal princess during a visit of the court to Mosul by the Mongol *shihna*, shown kneeling before the royal couple, and he was intentionally highlighting one of the skills for which his city was renowned.[50] That would explain the lack of wear on the reverse of the bag: like many diplomatic gifts, it may not have been appreciated and rarely, if ever, used.

Later work

Various changes have been made to the bag, which suggests that at some later date it was adapted for use as a lockable jewellery box. A ring was attached to the top of the lid which has left a small hole (now filled) and damaged the decorated area between the couple in the court scene. A square of solder on the interior base indicates that a metal compartment was soldered inside the bag. The interior is crisscrossed with incised lines. These lines are not original because they cut through later solder; they were probably done to help a later textile lining adhere to the surface of the brass. A rectangular hole was cut in the flap and its edges reinforced by attaching a frame of metal with four rivets, which remain visible inside. A corresponding hole was made in the wall of the bag just below the hole in the flap and a plaque was attached inside (five rivets remain and the surface is slightly dented). This plaque probably secured a metal loop which passed through the rectangular hole in the flap so that the bag could be locked with a padlock.[51]

49 There have been other attempts to connect the iconography on objects with specific events: see Holod 2012, Ward 2005, Abouseif 1989.

50 See Melville above, p. 21, for documented visits of the Il-Khanid court to Mosul/Iraq.

51 A note in the Courtauld Gallery Archives written by Kenneth M. Turner, Restorer and Conservator, dated 9 November 1965 lists the work he was to undertake for the Courtauld: "Remove ring at top of casket; Remove hasp from front; Remove hasp pin". According to Robinson (1967, p. 169) the removed ring was silver, but it may have been silvered copper like the suspension rings, and they might all three have been added when the bag was converted to a lockable box.

Conservation

DIANA HEATH

The Courtauld bag required carefully considered treatment in preparation for this exhibition, providing the opportunity for visual and microscopic examination. This enabled a better understanding of the original techniques used to create the bag and of several later interventions.

The overall structure of the bag was deemed sound, albeit repaired and altered over the centuries. There are multiple small dents, and parts of the hinges are flattened so the flap has to be handled carefully owing to distortion. Inevitably there is loss of inlay and the original strap is missing. These aspects were left unaltered as the 'historic' patch repairs remain physically stable and the lead solder uncorroded. The remaining silver and gold inlay appears well adhered and secure in spite of the damage and torn edges which are the result of age and varying uses.

Identification of the metals was recently carried out using X-ray fluorescence (XRF): the body of the bag was confirmed as brass.* The whole surface had developed a dull appearance with irregular patches of blue/black tarnish on the silver and darkening of the gold and copper alloy, caused by accretions of dirt and discoloured coatings.

Loss of gold and silver is apparent where there are dark, brown areas of 'oxidised' brass – where it has been 'exposed' to the atmosphere over a long period. However the underlying tool and 'keying' marks are visible, revealing the different preparation techniques of the brass prior to inlay and decoration.

Most of the original, black organic infill is lost from the recesses. In certain areas a light brown substance is visible. Examination shows it to be partly modern wax with polish residue, which, when deposited in the

Details of roundel with harpist, before and after conservation

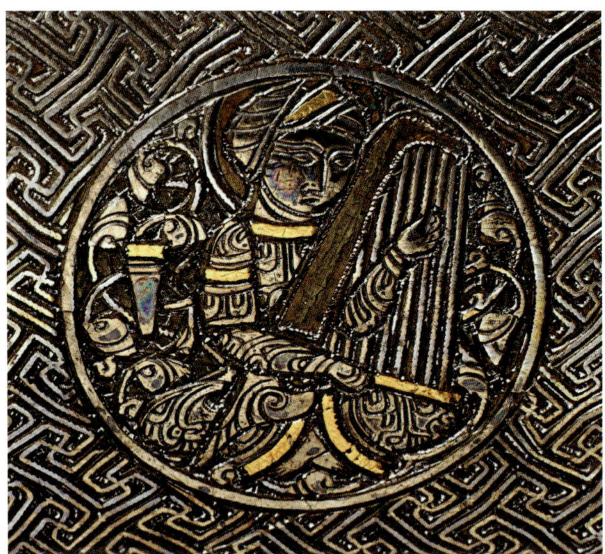
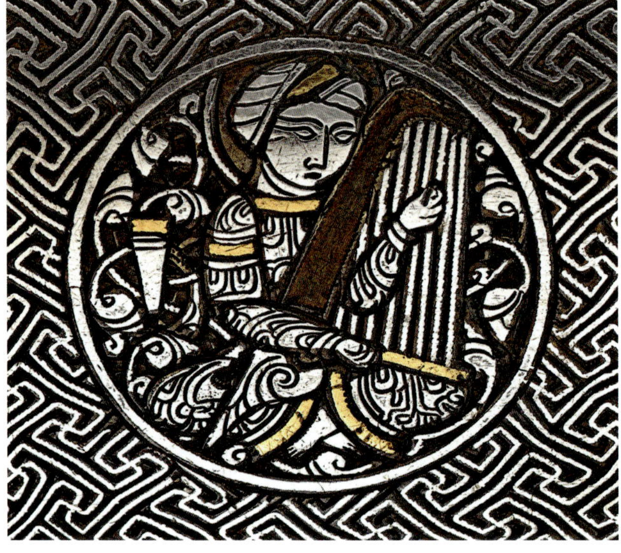

crevices, causes corrosion of the brass.

Records indicate that the bag was treated in 1966, when repair and surface treatment were carried out, possibly using an electrolytic process and polishing pastes. A nitro cellulose-based lacquer was apparently applied over the whole object. The practice is still current, but after forty-eight years the old lacquer has degraded and thus is no longer protective. Also in 1966 a ring on the centre of the lid (a later addition) was removed, the hole was filled and another patch of metal was inserted into the left side. Several lead patches from an earlier repair phase on the centre of the scene on the lid and on the central horseman on the front of the bag appear to have been toned in with powdered gold and brown resinous material.

After trials to check the solubility of the various materials on the bag, it was decided to remove the dirt and the discoloured, embrittled lacquer with swabs of Acetone, avoiding areas of retouch. Unstable modern wax and polish residue, under which there were sometimes crumbly green, copper corrosion products, was removed using fine wood and mother-of-pearl sticks and selected solvents on swabs. Selected hydro-carbon solvents removed any residue. This procedure was carried out under a binocular microscope. Silver and brass tarnish was removed or reduced with small pieces of soft, mineral-impregnated synthetic rubbers and impregnated silver cloth, and any residue locally removed.

This removed potentially corrosive material in the form of dirt, old polish, residue and coatings, as well as active corrosion products and tarnish which cause micro pitting of the metal surfaces. To prevent tarnish and corrosion re-forming during long term display, it was decided to coat the external surface in a colourless, nitro cellulose lacquer Frigilene*, carefully applied using sable hair brushes. The interior was waxed with microcrystalline wax. The treatment has succeeded in enlivening the surface and blending areas of previous repair, thus re-emphasising the contrast between the reflective metals and dark ground while maintaining the integrity of this unique bag.

NOTE ON THE TECHNICAL
* ANALYSIS OF METAL ALLOYS
Lucia Burgio, Aviva Burnstock, Diana Heath and Douglas Maclennan

The metal alloys of the bag were tested using X-ray fluorescence spectroscopy (XRF), a non-invasive technique that characterises the elemental composition. Analysis was performed using a Bruker Tracer III-SD (Rh-anode) portable XRF run at 40keV, 11.9μA for 60 seconds without filters, taking measurements at several points over the body of the bag and inside the lid. The x-ray beam of the instrument interacts with an area of approximately 6mm at the surface and to a depth of approximately 100 micrometers, with some variation depending on the elemental composition of the metal. Semi quantitative analysis was achieved by calibration using a set of standard alloys of copper and zinc (with trace elements less than 0.11%).

In almost all the points on the body and the lid, copper and zinc were the predominant elements and in most areas any impurities present were estimated to be less than 2% of the overall alloy. The ratio of copper to zinc on the main body of the bag averages 87 to 13 (+/- 3), which is high but compatible with alloys of the period from western Asia (Craddock *et al.* 1990; Ward *et al.* 1995; Attil, Chase and Jett 1985). The side fixings, which were cast, differ from this in their elemental composition. The repair on the proper left bottom corner of the lid, which the documentation suggests is dated to 1966, has a copper to zinc ratio of 72 to 28 (+/-3), which is fully consistent with modern manufacture.

This preliminary examination is part of a wider XRF investigative project to analyse comparative metalwork. We intend to follow this up by a more detailed technical publication.

2

Zal visits Rudaba in her palace, from the First Small *Shahnama*

Iraq or Iran, 1300–30
Written surface H: 15.5 cm, W: 12.5 cm
Dublin, Chester Beatty Library, Per 104.5

ILLUSTRATED VERSIONS of the *Shahnama* (Book of Kings) completed *c.* 1010 by Abu'l-Qasim Firdawsi became popular during the Il-Khanid period. This page is from one of a group of illustrated *Shahnama*s known, because of their size, as 'the Small *Shahnama*s',[1] which are amongst the earliest surviving illustrated *Shahnama* texts.[2] They are very heavily illustrated (one painting every two or three folios) and may have been produced for educational purposes, much as copies of Rashid al-Din's manuscripts were intended for dispatch to different cities each year (see cat. 16–18).[3]

This illustration is from the love story of Zal, the white-haired warrior from the court of Shah Manuchehr of Iran, and Rudaba, beautiful daughter of his enemy, the king of Kabul.[4] With the connivance of her Turkish maids, Rudaba arranged for Zal to visit her secretly one evening. The lovers are shown together on the edge of a couch: she is on his lap and they have their arms around each other's shoulders in an intimate embrace as he hands her a circular fruit, probably a pomegranate, symbol of fertility and beauty. Zal has removed his sword, which rests against the cushion. Rudaba wears an elaborate winged crown with a row of red stones and a blue diadem set in the front. Locks of her long hair – so long that she offered it to Zal to climb up the building – fall to the ground. Her cheeks are "blushed the colour of pomegranate blossoms".

The chamber was decorated specially for the occasion by Rudaba and her maids with a red carpet, hanging curtains in different colours and designs with contrasting linings, and gold trinkets hanging from the short red pelmet. Immediately above the couple is a gold lotus and in front of them a silver vase filled with white flowers on a silver tray (both now tarnished black). The high back of the couch might have afforded the couple some privacy but two maids peer over it at them. Two other attendants proffer them bowls of delicacies. One holds out a red bowl, probably filled with wine from the tall gold bottles behind her on the red table, and the other carries a wide silver bowl filled with fruit or sweetmeats. The attendants have their hair pinned up by golden ornaments in eastern Asian style; their robes are very fine, marking them out as companions and friends rather than servants. The text describes Rudaba decorating the room with Chinese textiles and it seems that the artist decided to depict contemporary Chinese or Mongol fabrics such as *nasij* (cloth of gold), as worn by the Mongol elite (figs. 48 and 49), for the textiles in the miniature are densely patterned with gold lotus and leaves.

None of the colophons of the Small *Shahnama*s have survived and so their date and place of production are unknown. Simpson suggested that they might have been produced in Baghdad in the late thirteenth century but other scholars favour a later date, perhaps 1320–30, at Baghdad or another Il-Khanid city.[5] They are unlikely to have been produced at a court atelier as they are stylistically distinct from royal manuscripts, such as the Great Mongol *Shahnama* (fig. 50), which favoured a new style with larger illustrations and a vertical rather than a horizontal format with a high viewpoint

NOTES

1 For a comprehensive study of the Small *Shahnama*s see Simpson 1979.
2 Scenes from the *Shahnama* are seen earlier on wall paintings, tiles and vessels. One of the medallions on the Blacas ewer (cat. 21), dated 1232, contains an image of Bahram Gur and Azada out hunting.
3 Fitzherbert 2001, pp. 366–73.
4 For an English translation of the story see Firdawsi/Davis 2007, pp. 70–103. For this illustration see Arberry and Minovi 1959–62, pp. 11–16, no. 104, pl. 4b; Simpson 1979, pl. 8; New York 2002, pp. 252–53, no. 33 and fig. 177.
5 Simpson 1979; New York 2002, pp. 252–53.

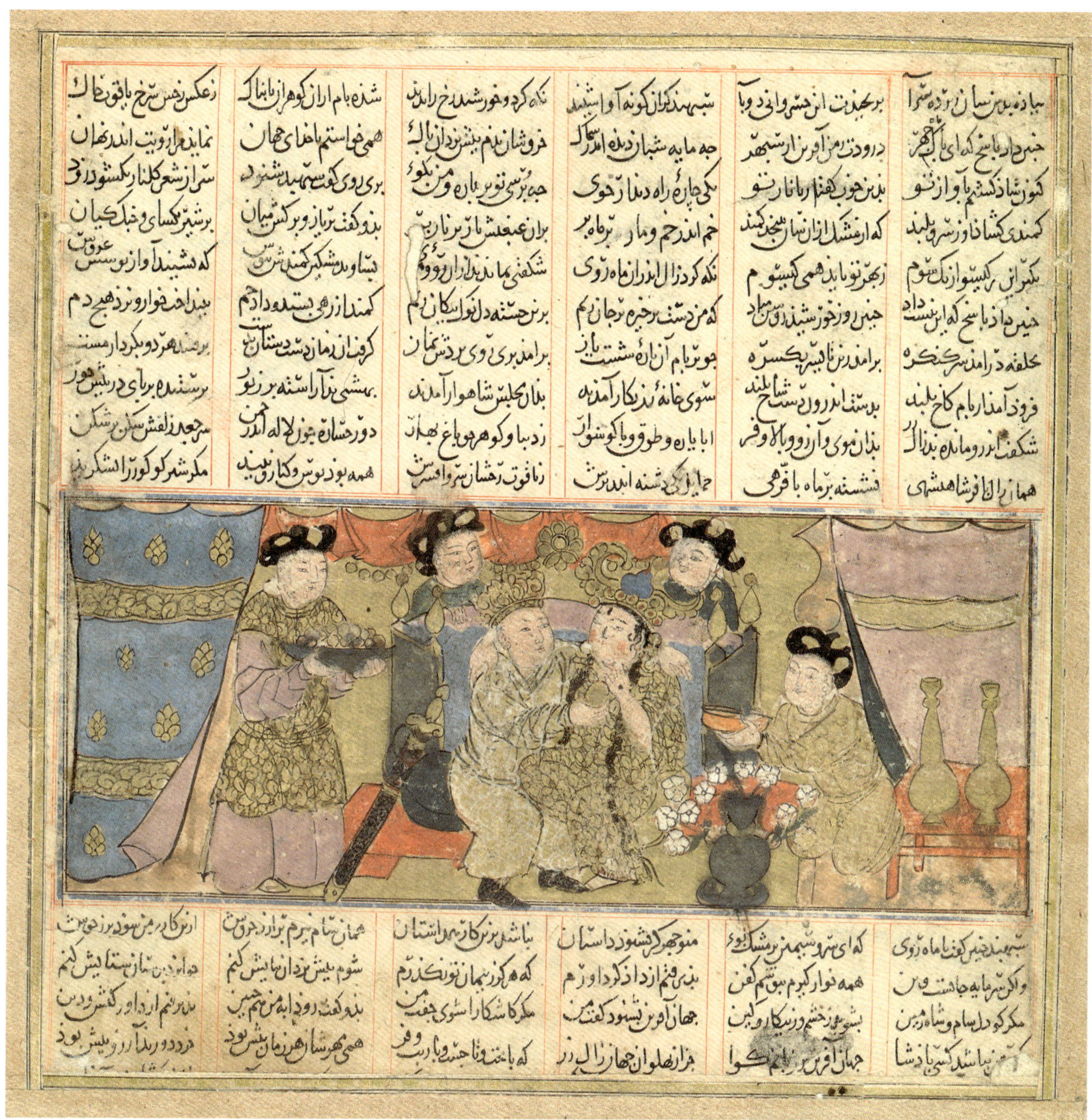

and smaller figures. The size and horizontal format of this painting, typical of the Small *Shahnama*s, was already old-fashioned, as were the proportions of the figures, which appear stunted with big heads and bodies shortened by the need to fit within the narrow space: if Zal and Rudaba stood up they would go way beyond the upper frame and Zal already has his foot over the lower one. The inclusion of Mongol ethnic types and customs and Chinese furniture and furnishings is only a veneer on a deeply traditional approach.

The size, format, scale of figures, even the mix of tradition with contemporary details in this painting, are remarkably similar to the court scene on the Courtauld bag (illustrated pp. 86–87) and suggests that, if a pictorial model was used for that court scene, it may have been composed by an artist working in a style akin to that of the Small *Shahnama*s.

3

Table

China, *c.* 1410
Red lacquer on a wood core, gold leaf
H: 28.3 cm, W: 94 cm, D: 41.2 cm
London, Victoria and Albert Museum, FE.1913-1993

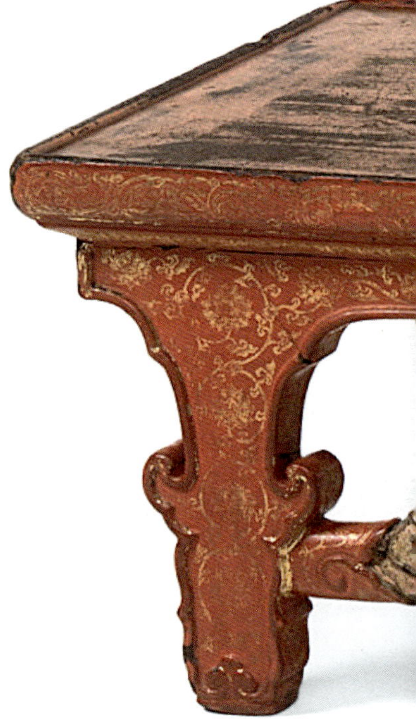

THIS CHINESE TABLE on four legs (originally with removable extensions) is remarkable for its lacquer decoration. The lacquer, the sap of the tree *rhus verniciflua*, was applied in layers to the wood base. The process took days, even months, because each layer had to dry before the next one was applied. When hard, lacquer is smooth like a modern plastic, and resistant to heat and water. Cinnabar mixed with the sap produces the red colour. When sufficient coats of lacquer had been applied to the base, it could be carved or incised. The red lacquer surface of this table was incised with scrolling blossoms and filled with gold leaf in the *qiang jin* technique. A stretcher on each long side was shaped into a leafy scroll and decorated with pigment and gilding.

Furniture in Chinese style appears regularly in paintings of Il-Khanid court scenes. The wide high-backed thrones with side panels in the two court scenes in the exhibition (cat. 16 and 17) each have a lotus at the centre and projecting finials of curling leaves; similar thrones in contemporary illustrations have dragon-headed finials. The feet of

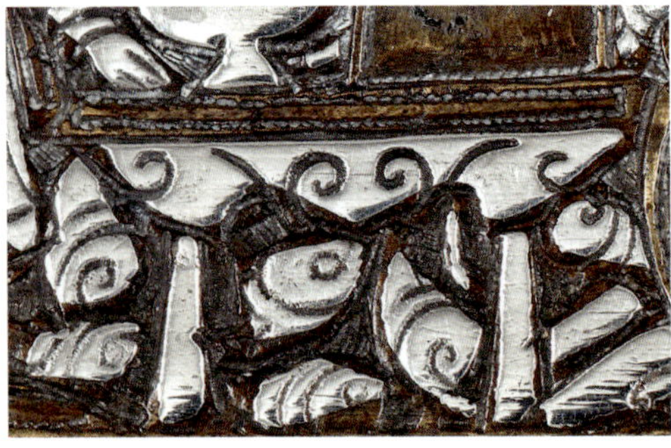

the thrones and their foot stools are also shaped like curling leaves. The double-page enthronement scene (cat. 16) also includes a box-like red table with pronounced crossbars, red benches (sat on by women at the top of the right-hand folio) and a red folding parasol stand. The elaborately carved apron beneath the tabletop on the left of the court scene on the Courtauld bag (detail below) includes lobed panels in Chinese style, as does the rather fantastical throne on the Tbilisi tray (cat. 20), which also has dragon finials.[1] The furniture seen here and in other Il-Khanid paintings and inlaid metalwork can also be parallelled in Chinese paintings of the period and has sometimes survived in miniature versions, placed in Chinese tombs.[2]

In the Il-Khanid paintings the furniture is coloured red, which suggests that it may represent Chinese lacquer. *Rhus verniciflua* only grows in eastern Asia and so, if lacquer furniture was used at the Il-Khanid court, it must have been imported from China. It is impossible to know whether the furniture depicted represents imported lacquer or local imitations in wood varnished red, but the Mongols imported huge quantities of vessels, including lacquer wares, textiles and other luxuries, from China, so it would be surprising if they were content to use imitation lacquer furniture at court.[3]

The present table is attributed to a lacquer workshop producing imperial commissions in China before the move of the capital to Beijing in 1423, and so was made long after the Courtauld bag.[4] However, it represents a tradition of lacquer furniture made in China of which earlier examples have not survived.

NOTES

1 For the development of these lobed panels from Chinese art see Rawson 1984, pp. 132–38.
2 For comparison between depictions of Il-Khanid and Chinese furniture see Rawson 1984, pp. 158–61, and figs. 140 and 141.
3 See Watson 1982 for a review of protective varnishes used in western Asia and India derived from insects (shellac or lac, which is naturally red in colour) or tree resin.
4 Low-Beer 1950.

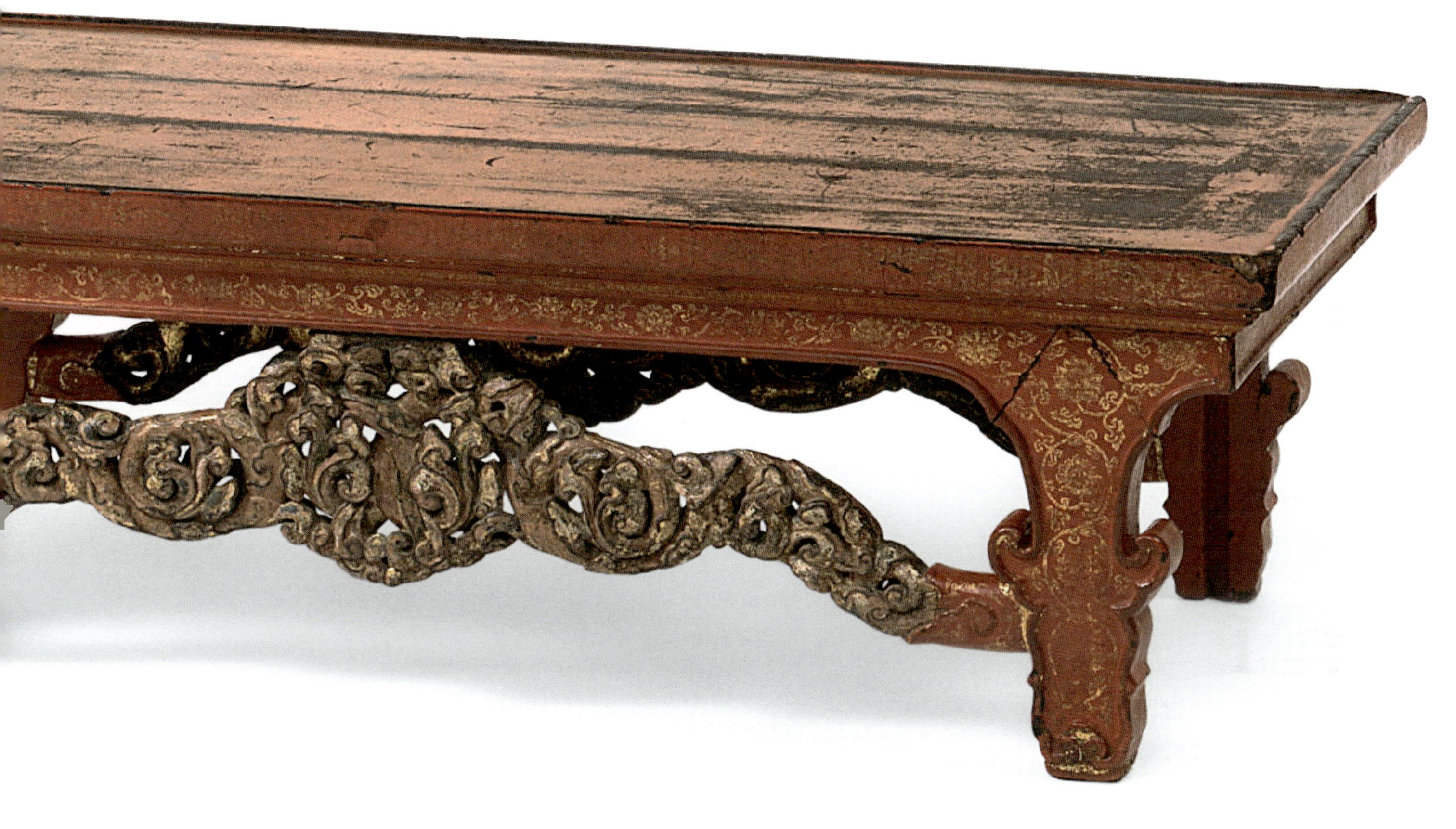

4

Bottle

Mamluk Egypt or Syria, *c.* 1330
Glass, blown, enamelled and gilded
H: 27.5 cm, Diam: 17.5 cm
London, British Museum, ME S.334

THE GLASS BOTTLE has a globular body, tall funnel neck and foot ring. The main area of the body is filled with birds amongst palmettes sketched in red enamel. The pacing lions in the roundels around the base of the neck were inspired by animal symbols used in the blazons of the early Mamluk sultans but here they are just decorative.[1] The inscription repeats a single word, 'the wise'.

The novelty of its enamelling technique made Mamluk glass highly prized and by the fourteenth century these colourful vessels were being exported across Asia as well as to Europe.[2] Mamluk titular inscriptions were replaced by inoffensive words such as 'the wise', as on the bottle here, and a range of appropriate floral and animal decoration was developed. Originally the surface of the bottle was heavily gilded but, unlike the enamels, which fused to the glass body during firing and have survived well, gilding was susceptible to abrasion and most of it has disappeared. When new, the gilding of the birds and foliage on this bottle would have resembled Mongol cloth of gold (figs. 48, 49).

Enamelled glass bottles in this shape were produced in the Mamluk empire in imitation of Chinese porcelain bottles and the lotus flowers in roundels and phoenix on the neck reflect this influence. A similar bottle, with a round body, low foot and tall funnel neck can be seen on the table in the court scene on the Courtauld bag (detail right, top) and also in two of its roundels (illustrated pp. 76, 78). The bottles could have been made from porcelain imported from China or from enamelled glass imported from the Mamluk empire.

Next to this bottle on the table is another which has no parallel in surviving vessels from the Il-Khanid period (detail right). It may have been made of leather. It is flat-based and almost straight-sided before narrowing at the shoulders and finishing with quite a wide mouth above a short neck. A handle (inlaid with gold wire) is attached just below the shoulders. An identical bottle is carried by the courtier second from right (detail right, bottom).

In the steppes, the Mongols relied on mare's milk (*kumis*) for nutrition as well as pleasure, as it became mildly alcoholic when fermented. John of Plano Carpini, who visited the Mongols in the 1240s, reported that the Mongols "have neither bread nor herbs nor vegetables nor anything else, nothing but meat …. They drink mare's milk in very great quantities if they have it; they also drink the milk of ewes, cows, goats and even camels." The bottles with carrying handles resemble milk churns and perhaps that is what they were – specialised containers for fermented milk drinks. Animal milk was only available in the steppes for about five months a year, but when the Mongols moved into Iran various stronger alcoholic drinks became available all year round – rice mead, rice ale, honey mead, red wine. Visitors to Mongol courts describe complicated apparatus which served several different drinks according to the taste of the guests present. Perhaps the different containers depicted in the court scene were meant to suggest that a variety of liquid refreshment was available to the assembled company.[3]

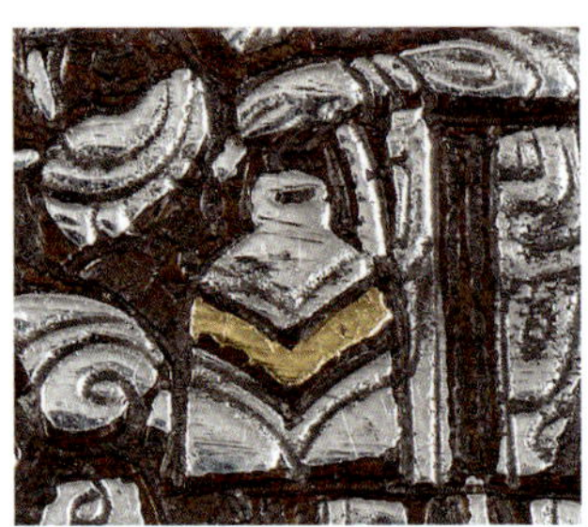

NOTES

1 Ward 1998, p. 31.
2 On the export of Mamluk glass to the Golden Horde Khanate, China and Europe see Kramarovsky 1998, Hardie 1998 and Ward 1998.
3 See Smith 2000 for Carpini and other quotations and for a account of the "dietary decadence" of the Mongols.

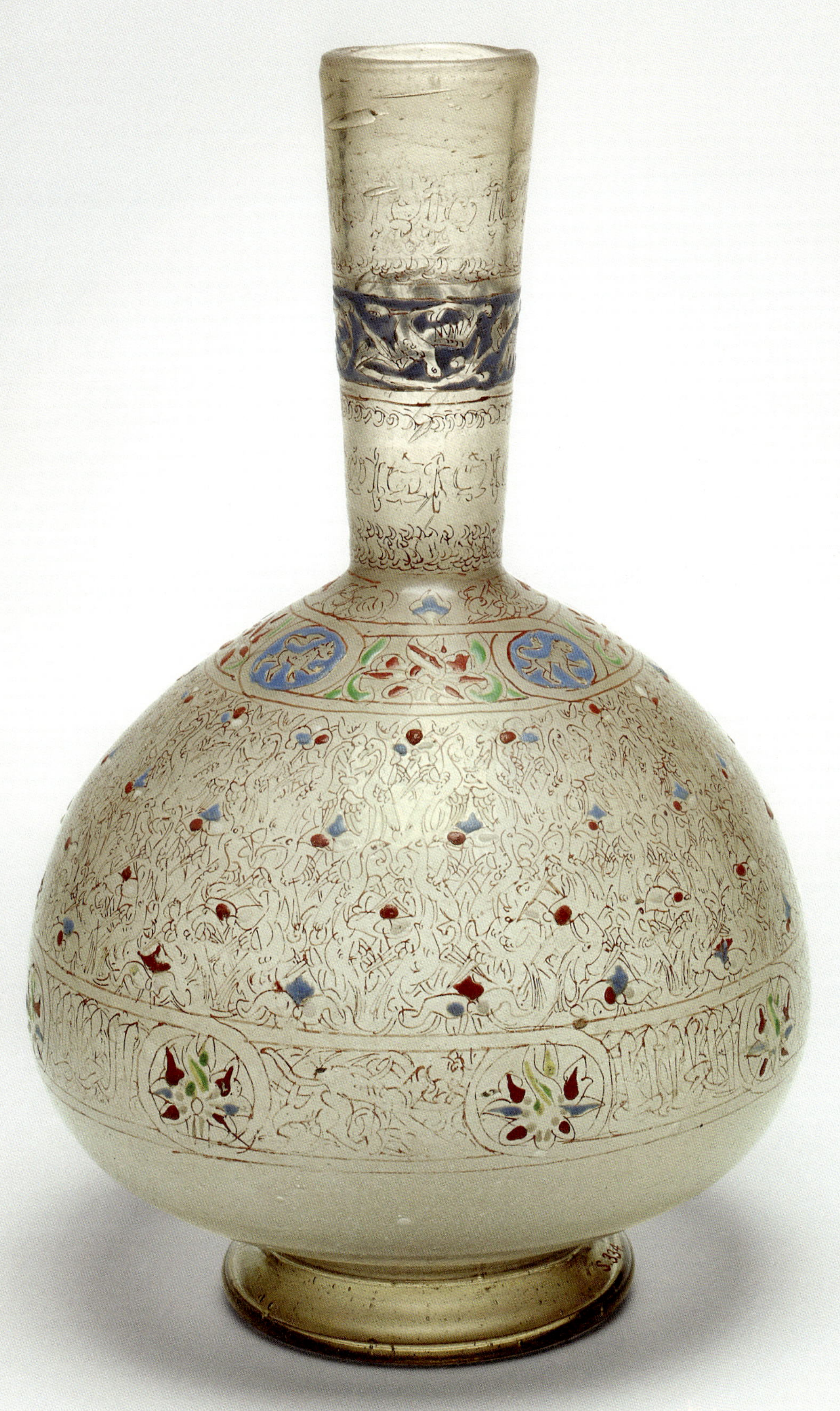

5

Pouring bowl

Western Iran or Central Asia, late 13th or early 14th century
Silver, raised, chased and gilded
H: 7 cm, L: (including spout) 21.5 cm, Diam: (bowl) 14.5 cm
London, Victoria and Albert Museum, M.194-1935

THE HEMISPHERICAL SILVER BOWL with a flat base and long curving spout was hammered to shape. The bowl was chased with a scrolling leafy stem around the rim and a leafy plant in a roundel inside, both on a punched ground; the decorated areas were then gilded. Chased below the spout at a later date is the woman's name 'Mihnaz'.

The lightness of sheet silver and gold was suited to the nomadic life of the Mongols. Numerous silver-gilt bowls, with and without spouts, have been excavated in the territories of the Golden Horde Khanate, which was ruled over by the descendants of Chinggis Khan's second son, Jochi.[1] An almost identical scroll appears on a gold cup with a dragon handle in the Hermitage Museum, which may have been acquired in Siberia.[2] Similar bowls were probably also made in the Il-Khanid regions. According to the registers of the Victoria and Albert Museum, this bowl, bought in Paris in 1935, was said to have been dug up at Hamadan in western Iran, which was well known for its goldsmiths' market in the fourteenth century.[3] Baer attributed the bowl to the twelfth century, but its decoration, especially the sinuous plant in the roundel inside, derives from East Asian designs unknown in Iran before the Mongol invasion.[4] Similar designs appear on Mongol textiles of the fourteenth century (figs. 48, 49).

Spouted bowls of this type were filled from a larger vessel (or used as a ladle to scoop up the liquid) and then used to pour liquid into a smaller bottle or drinking cup or beaker as required. They sometimes appear in illustrations stored next to a large vessel ready for use. In an image of Daqiqi killed by his slave in a palace interior, a large pottery jar in a wood stand is set within a tiled niche with a pouring bowl on a shelf above it.[5] In a famous painting of revelry in Saʿdi's *Bustan*, dated 893/1488, a spouted bowl is seen in action: it is being filled with wine from a large unglazed pottery jar while simultaneously funnelling the liquid into a long-necked glass bottle.[6]

In the court scene on the Courtauld bag (illustrated pp. 86–87), the attendant (second from left) has one hand touching the base of a bottle on the table as if he has just put it down, and is holding a spouted bowl aloft towards the couple on the dais, as if it were going to replenish the liquid in the beaker held by the man (detail above).

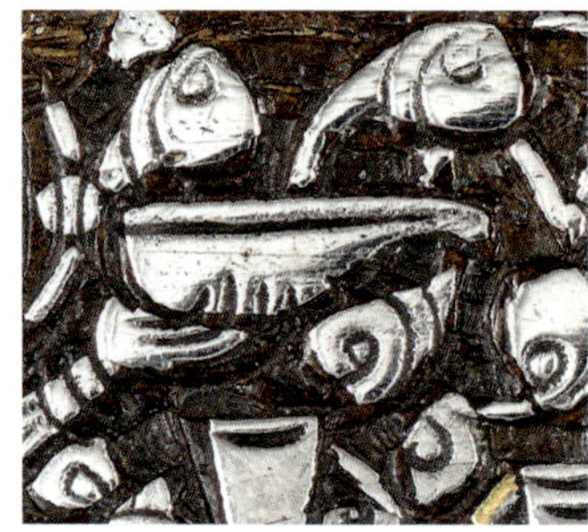

NOTES

1 A similar silver spouted bowl was discovered in the Crimea in 1967. It belonged to a Mongol official and had been hidden together with other possessions of his, including a Mongol passport (*pai-tsa*), in the early fourteenth century; see *Order of Lenin State Historical Museum* 1980.

2 New York 2002, no. 155, pp. 276–77 and fig. 197.

3 Ward 1993, p. 86.

4 Baer 1983, pp. 118–20 and fig. 96.

5 Topkapı Palace Library Ms H.2153, fol. 112r, illustrated in Soudavar 1996, fig. 45.

6 Illustrated in Washington 1989, pp. 260–61.

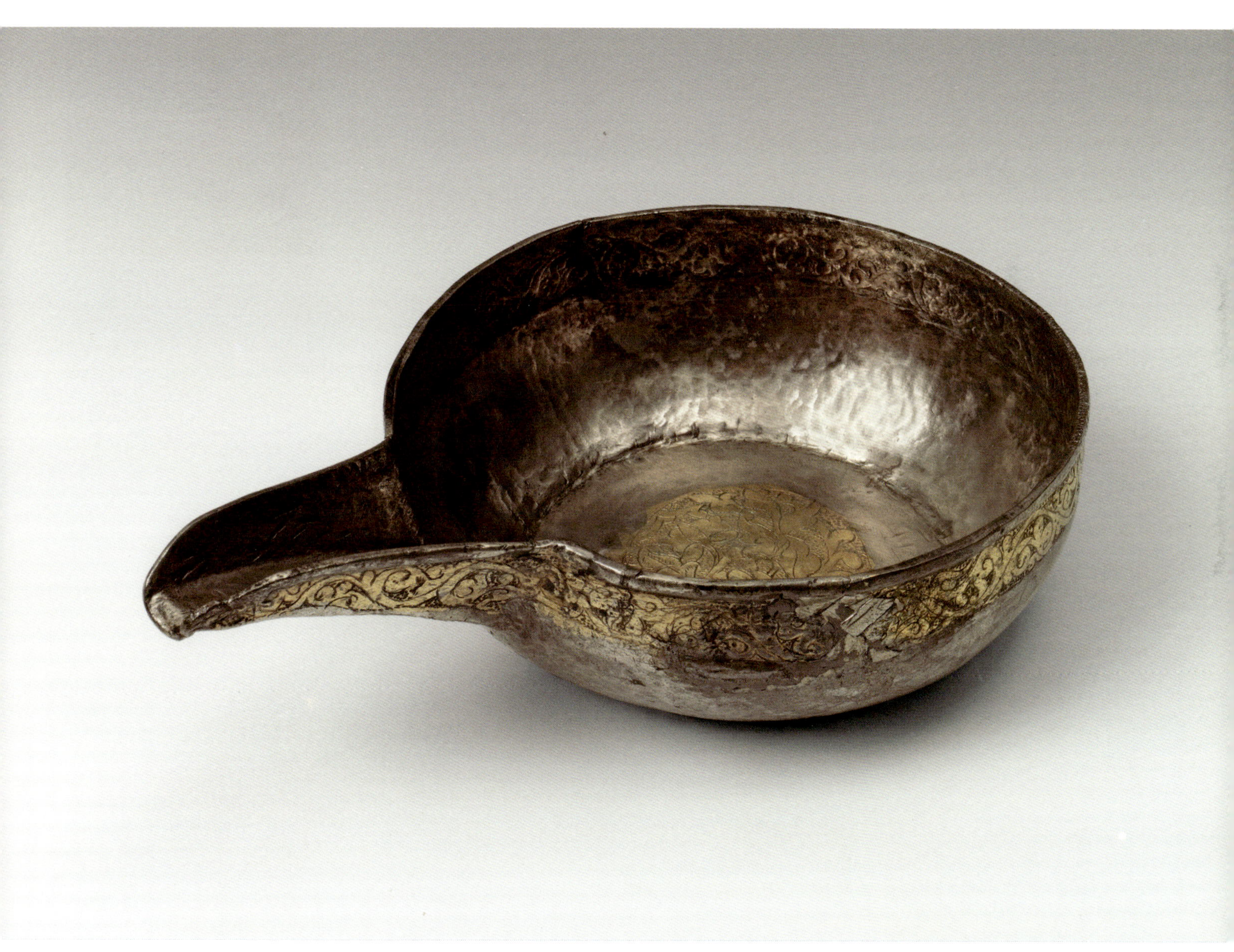

6

Bag

Afghanistan, 12th or 13th century
Leather, press-moulded and painted
H: 10.1 cm, W: 8.2 cm
Copenhagen, David Collection, 14/2001

THE BAG was made from two pieces of
leather stitched together down the sides,
the back continuing to form a flap in front,
which was secured by a button and loop.[1]
The design on both sides consists of a roundel
with animals and birds within and around it
other animals including harpies and sphinxes.
The design on the flap is a continuation of
the design below and the button was placed
at the centre of the roundel. The interior was
lined with thinner leather and paper, placed
between the lining and the outer leather. Later
the bag was re-stitched with beige cotton
thread. The motif of three hares running in a
circle with only three ears between them, in
the roundel on the back, was a popular motif
on thirteenth-century metalwork in Mosul,
and was probably inspired by similar designs
on metalwork from Afghanistan.

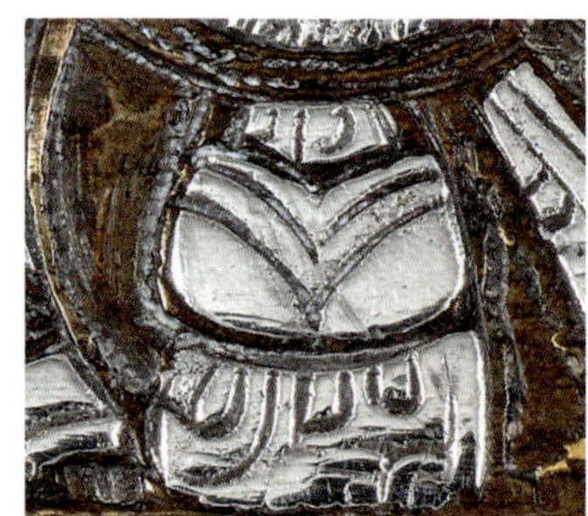

This is one of several small leather bags
that have been found in Afghanistan along
with carved stone moulds, used in their
production. A mural painting in the audience
hall at Lashkari Bazar (first half of the twelfth
century) depicts male courtiers with belts
from which such bags are suspended.[2] There
are likely to have been leather workshops
producing similar bags across western Asia,
because small bags are frequently worn by
noblemen in paintings and inlaid metalwork
from western Iran and northern Iraq
(see cat. 16 and 18, and the figure beside
the throne in fig. 22).

The kneeling courtier in the court scene
on the Courtauld bag (illustrated pp. 86–87)
wears a bag like this one suspended by two
straps from his belt (detail right).

NOTES

1 For a full description and
discussion of this bag and other
similar bags see Folsach 2004.
2 For images of stone moulds and
the painting at Lashkari Bazar see
again Folsach 2004.

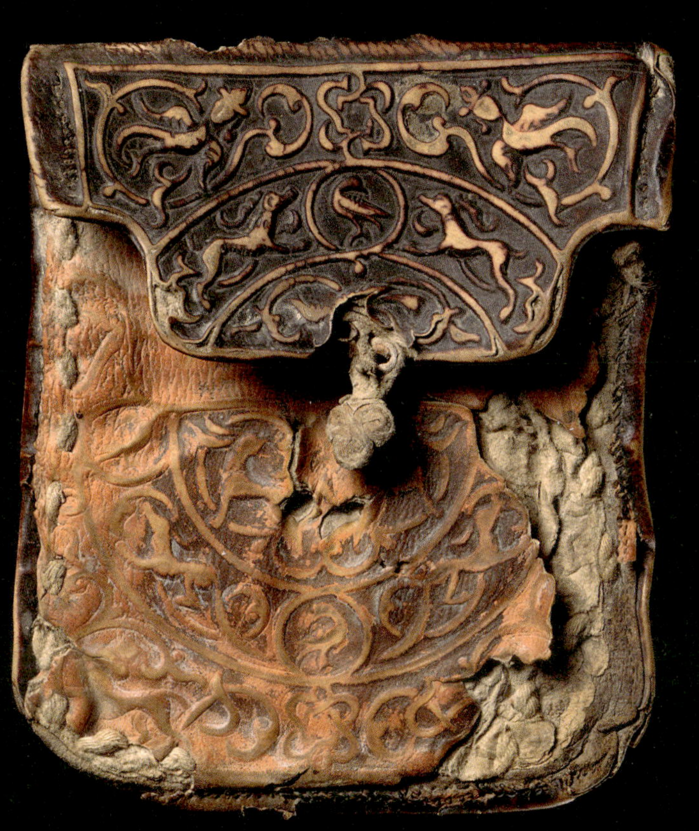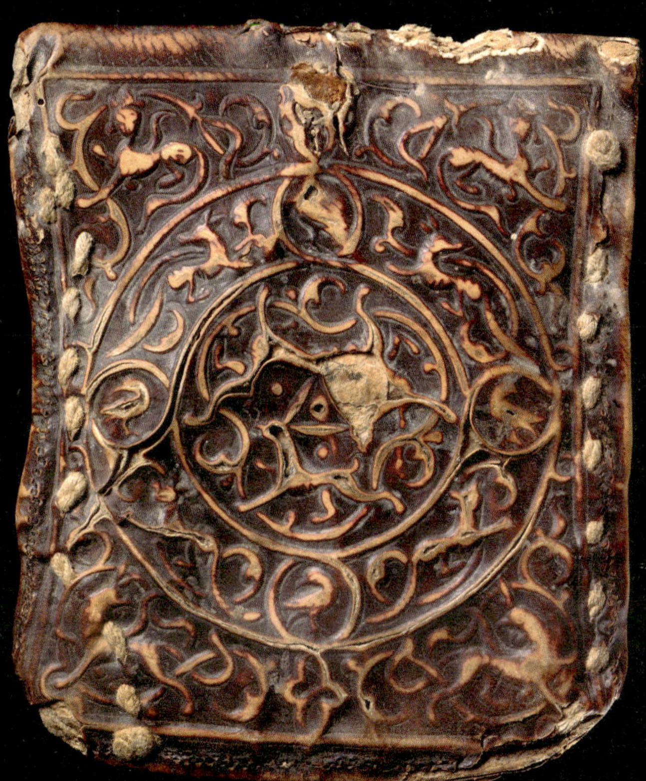

7–9

Spoon

Khurasan, early 13th century
High tin bronze, forged and inlaid with silver
L: *c.* 27 cm
London, Nasser D. Khalili Collection of Islamic Art, MTW 834

Dish

Khurasan, 13th century
Brass, raised, engraved and inlaid with silver
Diam: 30.45 cm
London, Nasser D. Khalili Collection of Islamic Art, MTW 557

Bowl

Golden Horde Khanate, 14th century
Silver, raised, chased and gilded
H: 7.5 cm, Diam: 11.5 cm
Copenhagen, David Collection, 47/1979

IN THE COURT SCENE of the Courtauld bag (illustrated pp. 86–87) a kneeling courtier with outstretched arms proffers a bowl to the seated couple. The bowl, on a low flaring foot, is of silver with a gold rim; it sits on a flat gold dish (the gold inlaid line indicating the profile of the dish has fallen out) and has a gold spoon with curving handle inside it ready for use (detail right). This arrangement of bowl, spoon and dish is often seen in paintings. For example, an attendant offers Humayun refreshment after her wedding night from a bowl on a dish and the bowl has a spoon inside it with a long curving handle (cat. 19).

Here the high tin bronze spoon (cat. 7) with long curving handle for serving within a bowl is inlaid with silver with a plait along the handle and a long-necked bird in a cartouche in the bowl of the spoon. The ladle shape would have made it suitable for sipping a fairly liquid food. A spoon with a ladle bowl is used to feed the mother of Muhammad after his birth in a painting in the *Compendium of Chronicles*.[1]

High tin bronze was a popular alternative to gold and silver for table wares because when new it was silvery gold in colour and, the high percentage of tin in the alloy (20% or more) protected it from corrosion and the unpleasant metallic taste of most copper alloys. It was less expensive than precious metal, but it was not cheap, because the tin had to be imported. High tin bronze was also extremely difficult to work. The tin made the alloy brittle when cold (the handle of this spoon is broken in two places) and so the spoon would have been forged to shape at red-hot heat. The inlaying was also problematic as the hard metal had to be engraved while hot or, if worked when cold, chipped with a sharp chisel like stone (chip marks can be seen, especially in the spoon bowl), which risked cracking the metal. As the product of very specialised workshops, items made of high tin bronze, especially when inlaid with silver, were treasured.

At least one workshop specialising in high tin bronze with inlaid decoration

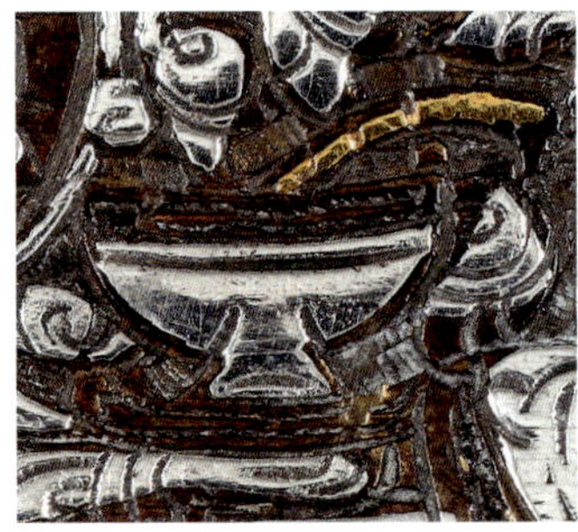

NOTES

1 New York 2002, p. 112, fig. 130, and no. 6, pp. 245–46.

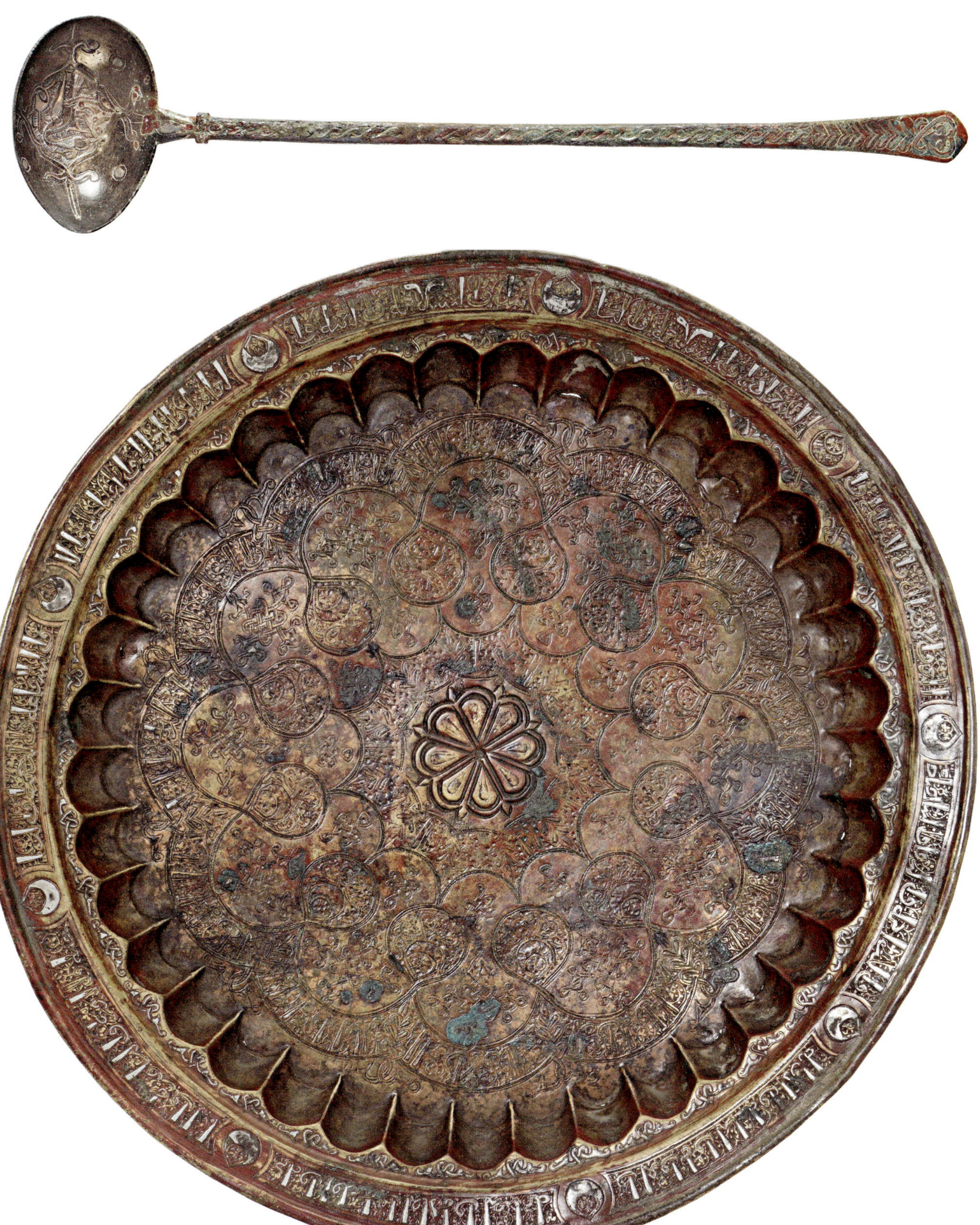

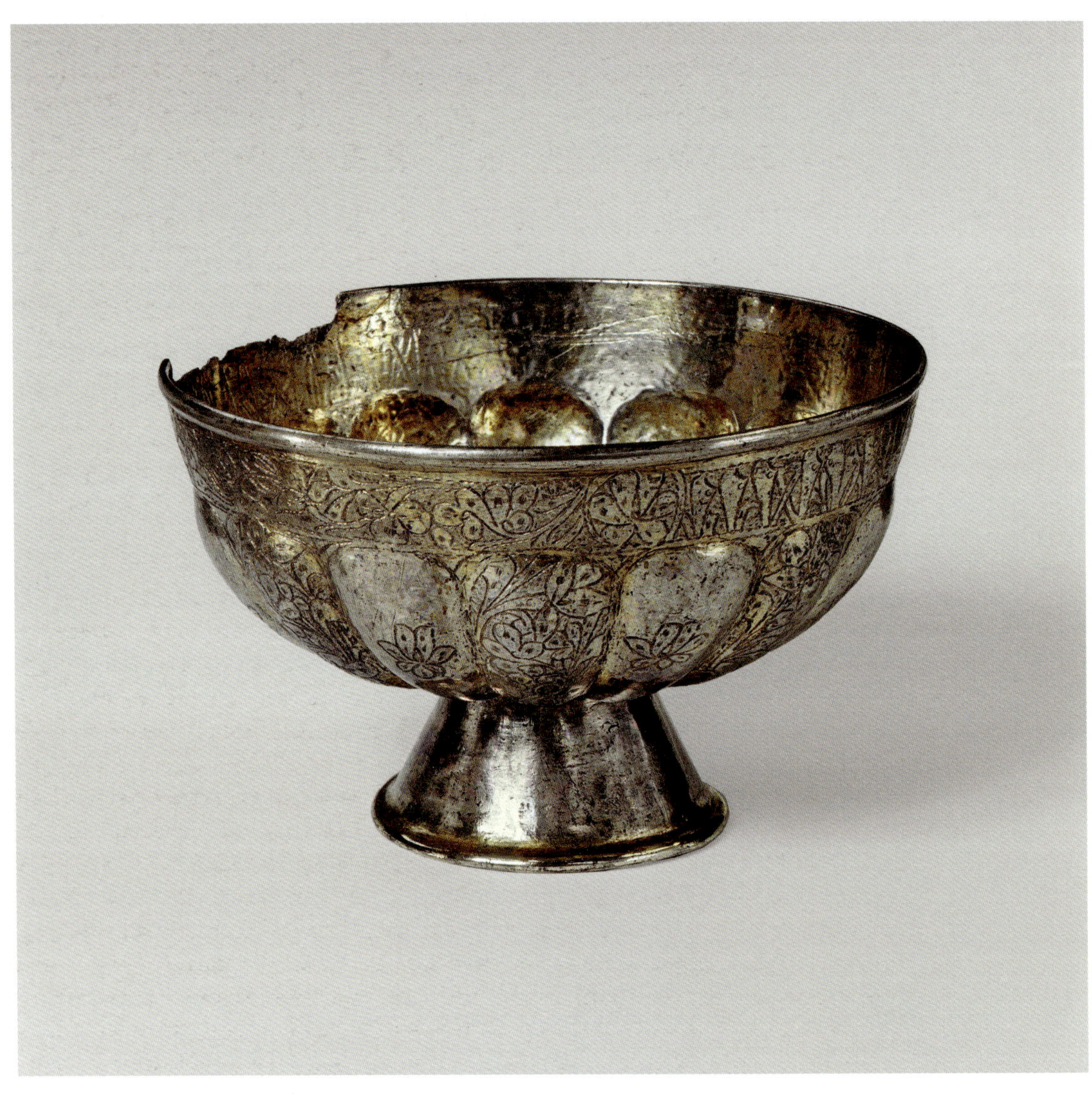

was established in Khurasan by the early thirteenth century. Another spoon with similar decoration of birds in a lobed cartouche and, on the reverse, a similar treatment of the ground has been attributed to the school of Shazi in Khurasan.[2] The long-necked bird on this spoon, and the way it is inlaid with just a line of silver down its breast, closely resembles the birds on pen boxes signed by Shazi and supports the attribution of both spoons to Khurasan.

The flat brass dish (cat. 8) has gadrooned sides and a narrow rim raised to shape probably with the help of a mould or form. The decoration includes two bands of benedictory inscriptions, both beginning *al-ᶜizz wa al-iqbāl wa al-dawlah wa al-saᶜādah* (glory and prosperity and good fortune and happiness), around a central rosette, all inlaid with silver. The shape and decoration of the dish is similar to vessels found in Khurasan and Central Asia.[3] Flat dishes like this one were placed beneath bowls and also other footed vessels such as incense burners (see the depiction in cat. 19).

The silver bowl (cat. 9) was beaten to shape, probably into a mould to ensure the regularity of the fourteen gadroons. The conical foot was made separately and soldered in place. Part of the rim is missing. The bowl was chased on the exterior with a scrolling stem and pseudo-inscription around the rim and a floral stem or single lotus flower on alternate gadroons; impressions from the blows of the hammer and chisel used in the decoration are clearly visible inside. The bowl was gilded inside and out.[4]

Gadrooned bowls were made in Iran in the early thirteenth century, but the style of decoration changed with the Mongol invasion to include lotus and other motifs from East Asia.[5] Silver bowls with similar decoration have been found in Russian excavations in the Golden Horde Khanate but they may have been made in other centres also.[6]

The bowl is a smaller version of the bowl in the Courtauld bag court scene. Footed bowls like this were usually presented on flat dishes while bowls without a foot were held in the hand and used as drinking vessels.

2 Melikian-Chirvani 1979, pp. 235–36 and pl. IV: 6, 7 (the spoon), pl. III: 3 (pen box with birds by Shazi).

3 For a similar gadrooned dish in the Ikramov Museum of the History of Culture and Art of the Uzbek SSR, Samarqand, see Pugachenkova and Khakimov 1988, fig. 181.

4 Folsach 1990, fig. 333; New York 2002, no. 156, p. 277, and p. 55, fig. 53.

5 For a gadrooned silver bowl in the name of an amir active in western Iran in the late twelfth and early thirteenth century see Ward 1993, p. 86 and fig. 65.

6 St Petersburg 2000; New York 2002, p. 112, fig. 130 and no. 6, pp. 245–46.

10

Ball joint

Mosul or western Iran, early 14th century
Cast brass, engraved and inlaid with silver, gold and a black material
H: 13 cm, Diam: 9.7 cm
London, Keir Collection, no. 132

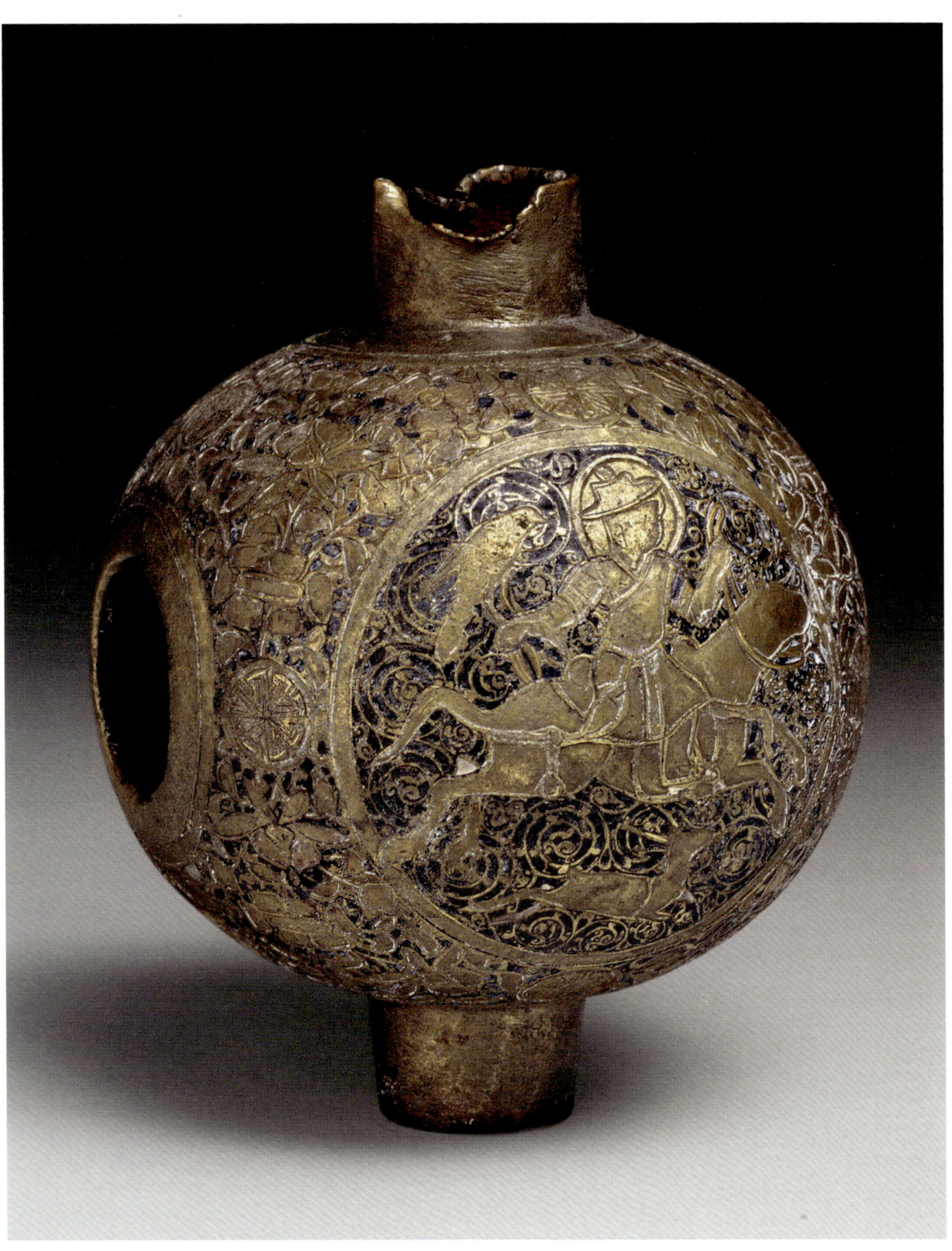

THE CAST-BRASS BALL JOINT is hollow, with openings at the four cardinal points. A rod would have been inserted through the simple opening to either side and the undecorated sockets above and below were each inserted into a slightly wider metal tube resting on the surface of the ball. The load bearing was vertical.[1]

Eight other inlaid brass ball joints are known. Three in the name of Sultan Öljeitü (ruled 1304–16) were in the Harari collection and must have come from the same source (see fig. 47).[2] A smaller one of similar form to this one and also decorated with a falconer was found in excavations at Sultaniyya.[3] Three more have distinctive articulated projecting sockets, two of them with nearly identical decoration.[4] Another ball joint is related in shape and decoration to others in the group, but, instead of being cast, it is made from sheet metal in two halves with round holes at the cardinal points. It could not have been load bearing and must have been a decorative cover for a ball joint in another material.[5]

The ball joints are usually described as coming from window grilles but they might instead have been part of internal screens, parapets or furniture. Illustrations of window grilles show small flat-sided joints, barely wider than the struts between them, to allow as much light to pass through as possible. Surviving ball joints measure 9–13 cm diameter, excluding the sockets (the one from Sultaniyya is unusually small at about 6.5 cm) and some of the sockets appear designed to join directly to the socket of another ball joint.[6] The dais on which the couple sit in the court scene on the Courtauld bag is supported on vertical struts with large balls between (detail below) and balls are shown as part of other furniture (for another dais see fig. 40).[7]

The ball joint is inlaid with silver, gold and black material in Mosul style. The brass ground was well recessed for the sheet silver inlays, but left as higher ridges for the gold wire, which was inlaid into parallel tracks of shallow pits. The ground was neatly stepped to receive black inlay and much of that has survived, showing what a deep contrast it provided for the figural and floral decoration.

The ball joint is decorated on both sides with a large roundel containing a falconer on horseback with a dog or deer running alongside. The falconer is in Mongol dress with a three-quarter-length tunic, which crosses his chest and attaches under his right arm, and boots. On one side he wears a wide-brimmed hat and on the other a three-pointed crown, both types of headgear seen in illustrated Il-Khanid manuscripts. The remaining areas are filled with lotus and peony flowers and small gold Z-medallions. The decoration is typical of the Il-Khanid court style but the inlay technique is quite different from other inlaid brass metalwork decorated with courtly iconography, such as the basin in the Victoria and Albert Museum (figs. 11–15), and closer to metalwork here attributed to Mosul. Designs appropriate for an Il-Khanid palace might have been supplied to the workshop in Mosul, as they were for the Courtauld bag; alternatively, a Mosul inlayer might have been employed on site for the duration of the work.

NOTES

1 Published in Fehérvári 1976, no. 132, pl. J; New York 2002, no. 171, p. 280, and fig. 145.

2 See Pope and Ackermann 1938–39, III, p. 2505, and IX, pl. 1357A for one of these. See Wiet 1933, pp. 45–46, for their dedicatory inscriptions.

3 Gandjavi 1979, fig. 5.

4 Los Angeles County Museum, M.73.5.124; Sotheby's, 6 October 2010, lot 164, and Aron Collection, inv. 34. See Allan 1986, no. 34, pp. 130–31, for an illustration of the ball joint in the Aron Collection and a discussion of the group.

5 Christie's, 4 October 2012, lot 80.

6 The Los Angeles, Aron and Sotheby's ball joints have articulated sockets which terminate in a plain collar with a wide lip around it which would not have been hidden by the crossbar of a window grille.

7 The throne on a tray in the British Museum attributed to Mosul, c. 1300 also has balls decrating its struts; Ward 1993, fig. 66.

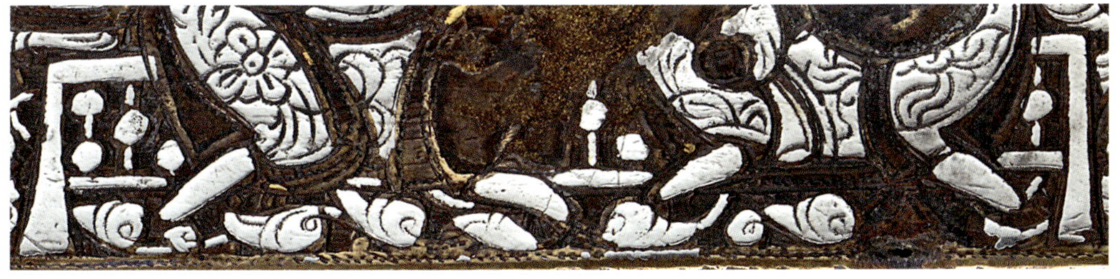

11

Beaker

Egypt or Syria, 1300–20
Glass, blown, enamelled and gilded
H: 11 cm
London, British Museum, ME 1879,0522.68

MAMLUK GLASS BEAKERS were often
decorated, as here, with gold fish outlined
with red enamel: flickering reflections on
the gold would have made them appear to
swim through the liquid within the glass.
This beaker also has an eel wriggling around
its foot – a touch of humour added by the
craftsman.[1]

Inspired by sheet-silver beakers (which
have not survived) beakers of this shape were
traditional for drinking vessels in the Arab
world and are often depicted in court scenes
in manuscript paintings (see figs. 20, 21) and
on inlaid metalwork. In Iran and Central
Asia, beakers of this type were also used
(see the image on the tile, cat. 33) but the
Il-Khanid elite usually drank from shallow
cups or bowls (see enthroned figures in
cat. 16, fig. 22). The seated man in the court
scene on the Courtauld bag is holding a
conical beaker (detail below), and other
beakers are held by, or placed close to, the
musicians and drinkers in the roundels.

This beaker was acquired in Qift, north
of Luxor in Egypt, but enamelled and gilded
glass beakers were popular items for export
and have been found in excavations of
Mongol sites.[2]

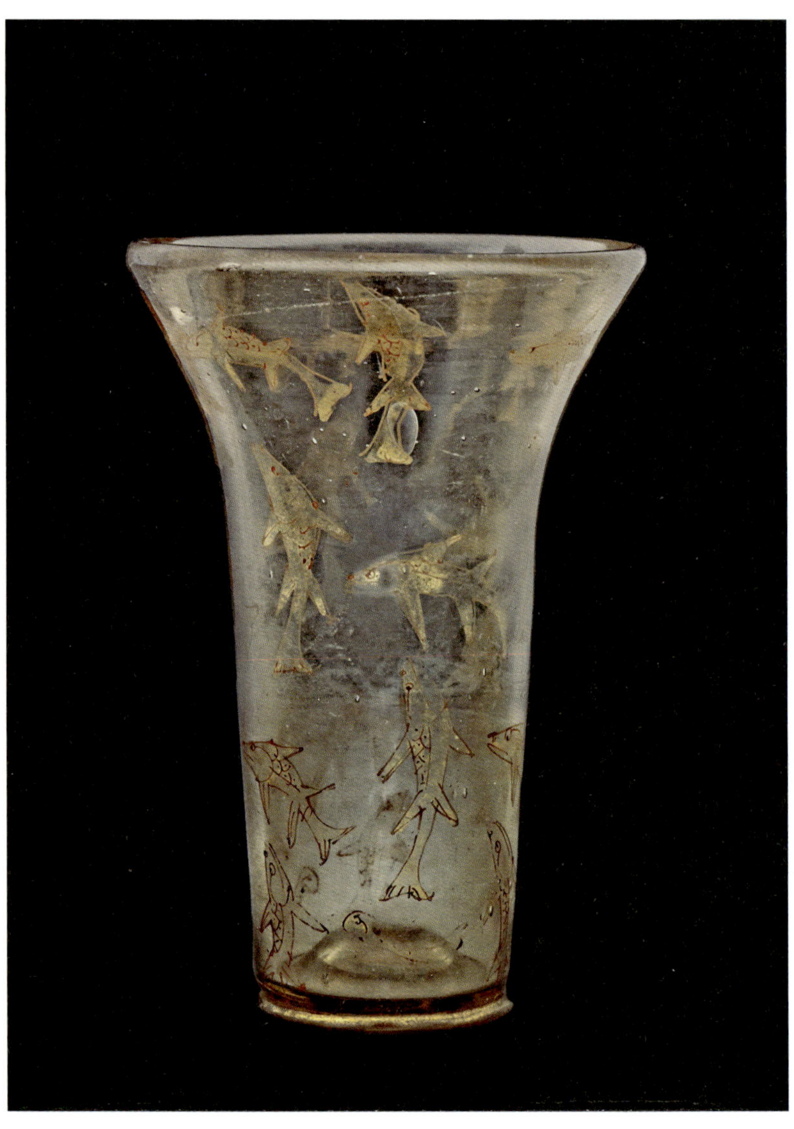

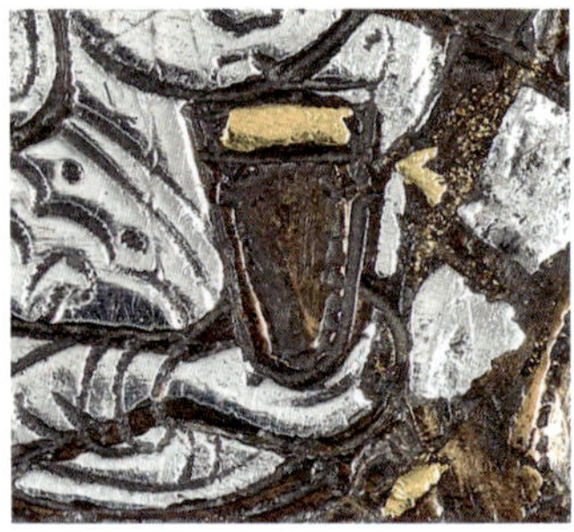

NOTES

1 London 1995, no. 7.60, p. 590.
2 See Kramarovsky 1998. A beaker
   this shape found with coins of
   the Golden Horde Khanate of the
   middle of the fourteenth century is
   in the British Museum, 1910,0416.2.

12

Pair of earrings

Iran or Iraq, 11–14th century
Gold sheet, wire and granulation
W: 3.2 cm, 3.4 cm; Wt: 16.9 g, 17.9 g
London, Nasser D. Khalili Collection of Islamic Art, JLY 1272

THE PAIR of crescent-shaped gold earrings are decorated with half-domes and twisted wire arranged to create spirals and figures of eight. Originally pearls or beads would have been strung around the outer edge of each side, held in place by the hoops that remain.[1]

Crescents have been popular shapes for earrings at all periods. These earrings are distinguished from similar earrings made in Syria and Egypt by their box-like construction and plain sheet domes without granulation. The dating of these earrings and other gold jewellery remains vague because of the traditional nature of gold jewellery and because very little such material has been found in a datable context.

Although the inlays have fallen out, the outline of the punched pits intended to secure them suggests that gold crescent-shaped earrings were shown worn by the woman on the Courtauld bag (detail below). Il-Khanid courtiers often wore earrings, usually a large pearl on a gold hoop (cat. 17), but none of the men on the bag are depicted with earrings, perhaps because of the tiny size of the image.

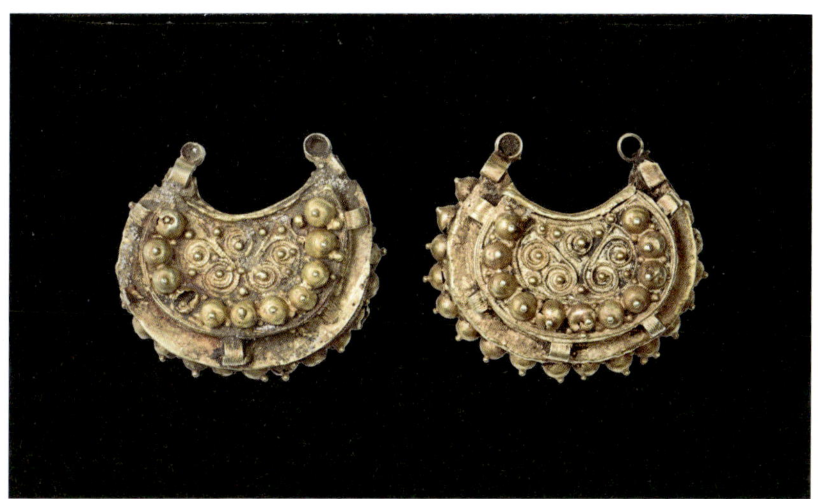

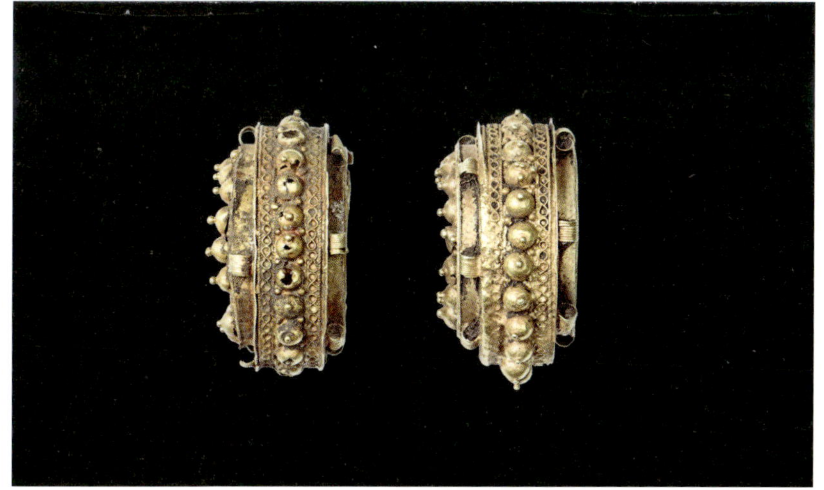

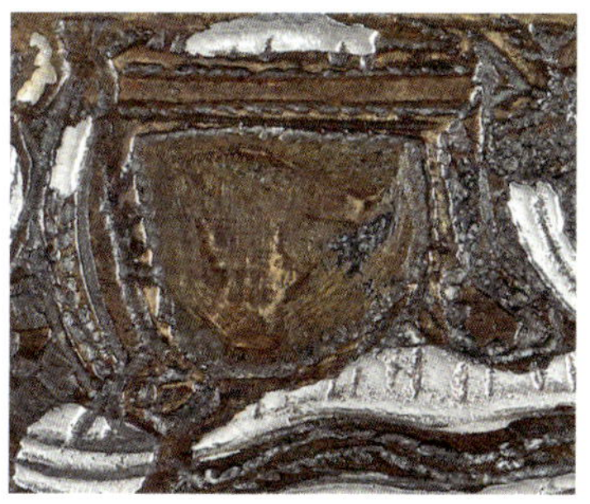

NOTE

1 Spink and Ogden 2013, I, no. 88, pp. 184–45.

13

Mirror

China, 12th century
Cast bronze
L: 23.2 cm, Diam: 12.9 cm
London, British Museum, Asia 1994.0129,8

THE CIRCULAR MIRROR on a long handle was cast with relief decoration on the back of two phoenix in flight. The alloy is high tin bronze, a copper alloy with about 25% tin, which allowed the flat front to be highly polished to a reflective silvery surface.

Chinese mirrors made of high tin bronze were greatly admired and had a strong influence on the shape and design of mirrors produced in Iran and Afghanistan.[1] Numerous round mirrors with a loop for suspension, their backs decorated with a pair of addorsed sphinxes or a border of running animals, were made in imitation of Chinese mirrors. In the twelfth century, some Chinese mirrors were given long handles and by the thirteenth some round mirrors in western Asia were also given handles but these were diminutive, a few centimetres in length. Mirrors with substantial handles do not survive from Iraq or Iran until the fifteenth century, probably because we are missing objects made of silver (recycled) and of steel (subject to corrosion).[2] A painting of Abraham with the Three Strangers in the *Compendium of Chronicles* shows his wife Sarah looking in a circular silver mirror mounted within a gold handle.[3]

The noblewoman on the Blacas ewer (see fig. 2) and the attendant on the Courtauld bag both hold round mirrors with substantial long handles (detail right). There is too little detail to identify the origin of the mirror in either scene but the handles suggest that they are locally made silver or steel mirrors or high tin bronze mirrors imported from China.

Mirrors are associated with marriage in several cultures. In China, marriage mirrors were carried by the bride during the wedding procession and were later hung over the marriage bed to protect against evil spirits and bring good fortune. Auspicious symbols, especially pairs of animals, were chosen to represent marital unity. Pairs of phoenixes were popular because, in Chinese tradition, the phoenix is monogamous and has a deep affection for its mate.[4] In Iran, a mirror continues to play an important part in the wedding ceremony, being placed so that the groom sees the bride's face reflected in the mirror when she removes her veil (traditionally, this would be the first time that he would see her face). The mirror with the reflected face in the court scene may refer to the marital status of the couple.

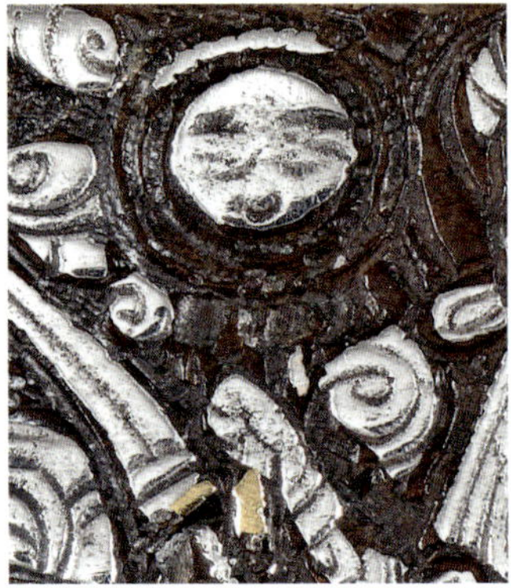

NOTES

1 Sources speak admiringly of the high tin alloy (*khar sini*) of Chinese mirrors and they have been found at various sites in Iran and Afghanistan and in the territory of the Golden Horde Khanate: Allan 1979, pp. 48–52, 61–62. Curiously, although the technology to make high tin bronze existed, surviving copper alloy mirrors from Iran contain only about 10–13% tin: Craddock *et al.* 1990, p. 98.

2 The Mamluks produced mirrors with long handles by the middle of the fourteenth century and a steel mirror (without its handle) made for the wife of a Mamluk amir is in the British Museum: London 1976, no. 228, p. 197.

3 Illustrated Gray 1961, p. 25.

4 Costello 2005, p. 6.

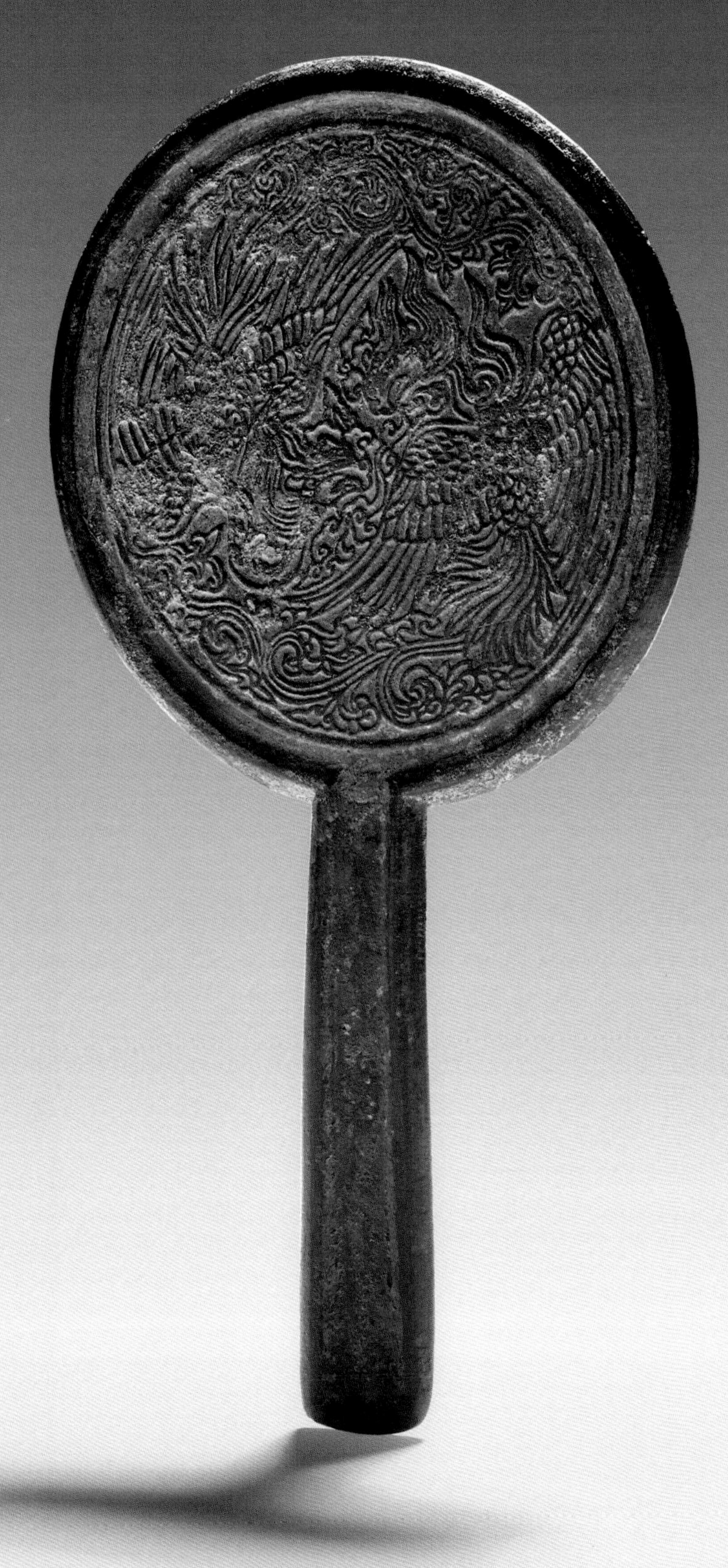

14

Fragment of *nasij* (cloth of gold)

Western Central Asia, mid 14th century
Polychrome lampas with gold thread
L: 30 cm, W: 10 cm
London, Victoria and Albert Museum, T&F 783-1875

THE STRIPED DESIGN includes panels of
lotus and blossoms and an Arabic inscription
reading 'the wise, the sultan' executed in gold
thread on differently coloured grounds of
silk.[1] The gold thread consists of strips of gilt
leather wound round a core of flax or hemp,
a technique associated with western Central
Asia.[2]

This fragment came from a set of vestments
made from the same or similar fabric for St
Mary's Church in Gdansk, Poland, and related
textiles have been found in other ecclesiastical
contexts in Europe.[3] Striped designs appear
to have been most popular in the Arab world
and these textiles may have been intended
for the Mamluk market.[4] The couple in the
court scene wear robes with leafy designs, and
textiles in contemporary Il-Khanid paintings
(see cat. 2) are usually plain with gold
embroidery or woven in gold with floral or
leafy designs similar to those on the woman's
tunic in the Mardjani Collection (figs. 48, 49).
No doubt both types of design were available
for sale in Mosul, which had a flourishing
market for local and imported textiles.

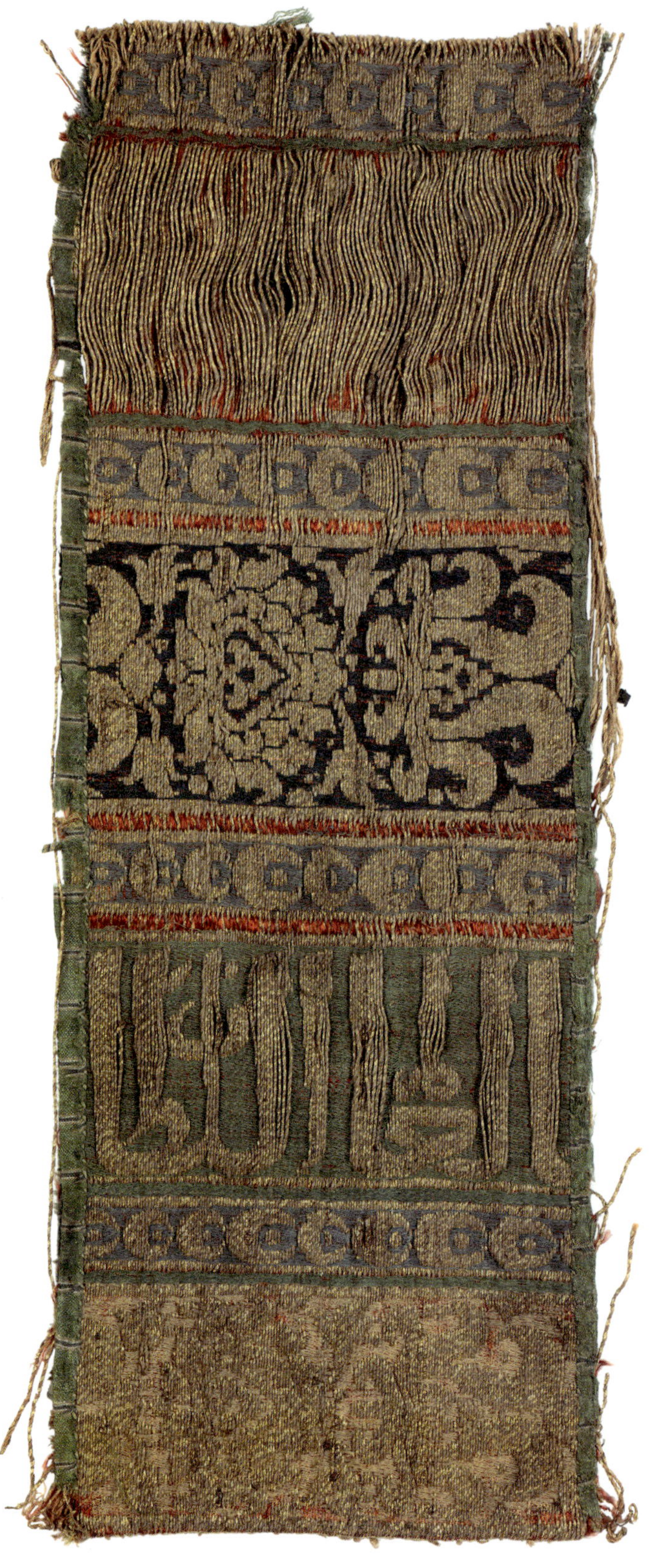

NOTES

1 Thanks to Helen Persson and Moya
   Carey for drawing our attention to
   this unpublished fragment.
2 Wardwell 1992, pp. 362–64.
3 See Mannowsky [*c.* 1936],
   pp. 10–11, for a description of
   material acquired from the
   treasury in the 1820s and 1830s
   by Johann Joseph Bock, curator at
   the Cologne Museum, who sold
   this fragment to the museum.
   He also illustrates a cope of the
   same material.
4 Kendrick 1924, no. 997, p. 67,
   pl. XXII. Washington 1991, p. 133,
   no. 17, is a dalmatic of very similar
   fabric in Berlin that probably also
   came from Gdansk. For more
   fragments in Berlin, see New York
   2002, no. 75.

15

Leather fragment, perhaps the side of a bag

Egypt, mid 14th–mid 15th century
Moulded leather, dyed and painted
H: 17.2 cm; W: 13.4 cm
Baltimore, Walters Art Museum, 73.109

THE LYRE-SHAPED FRAGMENT has relief decoration which was created by gluing strings to linen and then placing thin leather on top and tooling it so that the pattern of strings protruded. The resulting design consists of a medallion with an elaborate blossom terminating in a palmette and a plaited border running around its edge. The leather itself was dyed red and the design painted with yellow, green and black.

The fragment was acquired in Egypt by Richard Ettinghausen, who suggested that it was Coptic work dating from the seventh century, but others have suggested a later date.[1] The exotic blossom within a lobed medallion recalls Chinese or Il-Khanid designs. After peace was negotiated between the Mamluks and the Il-Khanids in the 1320s, imported luxuries created a fashion for 'chinoiserie' at the Mamluk court, and similar designs are seen in Mamluk art and architecture.[2]

The size and shape of the fragment is remarkably similar to the sides of the Courtauld bag (illustrated pp. 78–79), which also have plaited borders. A strap for suspension may have been attached where there are three cut holes in the upper part of the leather. An imported bag in metal, textile or leather may have inspired an Egyptian version, but leather has a poor survival rate so it is possible that leather bags were more widely available than the physical evidence suggests.

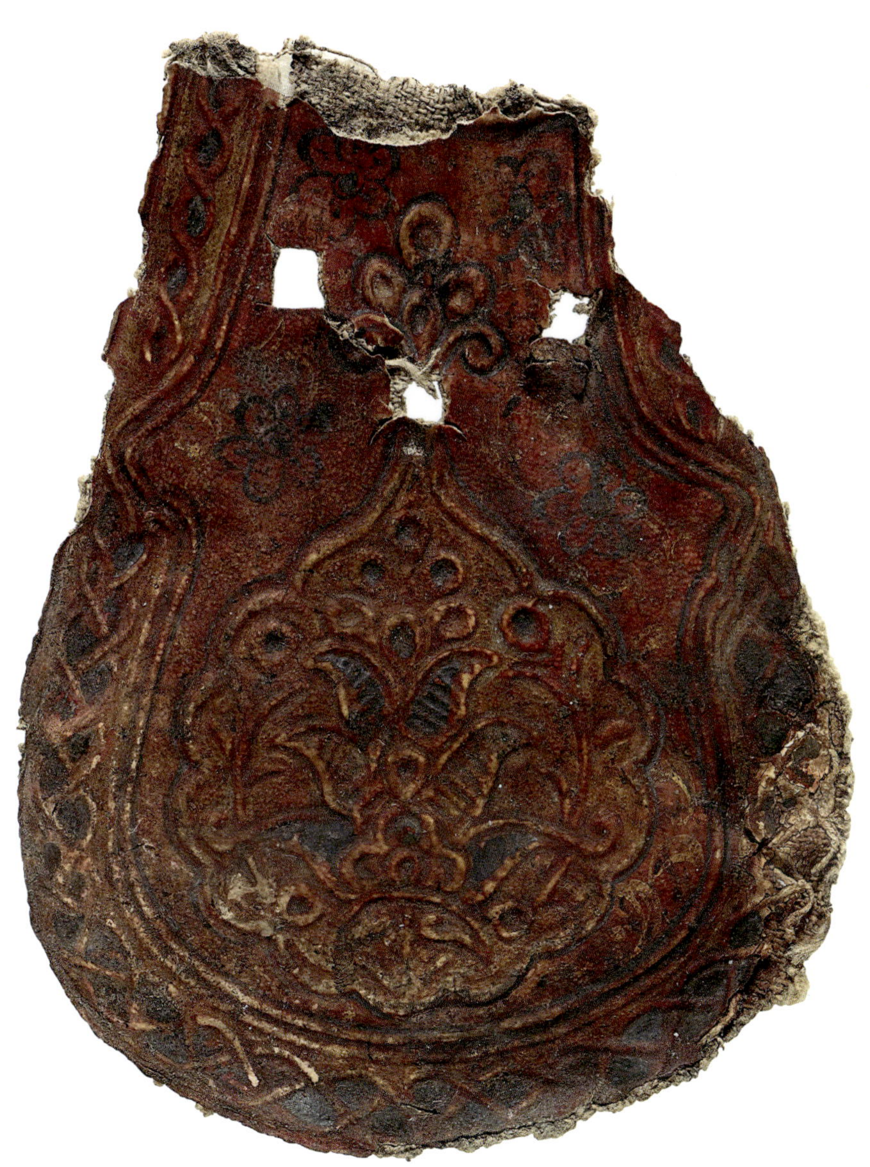

NOTES

1 Baltimore 1957, pp. 18–19, no. 32; Ettinghausen 1965, pp. 68–69; Petersen 1954, p. 51, n. 10, suggested it was Mamluk, late thirteenth to early fourteenth century. Folsach 2004, pp. 225–26 and fig. 1 also suggested that it was later than the seventh century. I am grateful to Kjeld von Folsach for reminding me of this leather fragment, to Alison Ohta for confirming its date, and to Amy Landau and colleagues for facilitating conservation and documentation for its exhibition.

2 See Washington 1981 pp. 232–33, no. 116, for similar Mamluk designs.

The Diez Albums

THE FIVE DIEZ ALBUMS were compiled by Heinrich Friedrich von Diez, who was Prussian chargé d'affaires at the Sublime Porte in Istanbul from 1786 to 1790.[1] They consist of a range of work on paper – paintings, drawings, calligraphy, patterns – which Diez amassed from local dealers and also from individuals in the Topkapı Palace, who sold him illustrated folios from manuscripts and albums kept in the women's quarters (harem) "to provide a source of recreation and conversation pieces".[2] Diez bequeathed the albums with the rest of his large library to the Königliche Bibliothek in 1817 and they are now in the Staatsbibliothek Preussischer Kulturbesitz in Berlin. The albums from which these folios came (Diez A, fols. 70, 71, 72) were disassembled and conserved in 1971–72, then mounted individually.

These four images share features of mounting with four similar illustrations in Topkapı Palace Museum Album H.2153, which is probably the album from which they were taken for sale to Diez.[3] They are amongst 49 illustrations in the Diez Albums (others are illustrated in figs. 5 and 7) which are related to surviving illustrated manuscripts of Rashid al-Din's *Compendium of Chronicles* (fig. 22).

Rashid al-Din (*c.* 1247–1318) was born in Hamadan, western Iran, to a Jewish apothecary and he himself trained as a physician.[4] Around the age of thirty he converted to Islam. He entered the service of the Il-Khanids as a physician and by 1298 he was deputy vizier to Ghazan Khan (1285–1304). During the reign of Ghazan's brother Öljeitü (1304–16), Rashid al-Din became even more powerful and wealthy and inevitably attracted jealousy from rivals, who often used his Jewish background to arouse suspicion against him. When Öljeitü died in 1316 Rashid al-Din was accused of murdering him, and was executed in 1318 during the reign of Abu Saʿid Khan (1316–35).

Rashid al-Din was commissioned by Ghazan to write a history of the Mongols, which he later expanded into a more comprehensive historical tome, the *Compendium of Chronicles*, covering the peoples of Eurasia, including China and the Franks. In 1309 Rashid al-Din wrote an endowment deed for a foundation attached to his tomb complex, built just outside Tabriz, which provided for the annual copying of a 30-volume Qur'an manuscript and a four-volume work on *hadith* (the sayings and deeds of Muhammad). Four years later he appended instructions for the production of two copies, one in Arabic and one in Persian, of all his own writings, including the *Compendium of Chronicles*, which were to be distributed to cities under Il-Khanid rule for educational purposes.[5]

The *Compendium of Chronicles* was divided into sections. The first covered the history of the Mongols, the second the history of the non-Mongol peoples. Illustrated copies of the second part have survived (see fig. 22) but none of the first.[6] The following paintings were intended to illustrate (or were inspired by illustrations from) the first part of the *Compendium of Chronicles*, *The History of the Mongols*. They have no writing on the back. It seems that the scriptorium may have been

NOTES

1 Diez A, fols. 70–74. On the Diez Albums see Roxburgh 1995; İpşiroğlu 1964.
2 Roxburgh 1995, p. 113.
3 Roxburgh 1995, p. 116.
4 For a biography of Rashid al-Din see Morgan 1995.
5 Blair 1996, p. 48.
6 The earliest illustrated version of the second part of the text, dated 714/1314–15, is divided between the Khalili Collection (Ms. 727) and Edinburgh University Library (Arabic Ms. 20). For a facsimile (and extended commentary) of the Khalili portion see Blair 1995.

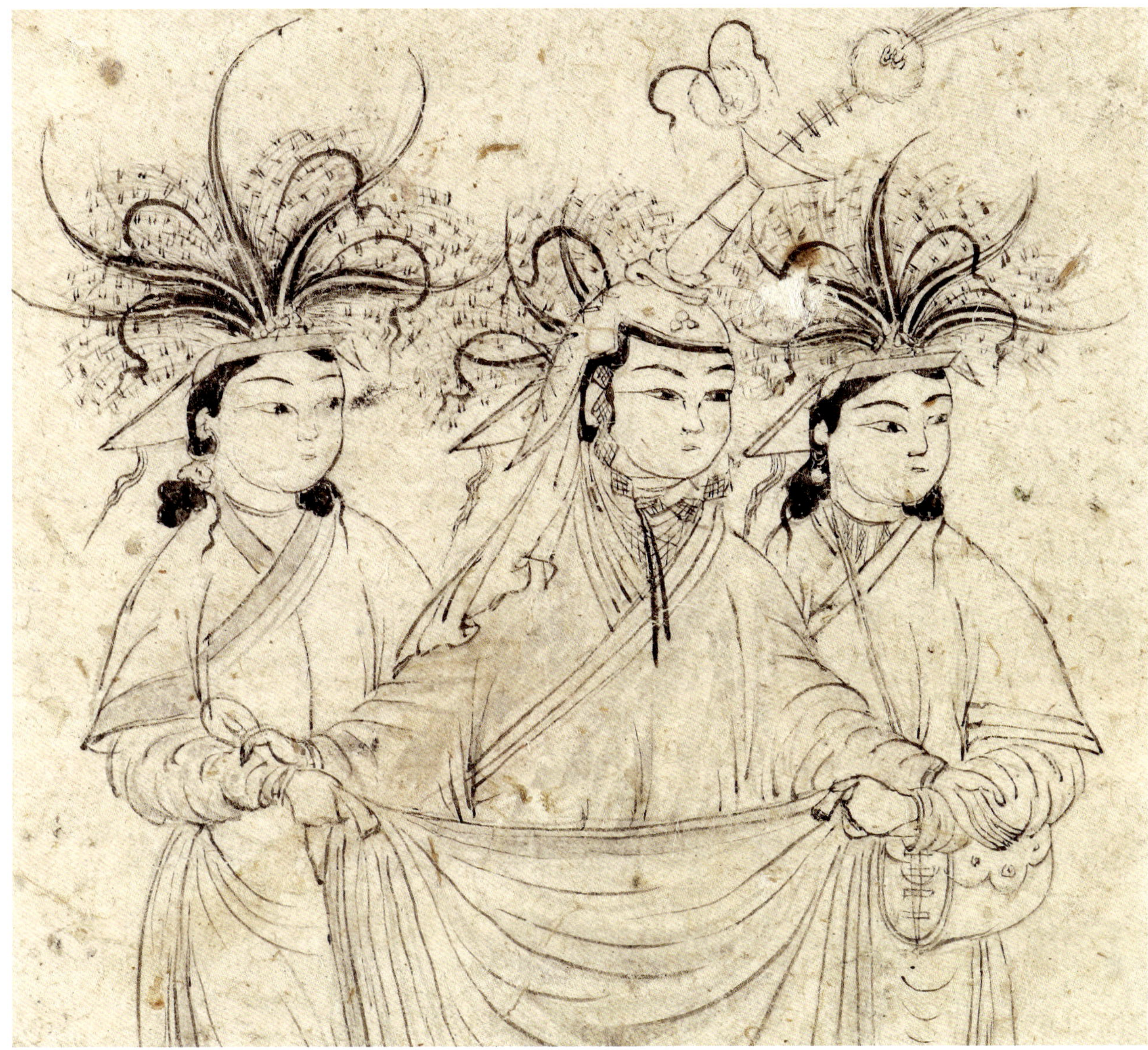

Cat. 18, detail

trying to save time by enabling the painters
to work on separate paper which would
have been pasted into the manuscript later.
Although some of these illustrations may
date into the second half of the fourteenth
century, they are based on images designed
for the original manuscript and so all reflect
the iconography, costume and distinctive
pen-and-wash technique seen in the early
fourteenth-century illustrations to the second
part of the *Compendium of Chronicles*
(fig. 22).

The illustrations can be divided by size
and subject matter, and the original location
of some of them has been identified by
comparison with later un-illustrated texts.
Couples appear in three different types
of painting – double-page compositions
depicting the enthronement of a new Khan
with his court (cat. 16), smaller scenes from
the life of the Khan (cat. 17–18), and tiny
images of a Khan and Khatun (fig. 7).[7]

7 Rührdanz 1997, pp. 295–306.

16

Enthronement scene

Iran, possibly Tabriz, early 14th century
Ink, colours and gold on paper
Unmounted, H: 39, W: 28.7 cm (left), H: 35.8, W: 29 cm (right)
Berlin Staatsbibliothek, Diez Album, fols. 70, S. 5 and 70, S. 2

SEVERAL DOUBLE-PAGE images depicting the enthronement of a new Khan with his court were introduced in Rashid al-Din's text as *surat-e takht,* literally 'picture of the throne'.[8] In this example both sides have been drastically trimmed along every edge, so some figures are sliced in half and others have the later framing lines running on top of them.[9]

On the right side the Khan and Khatun are enthroned at the top of the paper and close to the left edge. Originally the centrality of the enthroned couple would have been more obvious as they were at the apex of a visual circle, centred on the kneeling attendants, with the empty space around them fringed by further attendants. Both are seated in a relaxed pose and incline towards one another as if in conversation. Both hold a cup of red wine; the Khan holds a napkin and the Khatun holds a pomegranate. Their faces are smudged but it is possible to discern that the Khan is wearing an elaborate feathered hat and the Khatun is wearing a *boghtaq,* the Mongol headdress worn by married noblewomen.

Directly beside the Khatun is her young page carrying a bag (see detail in fig. 1, p. 11). It appears to have a fairly solid structure and a hinged lid with a flap in front shaped with a curving edge terminating in a point. The red strap goes under the bag and is held in place on both sides by two loops, one fixed to the bag and another to the lid. It is covered with fabric of some sort, which is woven or embroidered with birds, plants and water in black on a plain ground (although the colours may have been simplified, as in the rest of the scene). The edges of the bag are bordered in red and the strap is also red. A very similar bag is held by another young page in the third line of courtiers: on this a flying phoenix is clearly visible on the closing flap.

To the right are three rows of women of the court, dressed like the Khatun in *boghtaq*s. Some of them hold items like a napkin, a pomegranate, a bowl of wine. The three pages seated at the end of the third row, one carrying a bag, may be attendant on these women. Below them is a row of four secretaries each clutching a rolled scroll, and then a row of three falconers with their birds on their right arm; the falconer on the right has a hunk of meat in his left hand to keep the bird happy (if used as a lure it would have been attached to a long string).[10]

Below the throne, two kneeling attendants proffer flat dishes of food taken from a red lacquer table behind them which has bottles, bowls and a cup waiting for use. Various gesticulating courtiers around this table seem to be concerned with the provisioning of the Khan and his court. Two of them, holding a bowl and a pomegranate, approach the seated figure with a mace in the foreground – the master of ceremonies.

The left folio has male courtiers standing or seated in groups, most of them facing towards the enthroned couple. Those ranked down the left edge appear to be mere onlookers but others hold items indicating their function at court. Two sets of archers clasp their bows. The two on the top right have a snow leopard's tail attached to their bow cases. A bearded labourer at the top of the image, wearing non-Mongol garb (a turban, tunic joining centrally in front, fabric

8 Rührdanz 1997, p. 297.
9 There are several copies of each side of this enthronement scene in the Diez albums and there is no certainty which, if any, were intended to be seen together.
10 Personal communication, Teresa Fitzherbert.

tied around his waist) holds a large mallet and peg. He will be responsible for the erection of the large, richly decorated tents used by the Mongol court as they moved around their empire. His presence suggests that the scene should be visualised within one of these tents. The royal parasol is furled and waiting in its stand on the left, which confirms that the royal couple are not seated in direct sunlight.

Along the bottom of the illustration, musicians play the lute and harp and several figures dance or stamp their feet in time to the music. Several of the lower group are looking backwards, two with hands raised in surprise, towards a figure who enters from the left, but this may be a misunderstanding of dancers clapping hands in the original image. This is a formal scene, but the reality was probably rather more lively. William of Rubruck described the festivities of the Mongol court: "In summer they do not bother about anything except *kumis* …. When the master begins to drink, then one of the attendants cries out in a loud voice 'Ha' and a musician strikes his instrument. And when it is a big feast they are holding, they all clap their hands and also dance to the sound of the instrument, the men before the master and the women before the mistress. After the master has drunk, then the attendant cries out as before and the instrument player breaks off. Then they drink all around, the men and the women, and sometimes vie with each other in drinking in a really disgusting and gluttonous manner …. When they want to incite anyone to drink they seize him by the ears and pull them vigorously to make his gullet open, and they clap and dance in front of him."[11]

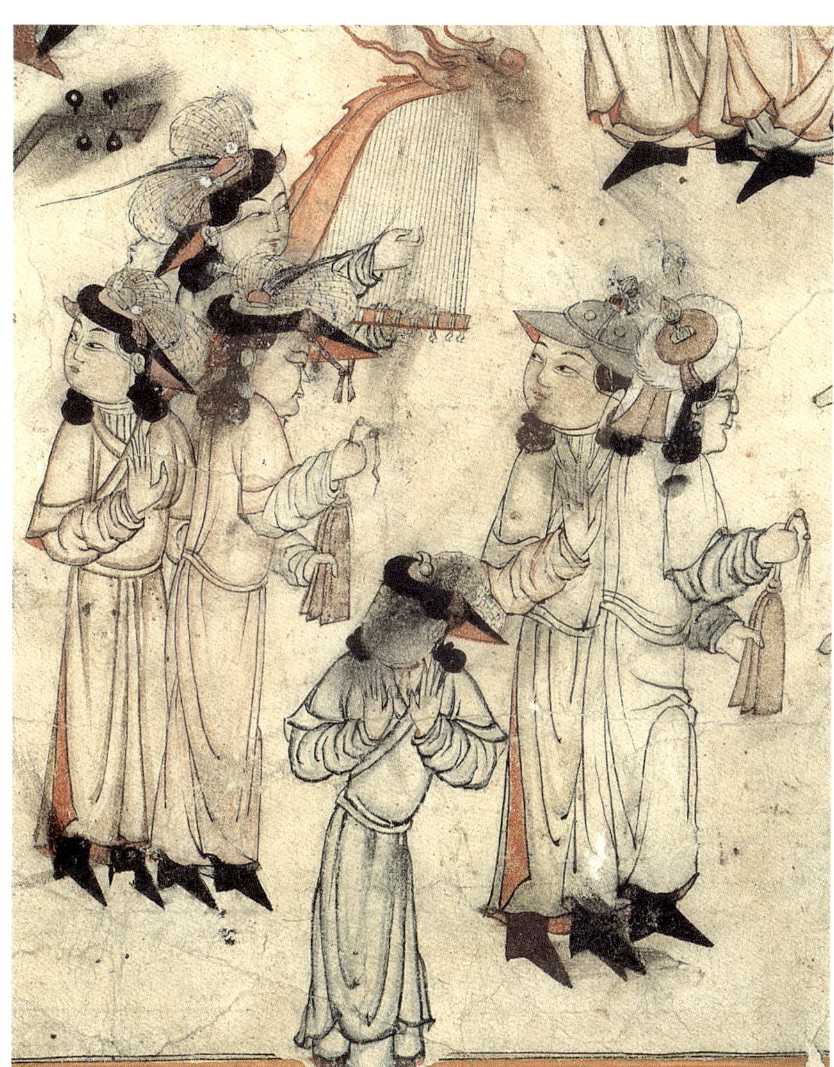

Cat. 16, detail

11 Quoted in Smith 2000, p. 38.

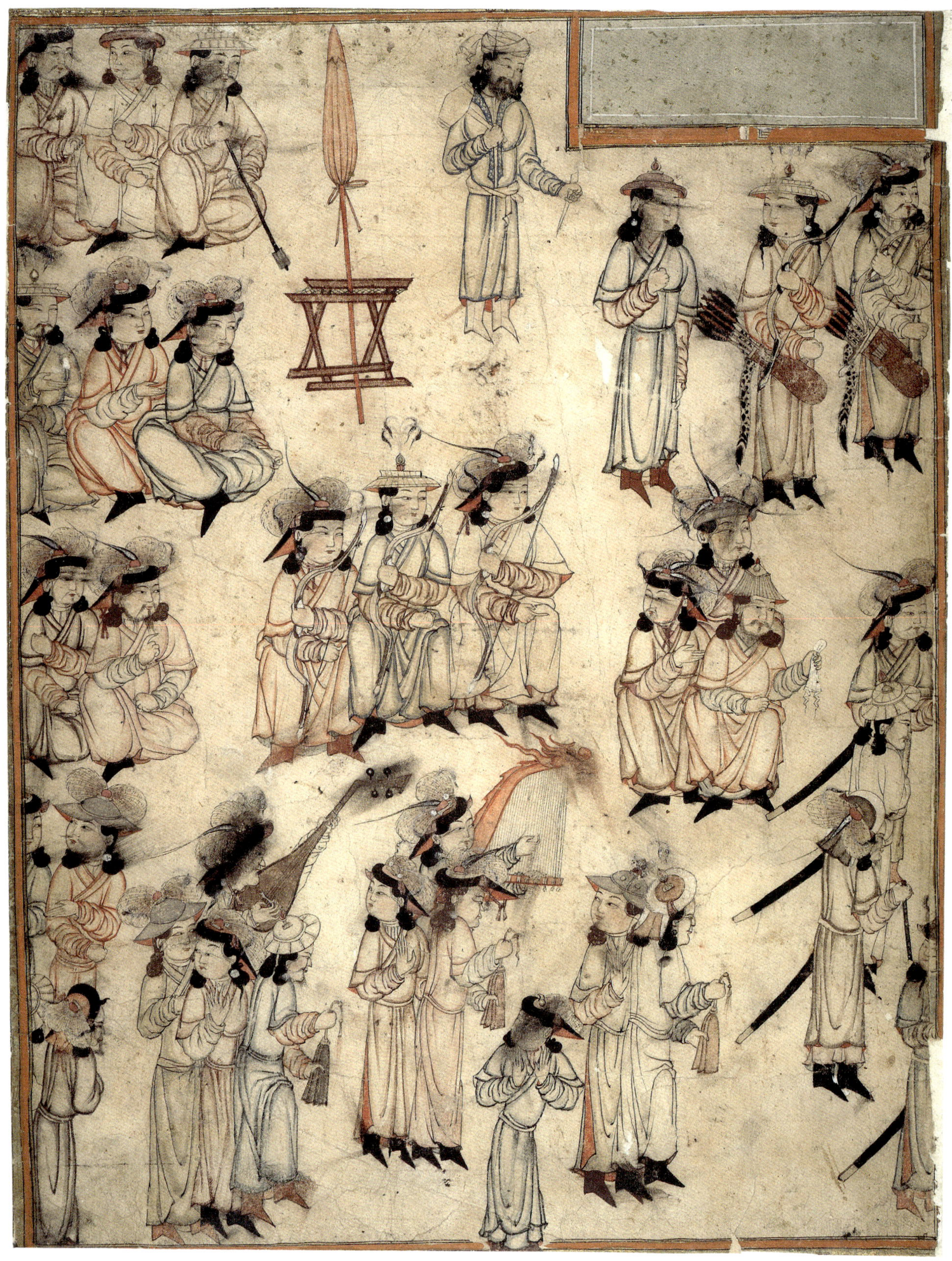

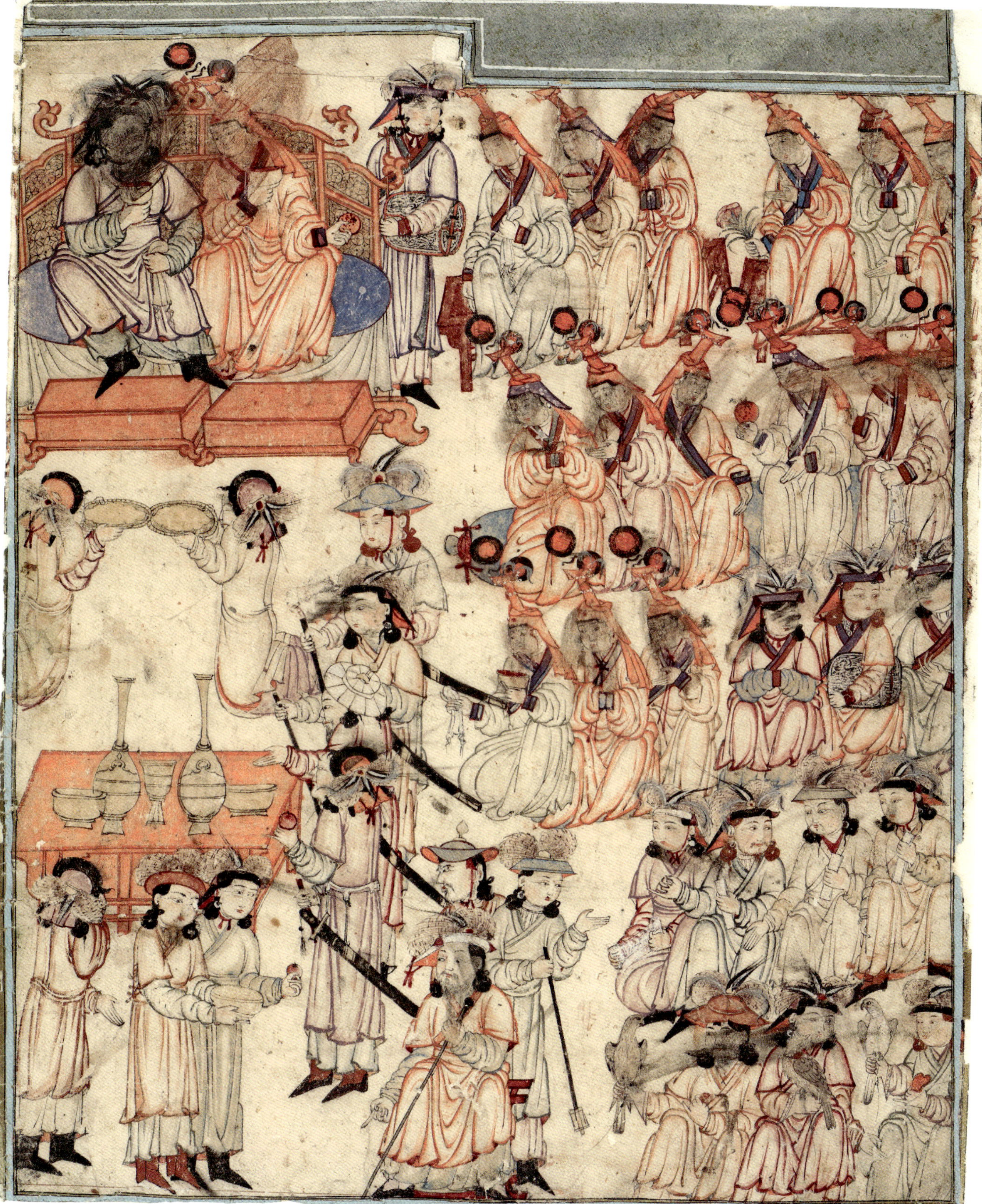

17

Enthronement scene

Iran, possibly Tabriz, early 14th century
Ink, colours and gold on paper
Unmounted, H: 19.2, W: 26.1 cm max.
Berlin, Staatsbibliothek, Diez A, fol. 71, S. 48

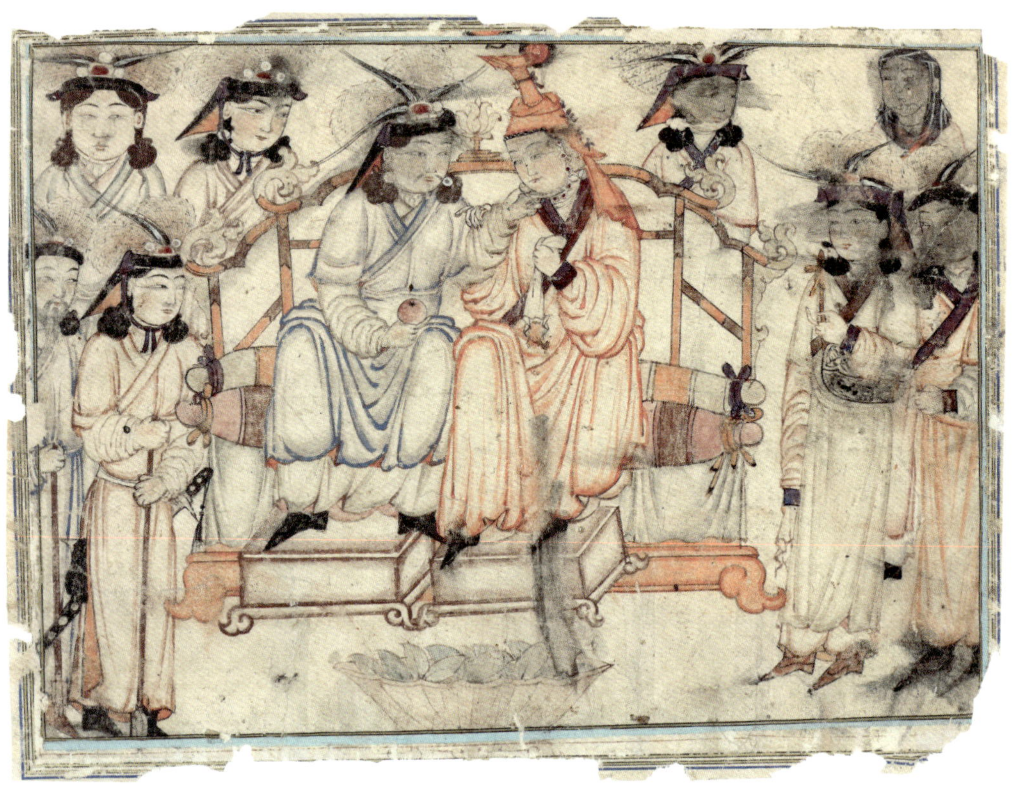

IN THIS SMALLER, more intimate scene of an enthroned Khan and his wife, the couple sit on a throne with two foot stools as in the large enthronement scene (cat. 16) and before them a large bowl of leaves. They are surrounded by courtiers and attendants including, beside the woman, a page carrying a bag and a napkin. The bag is smaller than the one in the previous scene, but like it has a rounded shape and a decorative flap with curving edge and red strap. It is covered in a textile with a design on it – not a pattern, perhaps an animal in foliage, as in the previous scene. A neighbouring page may also be carrying a bag but it is undefined, so he appears instead to be clutching his large belly. Behind the pages is a woman attendant wearing a *miqnaᶜa* of transparent material, perhaps the muslin for which Mosul was famous.[12]

The scenes illustrating events from the life of a Khan are difficult to interpret because the text which would have identified the event illustrated is missing, but this one may depict a Khan with a new bride: he holds her face in an appreciation of her beauty and proffers a pomegranate, again a reference to her fertility and the continuation of the dynasty; she accepts his offer by touching his shoulder and appearing compliant with a lowered head.

12 See Allan above, p. 53.

18

A lady walking with two pages

Iran, 14th century
Ink on paper
Unmounted, H: 9.5 cm, W: 14.4 cm max.
Berlin, Staatsbibliothek, Diez A, fol. 72, S. 11

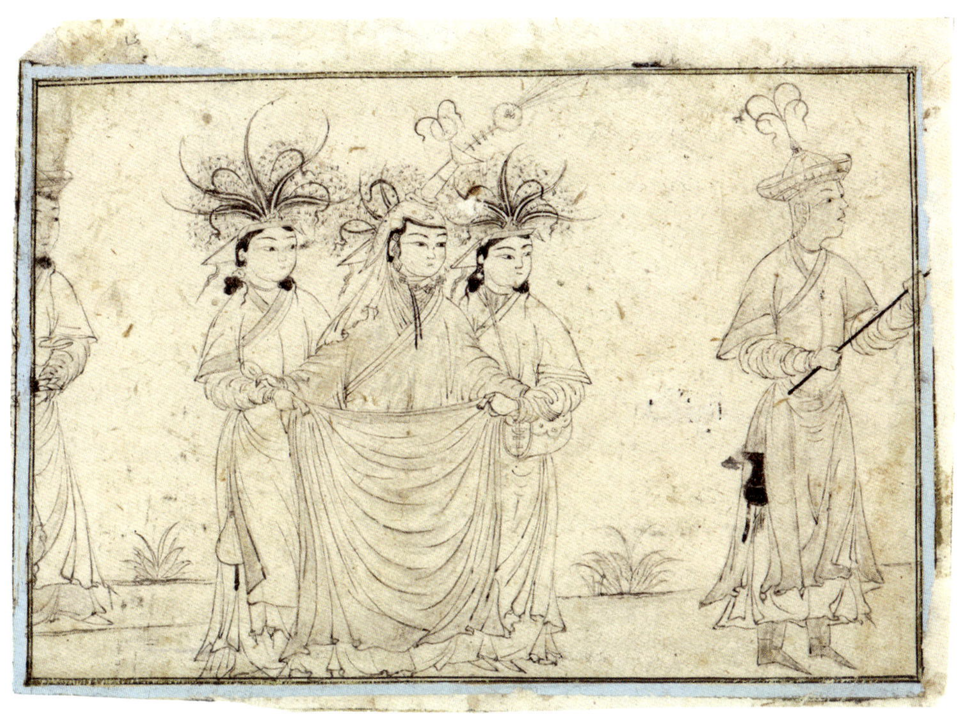

THIS DRAWING is inspired by a group of figures depicted in a scene of preparation for a party within a palace.[13] A finely dressed Mongol noblewoman, perhaps a royal wife, is supported on either side by two pages. She needs the support: her dress has quantities of surplus material, making it impossible for her to walk without it being lifted. A rope (presumably of an appropriate material, such as silk) has been threaded beneath it in such a way that the pages can lift the robe without touching it. The pages are themselves richly dressed, with very elaborate feathered hats, and the one on the left has a man-bag suspended from his waist. The one on the right is wearing the woman's bag beneath his left arm, suspended from a long strap which crosses his chest. It has a firm structure with loops attached to the sides of the body and the lid through which the strap is threaded. The closing flap has a decorative curving edge and three small buttons or decorative designs applied to it.

Behind this trio is a third page, in simpler headgear, indicating the woman and carrying something in his right hand, but he has been sliced in half by later trimming and so what he is carrying cannot be identified. They are all following a courtier holding a mace as if clearing their path. His hair is fair and short and his features look European. He has a small bag suspended from his waist with a feather dangling below it.

13 Diez A, fol. 70, S. 18, no. 1, illustrated New York 2002, fig. 86 and no. 30.

19

The *Khamsa* of Khwaju Kirmani

Baghdad, dated Jumada I 798/March 1396
Ink, colours and gold on paper
H: 32.3 cm, W: 23.3 cm (folio)
London, British Library, Add. 18113

THE MANUSCRIPT contains three of the five narrative poems from the *Khamsa* of Khwaju Kirmani.[1] Khwaju Kirmani (1290–*c.* 1349-52) was a poet and composer of verse on mystical themes who sought patronage from various rulers and powerful men in Iran and Iraq.[2] The manuscript was copied in 1396 by Mir ᶜAli ibn Ilyas al-Tabrizi in Baghdad, capital of the Jalayirid dynasty. The artist, Junayd Naqqash Sultani, signed his name within a panel below the arch above Humayun in the bedroom scene (fol. 45v).

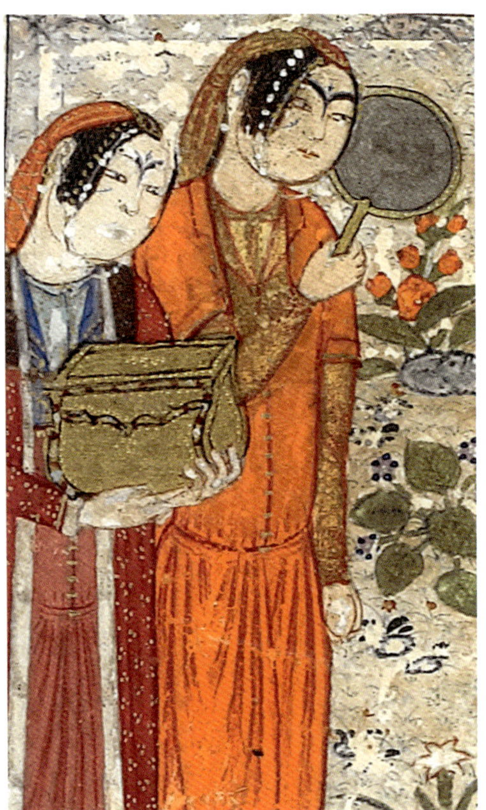

The illustration on show in the exhibition is 'Humay and Humayun in the garden', from the story of Humay and Humayun which was completed in 1331 in Baghdad and dedicated to the Il-Khan Abu Saᶜid and his vizier Ghiyath al-Din Muhammad (although it may never have been presented to them). It is a fairy tale with mystical overtones: while hunting, Prince Humay, Prince of Syria, is led by a ruby-lipped onager to the Queen of the Fairies, who shows him a portrait of Humayun, daughter of the Faghfur of China. Humay falls in love with the beautiful girl in the portrait and goes in search of her. There are various adventures and complications with the girl's father but he finally wins her and becomes ruler of the Chinese empire.

The painting depicts Humay and Humayun in a garden surrounded by courtiers and attendants who talk together, pick flowers and hold trays of money and food, while a group of musicians entertains them in the lower right corner. The couple are seated on a large divan with a high back, their hands clasped while she holds out a blossom to him and he lifts a shallow bowl to drink. In front of them is an animal skin swollen with liquid, a table with bottles of Chinese porcelain and various gold candlesticks and incense burners. By Humayun's side are her personal attendants carrying various items of use to her toilette – a gold container studded with precious stones, a silver mirror and perfume bottle and a rectangular object wrapped in fine cloth (detail left). The container is the same shape as the Courtauld bag, with a curved profile, flat rectangular top and lobed

NOTES

1 The paintings from this manuscript have been published frequently. For the British Library's digitised version of the manuscript, which allows you to see it in microscopic detail, go to http://www.bl.uk/manuscripts/Viewer.aspx?ref=add_ms_18113.

2 Fitzherbert 1991.

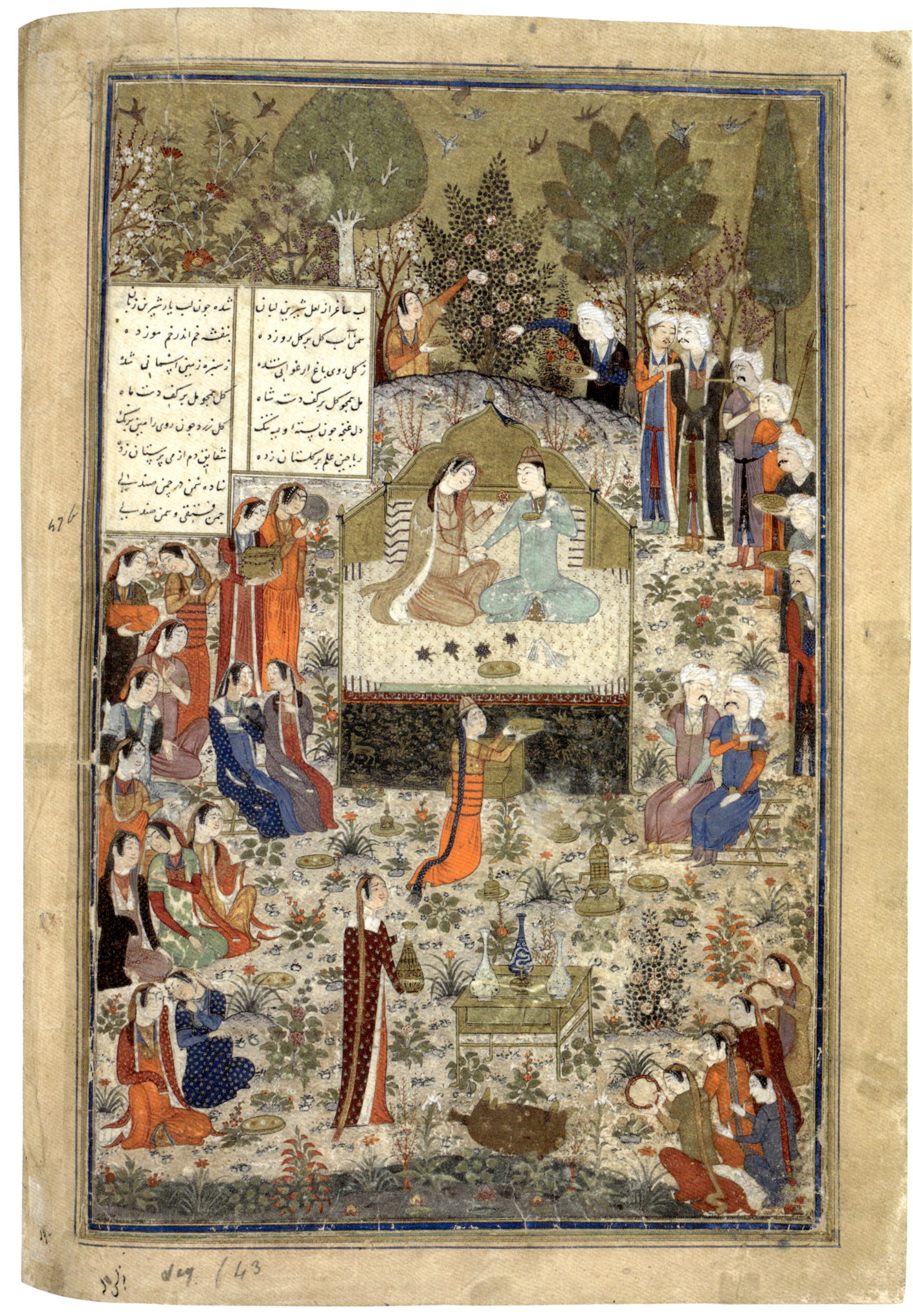

Fol. 40v
*Humay and Humayun
in the garden*

closing flap, but there is no evidence
(such as a strap) that it was used as a bag.

On folio 45v of the same manuscript
there is a painting of Humay leaving
Humayun's room after their wedding night.
Humayun leaves the bedchamber through a
door on the right and has gold coins poured
over him in celebration while courtiers kiss
the ground before him. Humayun remains
seated on the bed while the bloodied bed
sheet is displayed and covered in gold
coins. In the foreground are a group of wax
candles decorated with coloured paper in
candlesticks and incense burners. Humayun
is offered refreshment from a bowl furnished
with a spoon with a curved handle on a dish.
To her right, two attendants raise candles
aloft; one holds a silver perfume bottle on a
gold dish, the other holds a gold container
set with white gems (see detail, fig. 3, p. 15),
which is virtually identical to the container
in the previous illustration (fol. 40v) and, like
that one, is very similar to the Courtauld bag
– with a curved profile, flat rectangular top
and lobed closing flap.

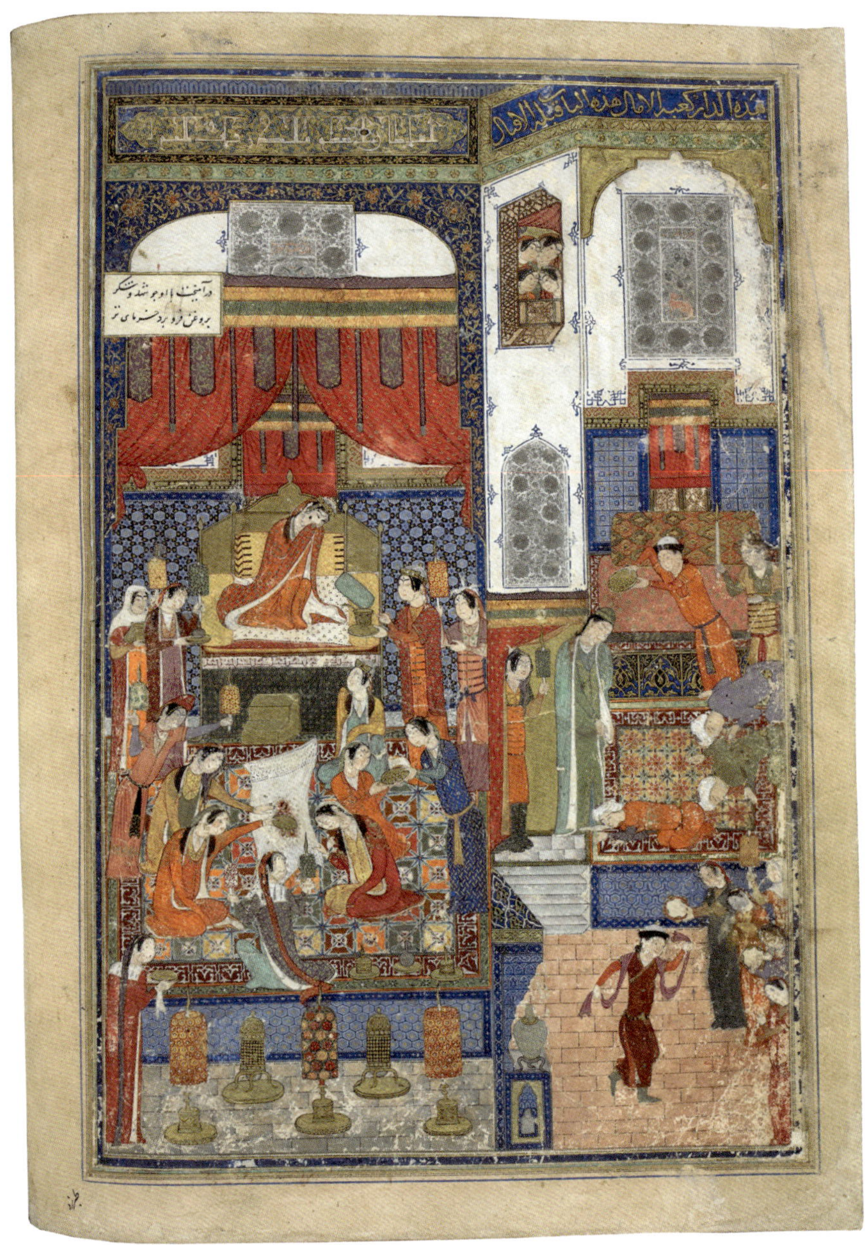

20

Tray

Probably Shiraz, 1345–60
Brass, raised, engraved and inlaid with silver, gold and a black material
Diam: 69 cm
Tbilisi, Georgian National Museum, Or. 3830

THE CIRCULAR TRAY is decorated with a series of inscriptions and floral and other designs around a large central roundel, the focus of the decoration, within which a couple sit enthroned surrounded by courtiers, attendants and angels.[1] The largest inscription is in praise of an unnamed sultan, the other inscriptions contain verses and wishes.[2]

The inscription, the sumptuous quality of the tray, the complexity of the composition and the emphasis on the divinity of the couple, with angels supporting their throne below as well as above so that they are literally airborne, all suggest that the couple are royal. The inscriptions include the title 'heir to the Kingdom of Solomon', which was used by the rulers of Shiraz, and the main inscription band and its roundels are similar to the decoration on bowls attributed to the Fars school.[3] However, the remaining decoration is closer to metalwork attributed to an Il-Khanid workshop, perhaps based at Tabriz, and the figural style relates to illustrations for the *Compendium of Chronicles* (cat. 16–18), the originals of which were created in Rashid al-Din's scriptorium just outside Tabriz. Grand Il-Khanid frontispieces do not survive; this roundel may be an indication of what we are missing.[4]

The fusion of styles and iconography is a reminder that craftsmen, manuscripts and objects moved from one centre to another (the stated intention of the *waqf* to Rashid al-Din's foundation was to distribute the manuscripts to cities around the Il-Khanid empire), influencing production and making simple stylistic groupings unreliable. Thus the tray may have been made in Tabriz or another Il-Khanid city as a diplomatic gift from the Il-Khans to their vassals in Shiraz, perhaps using a bowl or other metal object as model for the inscription band to ensure that the titulature was correct. Alternatively it may have been made in Shiraz using a design derived from an Il-Khanid painting as a model. Errors, such as the *boqhtaq* and *miqnaʿa* worn simultaneously by the woman, indicate that Il-Khanid iconography was not familiar to the metalworker, and therefore favour the second hypothesis. Wright has suggested that the rulers of Shiraz, notably Abu Ishaq (ruled 1343–57), appropriated royal Il-Khanid iconography in the 1340s as part of their justification for independent rule.[5] This tray may be an example of such appropriation.

Despite their different formats, the enthronement scene contains many of the same elements as the court scene on the Courtauld bag – a seated couple surrounded by courtiers, musicians and attendants providing refreshment from a Chinese table, the figures wearing Il-Khanid dress and headgear. Of particular interest are the attendants carrying items required for the toilette of the enthroned woman, including a mirror and a bag (the bag is viewed from the front and so appears flat, like a leather-bound codex, but it is carried by a female attendant of the enthroned woman and so is much more likely to be a bag). Both scenes are inspired by Il-Khanid iconography but the technique and style of the tray is completely different to those of the bag and of other metalwork here associated with Mosul and must have been made elsewhere.

NOTES

1 The tray is very abraded with only a few small traces of inlay. It appears to have been used as a work surface and was, until recently, covered in grime and oil. Conservation by Diana Heath, who was also responsible for conservation of the Courtauld bag, has transformed its appearance. Islamic metalwork in the Georgian National Museum is currently undergoing conservation and cleaning prior to an exhibition and publication of the most important objects, including this tray, which will be fully described with all of their inscriptions.

2 The tray was first published with a drawing of the roundel in Komaroff 1994, pp. 9–12 and fig. 7. The inscriptions are given in transliterated Arabic and translation on p. 31 note 29.

3 The title was observed by Komaroff 1994, p. 9. For the use of this title by rulers in Shiraz and an overview of the characteristics of the Shiraz school see Melikian-Chirvani 1971a, 1971b and 1982, pp. 147–52.

4 Komaroff 1974 emphasises the connection between painting and contemporary metalwork, including this tray.

5 Wright 2006, p. 265.

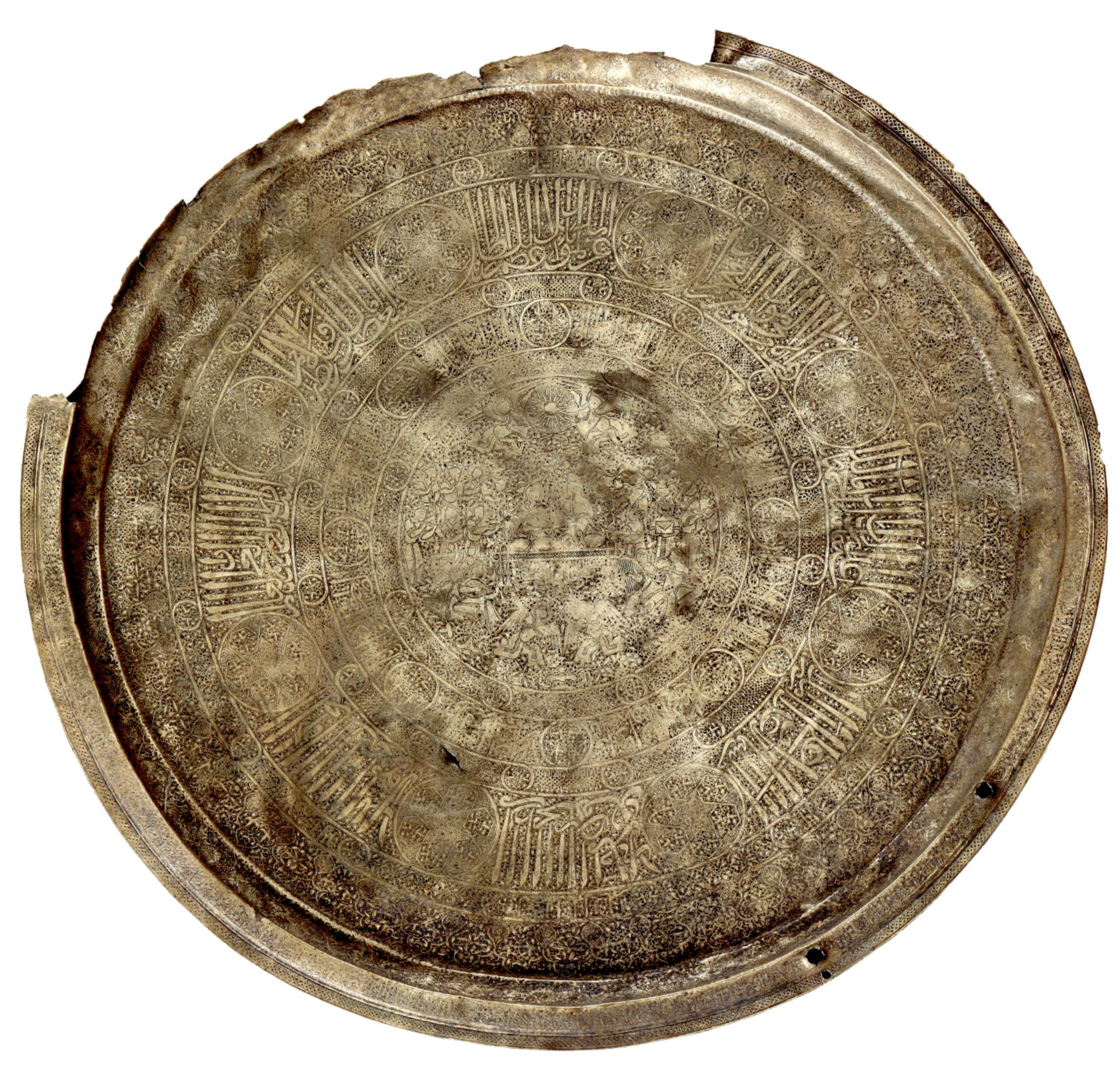

Detail of enthronement scene

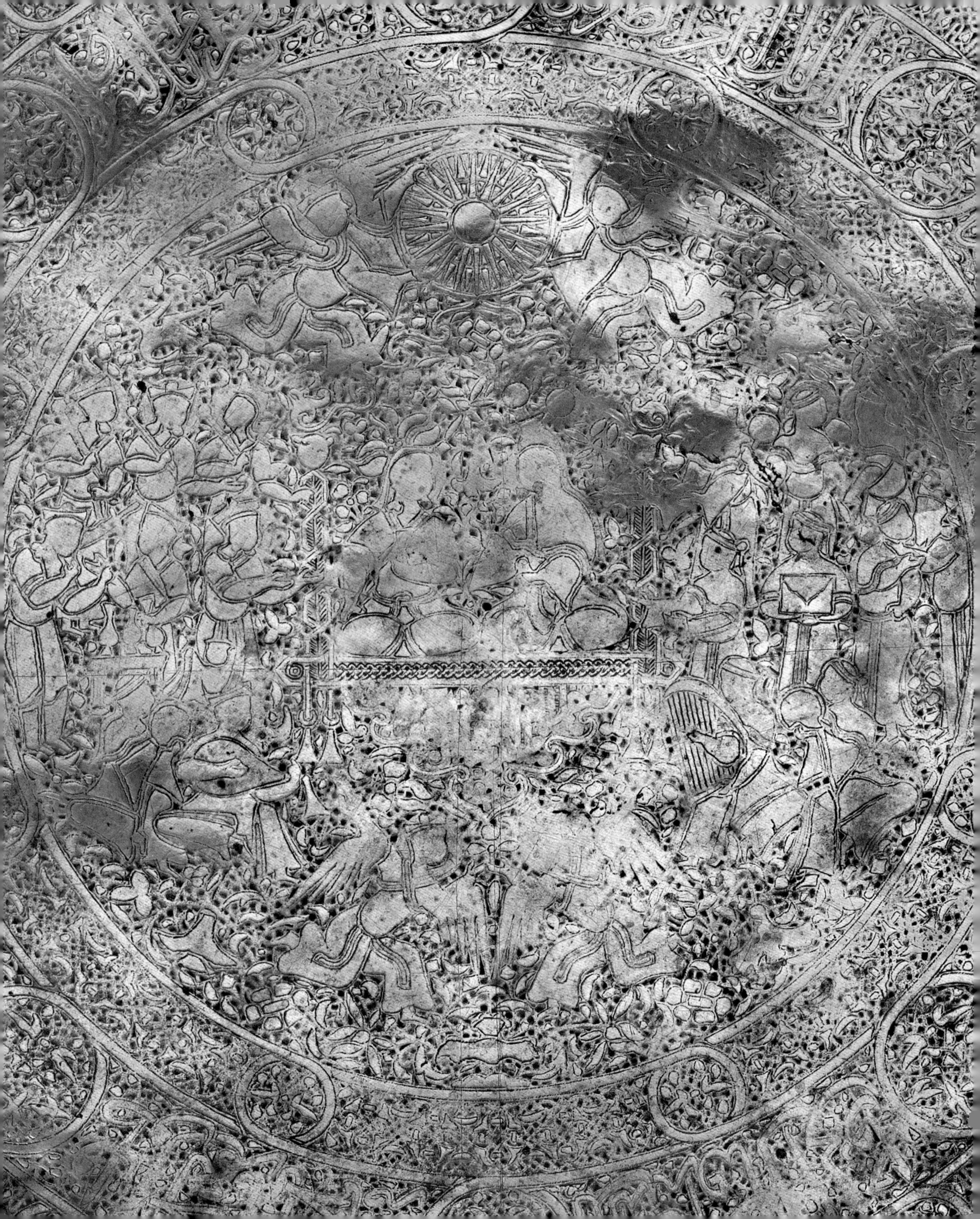

21

The Blacas ewer

Mosul, dated Rajab 629/April 1232
Brass, raised, engraved and inlaid with silver and copper
H: 30 cm, W: 20 cm
London, British Museum, ME 1866.12-29.61

THE BODY AND TALL NECK of the ewer are original but the body has been cut down and fitted with a replacement base and lid, its filter and spout are missing, and the handle and its collar are from another object. For an idea of its original shape and proportions see the ewer by ᶜAli ibn ᶜAbdallah (cat. 24). The brass ground was recessed to receive the sheet inlays and the wire inlays were inlaid into parallel tracks of fine pits. The background has been chased with different designs to add texture behind the decoration.

The decoration is laid out as a series of friezes and medallions on a geometric ground. The figural decoration in the medallions is very varied and includes enthroned rulers, battling soldiers, huntsmen, musicians (see fig. 23), Bahram Gur and Azada out hunting (a tale from the *Shahnama*), a lady with her maid (see fig. 2) and a lady on a camel with attendants.[1] Arabic wishes written in different calligraphic styles encircle the body of the ewer.[2] The maker's inscription, engraved and inlaid with silver, runs around the base of the neck: 'Decorated by Shujaᶜ bin Manᶜa al-Mawsili in the blessed month of God, the month of Rajab in the year six hundred and twenty nine in Mosul'.

Shujaᶜ ibn Manᶜa al-Mawsili is known only from this object but he must have been the head of a workshop in Mosul as another inlayer, Muhammad ibn Fattuh al-Mawsili, signed a candlestick describing himself as an employee of Shujaᶜ of Mosul.[3] The Blacas ewer and five objects bearing the name and titles of Badr al-Din Lu'lu' have provided the core group for the study of Mosul metalwork.[4] The range of styles included within this small group is consistent with a flourishing and prolific industry and numerous other objects can be attributed to the city by comparison with them. The Ibn Manᶜa family were one of the leading families of Mosul, prominent in the administrative and intellectual life of the city, which suggests that the inlaid metal industry was run by members of the educated class.[5]

The inlaid decoration on the body of the Blacas ewer is amongst the finest to have survived from thirteenth-century Mosul and it marks a major innovation in the style of inlay in that city. The earliest inlaid brasses from Mosul have figural medallions and inscription friezes lost amongst the swirling leaves that fill the background. Geometric patterns in medallions or borders were introduced to punctuate or frame the designs, and so create some visual order. The Blacas ewer goes one step further by introducing a geometric backdrop to contrast with the figural medallions and inscription friezes, which seem to float on top of it. The division of the surface into facets (this ewer is the earliest surviving in which this occurs) emphasises the regular layout of the decoration. The ewer also has larger, bolder inlays of silver and copper within the medallions so that the figural decoration stands out against the engraved brass ground. The clear, geometric style of the Blacas ewer, introduced in the 1230s, perhaps by Shujaᶜ ibn Manᶜa himself (his family in Mosul included Kamal al-Din ibn Manᶜa, a celebrated mathematician), became immensely influential and endured for more than a century – as demonstrated by the Courtauld bag (cat. 1).

NOTES

1 For illustrations of all the figural decoration, see Ward 1986.

2 See London 1976, p. 179, for two of the inscriptions on the body (with some errors) and the craftsman's inscription.

3 Cairo, Museum of Islamic Art, Harari Collection, inv. 1512; Ward 1993, fig. 11.

4 See Raby above, p. 56. See also Raby 2012 for an overview of the evidence for inlaid metalwork in Mosul before the Mongol conquest, with suggested criteria for expanding this small documentary group.

5 See Patton 1991, pp. 65–69, on the status of the Ibn Manᶜa family in Mosul.

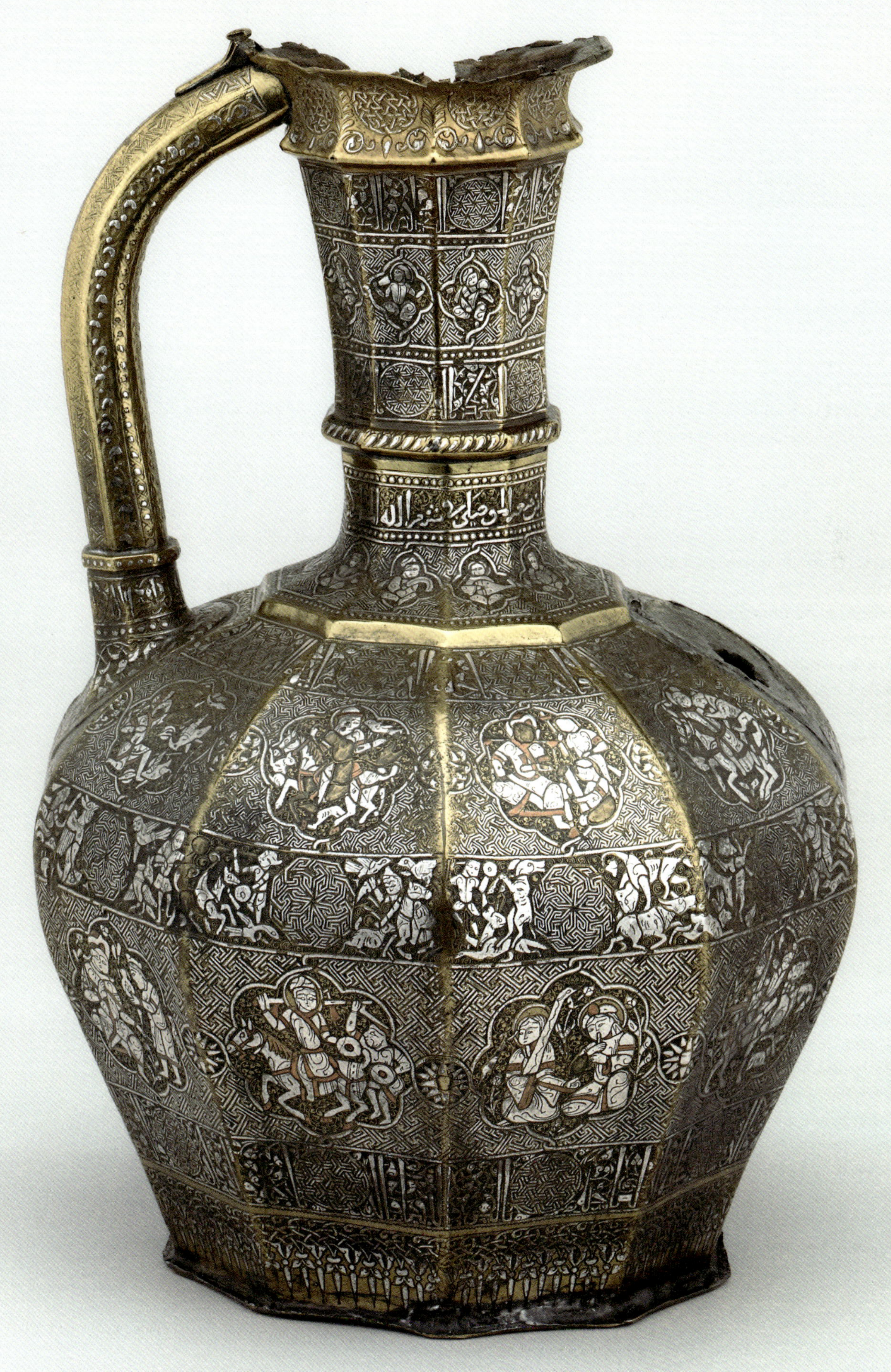

22

Incense burner

Mosul, 641/1243–44
Brass, cast, pierced, engraved and inlaid with silver
H: 19.5 cm, Diam: (lid rim) 9.2 cm
London, British Museum, ME 1878.12-30.678

23

Incense burner

Western Iran (Tabriz?), *c.* 1320–35
Brass, cast, pierced, engraved and inlaid with silver, gold and black material
H: 21.5 cm
Copenhagen, David Collection, 47/1967

MORE THAN FIFTY incense burners of the present type have survived.[1] The earliest date to 1230s, but they continued to be produced well into the fourteenth century. They are all made the same way – cast in two parts, the cylindrical container with its three legs and the domed lid. Piece moulds may have been used, which would have produced several vessels of identical size and shape before becoming too damaged for reuse. The burners are almost all missing the separately cast long handle which was riveted to the body – a space in the decoration of each reveals where it was attached. After the decoration had been planned, but before it was inlaid, the lid was pierced with holes through which the perfumed smoke could escape (see detail opposite).

The location of the foundry is likely to have been in or near Mosul because the incense burners have a traditional Iraqi shape (see cat. 19 for similarly shaped vessels in gold) and most of them appear to have been decorated there.[2] Most inlaid metalwork from Mosul is sheet brass, but there was always a need for heavy furniture and specialised objects such as astrolabes in cast brass and the foundry could also have supplied cast parts, such as

the handles for Mosul ewers (cat. 24).

The cursive inscription around the top of the domed lid of the British Museum burner (cat. 22) reads: 'Within me is the fire of hell but without float the perfumes of paradise. Made in the year six hundred and forty one'.[3]

The Kufic inscription on the body contains a series of wishes with qualifying adjectives seen on numerous Mosul objects: '*al-ᶜizz al-dā[ʾim wa] al-ᶜumr al-sālim wa al-baqāʾ li-ṣāḥibihi*' (eternal glory, secure life and long life to its owner). Longer versions of this inscription occur on the ewer by ᶜAli ibn ᶜAbdallah.

This incense burner is one of the earliest of the long series of incense burners. The similarity of its inlaid decoration to the Blacas ewer (cat. 21), some ten years earlier in date, suggests that it was decorated in Mosul, perhaps in the workshop of Shujaᶜ ibn Manᶜa.

Many of the decorative features on this incense burner reappear on the Courtauld bag (cat. 1), despite the period of time which separates them. The T-fret ground is most noticeable, but also the rosettes, the roundel with foliage around a Z-medallion, the quatrefoils with foliage interlace and the plaited borders.

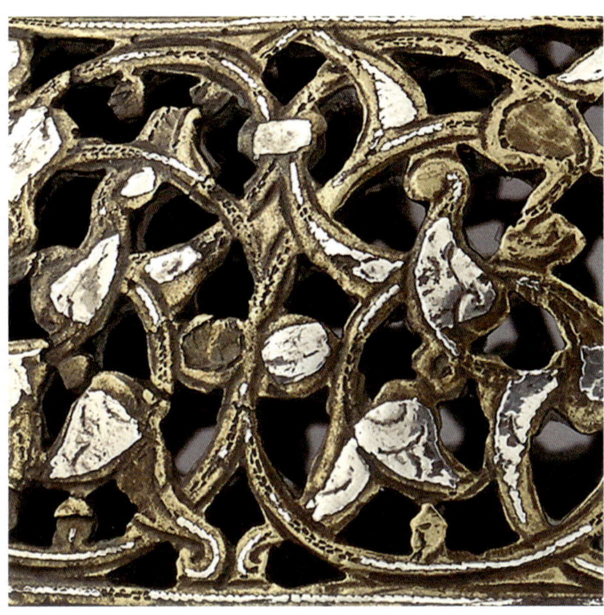

Cat. 22, detail showing pierced decoration done before the inlays were added

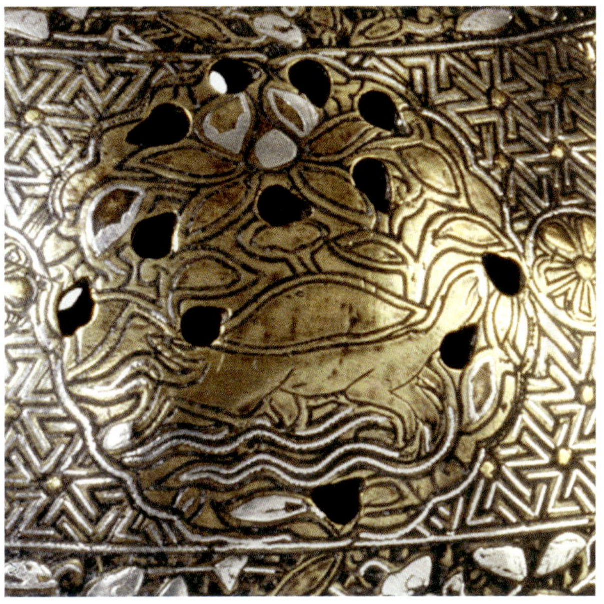

Cat. 23, detail showing pierced decoration done after the inlays were added

The David incense burner is quite different in style and inlay technique to both the British Museum incense burner and the Courtauld bag. The decoration includes figures in Mongol costume, lotus and other designs inspired by imported objects from eastern Asia. The areas for sheet inlays are not recessed and the hammered pits around their border are so close that they form a groove. A similar inlay technique is found on metalwork with distinctly Il-Khanid iconography, including Mongol court scenes, such as the facetted basin in the Victoria and Albert Museum (figs. 11–15). They are likely to have been made in a workshop located near the Il-Khanid court, perhaps in Tabriz.

The David incense burner seems to have been decorated and inlaid with silver without the metalworker being aware of its function, because clumsy holes were cut through the decoration after it had been inlaid – cutting through the silver inlays in some places (see detail above). This may be evidence that it was transported as a blank and decorated and pierced in a workshop where they had not seen such objects and/or were unskilled at cutting away metal in this manner.

NOTES

1 See Aga-Oglu 1945 and Ward 1992.
2 An incense burner of similar shape appears in an illustration to the *Maqamat* painted by al-Wasiti in Iraq in 634/1237; see Ettinghausen 1962, p. 121.
3 This inscription is published in Ward 1992, p. 80, fig. 14.

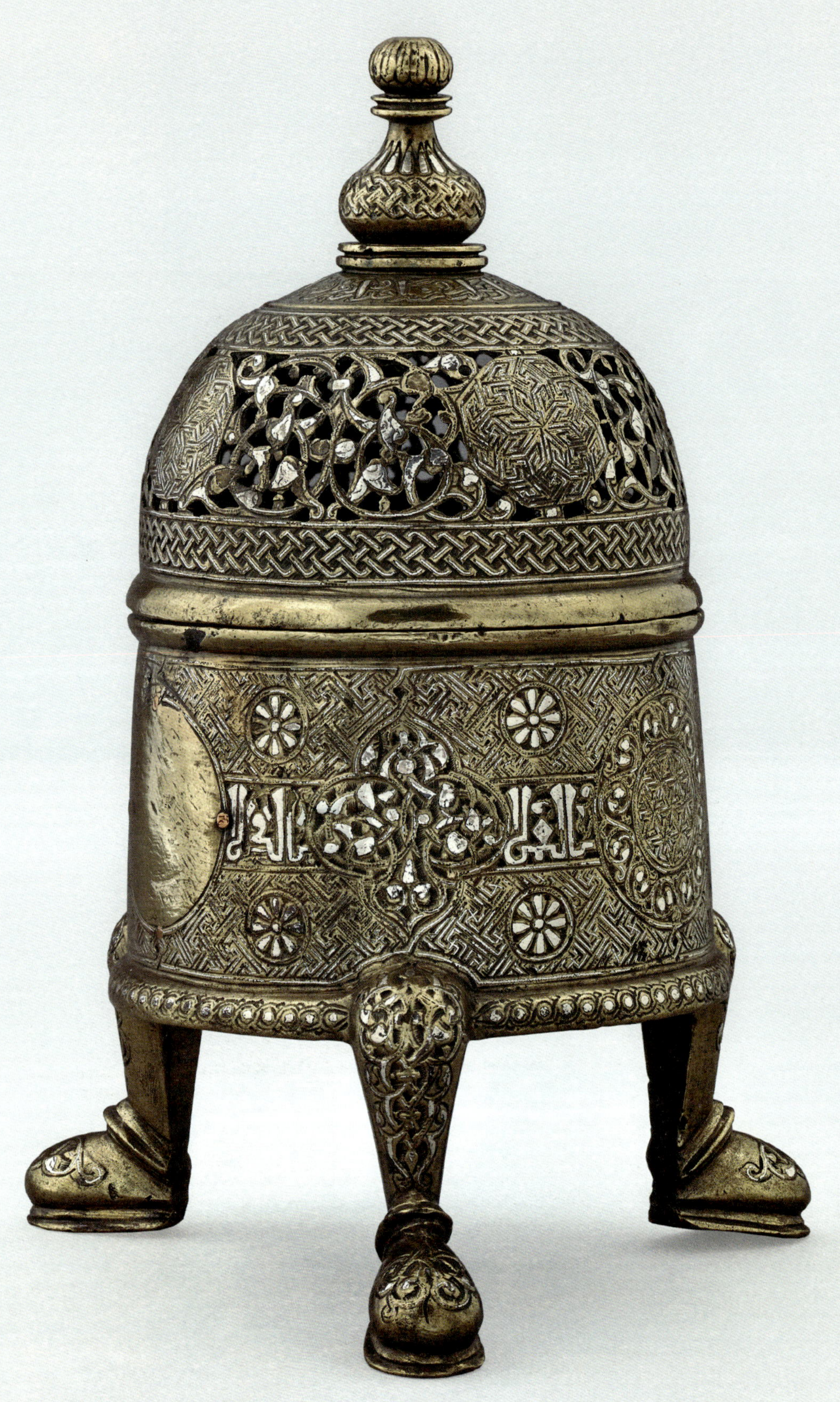

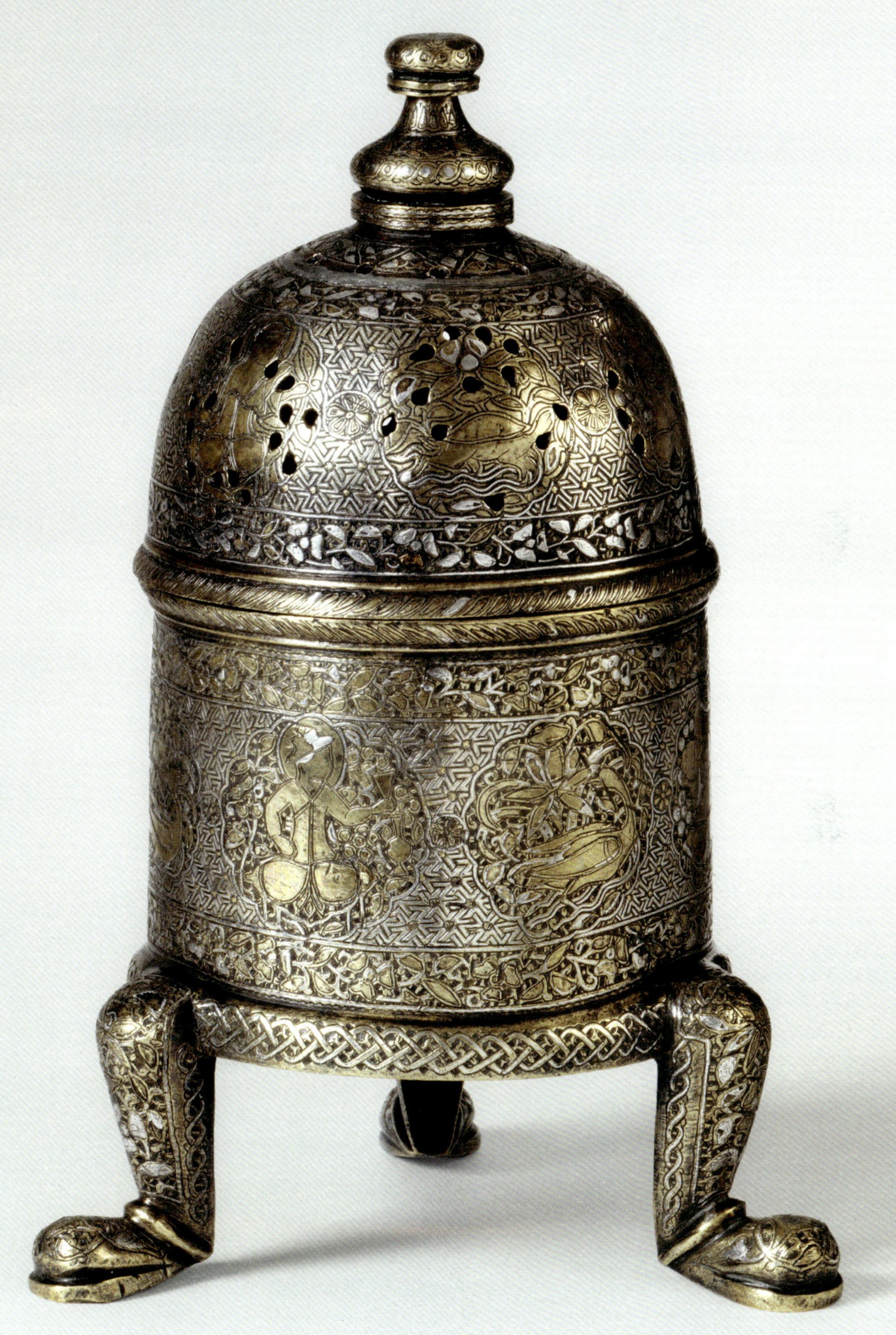

Ewer and basin

Mosul, *c.* 1275–1300
Brass, raised (ewer handle cast), engraved and inlaid with gold, silver and black material
H: (ewer) 37 cm, Diam: 20.6 cm; H: (basin) 17 cm, Diam: 43 cm
Berlin, Museum für Islamische Kunst, ewer I.6580, basin I.6581

THE EWER AND BASIN are signed by the inlayer on the underside of the flat lid of the ewer and under the lip of the basin: 'made by ᶜAli ibn ᶜAbdallah al-ᶜAlawi al-Naqqash al-Mawsili'. For a discussion of the work of ᶜAli ibn ᶜAbdallah and its relationship to other Mosul metalwork, see Raby above, pp. 63–65.[1] The ewer and basin were made and used as a set. A servant would have poured water from the ewer over the hands (or feet) of the owner or his guests before handing him a napkin to dry himself. While washing, the recipient would have had time to appreciate the decoration which reflected the pleasures and pursuits of the elite – ruling, hunting, feasting, astrology, calligraphy and poetry.

ᶜAli ibn ᶜAbdallah had a large and influential workshop which propagated particular compositions (see figs. 36–40), perhaps through the use of workshop pattern books. His style is softer than the geometric style seen on the Blacas ewer (cat. 21). He retains visual clarity without using a solidly patterned ground; instead he uses geometric designs to divide the composition into sections and give additional contrast where is it needed, for example around a figural medallion within a roundel. These vessels are the only signed examples of his work, although an incense burner of Mosul type in the British Museum repeats his distinctive figural style and provides additional evidence that ᶜAli ibn ᶜAbdallah's workshop was based in Mosul (see Ward above, p. 70).[2]

The Courtauld bag shows the influence of this craftsman's work. The seated figures in roundels are similar in scale and pose to his and much use is made of both birds and Z-pattern; but the startling contrast between the medallions and the T-pattern continues the geometric aesthetic first seen in the Blacas ewer by Shujaᶜ ibn Manᶜa.

The ewer has its original base, handle, spout and lid and so gives an accurate picture of the shape and manufacture of a Mosul ewer. The body was hammered to shape in one piece from foot to the moulding around the lower neck. The neck was made from a separate sheet hammered to shape and rolled into a funnel and soldered down the seam behind the handle. It was laid over the moulding, which helped to stop it slipping down into the body. The base, which was hammered into a decorative shape with relief petals radiating out from the centre, was separately applied and turned over the lower foot and soldered in place. The spout, like the neck, was rolled into a funnel then inserted into a separate collar soldered to the shoulder. A reinforcing ring was attached to the tip of the spout. A filter was inserted into the neck of the ewer and on top of it a separate flat sheet of brass with a hole cut in the centre, the cut brass then being hinged to the top to form an opening lid. The only cast element is the handle; the local foundry may have supplied these in bulk to various inlay workshops in Mosul because the same cast handles appear on ewers decorated in different styles.

The ewer is very finely inlaid in the traditional Mosul manner with deeply recessed areas bevelled towards the edge. The gold wire inlays were laid over parallel tracks of pits. Black inlays have now mostly

gone from the background. The four most
prominent roundels (on the neck and either
side of the spout) enclose a man enthroned
with roaring lions below and attendants to
either side playing a tambourine or flute or
handing him another beaker to replace the
one he is holding (fig. 39). The two remaining
roundels on the shoulder depict a nobleman
on horseback killing a lion and shooting
a bird (fig. 37). Around the base are eight
roundels, which is not the correct number for
a complete set either of the zodiac (twelve)
or of the planets (six). The craftsman chose
only the personifications of the zodiac (with
their planetary overlords) whose iconography
allowed seated figures (Jupiter in Pisces,
Venus in Libra, Mars in Scorpio, Mercury in
Virgo), and filled the other roundels with a
selection of seated figures of the planets alone
(Mars, Mercury, Sun, Moon). Presumably this
was to balance the images of enthroned rulers
on the shoulder and neck of the ewer.

The inscription round the lid and in
cartouches around the body contain wishes
arranged in rhyming pairs ending in *ā*,'
beginning *al-ʿizz wa al-baqā' wa'l-birr wa
al-ʿatā'* (glory and long life, godliness and
beneficence). First seen on metalwork from
Khurasan in the early thirteenth century,
inscriptions rhyming with *ā'* are found on
objects attributed to Mosul and western
Iran later in the century.[3] Round the foot are
wishes with qualifying adjectives beginning
al-ʿizz al-dā'im wa al-ʿumr al-sālim (eternal
glory, secure life) – a regular feature of earlier
Mosul metalwork (see cat. 22).

The basin was hammered to shape and
inlaid in the same manner as the ewer.
Around the basin is a band of inscription in
praise of an unnamed ruler (see Raby above,
p. 61) which is punctuated by medallions
with, alternately, an enthroned ruler flanked
by attendants, a horseman out hunting, two
revellers seated outside, one drinking, the
other playing a tambourine. Between them
are smaller roundels containing musicians
and drinkers. Inside the basin, enthroned
figures with attendants alternate with

horsemen hunting a variety of game, with
roundels between containing a personification
of the Moon. The base interior has a large
roundel with personifications of the planets
around the Sun, encircled by images of the
zodiac with their planetary overlord. Some of
the images are very unusual. Mars in Scorpio
has Mars with his trademark sword executing
a prisoner while a scorpion skulks behind
him, almost an afterthought. Venus playing
her lute has been joined by a backing band of
tambourinists (detail above).

The underside of the basin is engraved
and inlaid with silver almost as richly as
the visible surfaces. It has a large roundel
with intersecting circles in the centre which
could be a prototype for the designs on
the Courtauld bag (although filled with
arabesques rather than birds and geometric
designs). Around it is a narrow frieze of
decorative pseudo-Kufic interrupted by
medallions filled with arabesques. Rosettes
are scattered across the brass ground and
an elaborate plaited design runs around the
outer edge. Inscriptions around the basin
include verses seen on other metalwork
signed by craftsmen with the 'al-Mawsili'
nisba (see Raby above, pp. 61–62). Inside, the
inscriptions in the cartouches contain wishes
arranged in pairs ending in *ā'* as on the ewer.

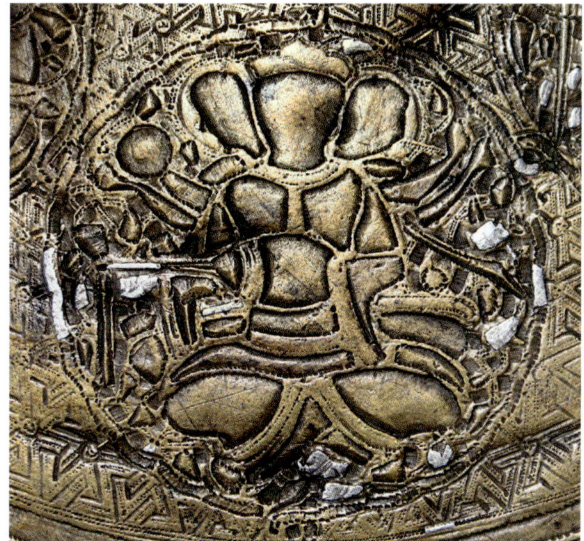

Cat. 25, detail of personification
of Venus from the interior base

NOTES

1 For the most recent publication
of the ewer and basin see Gladiss
2012, pp. 90–97.

2 For an illustration of the incense
burner see Ward 1993, fig. 61.

3 For inscriptions rhyming with
ā' in Khurasan see London 1976,
no. 188, p. 175, and Melikian-
Chirvani 1982, pp. 146, 154 note 46.
For the candlestick by Muhammad
ibn Fattuh see London 1976,
pp. 182–83. For similar inscriptions
on objects attributed to western
Iran see Melikian-Chirvani 1982,
nos. 75–77, pp. 169–78.

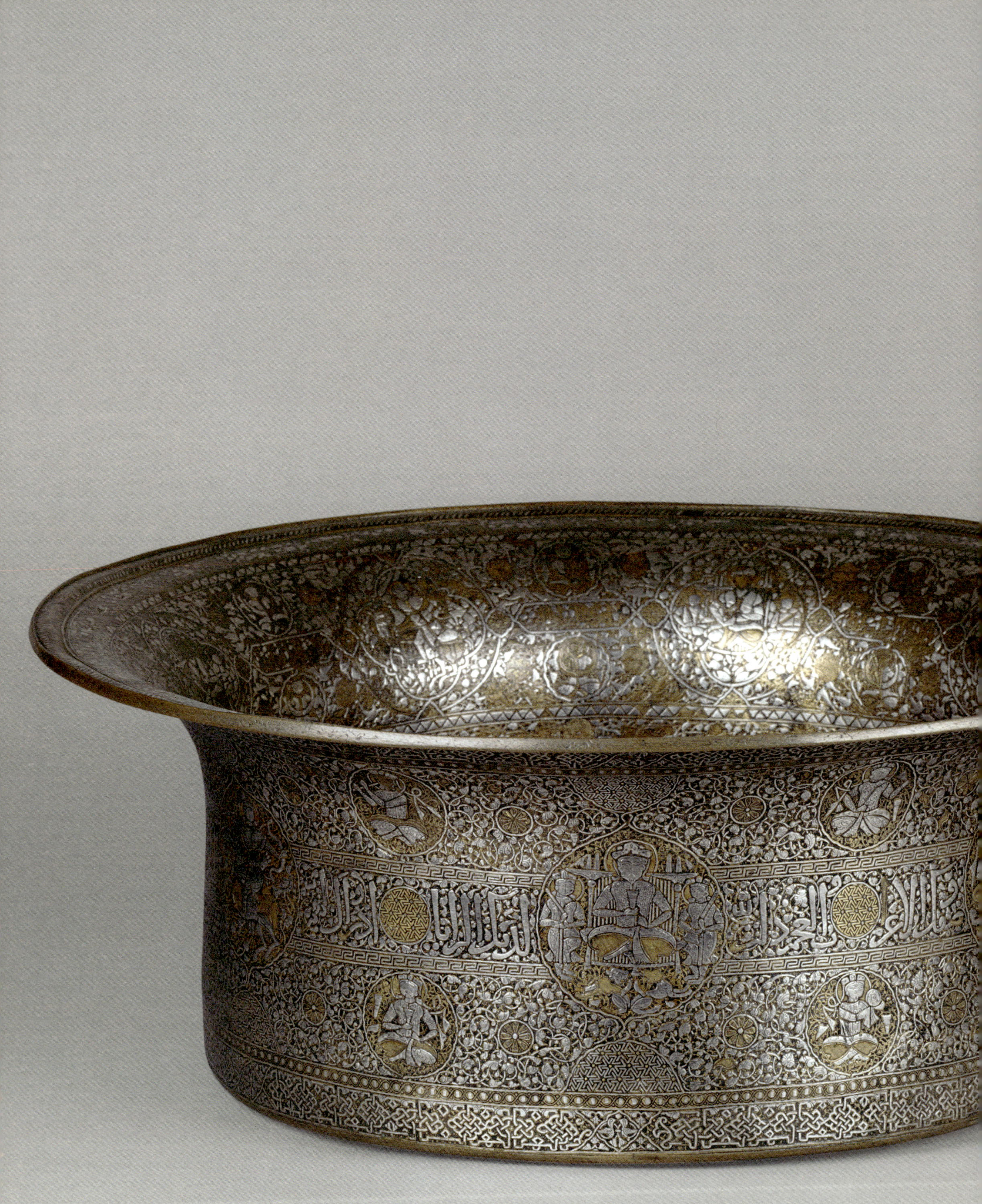

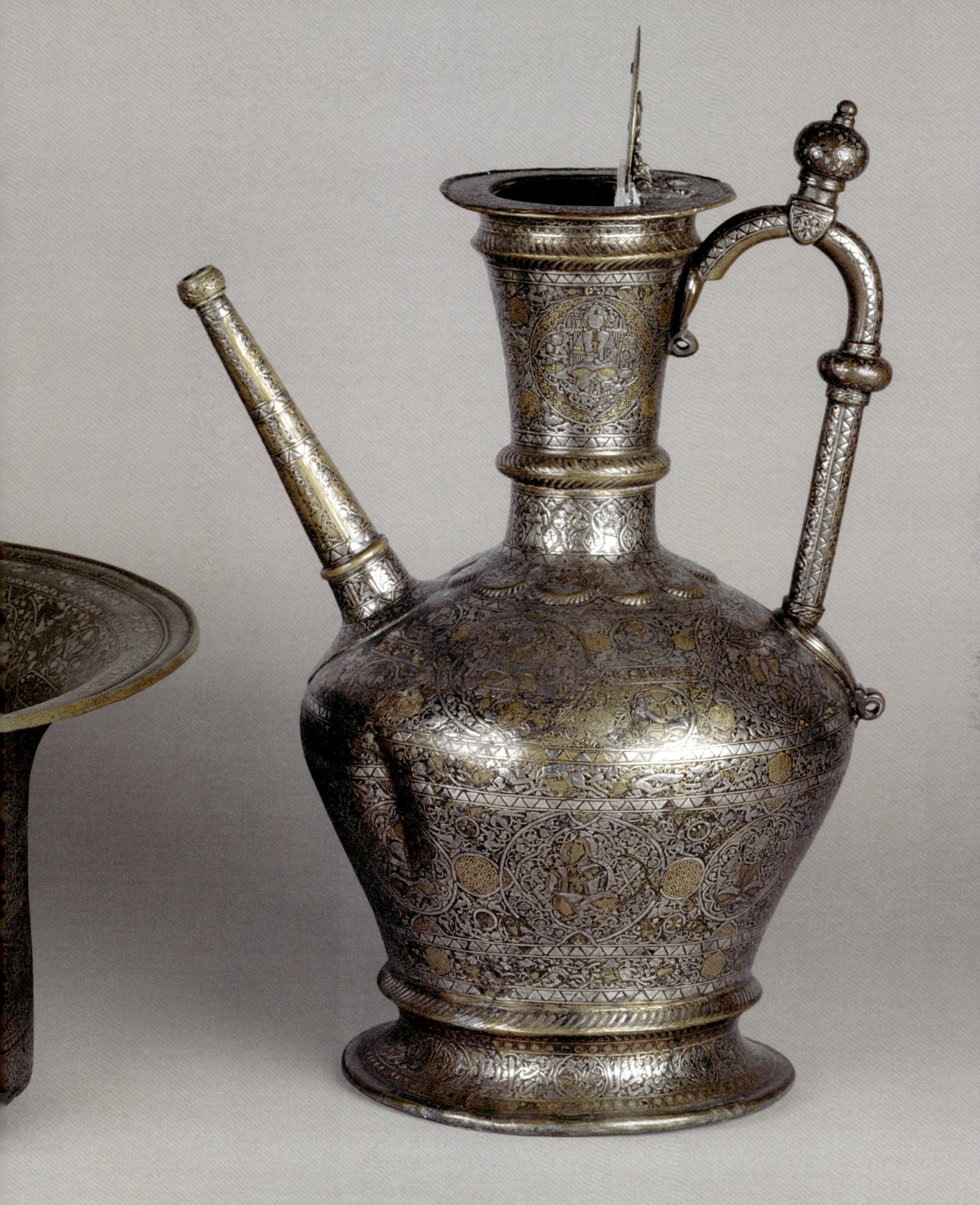

26

Candlestick

Mosul, 1300–30
Brass, raised, engraved and inlaid with silver, gold and black material
H: 19 cm, Diam: 24.5 cm
Copenhagen, David Collection, 27/1972

THIS NINE-SIDED brass candlestick, the socket of which is missing, was hammered in one piece up to and including the convex moulding at the base of the neck. A template is likely to have been used to achieve an accurate shape for the facetted body and sunken, gadrooned shoulder. A separate sheet was rolled into a tube to create the neck (the soldered join is still visible inside) then inserted within the moulding and soldered in place. Later a disk hammered to form a rosette in high relief was inserted inside to hide the mend.

The body of the candlestick is decorated with a series of large and small roundels linked by panels of gold inscription, with lozenges of paired birds providing a border above and below and a scattering of gold rosette medallions on the Z-pattern ground. The large roundels, spanning most of two facets, contain a design of intersecting circles filled with birds and Z-pattern. At its centre is a design in negative, the brass body chased with foliage on an inlaid silver ground. The small roundels fill just one facet and contain a 'cloud collar' design filled with T-pattern with paired birds outside. At its centre is another design in negative, the brass body chased with birds on an inlaid silver ground. The shoulder of the candlestick is decorated with a small inscription in gold. Z-pattern and leafy designs fill the sunken area and its gadrooned sides. The neck has roundels with a leafy border around a gold rosette medallions with more gold rosette medallions between on a Z-pattern.

The inscriptions on the body and the shoulder of the candlestick contain wishes with qualifying adjectives beginning *al-ʿizz al-dāʾim wa al-ʿumr al-sālim* (eternal glory, secure life and long life). Such inscriptions are typical of Mosul metalwork (see cat. 22, 24).

A range of facetted brass candlesticks was developed in the second half of the thirteenth century by sheet-metal workers and these continued into the fourteenth century, alongside imitations in cast brass.[1]

This candlestick shares many features with the Courtauld bag (cat. 1). It is a complex hammered object made of several separate sections for which moulds were used to ensure regularity. The silver inlays were inlaid into a recessed ground. Large roundels with intersecting circles filled with Z-pattern and birds and the gold rosette medallions on a geometric ground are seen again on all sides of the bag. The roundels with a cloud collar design or a leafy border around a circle in a row separated by gold rosette medallions recur on the base of the bag (see illustration p. 84). The small gold inscription is in a similar script, with rhyming wishes against a silver scroll, to the inscription which frames the court scene on the bag (see illustration pp. 86–87). They are likely to be contemporary products of the same workshop.[2]

NOTES

1 A nine-sided candlestick with a procession of standing courtiers encircling the body and the socket in the style of ʿAli ibn ʿAbdallah's ewer and basin was on the London art market in 2007.

2 Baer 1983, p. 30, attributes the candlestick to Syria but gives no reasons for doing so. Folsach 1990, fig. 328, labels it north-west Iran *c*. 1300.

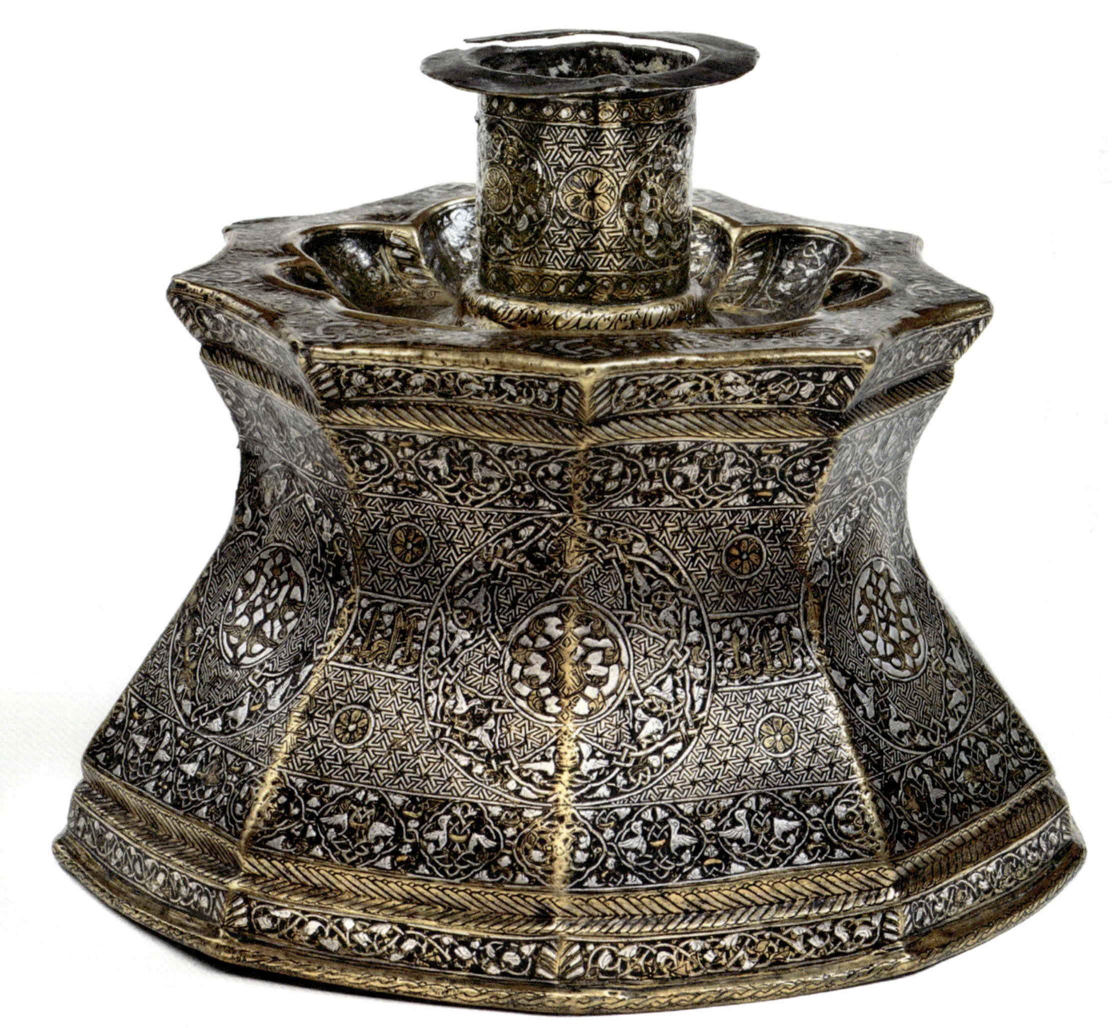

27

Box

Mosul, *c.* 1300–30
Brass, raised, engraved and inlaid with gold, silver and black material
H: 4.7 cm, W: 9.5 cm
London, British Museum, ME 1878,1230.677

THE KIDNEY SHAPE of the box is unique and its function is mysterious. It is tinned inside, which would suggest that the contents were perishable, but the tinning could have been done later. The silver fastenings are probably Ottoman additions but spaces left in the decoration of the lid suggest that it was intended to have fastenings, although there are no rivet holes so for some reason they were never fitted. Hinges were not standard on small boxes, which suggests that it was intended to contain something of high value. Presumably whatever it was required a box of this particular shape. Contents could be more precious than the surviving container: small boxes made in Mosul often carry the name of an Ayyubid sultan and probably functioned as packaging for a diplomatic gift to a royal neighbour.

Despite its small size, the box has a great variety of decoration with medallions containing birds and animals in interlaced foliage or interlaced foliage only, gold rosettes, Z-medallions, running animals, all on a Z-pattern. The inlays of gold and silver are carefully set into recessed areas of brass with undercut sides and the ground of the medallions and panels would have been filled with black material to add contrast.

Despite the differences in their scale, the parallels between the box and the Courtauld bag are striking. Both are containers of an unusual curving shape with a raised panel on the lid. Both have a similar inlay technique with a recessed brass ground. Both add colour and contrast with the generous use of gold and the solid black grounds of medallions which stand out against the pale silvery geometric designs. The decoration on both features rosettes, birds and Z-pattern and some of the chased details, such as the eyes of the birds or the veins of the leaves, are almost identical. The only scholar who has published the box is Baer, who attributed it to "North Mesopotamia or Syria, second half of thirteenth century", but it is likely to have been made in the same workshop and within a few years of the Courtauld bag, so may also be attributed to Mosul, *c.* 1300–30.[1]

NOTE
1 Baer 1983, pp. 80–81 and fig. 61.

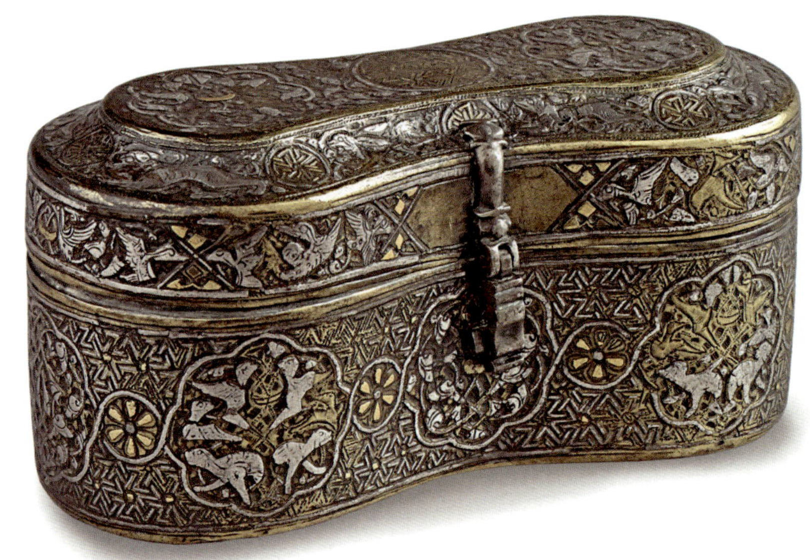

28

Pen box

Mosul, early 14th century
Brass, raised and inlaid with gold, silver
and black material
L: 22.2 cm
London, British Museum, ME 1881,0802.19

THE ROUND-ENDED PEN BOX is made
from sheet brass with two hinges and a
fastener made separately and soldered in
place. Inside the box was originally divided
into two sections. The long left section would
have had reed pens and a knife to sharpen
them. The smaller right section was originally
covered by a flat brass top from which were
suspended three containers, for wool soaked
with ink, starch and sand.

The lid and the base are finely decorated
on all sides with roundels containing seated
musicians and drinkers with birds and
geometric designs between. The sides have a
lattice design filled with birds and geometric
or leafy patterns.

Rounded-ended pen boxes were popular
products of the metal inlay workshops
in Mosul from the early thirteenth to the
mid fourteenth century. They are shown
in contemporary illustrations, for example
beside the scribes in fig. 16. This pen box
provides a bridge between the figural pen
boxes of the previous century and the non-
figural pen boxes of the fourteenth century
with their focus on lattice designs, paired
birds and geometric patterns (figs. 43–45).[1]

The combination of musicians and
revellers and details of style, such as the
manner in which drapery is depicted or
duff (tambourine) written on the frame drum
held by a musician within the pen box, are
directly comparable to the decoration of the
Courtauld bag and so the pen box is likely to
be a contemporary product, perhaps from the
same workshop.

NOTE

1 A pen box from the Nuhad es-Said
Collection also provides a bridge
between the earlier and later pen
boxes. See Allan 1982, no. 16,
pp. 90–92.

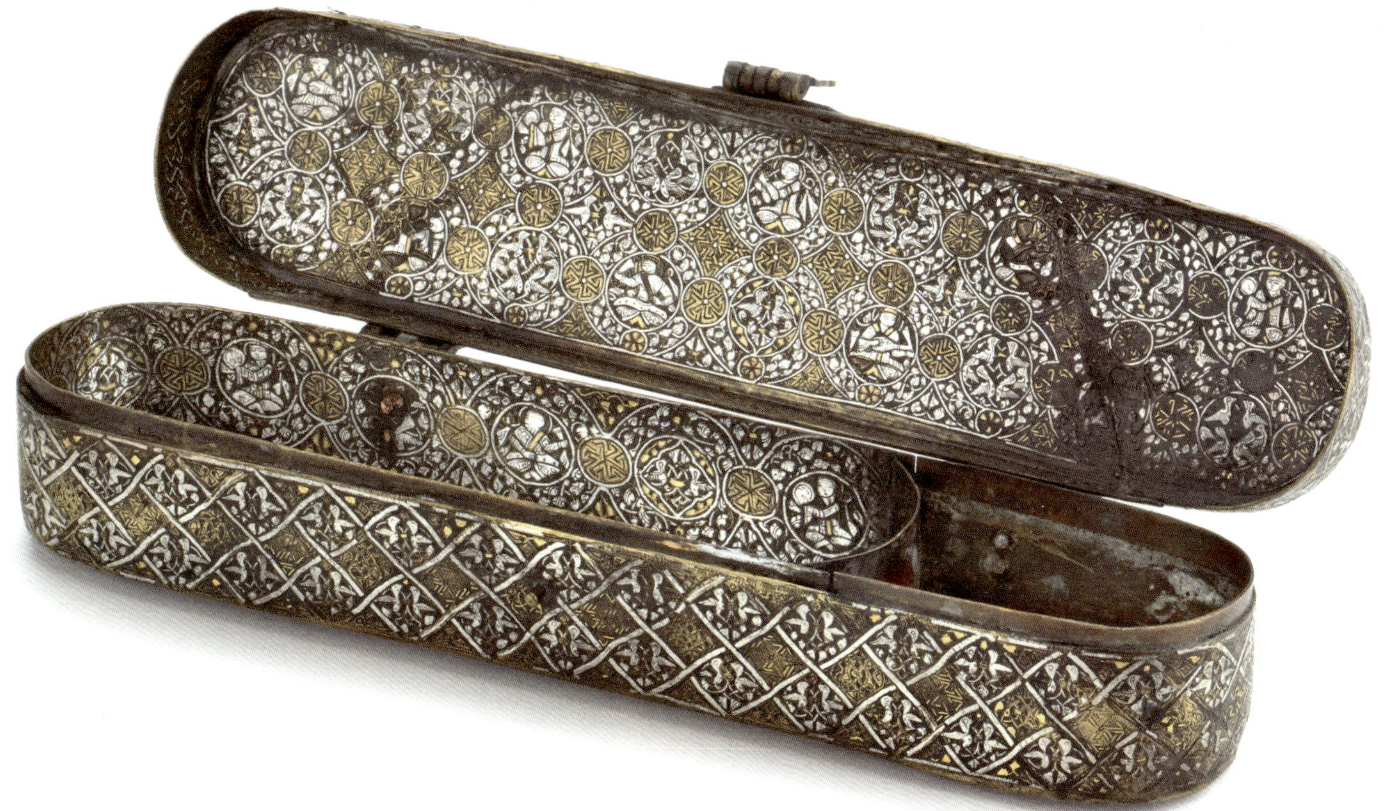

29

Pen box

Mosul, *c.* 1300–30
Brass, raised, engraved and inlaid with gold and silver; silver top added later
L: 25.1 cm, W: 3.1 cm
Baltimore, Walters Art Museum, 54.509

THE BODY of the pen box is raised from a single sheet of brass, the sides turned inwards to support the lid. The top is in two parts. The wider end originally consisted of a sheet of brass soldered to the sides, with holes cut through to hold containers for the ink etc. Most of it has since been replaced in silver and the surviving brass top has been re-attached about a centimetre too high, so that it does not fit properly with the decoration of the lid. The separate flat lid was reinforced by a decorative arched panel at the foot and narrow strips of metal along the sides. It was riveted through the foot so that it could swivel out to the left, through a gap where the top was not soldered to the side.

Inlays have been used extravagantly. The silver inlays are set into well recessed areas, but are of such thick sheet that they stand proud of the surface. The gold inlays are used for numerous details and are set into brass that has been only slightly recessed. There are no black inlays – perhaps because the metal inlays were so plentiful that little of the ground remained visible.

The lid is decorated with a series of horsemen out hunting in an ingenious composition that makes full use of the unusual shape of the space. The leader is chasing two deer who are disappearing into the arched top while he reaches for an arrow. Behind him, two horsemen attack the lion between them with bow and sword. A man on foot, carrying a sword and small shield, follows the horsemen and behind him a small hare cowers within the narrowing arch, as if hiding in his burrow. The horsemen in the hunting scene are Mongol in style, the front one with wide-brimmed hat and round face and nose similar to the figures in the court scene on the Courtauld bag (illustrated pp. 86–87).

Decoration on the underside of the pen box is drawn from the traditional Mosul repertoire made popular by the workshop of ʿAli ibn ʿAbdallah, with birds in interlace and rosettes on a Z-pattern and a short inscription reading 'eternal glory'. The sides have a monumental Kufic inscription which was specially designed for the tapering shape

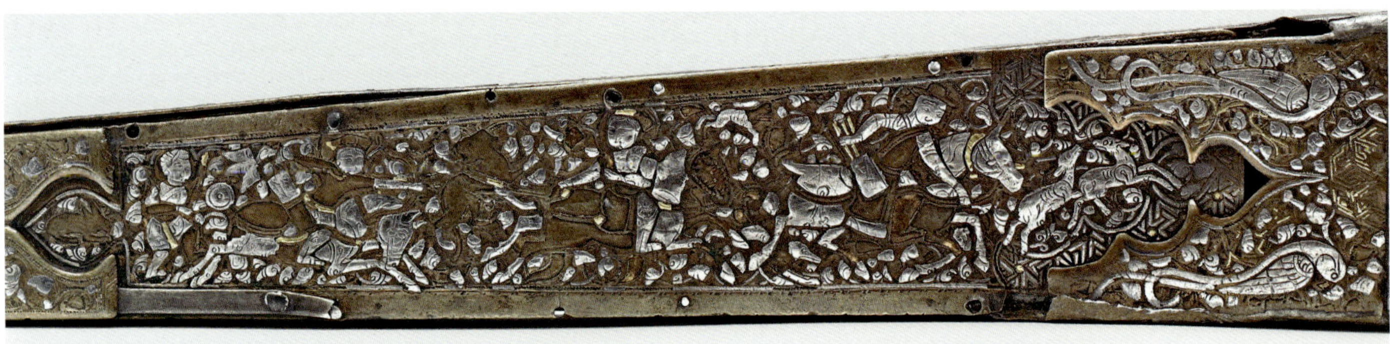

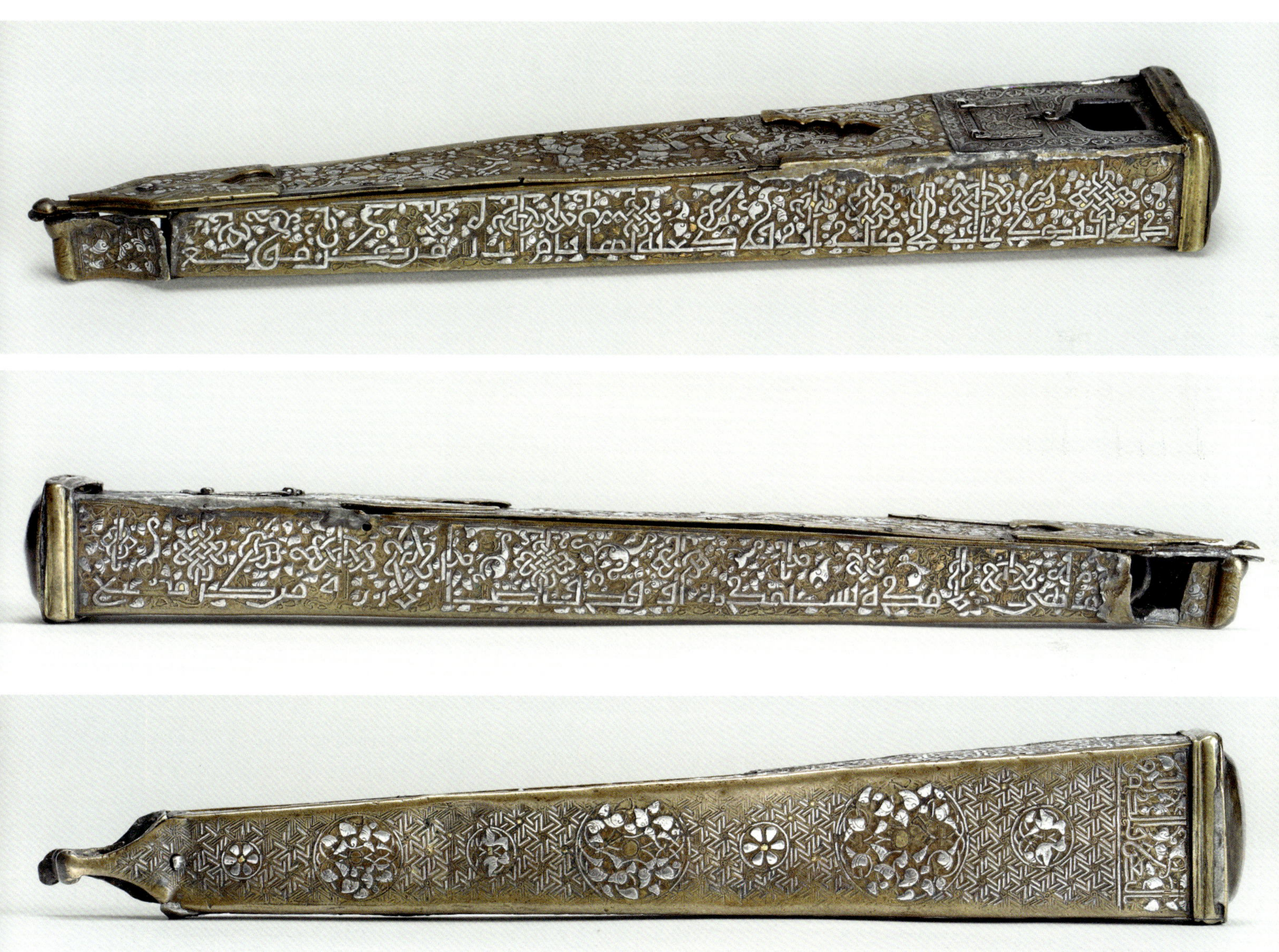

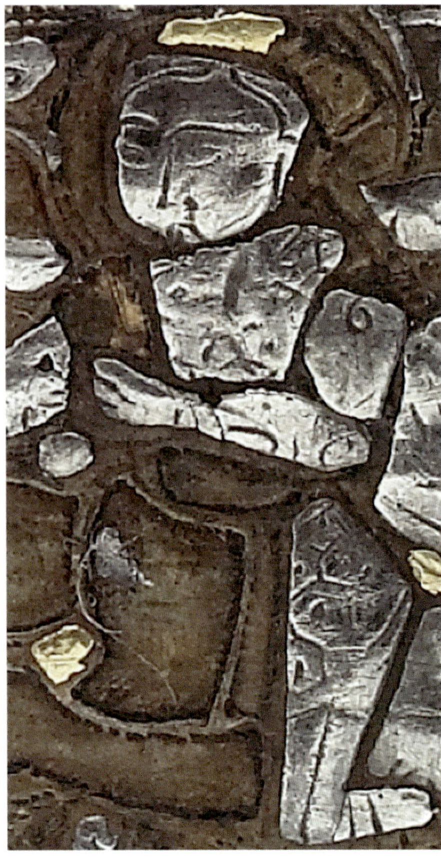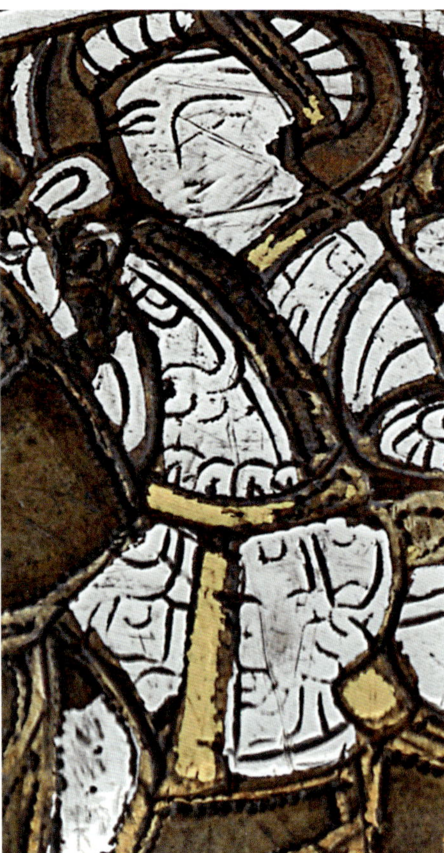

Cat. 29 and 1, details of horsemen from the Baltimore pen box and Courtauld bag showing similarities in style and inlay technique

of the pen box. Its content suggests that the owner was amongst the ruling elite, if not the Il-Khan himself. 'Your government shall rise without declining, if it has as its basis the largest number of people from every place.'[1]

This pen box is inspired by the narrow, tapering pen boxes, designed to be tucked inside a belt, which were popular in Khurasan between the twelfth and fifteenth century.[2] Previously attributed to north-west Iran and the twelfth to thirteenth century, it has many characteristics of metalwork here attributed to Mosul.[3] However, in Mosul, larger rectangular pen boxes, with round or square ends, were usually preferred, so this pen box is likely to have been made as a special commission.[4]

The pen box shares several features with the Courtauld bag (cat. 1). It is of an unusual shape with an ingenious opening mechanism made from sheet brass. The thick sheet inlays are set into well recessed areas yet stand proud of the surface. A contemporary Il-Khanid image that may derive from a pictorial model is combined with traditional Mosul designs. This image was given particular prominence on both objects: on one it was recessed and framed by surrounding metal, on the other it was raised and framed by an inlaid border and inscription. An inscription was specially composed and designed for both objects. Few workshops would have been capable of the complex manufacture and elaborate decoration of either object and small details such as the shape and veins of the leaves in the background and the sprinkling of rosette medallions support the attribution of them both to the same workshop.

NOTES

1 Reading from the Walters Art Museum website, http://art. thewalters.org/detail/13800/pen-and-ink-box.
2 For two examples dating to the fifteenth century see Komaroff 1992, pp. 163–65.
3 Pope and Ackerman 1938–39, pl. 1333B (Iran, thirteenth century); London 1976, no. 193 (north-west Persia, twelfth–thirteenth century).
4 Another tapering pen box with the same opening mechanism may also be from the western Il-Khanate; see Baer 1983, fig. 49.

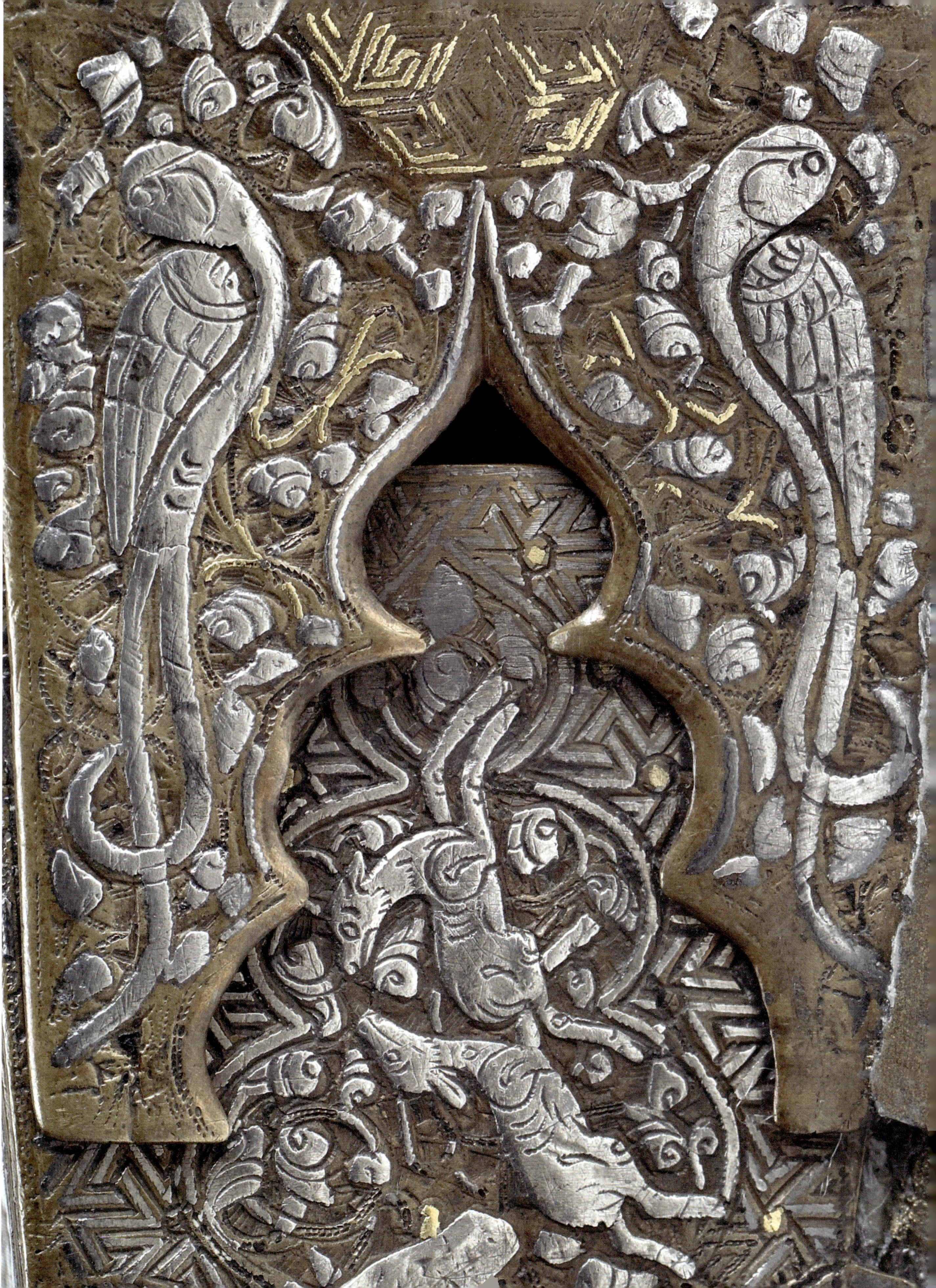

30

Spherical incense burner

Mosul, 1319–35 (1327–28?)
Brass, raised, engraved and inlaid with gold, silver and black material
Diam: 17 cm
Florence, Museo Nazionale del Bargello, inv. Dep. 6

THE SPHERICAL INCENSE BURNER is made in two halves, joined by a bayonet fitting. Burning incense would have been placed in a saucer suspended within gimbals inside, so that the ball could be rolled across the floor emitting fragrant smoke.[1]

The incense burner is lavishly inlaid with silver and gold on a black ground. The brass is recessed and the edges undercut to hold the inlays in place. A bold inscription is the main feature of the decoration. It is punctuated by large roundels with a design of intersecting circles filled with birds and Z-pattern and framed by a frieze of diamond shapes containing a leafy motif. The apex of both halves has a large lobed roundel filled with scrolling leaves.

The inscription of each half reads: 'Glory to your Lord, the Great Sultan, Dominant over the nations, the Sultan of the sultans of the Arabs and non-Arabs, ʿAla' al-Dunya wa'l-Din Bahadur Khan Sultan Abu Saʿid.'[2]

Sultan Abu Saʿid ruled the Il-Khanate between 1317 and 1335 but only received the title Bahadur Khan in 1319.[3] The inscription on the incense burner is very similar in content, layout and calligraphy to the inscription on the ball support from the Nisan Tası (fig. 46). They may both have been part of a much larger commission for Mosul inlaid metalwork from Abu Saʿid in 1327–28 (see Ward above, pp. 73–74).

Spherical incense burners of this type are usually attributed to a Syrian workshop, because several are in the name of Mamluk amirs and the Mamluks continued to make them for local use and for export into the fifteenth century.[4] However, at least one large incense burner was made in the workshop of ʿAli ibn ʿAbdallah (see fig. 38) and this one made for Abu Saʿid has nothing Mamluk about its decoration. It is very similar in size and decoration to another in the Metropolitan Museum, New York, inscribed with anonymous royal titles.[5] They both feature roundels with intersecting circles, geometric designs and paired birds and a lattice frieze with a leafy motif. They are typical of metalwork here attributed to Mosul in the early fourteenth century.

The bold letters of the titular inscription, with their large sheets of inlay, dominate the decoration on the incense burner and obscure the similarities between the remaining designs and those of the group of metalwork here attributed to Mosul – the large roundels filled with birds and geometric ornament, the lattice frieze, the six-sided medallions, and even the details of chasing on the background foliage and birds.

NOTES

1 For a discussion of these incense burners and the incense burnt in them see Ward 1992.

2 Inscriptions read and translated by Manijeh Bayani. The title Bahadur Khan appears before ʿAla' al-Dunya wa'l Din on the other half.

3 Melikian-Chirvani 1987, pp. 232–33.

4 Spallanzani 2010, p. 66 and fig. 40, attributes this incense burner to Syria.

5 Metropolitan Museum of Art inv. 17.190.2095. The museum has always labelled it Mamluk, but neither the inscription (which omits *al-sultan*) nor the decoration is Mamluk in style.

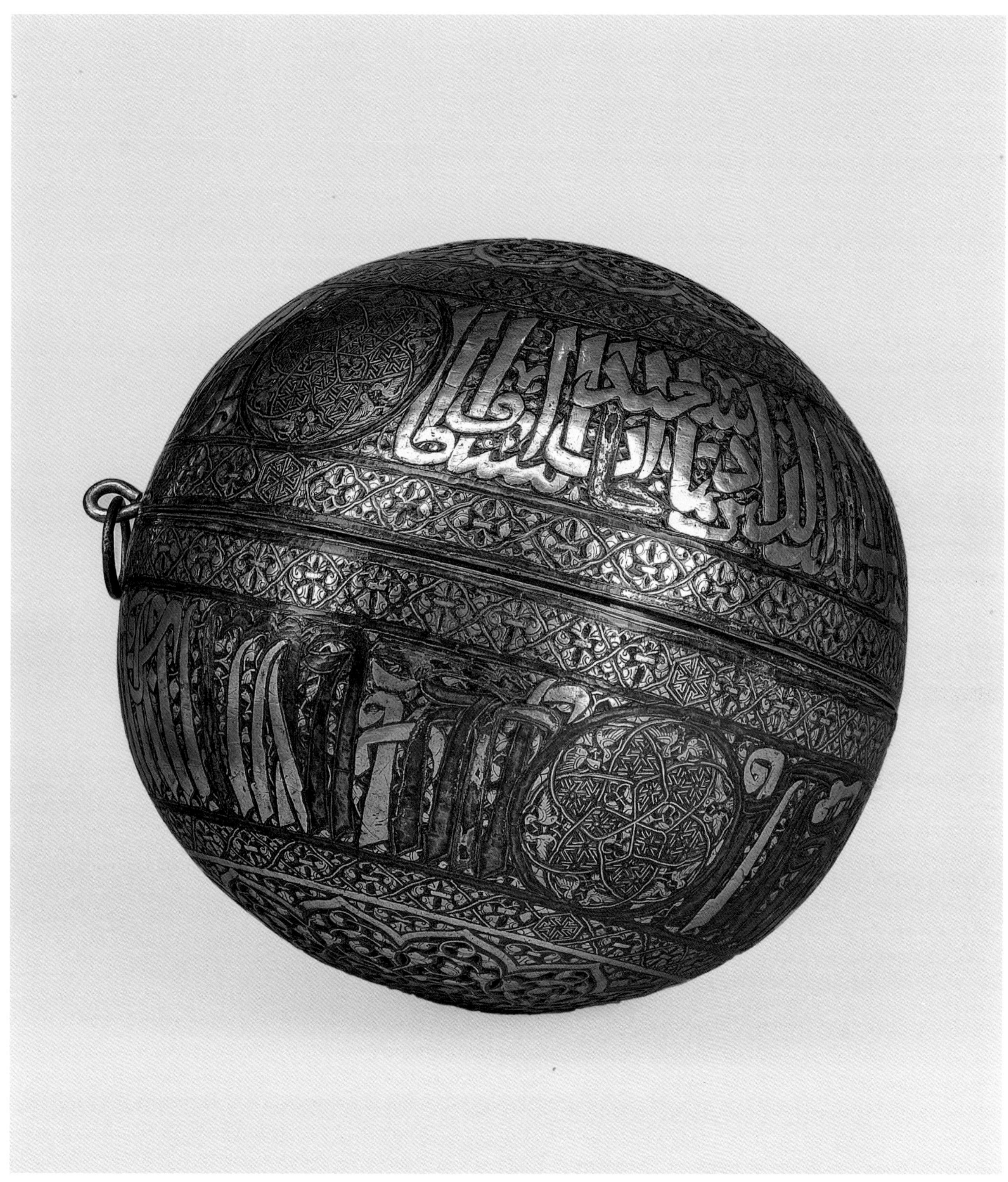

31–33

Three star tiles

Kashan, dated 739/1338–39 (cat. 31); 1330s (cat. 32 and 33)
Fritware, overglaze lustre painted
Diam: 21.5 cm, D: 1.9 cm (cat. 31); Diam: 12.5 cm, D: 0.9 cm (cat. 32); Diam: 20.7 cm, D: 1.3 cm (cat. 33)
London, British Museum, ME OA+1123 (cat. 31); ME Godman 221 (cat. 32); ME Godman 229 (cat. 33)

EIGHT-POINTED STAR TILES like these were produced in Kashan, Iran, in the thirteenth and fourteenth centuries.[1] They are decorated in lustre, an overglaze second firing of copper and silver oxides that created a metallic reflection which could appear quite golden. Tiles and vessels decorated in lustre were much admired and exported across Iran.

With the Mongol invasion, motifs seen on imported vessels and textiles from eastern Asia entered the artistic repertoire but the figural style remained traditional for longer, perhaps because figures are rare in Chinese decorative arts.[2] Figures on tiles surviving from Takht-i Sulaiman, the palace complex built for Abaqa Khan (ruled 1265–82) in the 1270s, are surrounded by lotus, dragons and phoenix, but they have no Mongol features.[3] The earliest surviving tiles decorated with Mongol courtiers with looped hair and feathered hats are dated 689/1290–91.[4] Kashan, like Mosul, was some distance from the heart of the Il-Khanid state. Wall paintings and illustrated manuscripts, which were produced within court circles, are likely to have seen developed Mongol iconography earlier, although nothing survives before the end of the thirteenth century.[5]

These tiles were probably destined for palaces, where each would have been displayed with others, to be seen together as an assembly like the roundels on the Courtauld bag (cat. 1). Visually the impact of large areas of star and cross tiles with small designs in each would have been similar to the carpet pages of contemporary Qur'ans (cat. 35 and 36).

In cat. 31, two figures are seated either side of a bowl of fruit on three tall legs. One is pouring liquid from a bottle, the other holds his hand up to indicate conversation. Two smaller faces behind them probably represent attendants. It is an exterior setting with flowers and foliage and a plump bird flying between them. The fabric of their tunics is richly patterned and their hats with back flaps and feathers are similar to two on the Courtauld bag. The stained lower right edge has been taken from another tile. The Persian inscriptions in informal cursive script contain poetry but also the date and the information that the tile was made in Kashan.[6]

In cat. 32, a seated figure plays the lute outside surrounded by plants and foliage. He wears a turban and a relatively simple spotted tunic, indicating that he is not a member of the Il-Khanid elite but represents one of the musicians who would have entertained guests to the palace. In cat. 33, a seated figure drinks from a beaker surrounded by plants. He wears a Mongol feathered headdress with a long flap at the back and a tunic of the same design as that of cat. 31. This is one of a set of four tiles acquired together, the other three being decorated with animals within a chinoiserie landscape.[7]

NOTES

1 For an account of the development of lustre wares in Iran see Watson 1985, especially the chapter on tiles and their uses pp. 122–56, and Porter 1995, pp. 32–54.

2 There are figures on some Yuan embroideries and tapestries: New York 1997b, nos. 25 and 59.

3 Watson 1985, fig. La.

4 For a Mongol courtier on a tile dated 689/1290–91 in a private collection see New York 2002, no. 111 and fig. 40. A similar tile is in the David Collection in Copenhagen.

5 The earliest dated depictions of Il-Khanid courtiers are in the double frontispiece to the *Tarikh-i jahan-gusha* (History of the World Conqueror), which has the author and companion both depicted in Mongol dress with lotus blossom on the tree behind and Chinese cloud scrolls behind the horse depicted opposite. The manuscript is dated 689/1290 and attributed to Iraq (Baghdad?). See New York 2002, no. 1, and fig. 201 on p. 173.

6 Porter 1995, p. 45 and fig. 35.

7 For an image of the four tiles together see Porter 1995, fig.17.

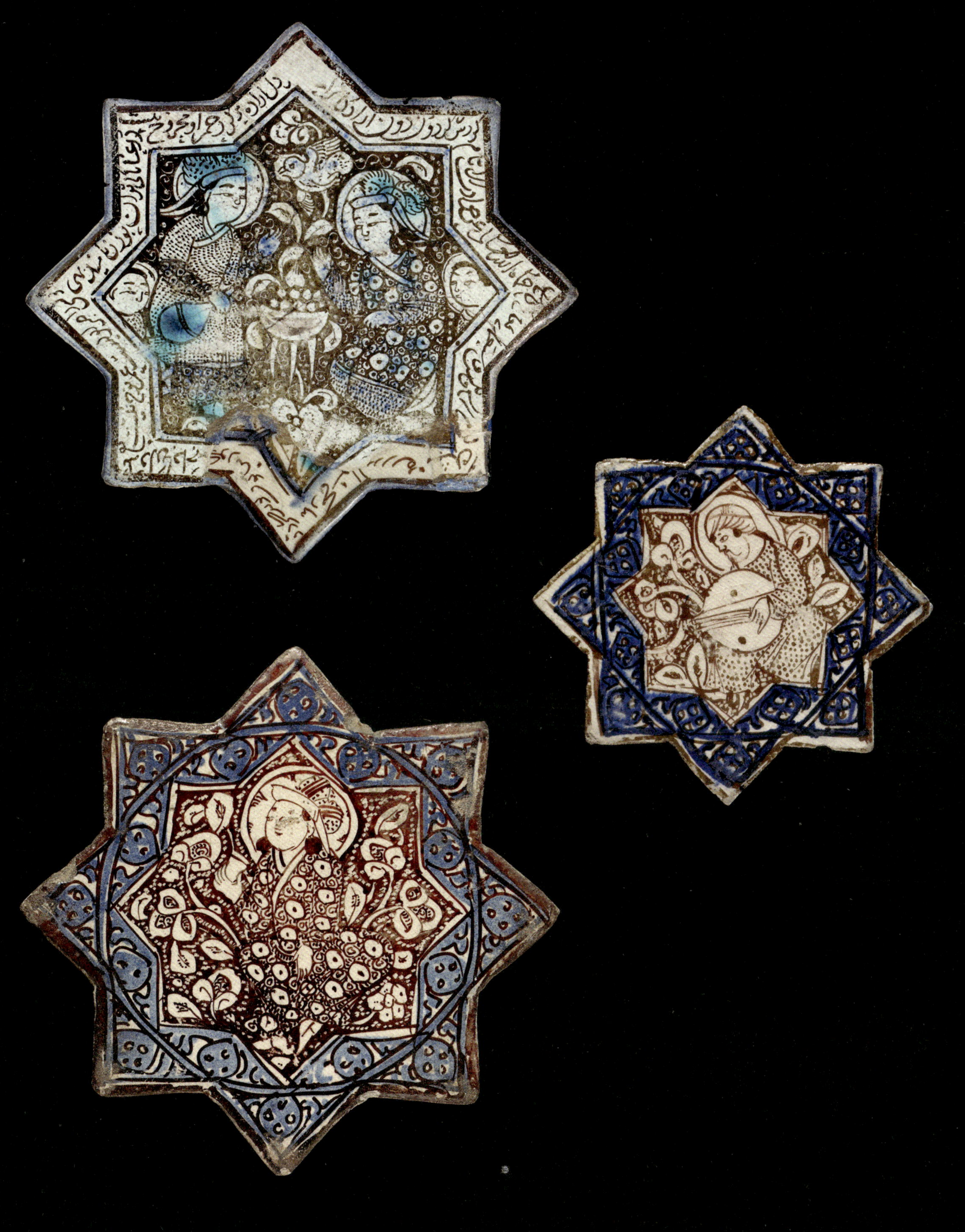

34

The Book of the Wonders of Creation and the Peculiarities of Existing Things

Jazira (possibly Mosul) or north-west Iran, 1295–1310
Ink, colours and gold on paper
H: 31.2 cm, W: 19.8 cm (page)
London, British Library, Or.14140

THE BOOK *of the Wonders of Creation and the Peculiarities of Existing Things* (*Kitāb ᶜAjā'ib al-makhlūqāt wa gharā'ib al-mawjūdāt*) was written by Muhammad ibn Mahmud al-Qazvini (*c.* 1203–1283) in Iraq in the 1270s and dedicated to ᶜAta-Malik Juvaini, Governor of Baghdad. It is divided into two sections, describing the wonders of the celestial and the terrestrial worlds. These paintings come from a lavishly illustrated copy of the text which has been attributed to Mosul by Carboni, who suggests that the city was producing other illustrated manuscripts, as well as illuminated Qur'ans, during the Il-Khanid period.[1]

This first folio comes from a section of the book which describes *jinn*s, spiritual creatures who live in a world invisible to humans but who can adopt different physical forms and can be both wicked and good.

The painting illustrates the tale of the singer Ibrahim, who has been locked in a cellar by his master and is visited by a *jinn* in the form of an old man, who offers him food and drink and orders him to sing.[2] The story ends with the *jinn* so amazed by Ibrahim's singing that he persuades his master to free him, and when he is told this story he rewards Ibrahim with 1700 dinars.[3] In the painting, Ibrahim sings and plays the lute while the *jinn*, a rather young-looking old man, holds out a beaker recently filled with red wine from the bottle in his other hand, in celebration of his music. The two figures are seen against a simple red background surrounded by a bricked structure representing the cellar.

The style of turban, the wide sleeves with brown/gold trim and *tiraz* bands, the

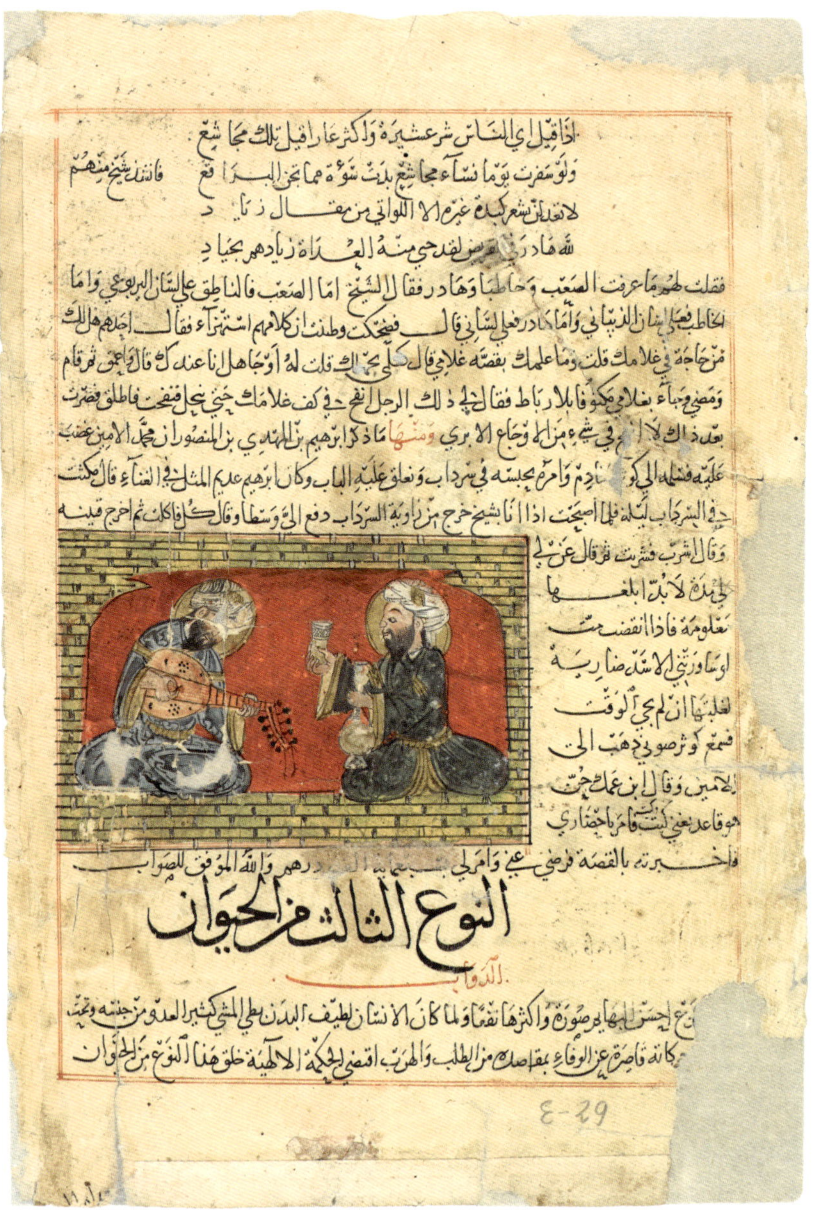

34a The singer Ibrahim and the Jinn (fol. 102v)

squiggly folds of Ibrahims's tunic, the shape of the bottle and the beaker all recur in the roundels of seated musicians and drinkers on the Courtauld bag and suggest that there was a close relationship between painting and inlaid metalwork at this period. Painters may have provided designs for the metal inlayers to copy.[4]

The painting in the second folio is damaged, with part of it missing on the left, although a section of furniture with a bolster suggests that it originally showed the king, mentioned in the text, waking in bed.[5] Al-Qazvini writes: 'It is said that on [New Year's] day … the king sits and all his servants and subjects go to him according to a curious custom: when [the king] wakes up, just as his eyes open, they see a handsome servant riding a beautiful horse and holding a pretty falcon in his hands'.[6]

"All his servants and subjects" are represented by a turbaned man leaning forward, his hand indicating conversation. Behind him is the handsome servant leading his horse and holding the falcon out towards the king on his red falconer's glove. The servant is a Mongol page with Asian features, looped hair and a splendid feathered hat. Other illustrations in the manuscript also show Mongol influence, which suggests that Mongol figures and motifs were already current in the Mosul area in the early fourteenth century, the proposed date of the Courtauld bag.

According to the text in the third folio, the spring in a village was dry for a month. The villagers put on their best clothes, took their musical instruments and played and danced near it and water started flowing once more.

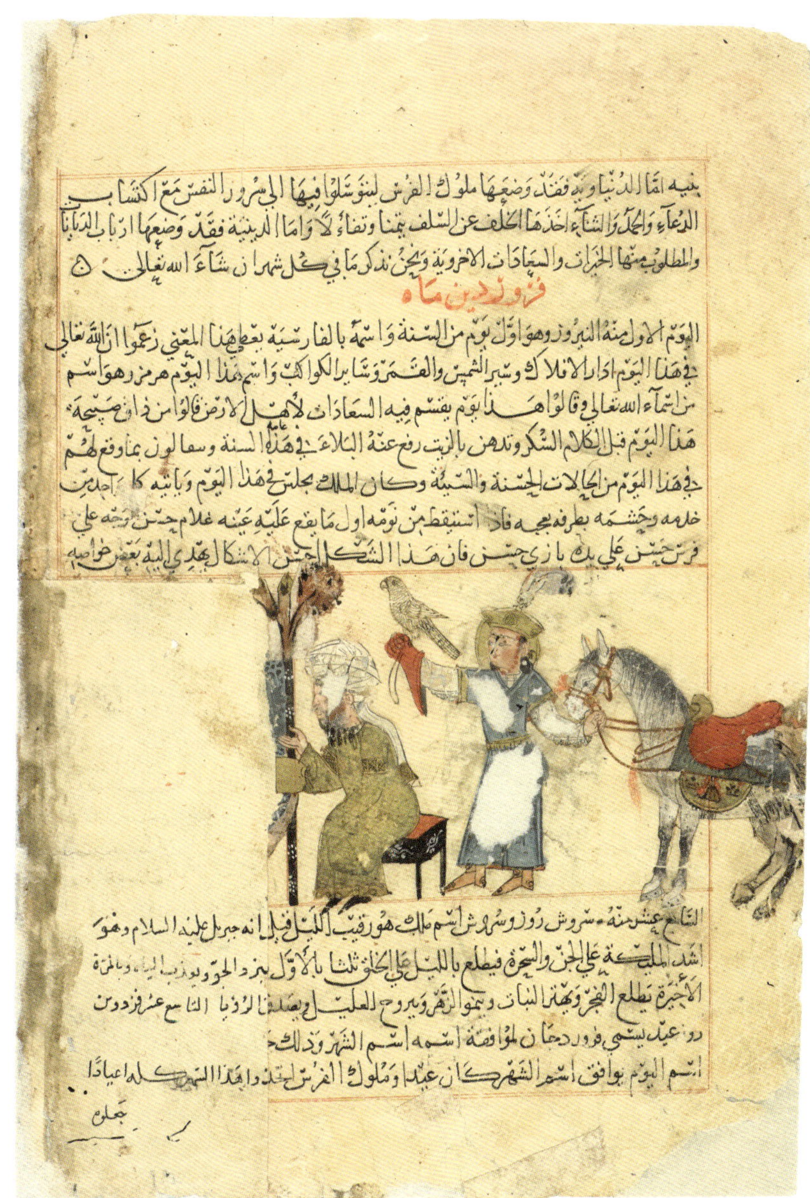

34b A custom of the Persian New Year's Day (fol. 20v)

The illustration depicts a woman dancing beside the spring (indicated by a small mound) to music played by four men on a lute, flute and two tambourines; the man on the far right appears to be an onlooker. The gold squares on the front of their robes and the *tiraz* bands on their arms indicate that they are in their finery.[6]

NOTES

1 For a detailed study of this manuscript see Carboni 1988–89 and 1992.

2 The painting has been published in Carboni 1988–89, pl. 7d; Carboni 1992, pp. 221–22; New York 2002, no. 15, p. 248, fig. 259.

3 For a translation of this part of the text see Carboni 1992, I, pp. 221–22.

4 Several craftsmen (including ᶜAli ibn ᶜAbdallah alᶜAlawai al-naqqash al-Mawsili; see cat. 24 and 25) describe themselves as *al-naqqāsh* (designer/decorator) in their signatures. This term is not specific to metalwork and they may have been working with other media also.

5 Carboni 1992, I, p. 88, suggests that the painting depicts a king enthroned but the angled side of the horizontal part suggests a bed rather than a throne and the turbaned man is looking down not up.

6 Translation Carboni 1992, I, p. 88.

7 See Carboni 1992, I, p. 148, for a translation of the text.

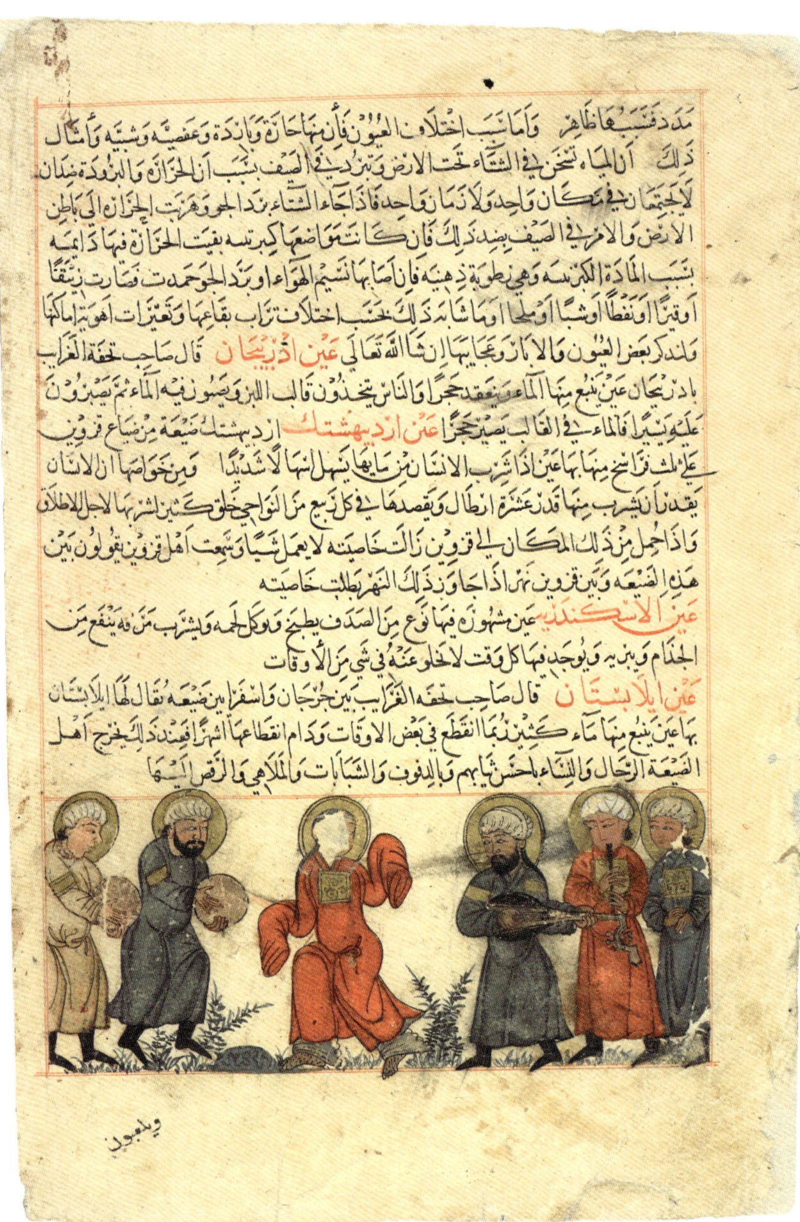

34c Musicians at the spring of Ilabustan (fol. 63v)

35–36

Two volumes from a Qur'an

Mosul, 710/1310
Ink, colour and gold on paper
Each page H: 57 cm, W: 40 cm
London, British Library, Or. 4945, volume 25, fols. 1v and 2r

Mosul, 706/1306–07
Ink, colour and gold on paper
Each page H: 47.7 cm, W. 34.2 cm (cut down)
UK, Sarikhani Collection, MS. 1030

THESE FOLIOS are from a magnificent thirty-volume Qur'an commissioned by the Il-Khanid Sultan Öljeitü (ruled 1304–16).[1] Each volume had a commissioning certificate on the opening page which read:[2]

The copying of this Noble Qur'an was ordered, seeking the favour of God, by our lord the Sultan, the greatest, Il-Khan, the exalted subjector of nations, Sultan of the Arab and non Arab sultans, King of the kings of the world, shadow of God on earth and His caliph over His subjects and domain, manifestor of the eternal truth by proof and example, Ghiyath al-Dunya wa'l-Din Uljaytu [Öljeitü] Sultan, Muhammad ibn al-Sultan al-Saᶜid Arghun Khan ibn al-Sultan al-Saᶜid Abaqa Khan ibn Hulaku [Hülegü] Khan ibn Tuli Khan ibn Jinkiz [Chinggis] Khan, may God preserve his kingdom for ever against the swings of fate and make it victorious unto the Day of Judgement, at the hands of his ministers, the greatest ones, the Sultans of ministers of the world, regulators of his eternal kingdom, Khwajah Rashid al-Haqq wa'l-Lin and Khwajah Saᶜd al-Haqq wa'l-Lin.[3]

The Qur'an was commissioned from ᶜAli ibn Muhammad al-Husayni, who signed his name, location (Mosul) and the date of completion at the end of each volume. So far no information about him has been found in contemporary sources and this Qur'an is the only known example of his work. He wrote the Qur'an in two phases, the first fifteen volumes between 1306 and 1307 and the second fifteen between 1310 and 1311. Fifteen volumes in one year is unusually fast progress for a Qur'an of this size and quality, but the gap of several years between volumes 15 and 16 is unexplained. It has been suggested that he may have stopped work to illuminate the first fifteen volumes.[4] But it was not usual for a calligrapher of this calibre to spend time on illumination and he does not claim to be the illuminator in any of his colophons. It is more likely that he was working on something else during this period, presumably for Öljeitü, because he is unlikely to have interrupted a royal project for anyone else.

The Qur'an is of the highest quality with no expense spared on materials. The text pages each have five lines written in *muhaqqaq*, a bold script with dramatic, rhythmic lines, well suited to such a large Qur'an. The letters are gold outlined with black and the vowel signs are also in black. Roundels inscribed *ayah* (verse) mark the end of each verse. The carpet pages, which preceded the text of each volume, are illuminated with complex geometric patterns filled with smaller designs and motifs.

This Qur'an is evidence that by the early fourteenth century Mosul was producing luxury manuscripts and objects for the victorious Il-Khanid dynasty. The Qur'an may have been intended for the spectacular mausoleum which Sultan Öljeitü built at Sultaniyya because it coincides precisely with the period of work on the building (1305–14).

NOTES

1 See James 1988, pp. 100–03; Lings and Safadi 1976, no. 99 *Sarikhani Collection* [2011], pp. 64–67; Baker 2007, pp. 56–65.

2 The certificate in the British Library volume is illustrated by Baker 2007, p. 59.

3 Based on the translation by James 1988, p. 100. The inclusion of the names of Öljeitü's viziers Rashid al-Din and Saᶜd al-Din at the end of the certificates is highly unusual. It suggests that they were in some way involved: perhaps they organised and even paid for the production of the Qur'an while giving the credit for its commission to the Il-Khan.

4 James 1988, p. 101.

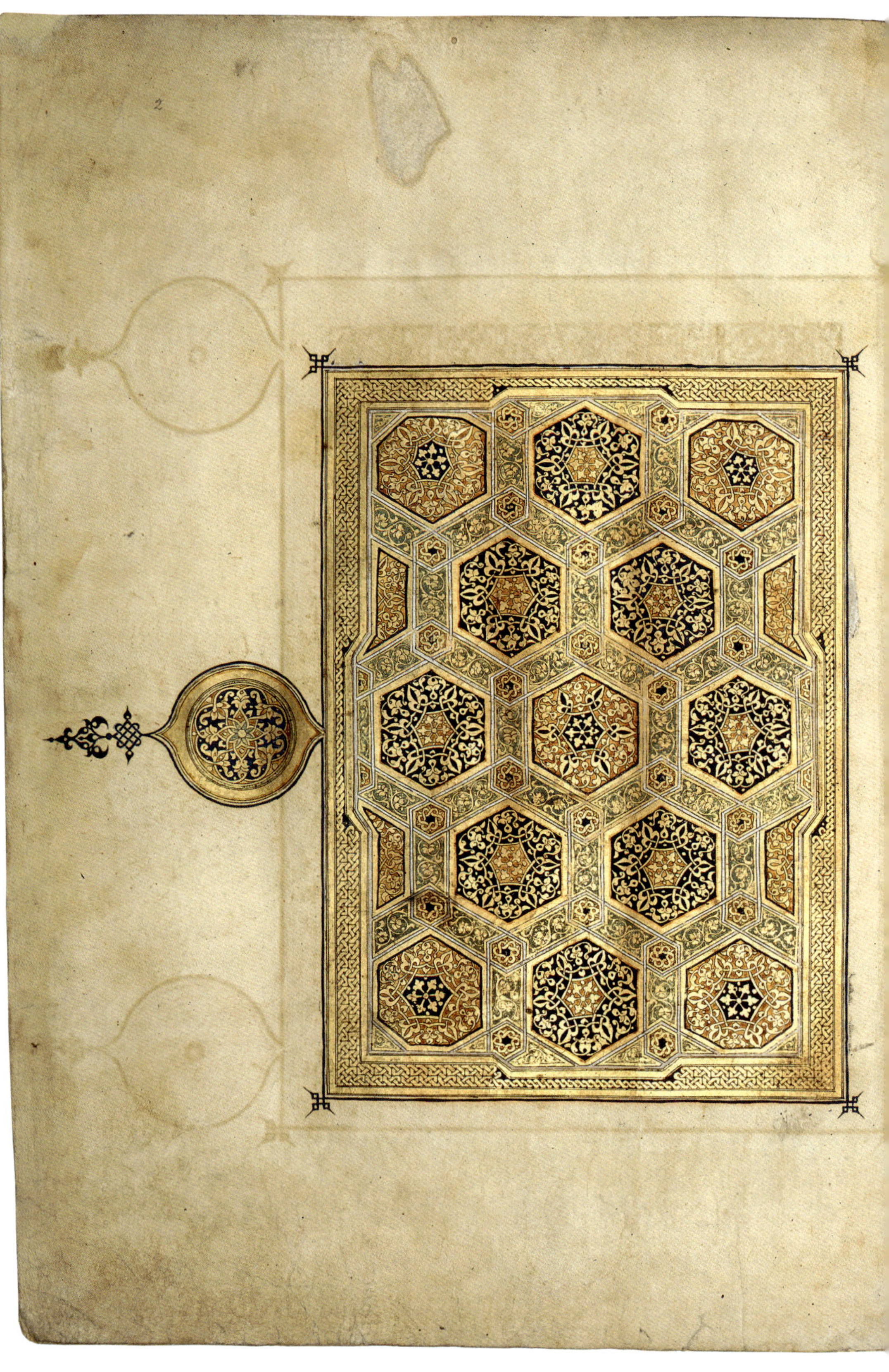

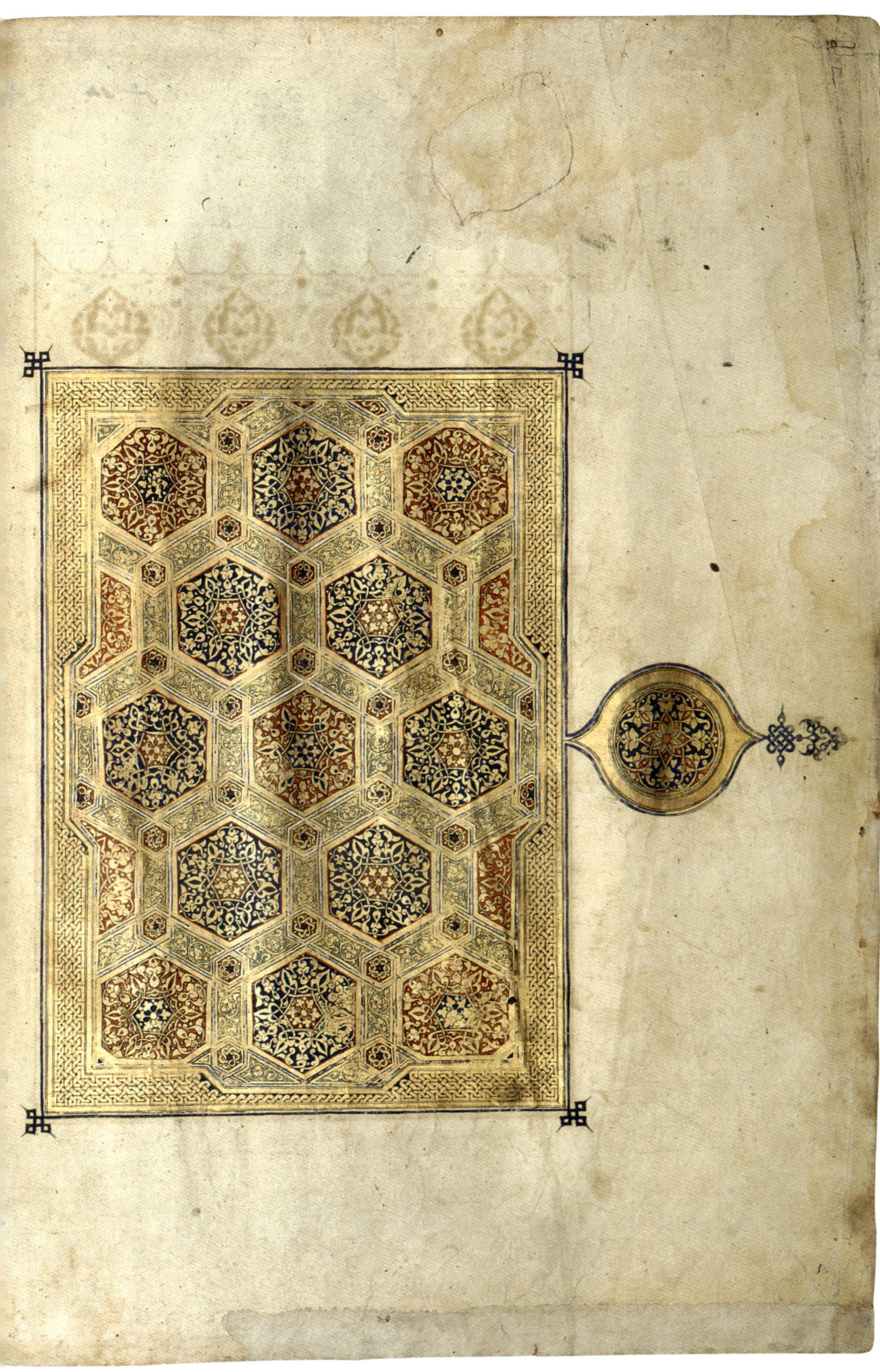

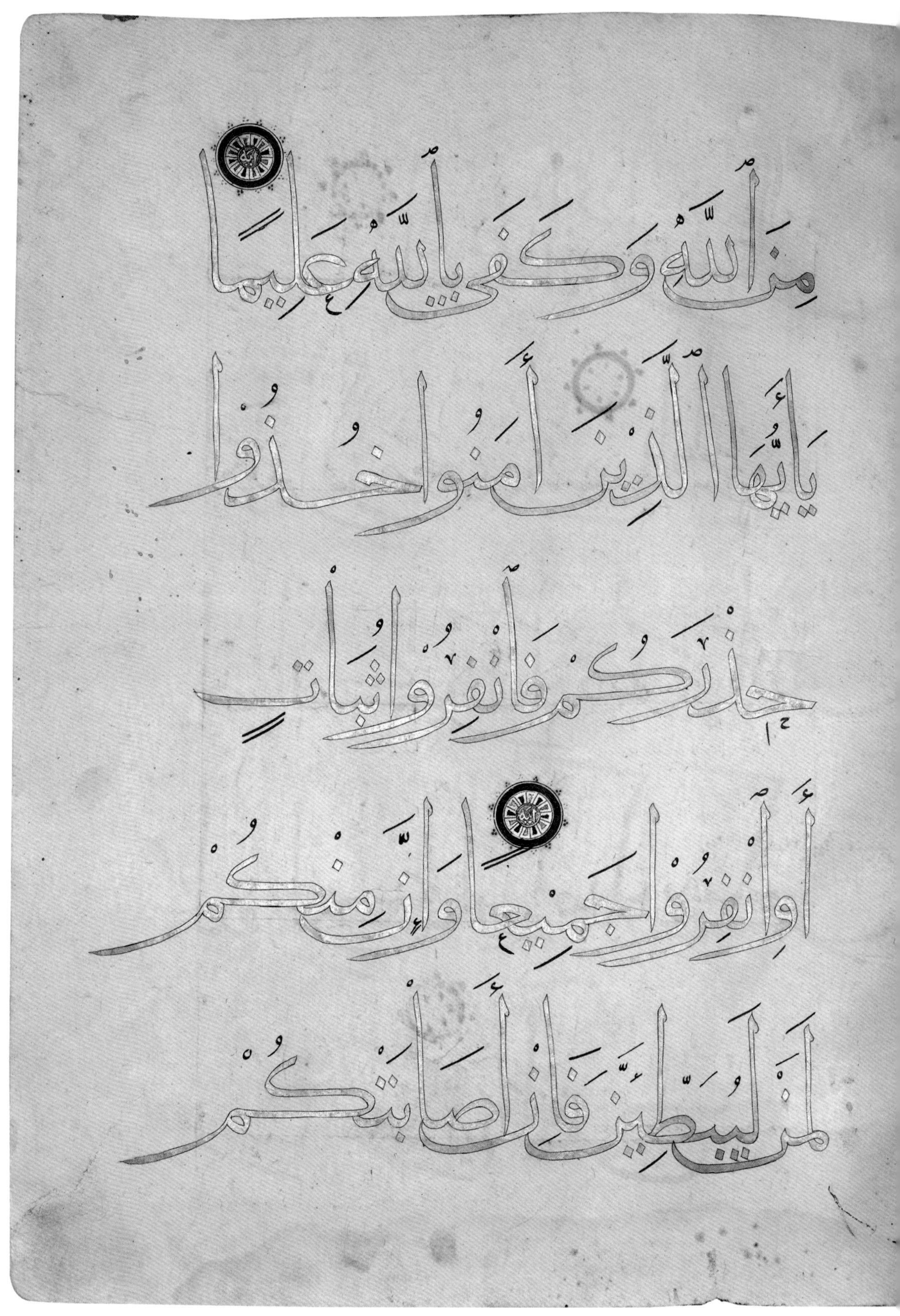

مِنَ اللَّهِ وَكَفَىٰ بِاللَّهِ عَلِيمًا ۝

يَا أَيُّهَا الَّذِينَ آمَنُوا خُذُوا

حِذْرَكُمْ فَانفِرُوا ثُبَاتٍ

أَوِ انفِرُوا جَمِيعًا ۝ وَإِنَّ مِنكُمْ

لَمَن لَّيُبَطِّئَنَّ فَإِنْ أَصَابَتْكُم

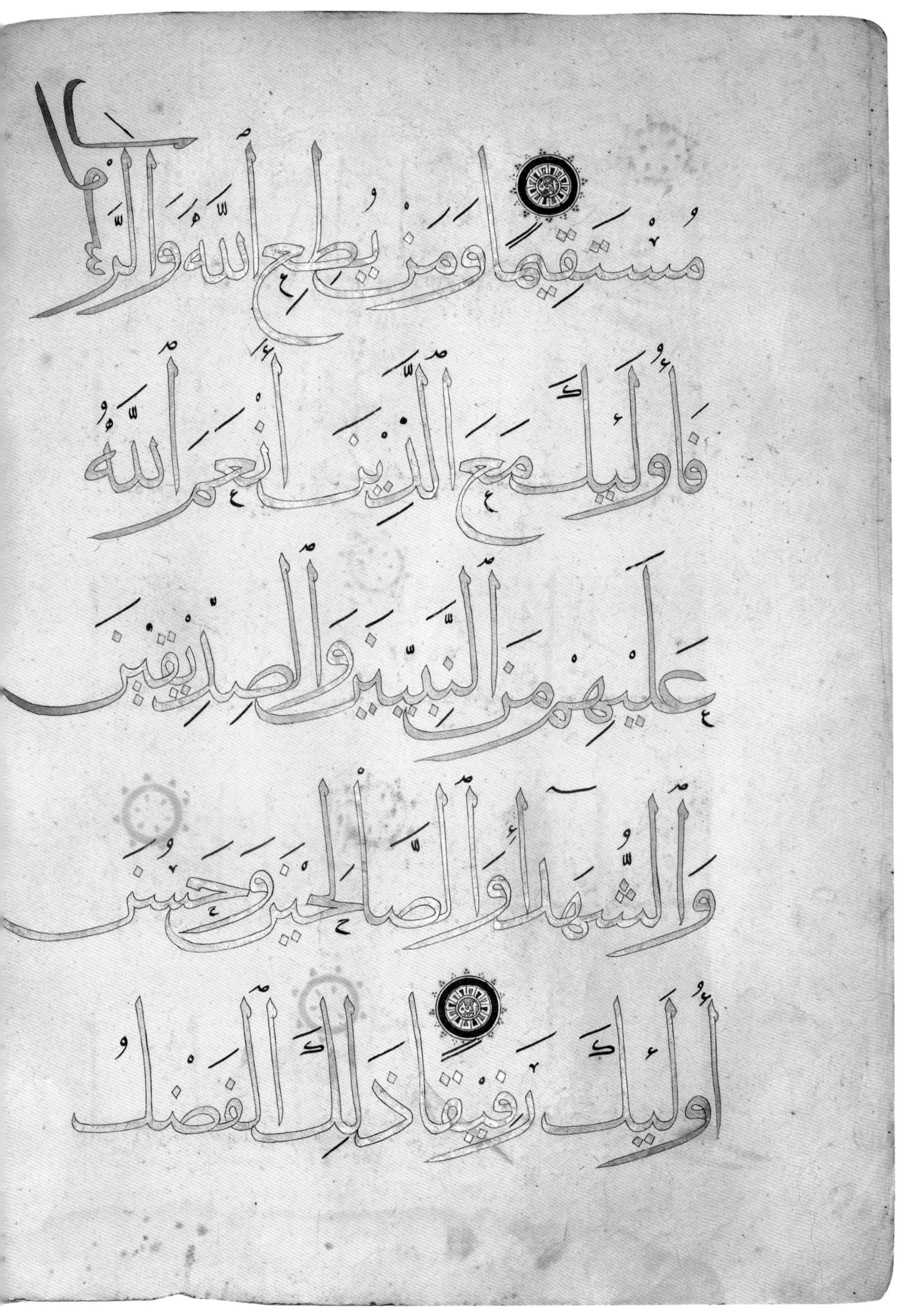

مستقيمًا ومن يطع الله والرسو

ل فأولئك مع الذين أنعم الله

عليهم من النبيين والصديقين

والشهداء والصالحين وحسن

أولئك رفيقًا ذلك الفضل

Bibliography

Abouseif 1989
Doris Abouseif, 'The Baptistère de St. Louis: A Reinterpretation', *Islamic Art*, 3, 1989, pp. 3–13

Adamova and Giuzal'ian 1985
Adel' Tigranovna Adamova and Leon Tigranovich Giuzal'ian, *Miniatiury rukopisi poémy "Shakhname" 1333 goda*, St Petersburg, 1985

Aga-Oglu 1945
Mehmet Aga-Oglu, 'About a type of Islamic incense burner', *Art Bulletin*, 37, March 1945, pp. 28–45

Ahri 2010
Abu Bakr Ahri, *Tarikh-i Shaikh Uvais*, ed. Iraj Afshar, Tabriz, 2010

Ahsan 1979
Muhammad Manazir Ahsan, *Social Life Under the Abbasids*, London and New York, 1979

Aigle 1997
Denise Aigle (ed.), *L'Iran face à domination mongole*, Tehran: Institut français de recherche en Iran, 1997

Aigle 2008
Denise Aigle, 'L'œuvre historiographique de Barhebraeus. Son apport à l'histoire de la période mongole', *Parole de l'Orient*, 33, 2008, pp. 25–61

Akasoy 2007
Akasoy, 'The Influence of the Arabic Tradition of Falconry and Hunting on Western Europe', in *Islamic Crosspollinations: Interactions in the Medieval Middle East*, ed. A. Akasoy and P.E. Pormann (Gibb Memorial Trust), Warminster, 2007, pp. 46–64

Allan 1979
James W. Allan, *Persian Metal Technology 700–1300 AD*, London, 1979

Allan 1982
James W. Allan, *Islamic Metalwork: The Nuhad Es-Said Collection*, London, 1982

Allan 1986
James W. Allan, *Metalwork of the Islamic World: The Aron Collection*, London, 1986

Allan and Maddison 2002
James W. Allan, with a contribution by Francis R. Maddison, *Metalwork Treasures from the Islamic Courts*, Doha and London, 2002

Allouche 1990
Adel Allouche, 'Tegüder's Ultimatum to Qalawun', *International Journal of Middle East Studies*, 22, 1990, pp. 437–46

Allsen 1997
Thomas T. Allsen, *Commodity and Exchange in the Mongol Empire. A Cultural History of Islamic Textiles*, Cambridge, 1997

Allsen 2001
Thomas T. Allsen, *Culture and Conquest in Mongol Eurasia*, Cambridge: Cambridge University Press, 2001

Allsen 2006
Thomas T. Allsen, *The Royal Hunt in Eurasian History*, Philadelphia, 2006

Amitai 2005
Reuven Amitai, 'The resolution of the Mongol–Mamluk war', in *Mongols, Turks, and others. Eurasian nomads and the sedentary world*, ed. Reuven Amitai and Michal Biran, Leiden, 2005, pp. 359–90

Amitai-Preiss 1995
Reuven Amitai-Preiss, *Mongols and Mamluks. The Mamlūk–Īlkhānid war, 1260–1281*, Cambridge, 1995

Amuli 1379/1959
Shams al-Dīn Muḥammad ibn Maḥmūd Āmulī, *Nafāʾis al-funūn fī ʿarāʾis al-ʿuyūn*, ed. Mīrzā Abū al-Ḥasan Shaʿrānī, 3 vols., Tehran, 1379/1959

Arberry 1962
Arthur John Arberry, *Fifty Poems of Ḥāfiẓ*, Cambridge, 1962

Arberry 1965
Arthur John Arberry, *Arabic Poetry. A Primer for Students*, Cambridge, 1965

Arberry 1967
Arthur John Arberry, *Aspects of Islamic Civilization As Depicted in the Original Texts*, Ann Arbor, 1967

Arberry and Minovi 1959–62
Arthur John Arberry and Mojtaba Minovi, *The Chester Beatty Library: A Catalogue of the Persian Manuscripts and Miniatures*, 3 vols., Dublin, 1959–62

Aydın and Aykut 1992
Şennur Aydın and Tunçay Aykut, *Ak Akçe. Moğol ve İlhanlı Sikkeleri/Mongol and Ilkhanid Coins*, Istanbul: Yapı Kredi Yayınları, 1992

Azarnouche 2013
S. Azarnouche (ed. and tr.), *Husraw Ī Kawādān ud Redag-ē. Khosrow fils de Kawād et un Page*, Cahiers de Studia Iranica 49, Paris, 2013

Baer 1973–74
Eva Baer, 'The Nisan Tası. A study in Persian–Mongol metal ware', *Kunst des Orients*, 9, 1973–74, pp. 1–46

Baer 1983
Eva Baer, *Metalwork in Medieval Islamic Art*, Albany, NY, 1983

Baer 1989
Eva Baer, *Ayyubid Metalwork with Christian Images* (Studies in Islamic Art and Architecture, Supplements to Muqarnas IV), Leiden, 1989

Baker 2007
Colin F. Baker, *Qurʾan Manuscripts: Calligraphy, Illumination, Design*, London, British Library, 2007

Ballian 2009
Anna Ballian, 'Three Medieval Islamic Brasses and the Mosul Tradition of Inlaid Metalwork', Μουσείο Μπενάκι, 9, 2009, pp. 113–41

Baltimore 1957
The History of Bookbinding 525–1950 AD, exh. cat., Baltimore Museum of Art, 1957–58

al-Baqli 1984
Muḥammad Qandīl al-Baqlī, *Al-tarab fī al-ʿaṣr al-mamlūkī: al-ghināʾ, al-raqs, al-mūsīqā*, Cairo: Al-hayʾa al-miṣriyya al-ʿāmma li-l-kitāb, 1984

Bar Hebraeus/Bruns and Kirsch 1789
Bar Hebraeus, *Chronicon Syriacum, e codicibus Bodleianis descripsit*, ed. Paul Jacob Bruns and Georg Wilhelm Kirsch, Leipzig, 1789

Bar Hebraeus/Budge 1932
Bar Hebraeus, *The Chronography of Gregory Abū'l Faraj the son of Aaron, the Hebrew Physician commonly known as Bar Hebraeus. Being the first part of his political history of the world*, translated from the Syriac by Ernest A. Wallis Budge, London, 1932

Bar Hebraeus/Salihani 1890
Tārīkh mukhtaṣar al-duwal / lil-ᶜallāmah Ghrīghūryūs Abī al-Faraj ibn Hārūn al-ṭabīb al-Milaṭī al-maᶜrūf bi-Ibn al-ᶜIbrī, ed. Anṭūn Ṣāliḥānī al-Yasūᶜī, Beirut, 1890

Barry 2010
Michael Barry, 'The Persianised East and the Royal Tradition', in *Treasures of the Aga Khan Museum. Masterpieces of Islamic Art*, exh. cat., ed. V. Daiber and B. Junod, Berlin, 2010, pp. 149–52

Bencheikh 1978
Jamal Eddine Bencheikh, 'Khamriyya', in *Encyclopaedia of Islam*, 2nd edn, IV, 1978, pp. 998a–1009a

Berchem 1906
Max van Berchem, 'Monuments et inscriptions de l'atābek Lu'lu' de Mossoul', in *Orientalische Studien Theodor Nöldeke zum siebzigsten geburtstag (2. März 1906)*, ed. C. Bezold, I, Gieszen, 1906, pp. 197–210

Berlin 2006
Die Dschazira: Kulturlandschaft zwischen Euphrat und Tigris, exh. cat., ed. Almut von Gladiss, Museum für Islamische Kunst, Staatliche Museen zu Berlin, 2006

Binbaş 2011
İlker Evrim Binbaş, 'Structure and Function of the Genealogical Tree in Islamic Historiography (1200-1500)', in *Horizons of the World: Festschrift for İsenbike Togan*, ed. İlker Evrim Binbaş and Nurten Kılıç-Schubel, Istanbul: İthaki, 2011, pp. 465–544

Bira 2004
Shagdaryn Bira, 'Mongolian Tenggerism and modern globalism. A retrospective outlook on globalisation', *Journal of the Royal Asiatic Society*, series 3, 14, part 1, April 2004, pp. 1–12

Blair 1995
Sheila S. Blair, *A Compendium of Chronicles : Rashid al-Din's Illustrated History of the World*, London, Nour Foundation, 1995

Blair 1996
Sheila S. Blair, 'Patterns of Patronage and Production in Ilkhanid Iran, The Case of Rashid al-Din', in *The Court of the Il-Khans 1290–1340*, ed. J. Raby and T. Fitzherbert (Oxford Studies in Islamic Art XII), Oxford, 1996

Blochet 1910
Edgard Blochet, *Introduction à l'Histoire des Mongols de Fadl Allah Rashid ed-Din*, Leyden: E.J. Brill, and London: Luzac & Co., 1910

Bloom 2001
Jonathan Bloom, *Paper before Print: The History and Impact of Paper in the Islamic World*, New Haven and London: Yale University Press, 2001

Bonn 2005
Dschingis Khan und seine Erben: das Weltreich der Mongolen, exh. cat., ed. W. Jacob and C. Müller, Kunst- und Ausstellungshalle der Bundesrepublik Deutschland, Bonn, 2005 (and Staatlisches Museum für Völkerkunde, Munich, 2005–06)

Bosworth 2006
Clifford Edmund Bosworth, 'Ḵātun' *Encyclopaedia Iranica*, XVI/2, 2006, pp. 129–30

Boyle 1968a
Boyle, J.A., 'Dynastic and Political History of the Īl-Ḵhāns', *The Cambridge History of Iran*. vol. 5, *The Saljuq and Mongol Periods*, Cambridge 1968, pp. 303–421

Boyle 1968b
Boyle, J.A., 'A Mongol Hunting Ritual', in "Die Jagd bei den Altaischen Völkern", Walter Heissig, Herbert Franke, Nikolaus Poppe and Omeljan Pritsak eds, *Asiatische Forschungen: Monographienreihe zur Geschichte, Kultur und Sprache der Völker Ost- und Zentralasiens*, vol. 26, Wiesbaden 1968, pp. 1–7

Boyle 1978a
Boyle, J.A., 'The Attitude of the Thirteenth-Century Mongols Towards Nature', *Central Asiatic Journal*, XXII, no. 3–4, Wiesbaden 1978, pp. 177–185

Boyle 1978b
J.A. Boyle, 'Ḵātūn', in *Encyclopaedia of Islam*, 2nd edn, IV, 1978, p. 1133

Brack 2011
Yoni Brack, 'A Mongol Princess Making *hajj*: The Biography of El Qutlugh Daughter of Abagha Ilkhan (r. 1265–82)', *Journal of the Royal Asiatic Society*, 21, no. 3, 2011, pp. 331–59

Broadbridge 2008
Anne F. Broadbridge, *Kingship and Ideology in the Islamic and Mongol Worlds*, Cambridge, 2008

Caiger-Smith 1985
Alan Caiger-Smith, *Lustre Pottery*, London, 1985

Cammann 1951
Schuyler Cammann, 'The Symbolism of the Cloud Collar Motif', *The Art Bulletin*, 33, no. 1, March 1951, pp. 1–9

Carboni 1988–89
Stefano Carboni, 'The London Qazwīnī: An Early Fourteenth-Century Copy of the ᶜAjā'ib al-makhlūqāt', *Islamic Art*, 3, 1988–89, pp. 15–31

Carboni 1992
Stefano Carboni, 'The *Wonders of Creation* and the Singularities of Ilkhanid Painting: A Study of the London Qazwini, British Library MS. Or. 14140', PhD thesis, School of Oriental and African Studies, University of London, 1992, available on line at ethos.bl.uk

Carey 2009
Moya Carey, 'The Gold and Silver Lining: Shams al-Dīn Muhammad b. Mu'ayyad Al-'Urdī's Inlaid Celestial Globe (c. AD 1288) from the Ilkhanid Observatory at Marāgha', *Iran*, 47, 2009, pp. 97–108

de Chamerlat 1987
Christian Antoine de Chamerlat, *Falconry and Art*, Sotheby's Publications, London 1987

Christie's 2012
Christie's, *Art of the Islamic and Indian Worlds*, sale, London, 4 October 2012

Clinton 1972
Jerome W. Clinton, *The Diwan of Manūchihrī Dāmghānī. A Critical Study*, Minneapolis, 1972

Combe 1931
Étienne Combe, 'Cinq cuivres musulmans datés des XIIIe, XIVe et XVe siècles, de la Collection Benaki', *Bulletin de l'Institut Français d'Archéologie Orientale*, 30, 1931, pp. 49–58

Combe, Sauvaget and Wiet *et al.* 1931–
Étienne Combe, Jean Sauvaget and Gaston Wiet *et al.* (eds., trans.), *Répertoire chronologique d'épigraphie arabe*, 18 vols., Cairo, 1931–

Conrad 1994
Lawrence I. Conrad, 'On the Arabic Chronicle of Bar Hebraeus', *Parole de l'Orient : revue semestrielle des études syriaques et arabes chrétiennes : recherches orientales : revue d'études et de recherches sur les églises de langue syriaque*, 19 (Actes du 4e congrès international d'études arabes chrétiennes, Cambridge, septembre 1992), 1994, pp. 319–78

Contadini 2005
Anna Contadini, 'Fatimid Ivories within a Mediterranean Culture', in Kjeld von Folsach and Joachim Mayer (eds.), *The Ivories of Muslim Spain (The Journal of the David Collection, 2, no. 2)*, pp. 226–47

Contadini 2012
Anna Contadini, *A World of Beasts: A Thirteenth-Century Illustrated Book on Animals (the* Kitāb Naᶜt al-ḥayawān*) in the Ibn Bakhtīshūᶜ Tradition*, Leiden and Boston: Brill, 2012

Costello 2005
Susan D. Costello, 'An Investigation of Early Chinese Bronze Mirrors at the Harvard University Art Museums', ANAGPIC, 2005 (*www.ischool.utexas.edu/~anagpic/pdfs/Costello.pdf*)

Craddock *et al.* 1990
Paul T. Craddock, Susan C. La Niece and Duncan
R. Hook, 'Brass in the Medieval Islamic World' in
P.T. Craddock (ed.), *2000 Years of Zinc and Brass*,
London: British Museum Press, 1990

Curtin 1907
Jeremiah Curtin, *The Mongols: A History*, Boston,
1907

Dawson 1966
Christopher Dawson, *Mission to Asia*, New York:
Harper & Row, 1966

Defrémery 1844
Charles Defrémery, 'Mémoire historique sur la
destruction de la dynastie des Mozafferiens, part
1', *Journal Asiatique*, series 4, 4, 1844, pp. 93–114

De Nicola 2011
Bruno De Nicola, 'Unveiling the Khātūns: Some
Aspects of the Role of Women in the Mongol
Empire', PhD thesis, University of Cambridge,
2011

Derenk 1974
Dieter Derenk, *Leben und Dichtung des
Omaiyadenkalifen al-Walid ibn Yazid: ein
quellenkritischer Beitrag*, Frankfurt, 1974

al-Dhahabi/Negre 1979
Muhammad ibn Aḥmad al-Dhahabī, *Kitāb duwal
al-Islām*, trans. Arlette Negre, Damascus, 1979

Dihkhuda
ᶜAlī Akbar Dihkhudā, 'Miqnaᶜa', *Lughatnāma*:
http://www.loghatnaameh.org

Diler 2006
Ömer Diler, *İlhanlar, İran Moğollarının Sikkeleri*,
Istanbul: Turkuaz Kitapçılık, 2006

Dimand 1947
Maurice Dimand, *A Handbook of Muhammadan
Art*, New York, 1947

Doerfer 1963–75
Gerhard Doerfer, *Türkische und Mongolische
Elemente im Neupersischen*, 4 vols., Wiesbaden:
Franz Steiner, 1963–75

Donaldson 1939
Dwight M. Donaldson, 'The Qualities of the
Planets: Astrology in Islam', *Moslem World*, 29,
1939, pp. 151–57

Drouot-Richelieu 1998
Drouot-Richelieu, *Art Arabe des Collections du
Comte de Toulouse-Lautrec*, Paris, 25 September
1998

Enderlein 1973
Volkmar Enderlein, 'Das Bildprogramm des
Berliner Mosul-Beckens', in *Forschungen und
Berichte* (Staatliche Museen zu Berlin) 15, 1973,
pp. 7–40

d'Erlanger 1930
Rudolphe d'Erlanger, *La musique arabe*, Paris:
Geuthner, vol. 1, 1930

Esin 1969
Emel Esin, '"AND". The cup rites in Inner-
Asian and Turkish art", in O. Aslanapa and R.
Naumann (eds), *Forschungen zur Kunst Asiens. In
Memoriam Kurt Erdmann. 9. September 1901-30.
September 1964*, Istanbul Universitesi Edebiyat
Fakültesi Türk ve Islam Sanati Kürsüsü, Istanbul,
1969, pp. 224–61

Esin 1970
Emel Esin, '*Bedük börk*: the iconography of
Turkish honorific headgears', in *Proceedings of
the IXth meeting of the Permanent International
Altaistic Conference, Ravello, 26–30 September
1966*, Naples: Istituto Universitario Orientale
Seminario di Turcologia, 1970, pp. 71–138

Ettinghausen 1962
Richard Ettinghausen, *Arab Painting*, Geneva,
1962

Ettinghausen 1965
Richard Ettinghausen, 'Foundation-moulded
leatherwork – a rare Egyptian technique also
used in Britain', in *Studies in Islamic Art and
Architecture in Honour of Professor K.A.C.
Creswell*, ed. C.L. Geddes *et al.*, Cairo, 1965, pp.
63–71

Ettinghausen 1979
Richard Ettinghausen, 'Bahram Gur's hunting
feats', *Iran*, 17, 1979, pp. 25–31

Farmer 1929/1973
Henry George Farmer, *A History of Arabian
Music to the XIIIth Century*, London: Luzac, 1929,
repr. 1973

Farmer 1976
Henry George Farmer, *Islam* (Musikgeschichte
in Bildern. Band III: Musik des Mittelalters und
der Renaissance, Lieferung 2), Leipzig: VEB
Deutscher Verlag für Musik, 1976

Federico II/Trombetti Budriesi 2009
Federico II di Svevia, *De arte venandi cum
avibus. L'arte di cacciare con gli uccelli. Edizione e
traduzione italiana del ms. Lat. 71 della Biblioteca
Universitaria di Bologna collazionato con il ms.
Pal. Lat. 1071 della Biblioteca Apostolica Vaticana*,
ed. and trans. Anna Laura Trombetti Budriesi,
Rome and Bari 2009

Fehérvári 1976
Géza Fehérvári, *Islamic Metalwork of the Eighth
to the Fifteenth century in the Keir Collection*,
London, 1976

Fehérvári 1985
Géza Fehérvári, *La Ceramica Islamica*, Milan:
Arnoldo Mondadori, 1985

Feldman 1996
Walter Feldman, *Music of the Ottoman
Court: makam, composition and the early
Ottoman instrumental repertoire* (Intercultural
Music Studies, 10), Berlin: VWB - Verlag für
Wissenschaft und Bildung, 1996

Fiey [1959]
Jean Maurice Fiey, *Mossoul Chrétienne. Essai
sur l'histoire, l'archéologie et l'état actuel des
monuments chrétiens de la ville de Mossoul*,
Beirut, n.d. [1959]

Fiey 1975
Jean Maurice Fiey, *Chrétiens syriaques sous les
Mongols (Il-Khanat de Perse, XIIIe-XIVe s.)*,
Louvain, 1975

Firdawsi/Davis 2007
Abolqasem Ferdowsi, *Shahnameh, The Persian
Book of Kings*, trans. Dick Davis, Washington,
2007

Fitzherbert 1991
Teresa Fitzherbert, 'Khwājū Kirmānī (689–753/
1290–1352): An Éminence Grise of Fourteenth
Century Persian Painting', *Iran*, 29, 1991,
pp. 137–51

Fitzherbert 2001
Teresa Fitzherbert, *"Balᶜami's Tabari". An
illustrated manuscript of Balᶜami's Tārjama-
yi Tārīkh-i ṭabarī, in the Freer Gallery of Art,
Washington*, PhD thesis, University of Edinburgh,
2001, available on line at ethos.bl.uk

Fitzherbert 2006
Teresa Fitzherbert, 'Religious diversity under
Ilkhanid rule c. 1300 as reflected in the Freer
Balᶜami', in L. Komaroff (ed.) *Beyond the legacy of
Genghis Khan*, Leiden, 2006, pp. 390–406

Folsach 1990
Kjeld von Folsach, *Islamic art: The David
Collection*, Copenhagen, 1990

Folsach 2001
Kjeld von Folsach, *Art from the World of Islam in
the David Collection*, Copenhagen, 2001

Folsach 2004
Kjeld von Folsach, 'Three Eastern Islamic Leather
Wallets and Three Related Stone Press-moulds
in the David Collection', in K. von Folsach, H.
Thrane, I. Thrane (eds.), *From Handaxe to Khan,
Essays presented to Peder Mortensen on the
occasion of his 70th Birthday*, Aarhus: Aarhus
University Press, 2004, pp. 225–39

Folsach 2013
Kjeld von Folsach, 'A set of Silk Panels from the
Mongol Period', in *God is Beautiful and Loves
Beauty*, ed. Sheila Blair and Jonathan Bloom, New
Haven, London and Qatar: Yale University Press,
2013

Franke 1994
Herbert Franke, 'Women under the dynasties of
conquest', in *La donna nella Cina imperiale nella
Cina repubblicana*, ed. L. Lanciotti, Florence,
1980; reprinted in H. Franke, *China under Mongol
Rule*, Aldershot, 1994, pp. 23–43

Franke and Neubauer 2000
Daniël Franke and Eckhard Neubauer (eds.),
*Museum des Institutes für Geschichte der
Arabisch-Islamischen Wissenschaften*, Teil I:
Musikinstrumente, Frankfurt am Main, 2000

Fulton 1948
Alexander Strathern Fulton, 'Fīrūzābādī's "wine-
list"', *Bulletin of the School of Oriental and African
Studies*, 12/3–4, 1948, pp. 579–85

Gabrieli and Scerrato 1979
Francesco Gabrieli and Umberto Scerrato, *Gli
Arabi in Italia. Cultura, contatti, e tradizioni*,
Milan, 1979

Gandjavi 1979
S. Gandjavi, 'Prospection et fouilles à Sultaniyeh',
in *Akten des VII. Internationalen Kongresses für
Iranische Kunst und Archäologie, München, 1976*,
Berlin, 1979, pp. 523–26

Gerstein 2013
Alexandra Gerstein, 'Thomas Gambier Parry:
Collecting in the Gothic Revival', in J. Lowden,
*Medieval and Later Ivories in the Courtauld
Gallery*, London, 2013, pp. 26–36

Ghouchani 1999
ᶜAbd Allāh Ghouchani, 'Some 12th Century
Iranian Wine Ewers and Their Poems', *Bulletin of
the Asia Institute*, new series, 13, 1999, pp. 141–50

Ghouchani and Adle 1992
ᶜAbd Allāh Ghouchani and Chahryar Adle, 'A
Sphero-Conical Vessel as *Fuqqā*'a, or a Gourd for
"Beer"', *Muqarnas*, 9, 1992, pp. 72–92

Gierlichs 1996
Joachim Gierlichs, *Mittelalterliche Tierreliefs
in Anatolien und Nordmesopotamien:
Untersuchungen zur figürlichen Baudekoration der
Sedjschuken, Artuqiden und ihrer Nachfolger bis
ins 15. Jahrhundert*, Tübingen, 1996

Gilli-Elewy 2012
Hend Gilli-Elewy, 'On Women, Power, and
Politics During the Last Phase of the Ilkhanate',
Arabica, 59, 2012, pp. 709–23

Giuzalian 1960
Leon Tigranovich Giuzal'ian, 'Three Injuid bronze
vessels (On the problem of localization of the
South-West group of medieval Iranian bronze
objects of art)', separately printed paper from *XXV
International Congress of Orientalists: papers
presented by the USSR delegation*, Moscow, 1960

Gladiss 2012
Almut von Gladiss, *Glanz und Substanz:
Metallarbeiten in der Sammlung des Museums für
Islamische Kunst (8. bis 17. Jahrhundert)*, Berlin,
2012

Grabar and Blair 1980
Oleg Grabar and Sheila Blair, *Epic Images and
Contemporary History, The Illustrations of the
Great Mongol Shahnama*, Chicago and London,
1980

Gray 1961
Basil Gray, *Persian Painting*, Geneva, 1961

Grigor of Akancᶜ/Blake and Frye 1949
Grigor of Akancᶜ, 'History of a Nation of Archers
(The Mongols)', ed. and trans. Robert P. Blake
and Richard N. Frye (*Harvard Journal of Asiatic
Studies*, 12, 1949, pp. 269–393)

Gunther 1932
Robert T. Gunther, *Astrolabes of the World*, 2
vols., Oxford, 1932

Hafiz 1941
Ḥafiz, *Dīvān-i ḥāfiz*, ed. Muḥammad Qazvīnī and
Qāsim Ghanī, Tehran, 1320/1941

Hamilton 1959
Robert W. Hamilton, *Khirbat al Mafjar. An
Arabian Mansion in the Jordan Valley*, Oxford,
1959

Hamilton 1988
Robert W. Hamilton, *Walid and his Friends. An
Umayyad Tragedy* , Oxford, 1988

Hardie 1998
Peter Hardie, 'Mamluk glass from China?' in R.
Ward (ed.), *Gilded and Enamelled Glass from
the Middle East*, London: British Museum Press,
1998, pp. 85–90

Harrak and Ruji 2004
Amir Harrak and Niu Ruji, 'The Uighur
Inscription in the Mausoleum of Mār Behnam',
Journal of the Canadian Society for Syriac Studies,
4, 2004, pp. 66–72

Hawadith 1997
[Anonymous], *Kitab al-hawadith*, ed. Bashshār
ᶜAwwād Maᶜrūf and 'Imād ᶜAbd al-Salām Ra'ūf,
Beirut, 1997

Heissig/Samuel 1980
Walther Heissig, *The Religions of Mongolia*, trans.
Geoffrey Samuel, London and Henley, 1980

Herzfeld and Sarre 1911–20
Ernst Herzfeld and Ernst Sarre, *Archäeologische
Reise im Euphrat und Tigris Gebiet*, 4 vols., Berlin
1911–20

Hillenbrand (Carole) 1981
Carole Hillenbrand, 'The career of Najm al-Din
Il-Ghazi', *Der Islam*, 58/2, 1981, pp. 250–92

Hillenbrand (Carole) 1990
Carole Hillenbrand, *A Muslim Principality
in Crusader Times. The Early Artuqid State*,
Istanbul, 1990

Hillenbrand (Carole) 1995
Carole Hillenbrand, 'Ibn al-'Adim's biography of
the Seljuq sultan, Alp Arslan', in C.V. de Bonito
and M.A.M. Rodriguez (eds.), *Actas XVI Congreso
UAEI*, Salamanca, 1995, pp. 237–42

Hillenbrand (Carole) 2001
Carole Hillenbrand, 'The career of Zengi', in J.
Phillips and M. Hoch (eds.), *The Second Crusade:
Scope and Consequences*, Manchester, 2001,
pp. 111–32

Hillenbrand (Carole) 2011
Carole Hillenbrand, 'What's in a Name?
Tughtegin – "The Minister of the Antichrist"?', in
O.A. de Unzaga (ed.), *Fortresses of the Intellect.
Ismaili and other Islamic Studies in Honour of
Farhad Daftary*, London and New York, 2011,
pp. 459–71

Hillenbrand (Robert) 1996
Hillenbrand, Robert, "The Iskandar Cycle in the
Great Mongol Shahnama", in *The Problematics of
Power. Eastern and Western Representations of
Alexander the Great*, M. Bridges and C. Bürgel
(eds), Bern, 1996, pp. 203–29

Hillenbrand (Robert) 1982
Robert Hillenbrand, '*La dolce vita* in early Islamic
Syria: the evidence of later Umayyad palaces', *Art
History*, 5/1, 1982, pp. 1–35

Holmgren 1986
Jennifer Holmgren, 'Observations on marriage
and inheritance practices in early Mongol and
Yuan society with particular reference to the
Levirate', *Journal of Royal Asian History*, 20/2,
1986, pp. 146–67

Holod 2012
Renata Holod, 'Event and Memory: The Freer
Gallery's Siege Scene Plate', *Ars Orientalis*, 42,
2012, pp. 194–220

Holt 1986
Peter Malcolm Holt, 'The Īlkhān Aḥmad's
Embassy to Qalāwūn: Two Contemporary
Accounts', *Bulletin of the School of Oriental and
African Studies*, 49, 1986, pp. 129–32

Howorth 1876–88
Henry Hoyle Howorth, *History of the Mongols
from the 9th to the 19th Centuries*, London,
1876–88

Ibn al-Athir/Richards 2008
Ibn al-Athir, *The Chronicle of Ibn al-Athīr for
the Crusading Period from al-Kāmil fi'l-ta'rīkh*,
Part 3. *The Years 589-629/1193-1231. The Ayyubids
after Saladin and the Mongol Menace*, trans. D.S.
Richards, Aldershot 2008

Ibn Fadlan 1939
Ibn Fadlān, *Rihlat Ibn Fadlān*. Ed. A. Zeki Validi
Togan. *Ibn Fadlān's Reisebericht* (Abhandlungen
für die Kunde des Morgenlandes, Bd. XXIV, 3).
Leipzig: Deutsche Morgenländische Gesellschaft,
1939

Ibn al-ᶜIbri 1986
Ibn al-ᶜIbri, *Ta'rīkh al-zamān*, Arabic trans. P.
Isḥāq Armaleh, Beirut, 1986

Ibn Jubayr/Broadhurst 1952
Muhammad ibn Ahmad ibn Jubayr, *The Travels of Ibn Jubayr*, ed. and trans. Ronald J.C. Broadhurst, London, 1952

Ibn al-Tiqtaqa 1960
Muḥammad ibn ᶜAlī ibn al-Ṭiqṭaqā, *Kitāb al-Fakhrī*, Beirut, 1960

Ibn al-Tiqtaqa/Whitting 1947/1990
Muḥammad ibn ᶜAlī ibn al-Ṭiqṭaqā, *al-Fakhrī, on the systems of government and the Moslem dynasties*, trans. C.E.J. Whitting, London, 1947, repr. 1990

İnan 1968-91
Abdülkadir İnan, 'Orun' ve 'ülüş' meselesi. I-Mevki-Orun Hukuku,' in *idem, Makaleler ve İncelemeler*, 2 vols., Ankara: Türk Tarih Kurumu, 1968–91

Ipsiroglu 1964
Mazhar S. Ipsiroglu, *Saray-Alben: Diezsche Klebebände aus den Berliner Sammlungen: Beschreibung und stilkritische Anmerkungen*, Wiesbaden, 1964

Ipsiroglu/Phillips 1967
Mazhar S. Ipsiroglu, *Painting and Culture of the Mongols*, trans. E.D. Phillips, London, 1967

Jackson 2005
Peter Jackson, *The Mongols and the West*, London, 2005

Jahiz /Pellat 1969
'Amr ibn Baḥr Jāḥiz, *The Life and Works of Jāḥiz*, ed. and trans. Charles Pellat; trans. from the French by D.M. Hawke, London, 1969

James 1988
David James, *Qur'āns of the Mamlūks*, London 1988

Jenkins and Keene 1982
Mariyn Jenkins and Manuel Keene, *Islamic Jewelry in the Metropolitan Museum of Art*, New York, 1982

Juvaini 1912–37
ᶜAṭā' Malik Juvainī, *Ta'rīkh-i Jahān-gushā*, ed. Mīrzā Muḥammad Qazvīnī, 3 vols., Leiden and London, 1912–37

Juvaini/Boyle 1958/1997
ᶜAṭā' Malik Juvainī, *Genghis Khan. The History of the World-Conqueror*, trans. John Andrew Boyle, 2 vols., Manchester 1958; reprinted Seattle: University of Washington Press, 1997

Karamağaralı 1971a
Haluk Karamağaralı, 'Erzurum'daki Hâtuniye Medresesi'nin tarihi ve bânisi hakkında mülâhazalar', *Selçuklu Araştırmaları Dergisi*, 3, 1971, pp. 20–42

Karamağaralı 1971b
Haluk Karamağaralı, 'Einige Bemerkungen zur Geschichte und über die Stifterin der Hatuniye Medrese in Erzurum (Zusammenfassung)', *Selçuklu Araştırmaları Dergisi*, 3, 1971, pp. 243–47

Karic 2002
Enes Karic, 'Intoxicants', in *Encyclopaedia of the Qur'an*, ed. J.D. McAuliffe, Leiden and Boston, 2002, II, pp. 555–57

Kendrick 1924
A.F. Kendrick, *Catalogue of Muhammadan Textiles of the Medieval Period*, London: Victorian and Albert Museum, 1924

Kennedy 1997
Philip F. Kennedy, *The Wine Song in Classical Arabic Poetry. Abū Nuwās and the Literary Tradition*, Oxford, 1997

Kirmani 1328/1949
Nāṣir al-Dīn Munshī Kirmānī, *Simṭ al-ᶜulā li al-ḥadrat al-ulyā*, ed. ᶜAbbās Iqbāl Āshtiyānī, Tehran: Intishārāt-i asāṭīr, 1328/1949

Komaroff 1988
Linda Komaroff, 'Pen-case and Candlestick: Two Sources for the Development of Persian Inlaid Metalwork', *Metropolitan Museum Journal*, 23, 1988

Komaroff 1992
Linda Komaroff, *The Golden Disk of Heaven: Metalwork of Timurid Iran*, Costa Mesa CA and New York, 1992

Komaroff 1994
Linda Komaroff, 'Paintings in Silver and Gold: The Decoration of Persian Metalwork and its Relationship to Manuscript Illustration', *Studies in the Decorative Arts*, 2/1, Fall 1994

Komaroff 2006/2013
Linda Komaroff (ed.), *Beyond the legacy of Genghis Khan* (Islamic History and Civilization: Studies and Texts, vol. 64) Leiden: Brill, 2006; reprint 2013

Kramarovsky 1998
Mark Kramarovsky, 'The import and manufacture of glass in the territories of the Golden Horde', in R. Ward (ed.) *Gilded and Enamelled Glass from the Middle East*, London: British Museum Press, 1998, pp. 96–100

Kühnel 1924–25
Ernst Kühnel, 'Three Mosul bronzes at Leningrad', *The Year Book of Oriental Art and Culture*, 1924–25, pp. 100–01

Kühnel 1938
Ernst Kühnel, *Die Sammlung türkischer und islamischer Kunst im Tschinili Köschk*, Berlin, 1938

Kühnel 1939
Ernst Kühnel, 'Zwei Mosulbronzen und ihr Meister', *Jahrbuch der preussischen Kunstsammlungen*, 60, 1939, pp. 1–20

Kühnel 1963
Ernst Kühnel, *Islamic Arts*, trans. K. Watson, London, 1963

La Niece 2003
Susan La Niece, 'Medieval Islamic metal technology', in *Scientific research in the field of Asian art: Proceedings of the First Forbes Symposium at the Freer Gallery of Art*, ed. P. Jett with J.G. Douglas, B. McCarthy and J. Winter, London: Archetype Publications, 2003, pp. 90–96

Lambton 1981
Ann K.S. Lambton, 'Reflections on the role of agriculture in medieval Persia', in *The Islamic Middle East, 700-1900 : Studies in Economic and Social History*, ed. A.L. Udovitch, Princeton: The Darwin Press, 1981, pp. 283–312

Lambton 1988
Ann K.S. Lambton, *Continuity and Change in Medieval Persia: Aspects of Administrative, Economic, Social History in 11th–14th Century Persia*, London: I.B. Tauris, 1988

Lane 2003
George Lane, *Early Mongol Rule in Thirteenth-century Iran. A Persian Renaissance*, London, 2003

Lings and Safadi 1976
Martin Lings and Yasin Safadi, *The Qur'ān*, London: British Library, 1976

Little 2006
Donald P. Little, 'Diplomatic Missions and Gifts Exchanged by Mamluks and Ilkhans,' in *Beyond the Legacy of Genghis Khan*, ed. L. Komaroff (Islamic History and Civilization: Studies and Texts, vol. 64) Leiden: Brill, 2006, pp. 30–42

Lockhart 1968
Laurence Lockhart, 'The Relations Between Edward I and Edward II of England and the Mongol Il-khans of Persia', *Iran*, 6, 1968, pp. 23–31

London 1931
S.A.T. Wilson (ed.), *Catalogue of the International Exhibition of Persian Art: Patrons: His Majesty the King, His Majesty Rizā Shāh Pahlavi: 7th January to 7th March, 1931, Royal Academy of Arts, London*, exh. cat., Royal Academy of Art, London, 1931

London 1976
The Arts of Islam, exh. cat., Hayward Gallery, London, 1976

London 1988
J.M Rogers and Rachel Ward, *Süleyman the Magnificent*, exh. cat, British Museum, London, 1988

London 1995
Africa, Art of a Continent, exh. cat., ed. Tom Phillips, London, 1995

Los Angeles 2011
Gifts of the Sultan: The Arts of Giving at the Islamic Courts, exh. cat., ed. L. Komaroff, Los Angeles County Museum of Art, 2011

Louisiana 1987
Art from the World of Islam, 8th–18th century, ed. K. von Folsach, exh. cat., The Louisiana Museum of Modern Art, 1987, published in *Louisiana Revy*, 27, no. 3, 1987

Low-Beer 1950
Fritz Low-Beer, 'Chinese Lacquer of the Early 15th Century', *Bulletin MFEA*, 22, 1950, pp. 145–67

Macdonald 2006
Helen Macdonald, *Falcon*, London, 2006

Mannowsky [*c.* 1936]
Walter Mannowsky, *Der Kirchenschatz von St. Marien in Danzig*, Danzig, n.d. [*c.* 1936]

Manz 2003
Beatrice Forbes Manz, 'Women in Timurid dynastic politics', in *Women in Iran: from the rise of Islam to 1800*, ed. Guity Nashat and Lois Beck, Urbana and Chicago: University of Illinois Press, 2003, pp. 121–39

al-Maraghi 1987
ᶜAbd al-Qādir al-Māraghī, *Jāmiᶜ al-alḥān*, ed. Taqī Bīniš, Tehran, 1987

Mar Jabalaha/Budge 1928
The Monks of Kûblâi Khân Emperor of China, trans. E.A. Wallis Budge, London, 1928

Mayer 1956
Leo A. Mayer, *Islamic Astrolabists and their Works*, Geneva, 1956

Mayer 1959
Leo A. Mayer, *Islamic Metalworkers and their Works*, Geneva, 1959

McAuliffe 1984
Jane Dammen McAuliffe, 'The Wines of Earth and Paradise. Qur'anic Proscriptions and Promises', in R.M. Savory and D.A.Agius (eds.), *Papers in medieval studies. 6. Logos Islamikos. Studia Islamica in Honorem Georgii Michaelis Wickens*, Toronto, 1984, pp. 159-74

McChesney 1983
Robert D. McChesney, 'The Amirs of Muslim Central Asia in the XVIIth Century', *Journal of the Economic and Social History of the Orient*, 26, 1983, pp. 33–70

Melikian-Chirvani 1971a
Assadullah Souren Melikian-Chirvani, 'M.C.A.B.I. XII: Nouvelles remarques sur l'école du Fars', *Bulletin des Musées et Monuments Lyonnais*, 4, no. 3, 1971, pp. 361–91

Melikian-Chirvani 1971b
Assadullah Souren Melikian-Chirvani, 'Le royaume de Salomon: Les inscriptions persanes des sites achéménides', *Le Monde Iranien et l'Islam, sociétés et cultures* (Haute études islamiques et orientales d'histoire comparée, no. 4), Geneva and Paris, 1971

Melikian-Chirvani 1973
Assadullah Souren Melikian-Chirvani, *Le Bronze Iranien*, Paris, 1973

Melikian-Chirvani 1979
Assadullah Souren Melikian-Chirvani, 'Les Bronzes du Khorâssân – VII', *Studia Iranica*, 8/2, 1979, pp. 233–43

Melikian-Chirvani 1982
Assadullah Souren Melikian-Chirvani, *Islamic Metalwork from the Iranian World, 8th–18th Centuries. Victoria and Albert Museum Catalogue,* London: Victoria and Albert Museum, 1982

Melikian-Chirvani 1985
Assadullah Souren Melikian-Chirvani, 'Anatolian candlesticks: the eastern element and the Konya school', *Rivista degli Studi Orientali*, 59, nos. 1–4, 1985, pp. 225–66

Melikian-Chirvani 1987
Assadullah Souren Melikian-Chirvani, 'The lights of Sufi shrines', *Islamic Art*, 2, 1987, pp. 117–47

Melikian-Chirvani 1991
Assadullah Souren Melikian-Chirvani, 'Les taureaux à vin et les cornes à boire de l'Iran islamique', in P. Bernard and F. Grenet (eds.), *Histoire et cultes de l'Asie Centrale préislamique*, Paris, 1991, pp. 101–25

Melikian-Chirvani 1992
Assadullah Souren Melikian-Chirvani, 'The Wine-Bull and the Magian Master', *Studia Iranica (*Cahier 11, Recurrent Patterns in Iranian Religions), Paris, 1992, pp. 101–34

Melikian-Chirvani 1995
Assadullah Souren Melikian-Chirvani, 'The Wine Birds of Iran from Pre-Achaemenid to Islamic Times', *Bulletin of the Asia Institute*, new series, 9, 1995, pp. 41–97

Melikian-Chirvani 1996
Assadullah Souren Melikian-Chirvani, 'The Iranian Wine Horn from Pre-Achaemenid Antiquity to the Safavid Age', *Bulletin of the Asia Institute*, new series, 10, 1996, pp. 85–139

Melikian-Chirvani 1997a
Assadullah Souren Melikian-Chirvani, 'Conscience du passé et résistance culturelle dans l'Iran mongol', in *L'Iran Face à la Domination Mongole*, ed. D. Aigle, Tehran: Insitut français de recherché en Iran, 1997, pp. 135–77

Melikian-Chirvani 1997b
Assadullah Souren Melikian-Chirvani, 'The Iranian Wine Leg from Prehistory to Mongol Times', *Bulletin of the Asia Institute*, new series, 11, 1997, pp. 65–91

Melville 1990a
Charles Melville, 'The Itineraries of Sultan Öljeitü, 1304–16', *Iran*, 28, 1990, pp. 55 70

Melville 1990b
Charles Melville, 'Pādshāh-i Islām. The conversion of Sultan Maḥmūd Ghāzān Khān', *Pembroke Papers*, 1, 1990, pp. 159-77

Melville 1997a
Charles Melville, 'Ebn al-Fowaṭī', in *Encyclopaedia Iranica*, VIII/1, 1997, pp. 25–26

Melville 1997b
Charles Melville, 'Ebn al-ṭeqṭaqā', in *Encyclopaedia Iranica*, VIII/1, 1997, pp. 58–59

Melville 1998
Charles Melville, 'Boloğān Ḳātun', *Encyclopaedia Iranica*, IV/4, 1998, pp. 338–39

Melville 1999
Charles Melville, *The Fall of Amir Chupan and the Decline of the Ilkhanate, 1327-37: A Decade of Discord in Mongol Iran*, Bloomington, Indiana 1999

Melville 2006
Charles Melville, 'The *Keshig* in Iran: The Survival of the Royal Mongol Household', in *Beyond the Legacy of Genghis Khan*, ed. L. Komaroff, Leiden and Boston 2006, pp. 135–64

Mernissi 1993
Fatima Mernissi, 'The Mongol Khatuns', in *eadem, Forgotten Queens of Islam*, trans. Mary Jo Lakeland, Oxford: Polity Press/Blackwells, 1993, pp. 99–107

Mez 1937
Adam Mez, *The Renaissance of Islam*, trans. S. Khuda Bakhsh and D.S. Margoliouth, Patna, 1937

Mirza 1996
Mīrza Muḥammad Ḥaydar Dughlat, *Tarīkh-i Rashīdī. A History of the Khans of Moghulistan*, Persian text, ed. W.M. Thackston (Sources of Oriental Languages and Literatures 37, ed. Ş. Tekin and G. Alpay Tekin; Central Asian Sources II), Cambridge MA, 1996

Mirza/Thackston 1996
Mīrza Muḥammad Ḥaydar Dughlat, *Tarīkh-i Rashīdī. A History of the Khans of Moghulistan*, English trans. W.M. Thackston (Sources of Oriental Languages and Literatures 38, ed. Ş. Tekin and G. Alpay Tekin; Central Asian Sources III), Cambridge MA, 1996

Monneret de Villard 1940
Ugo Monneret de Villard, 'Le Chiese della Mesopotamia', *Orientalia Christiana Periodica*, 128, 1940, pp. 1–115

Morgan 1995
David O. Morgan, 'Rashīd al-Dīn Ṭabīb', in *Encyclopaedia of Islam*, 2nd edn, VIII, 1995, pp. 443–44

Moscow 2013
Ninety-nine Names of God, Classical Art of Islamic World from IX to XIX Centuries, exh. cat., Pushkin State Museum of Fine Arts, Moscow, 2013

Mustawfi Qazvini 1999
Ḥamd Allāh Mustawfī Qazvīnī, *Ẓafarnāma*, facsimile edn, ed. N. Pourjavadi and N. Rastegar, Tehran and Vienna, 1999

Mustawfi Qazvini/ Stephenson 1928
Ḥamd Allāh Mustawfī Qazvīnī, *The Zoological Section of the Nuzhatu-l-qulūb of Ḥamdullāh al-Mustaufī al-Qazwīnī* , ed., trans. and annotated J. Stephenson (Oriental Translation Fund, New Series, vol. XXX), London, 1928

Neubauer 1993
Eckhard Neubauer, 'Der Bau der Laute und ihre Besaitung nach arabischen, persischen und türkischen Quellen des 9. bis 15. Jahrhunderts', *Zeitschrift für Geschichte der Arabisch-Islamischen Wissenschaften*, 8, 1993, pp. 279–378

New York 1997a
Stefano Carboni, *Following the Stars: Images of the Zodiac in Islamic Art*, exh. cat., Metropolitan Museum of Art, New York, 1997

New York 1997b
When Silk was Gold : Central Asian and Chinese Textiles, exh. cat., ed. James C.Y. Watt and Anne E. Wardwell, Metropolitan Museum of Art, New York, 1997

New York 2002
Linda Komaroff and Stefano Carboni (eds.), *The Legacy of Genghis Khan: Courtly Art and Culture in Western Asia, 1256-1353*, exh. cat., New York, New Haven and London, 2002

Noorani 2004
Yaseen Noorani, 'Heterotopia and the wine poem in early Islamic culture', *International Journal of Middle East Studies*, 36, 2004, pp. 345–66

Northrup 1998
Linda S. Northrup, *From Slave to Sultan. The Career of al-Mansur Qalawun and the consolidation of Mamluk rule in Egypt and Syria (678–689 A.H. / 1279–1290 A.D.)*, Stuttgart, 1998

Nurbakhsh 1980
Javad Nurbakhsh, *What the Sufis Say*, New York, 1980

Oral 1954
M. Zeki Oral, *Hazret-i Mevlana Dergahındaki Şaheserlerden Nisantası*, Ankara, 1954

Order of Lenin State Historical Museum 1980
Order of Lenin State Historical Museum, *The Simferopol Treasure*, Moscow, 1980

Paris 2002
Chevaux et cavaliers arabes dans les arts d'Orient et d'Occident, exh. cat., Institut du monde arabe, Paris, 2002–03

Patton 1991
Douglas L. Patton, *Badr al-Dīn Lu'lu', Atabeg of Mosul, 1211–1259*, Seattle and London, 1991

Paviot 2000
Jacques Paviot, 'England and the Mongols (c. 1260–1330)', *Journal of the Royal Asiatic Society*, third series, 10/3, November 2000, pp. 305–18

Petersen 1954
Theodore C. Petersen, 'Early Islamic Bookbindings and Their Coptic Relations Source', *Ars Orientalis*, 1, 1954, pp. 41–64

Pevzner 1969
Sergeï Borisovich Pevzner, 'Bronnzoví penal b sobranii Gosudarstvennogo Muzeya kul'turi i iskusstva narodov vostoka', *Epigrafica Vostoka*, 19, 1969, pp. 51–58

Pfeiffer 2003
Judith Pfeiffer, 'Conversion to Islam among the Ilkhans in Muslim narrative traditions: The case of Aḥmad Tegüder', PhD thesis, The University of Chicago, 2003

Philon 1980
Helen Philon, *Benaki Museum Athens: Early Islamic Ceramics: Ninth to Late Twelfth Centuries*, London: Islamic Art Publications, 1980

Pinder-Wilson 1976
Ralph H. Pinder-Wilson, 'The Malcolm Celestial Globe', *British Museum Yearbook*, 1, 1976, pp. 297–321

Polo/Yule 1875
Marco Polo, *The book of Ser Marco Polo, the Venetian*, trans. Sir Henry Yule, London, 1875

Polo/Yule-Cordier 1903/1993
Marco Polo, *The Book of Ser Marco Polo the Venetian Concerning the Kingdoms and Marvels of the East*, trans. H. Yule, revised H. Cordier, 2 vols., New York 1903; reprinted 1993

Pope and Ackermann 1938–39
Arthur Upham Pope and Phyllis Ackermann (eds.), *A Survey of Persian Art from Prehistoric Times to the Present*, 6 vols., London, New York, 1938–39

Porter 1995
Venetia Porter, *Islamic Tiles*, British Museum Press, London, 1995

Potapov and Sale 2005
Eugene Potapov and Richard Sale, *The Gyrfalcon*, London, 2005

Pugachenkova and Khakimov 1988
Galina Pugachenkova and Akbar Khakimov, *The Art of Central Asia*, Leningrad: Aurora Publishers, 1988

Qashani 1348/1969
Abū al-Qāsim Qāshānī, *Tārīkh-i Öljeitü*, ed. Mahin Hambly, Tehran: Intishārāt-i Bungāh-i Tarjuma va Nashr-i Kitāb, 1348/1969

Quade-Reutter 2003
Karin Quade-Reutter, *"… denn sie haben einen unvollkommenen Verstand" – Herrschaftliche Damen im Grossraum Iran in der Mongolen- und Timuridenzeit (ca. 1250–1507)*, Aachen: Shaker Verlag, 2003

Raby 2012
Julian Raby, 'The Principle of Parsimony and the Problem of the 'Mosul School of Metalwork', in *Metalwork and Material Culture in the Islamic World*, ed. V. Porter and M. Rosser-Owen, London, 2012, pp. 11–85

Rashid al-Din n.d.
Rashīd al-Dīn, *Shuʿabi panjgāna*, Istanbul, Ms. Ahmet III. 2937

Rashid al-Din 1983
Rashīd al-Dīn, *Jāmiʿ al-tawārīkh*, ed. Bahman Karīmī, Tehran, 1983

Rashid al-Din 1994
Rashīd al-Dīn, *Jāmiʿ al-tawārīkh*, ed. Muḥammad Rawshan and Muṣṭafā Mūsavī, 4 vols., Tehran: Nashri Alburz, 1373/1994

Rashid al-Din/Boyle 1971
Rashīd al-Dīn, *The Successors of Genghis Khan*, trans. A. Boyle, New York and London: Columbia University Press, 1971

Rashid al-Din/Quatremère 1836
Rashīd al-Dīn, *Histoire des Mongols de la Perse*, ed. and trans. Etienne Quatremère, Paris, 1836

Rashid al-Din/Thackston 1998–99
Rashīd al-Dīn, *Rashiduddin Fazlullah's Jamiʿ u't-tawarikh: Compendium of Chronicles. A History of the Mongols*, 3 vols., trans. Wheeler M. Thackston, Cambridge MA: Harvard University Department of Near Eastern Languages and Civilizations, 1998–99

Rawson 1984
Jessica Rawson, *The Lotus and the Dragon*, London: British Museum Press, 1984

Reinaud 1828
Joseph Toussaint Reinaud, *Monumens arabes, persans et turcs, du cabinet de M. le duc de Blacas, et d'autres cabinets*, 2 vols., Paris, 1828

Reynolds 2006
Dwight F. Reynolds, 'Musical aspects of Ibn Sana' al-Mulk's Dar al-ṭirāz' in E. Emery (ed.), *Muwashshah!: Proceedings of the International Conference on Arabic and Hebrew Strophic Poetry and its Romance Parallels, School of Oriental and African Studies [SOAS], London, 8-10 October 2003*, 2006, pp. 211–27

Rice (David Storm) 1952
David Storm Rice, 'Studies in Islamic Metalwork I', *Bulletin of the School of Oriental and African Studies*, 14/3, 1952, pp. 564–78

Rice (David Storm) 1953
David Storm Rice, 'The Aghani miniatures and religious painting in Islam', *Burlington Magazine*, 95, 1953, pp.128-134

Rice (David Storm) 1954
David Storm Rice, 'The Seasons and Labours of the Months in Islamic Art', *Ars Orientalis*, 1, 1954, pp. 1–39

Rice (David Storm) 1957
David Storm Rice, 'Inlaid Brasses from the Workshop of Aḥmad al-Dhakī al-Mawṣilī', *Ars Orientalis*, 2, 1957, pp. 283–326

Rice (David Storm) 1958
David Storm Rice, 'Deacon or drink? Some paintings from Samarra re-examined', *Arabica*, 5, 1958, pp. 15–33

Rice (David Talbot) 1976
David Talbot Rice, *The illustrations to the 'World History of Rashīd al-Dīn'*, ed. B. Gray, Edinburgh: Edinburgh University Press, 1976

Riefstahl 1922
Rudolf Meyer Riefstahl, *The Parish-Watson Collection of Mohammadan Potteries*, New York, 1922

Robinson 1967
Basil Robinson, 'Oriental metalwork in the Gambier-Parry collection', *Burlington Magazine*, 109, March 1967, pp. 169–73

Rossabi 1998
Morris Rossabi, 'Behind the silk screen: movements of weavers in Asia, seventh to fourteenth centuries', *Orientations*, 29, 1998, pp. 84–89

Rotter 2004
Gernot Rotter, *Abu l-Faradsch. Und der Kalif beschenkte ihn reichlich*, Lenningen, 2004

Roux 1984
Jean-Paul Roux, *La religion des Turcs et des Mongols*, Paris, 1984

Roxburgh 1995
David J. Roxburgh, 'Heinrich Friedrich Von Diez and His Eponymous Albums: Mss. Diez a. Fols. 70–74', *Muqarnas*, 12, 1995, pp. 112–36

Rubruck/Jackson 2009
Friar William of Rubruck, *The Mission of Friar William of Rubruck, his journey to the court of the Great Khan Möngke, 1253–1255*, trans. Peter Jackson, Cambridge, 2009

Rührdanz 1997
Rührdanz, K., 'Illustrationen zu Rašīd al-Dīn's *Taʾrīḫ-i Mubārak-i Ġāzānī* in den Berliner Diez-Alben', in Denise Aigle (ed.), *L'Iran face à domination mongole*, Tehran: Institut français de recherche en Iran, 1997, pp. 295–306

Rumi/Barks 1999
Jalāl al-Dīn Rūmī, *The Essential Rumi*, trans. Coleman Barks, London, 1999

Sadan 1977
Joseph Sadan, 'Vin – fait du civilisation', in M. Rosen-Ayalon (ed.), *Studies in Memory of Gaston Wiet*, Jerusalem, 1977, pp. 129–60

Safa 1358/1980
Zabīh Allāh Ṣafā, *Tārīkh-i adabiyāt dar Īrān*, vol. 3/1 *(Az avāyili qarni haftum tā pāyāni qarni hashtumi hijrī)*, Tehrān: Chāpkhānayi Dānishgāhi Tehrān, 1358/1980

Sarikhani Collection [2011]
The Sarikhani Collection, an introduction, London: Paul Holberton, n.d. [2011]

Sarre and Martin 1912
Friedrich Paul Theodor Sarre and Fredrik Robert Martin, *Die Ausstellung von Meisterwerken Muhammedanischer Kunst in München 1910*, 3 vols., Munich, 1912

Sarre and Mittwoch 1906
Friedrich Sarre and Eugen Mittwoch, *Sammlung F. Sarre: Erzeugnisse Islamischer Kunst. Teil I: Metall*, Berlin, 1906

Savage-Smith 1985
Emilie Savage-Smith, *Islamicate Celestial Globes*, Washington DC, 1985

Savory 1960
Roger M. Savory, 'Baghdād Khātūn', in *Encyclopaedia of Islam*, 2nd edn, I, 1960, pp. 908–09

Sawa 1989
George Dimitry Sawa, *Music Performance Practice in the Early ʿAbbāsid Era*, Toronto: Pontifical Institute of Medieval Studies, 1989

Scerrato 1967
Umberto Scerrato, *Arte islamica a Napoli: Opere delle raccolte pubbliche napoletane*, 1967

Schroeder 1955
Eric Schroeder, *Muhammad's People*, Portland, Maine, 1955

Secret History/Rachewiltz 2004
The Secret History of the Mongols: A Mongolian epic chronicle of the thirteenth century, trans. with historical and philological commentary, Igor de Rachewiltz (Brill's Inner Asian Library 7, ed. N. Di Cosmo, D. Deweese and C. Humphrey), 2 vols., Leiden 2004

Serjeant 1942
Robert Bertram Serjeant, 'Material for a history of Islamic textiles up to the Mongol conquest', *Ars Islamica*, 9, 1942, pp. 54–92

Serjeant 1951
Robert Bertram Serjeant, 'Material for a history of Islamic textiles up to the Mongol conquest', *Ars Islamica*, 15–16, 1951, pp. 29–85

Shabankara'i 1984
Muḥammad ibn ʿAlī ibn Muḥammad Shabānkārāʾī, *Majmaʿ al-ansāb*, ed. Hāshim Muḥaddith, Tehran, 1984

Shields 2000
Sarah Shields, *Mosul before Iraq: like bees making five-sided cells*, Albany NY, 2000

Shir 2006
Shai Shir, '"The Chief Wife" at the Courts of the Mongol Khans during the Mongol World Empire (1206–1260)', MA thesis (in Hebrew), The Hebrew University of Jerusalem, 2006

Simpson 1979
Marianna Shreve Simpson, *The Illustration of an Epic: the Earliest Shahnama Manuscripts*, New York: Garland, 1979

Simpson 2006
Marianna Shreve Simpson, 'In the Beginning: Frontispieces and Front Matter in Ilkhanid and Injuid Manuscripts', in Linda Komaroff (ed.), *Beyond the Legacy of Genghis Khan (Islamic History and Civilization: Studies and Texts, vol. 64)*, Leiden: Brill 2006; reprinted 2013

Simpson 2013
Marianna Shreve Simpson, 'A medieval representation of Kay Khusraw's jäm-i gītī namāy', in R. Hillenbrand, A.C.S. Peacock and F. Abdullaeva (eds.), *Ferdowsi, the Mongols and the History of Iran. Art, Literature and Culture from Early Islam to Qajar Persia: Studies in Honour of Charles Melville*, London and New York, 2013, pp. 351–58

Smith 2000
John Masson Smith, 'Dietary Decadence and Dynastic Decline in the Mongol Empire', *Journal of Asian History*, 34, no. 1, 2000, pp. 35–52; also available as a pdf online

Snelders 2010
Bas Snelders, *Identity and Christian-Muslim Interaction: Medieval Art of the Syrian Orthodox from the Mosul Area*, Leuven, 2010

Sotheby's 1992
Sotheby's, *Islamic Paintings and Works of Art*, sale, London, 22 October 1992

Sotheby's 2003
Sotheby's, *Arts of the Islamic World*, sale, London, 30 April 2003

Sotheby's 2010
Sotheby's, *Arts of the Islamic World*, sale, London, 6 October 2010

Sotheby's 2013
Sotheby's, *Arts of the Islamic World*, sale, London, 10 October 2013

Soudavar 1996
Abolala Soudavar, 'The Saga of Abu-Saʿid Bahādor Khān: The Abu-Saʿidnāmé', in Julian Raby and Teresa Fitzherbert (eds.), *The Court of the Il-Khans 1290-1340* (Oxford Studies in Islamic Art XII), Oxford, 1996

Spallanzani 2010
Marco Spallanzani, *Metalli islamici a Firenze nel Rinascimento*, Florence, 2010

Spink and Ogden 2013:
Michael Spink and Jack Ogden, *The Art of Adornment. Jewellery of the Islamic World* (Nasser D. Khalili Collection of Islamic Art, XVII, Part One), London, 2013

Spuler 1982
Bertold Spuler, 'Ābeš Ḵātūn', in *Encyclopaedia Iranica*, I/2, 1982, p. 210

Spuler 1985
Bertold Spuler, *Die Mongolen in Iran. Politik, Verwaltung und Kultur der Ilchanzeit 1220–1350*, 4th revised and expanded edn, Leiden, 1985

Spuler and Sourdel-Thomine 1973
Bertold Spuler and Janine Sourdel-Thomine (eds), *Die Kunst des Islam*, Propyläen Verlag, Berlin, 1973

St Petersburg 2000
The Treasures of the Golden Horde, exh. cat., Hermitage Museum, St Petersburg, 2000

Steingass 1892/1975
Francis Joseph Steingass, *Persian-English Dictionary*, Beirut: Librairie du Liban, 1892/1975

Stewart 1967
Desmond Stewart, *Early Islam*, Weert, 1967

Subtelny 1984
Maria E. Subtelny, 'Scenes from the literary life of Tīmūrid Herāt', in R.M. Savory and D. Agius (eds.), *Logos islamikos: Studia islamica in honorem Georgii Michaelis Wickens* (Papers in Medieval Studies, 6), Toronto: Pontifical Institute of Medieval Studies, 1984, pp. 137–55

Swietochowski and Carboni 1994
Marie Lukens Swietochowski and Stefano Carboni, *Illustrated Poetry and Epic Images: Persian Painting of the 1330s and 1340s*, New York: Metropolitan Museum of Art, 1994

Togan 1999
İsenbike Togan, 'In Search for an Approach to the History of Women in Central Asia', in Korkut Ertürk (ed.), *Rethinking Central Asia*, Reading: Ithaca University Press, 1999, pp. 163–95

Togan 2006
İsenbike Togan, 'The Qongrat in History', in *History and Historiography of Post-Mongol Central Asia and the Middle East. Studies in Honor of John E. Woods*, ed. Judith Pfeiffer and Sholeh A. Quinn, Wiesbaden: Harrassowitz, 2006, pp. 61–83

Tsuge 2013
Gen'iche Tsuge, 'Musical instruments described in a fourteenth-century Persian treatise, *Kanz al-tuḥaf*', *The Galpin Society Journal*, 66, 2013, pp. 165–84

Usama ibn Munqidh 1930
Usāma ibn Munqidh, *Kitāb al-Iʿtibār*, ed. Philip K. Hitti, Princeton, 1930

Usama/Cobb 2008
Usāma ibn Munqidh, *The Book of Contemplation. Islam and the Crusades*, trans., intro. and notes, P.M. Cobb, London: Penguin Classics, 2008

Vainker 2004
Shelagh Vainker, *Chinese Silk*, London, 2004

Vassaf 1853
ʿAbd Allāh ibn Fazl Allāh Vaṣṣaf, *Tajzīyat al-amṣār wa-tazjīyat al-aʿṣār*, Bombay, 1853

Vassaf 1967
ʿAbd Allāh ibn Fazl Allāh Vaṣṣāf, *Taḥrir-i Tarikh-i Vaṣṣaf*, ed. ʿAbd al-Muḥammad Āyatī, Tehran, 1967

Venice 1993
Eredità dell'Islam. Arte Islamica in Italia, exh. cat., ed. Giovanni Curatola, Palazzo Ducale, Venice, 1993–94

Ward 1986
Rachel Ward, 'High Life in Mosul: 1232 A.D', in *Arts of Asia*, 16/3, May–June 1986, pp. 119–24

Ward 1992
Rachel Ward, 'Incense and incense burners in Mamluk Egypt and Syria', *Transactions of the Oriental Ceramic Society* [1990–91], 55, 1992, pp. 67–82

Ward 1993
Rachel Ward, *Islamic Metalwork*, London: British Museum Press, 1993

Ward 1995
Rachel Ward, 'Tradition and Innovation: A group of candlesticks made in Mamluk Egypt', in *Islamic Art in the Ashmolean Museum*, ed. J.W. Allan (Oxford Studies in Islamic Art, vol. 10), 1995, II, pp. 147–58

Ward 1998
Rachel Ward (ed.), *Gilded and Enamelled Glass from the Middle East*, London: British Museum Press, 1998

Ward 1999
Rachel Ward, 'The Baptistère de Saint Louis – a Mamluk basin made for export to Europe', in *Islam and the Italian Renaissance*, ed. N. Mann and A. Contadini, London: Warburg Institute, 1999, pp. 113–32

Ward 2004
Rachel Ward, 'Brass, Gold and Silver: Metal Vessels Made for Sultan Al-Nāsir Muhammad. A Memorial Lecture for Mark Zebrowski. Given at the Royal Asiatic Society on 9 May 2002. By Rachel Ward', *Royal Asiatic Society Journal*, third series, 14/1, April 2004, pp. 59–73

Ward 2005
Rachel Ward, 'Style versus Substance: The Christian Iconography on Two Vessels made for the Ayyubid Sultan al-Salih Ayyub', in *The Iconography of Islamic Art, Studies in Honour of Robert Hillenbrand*, ed. Bernard O'Kane, Edinburgh, 2005, pp. 309–24

Ward et al 1995
Rachel Ward, Susan La Niece, Duncan Hook and Raymond White, 'Veneto-Saracenic metalwork: an analysis of the bowls and incense burners in the British Museum', in *Trade and Discovery: the scientific study of artefacts from post-medieval Europe and beyond* (British Museum Occasional Paper 109, ed. D. Hook and D. Gaimster), London: British Museum Press, 1995, pp. 235–58

Wardwell 1989
Anne Wardwell, '*Panni tartarici*: Eastern Islamic Silks woven with Gold and Silver (13th and 14th centuries)', *Islamic Art*, 3, 1988–89, pp. 95–173

Wardwell 1992
Anne E. Wardwell, 'Two Silk and Gold Textiles of the Early Mongol Period', *The Bulletin of the Cleveland Museum of Art*, 79/10, December 1992, pp. 354–78

Washington 1981
Esin Atıl, *Renaissance of Islam: Art of the Mamluks*, exh. cat., National Museum of Natural History, Smithsonian Institution, and other institutions, Washington, D.C., 1981

Washington 1989
Timur and the Princely Vision, ed. Thomas W. Lentz and Glenn D. Lowry, exh. cat., Arthur M. Sackler Gallery, Smithsonian Institution, Washington, D.C. (and the Los Angeles County Museum of Art), 1989

Washington 1991
Circa 1492, Art in the Age of Exploration, exh. cat., ed. Jay A. Levenson, National Gallery of Art, Washington, 1991

Watson 1982
Oliver Watson, 'An Islamic "lacquered" dish', in *Lacquerwork in Asia and Beyond*, ed. William Watson (Colloquies on Art and Archaeology in Asia no. 11), London: University of London, 1982, pp. 232–46

Watson 1985
Oliver Watson, *Persian Lustre Ware*, London: Faber, 1985

Wensinck 1978
Arent Jan Wensinck, 'Khamr', in *Encyclopaedia of Islam*, 2nd edn, IV, 1978, pp. 994b–97a

Wiet 1931
Gaston Wiet, 'Un nouvel artiste de Mossoul', *Syria*, 12, 1931, pp. 160–62

Wiet 1933
Gaston Wiet, *L'Exposition persane de 1931*, Cairo, 1933

Woods 1999
John E. Woods, *The Aqquyunlu: Clan, Confederation, Empire. Revised and Expanded Edition*, Salt Lake City: The University of Utah Press, 1999

Wright 2006
Elaine Wright, 'Patronage of the arts of the book under the Injuids of Shiraz', in Linda Komaroff (ed.), *Beyond the legacy of Genghis Khan (Islamic History and Civilization: Studies and Texts, vol. 64)*, Leiden:Brill 2006; reprint 2013, pp. 248–68

Wyatt and Wardwell 1997
James C.Y. Wyatt and Anne E. Wardwell, *When Silk was Gold*, exh. cat., Metropolitan Museum of Art, New York, 1997

Yaqut 1866–70
Shihāb al-Dīn Yāqūt al-Rūmī, *Kitāb mu'jam al-buldān*, ed. F. Wüstenfeld, 6 vols., Leipzig, 1866–70

Zhao 1999
Feng Zhao, *Treasures in Silk*, Hongkong, 1999

Zhao 2008
George Qingzhi Zhao, *Marriage as Political Strategy and Cultural Expression: Mongolian Royal Marriages from World Empire to Yuan Dynasty*, New York: Peter Lang, 2008

Copyright © 2014
Texts copyright © the authors

All rights reserved. No part of this publication may be transmitted in any
form or by any means, electronic or mechanical, including photocopy,
recording or any storage or retrieval system, without the prior permission
in writing from the copyright holder and publisher.

ISBN 978 1 907372 65 0

British Library Cataloguing in Publication Data
A catalogue record for this book is available from the British Library

Produced by Paul Holberton publishing
89 Borough High Street, London SE1 1NL, uk
www.paul-holberton.net

Designed by Laura Parker

Origination and printing by E-graphic, Verona, Italy

FRONT The Courtauld bag (cat. 1)
BACK The Courtauld bag (cat. 1) detail of court scene
FRONTISPIECE The Courtauld bag (cat. 1) detail of horseman roundel
PAGE 9 The Courtauld bag (cat. 1)